Conventions
OF FORM AND THOUGHT
IN EARLY GREEK EPIC POETRY

Conventions
of Form and Thought
in Early Greek Epic Poetry

William G. Thalmann

THE JOHNS HOPKINS UNIVERSITY PRESS
BALTIMORE AND LONDON

This book was brought to publication with the generous assistance
of the Frederick W. Hilles Publication Fund of Yale University
and the Andrew W. Mellon Foundation.

The Johns Hopkins University Press
Baltimore, Maryland 21218
The Johns Hopkins Press Ltd., London

The paper in this book is acid-free and meets the guidelines for
permanence and durability of the Committee on Production Guidelines
for Book Longevity of the Council on Library Resources.

Library of Congress Cataloging in Publication Data

Thalmann, William G., 1947–
    Conventions of form and thought in early Greek Epic
poetry.

    Bibliography: p. 237
    Includes indexes.
    1. Greek poetry—History and criticism.   2. Hexameter.
3. Homer—Criticism and interpretation.   4. Hesiod—
Criticism and interpretation.   5. Homeric hymns.
I. Title.
PA3092.T48   1984   883'.01'09   84-47944
ISBN 0-8018-3195-4

To Susan

🔁 Contents 🔁

▣ Acknowledgments ▣

I AM GRATEFUL TO YALE UNIVERSITY for a Morse Junior Faculty Fellowship during 1979–80, which enabled me to do the necessary reading for this book and to write a first draft of it, and to the Council of Fellows of the Whitney Humanities Center for a grant from the A. Whitney Griswold Faculty Research Fund to defray the cost of typing the manuscript. But Yale has provided more than financial support for this book. It has been a privilege to have the university's superb resources at my disposal and to work in the congenial atmosphere of the Yale Classics Department. I would like to thank all those colleagues and students who listened receptively to my ideas, in particular Jeffrey Hurwit and Sheila Murnaghan, both of whom read and commented generously on a version of Chapter 6. I am also grateful to the anonymous reader for The Johns Hopkins University Press for advice and criticism.

My debts to the published work of other scholars will be obvious from the notes. My reading has not been limited to those works listed in the Bibliography, but I could not, of course, master in their entirety the huge bibliographies on the poets treated here; and I regret that I have not been able to give systematic coverage to books and articles that have appeared since 1980.

Special thanks are due to the staff of The Johns Hopkins University Press for its professionalism and efficiency, particularly to William Sisler, Eric Halpern, Jane Warth, Jackie Wehmueller, and Cynthia Foote.

Most of all I would like to thank my wife, Susan, for her perceptive comments on the manuscript and for her forebearance, understanding, and encouragement during the years of writing and rewriting, when circumstances often tested those qualities in her. I dedicate this book to her, in order to make what return I can for her indispensable help.

▣ Introduction ▣

THE WORD *EPIC* IN MY TITLE is meant, not in the sense it has come to have for us today, but in the way the Greeks, by the fifth century B.C. if not earlier, used the term from which it is derived, *ta epea:* to designate poems composed in dactylic hexameter. It is thus intended to convey my sense of a fundamental kinship among all early Greek poems in this meter. In the body of this book I sometimes refer to *epic* without qualification, and when I do the word should be understood in this wider sense; but generally I prefer the more precise though somewhat forbidding and clumsy phrase *hexameter poetry.* The period to which the major surviving examples of this poetry belong, and to which the word *early* in the title refers, spans the later geometric and the archaic ages—that is, the time from the eighth through the sixth centuries B.C. Hexameter poetry continued to be produced during the fifth century, but I have found nothing of use for my purposes among what little survives from that period. The body of poetry that I treat thus includes principally the *Iliad,* the *Odyssey,* Hesiod's *Theogony* and his *Works and Days,* and the Homeric Hymns, especially the four longer hymns (numbers 2-5 in the manuscript collection), those to Demeter, Apollo, Hermes, and Aphrodite, respectively. Where something can profitably be said about them, I also discuss the shorter Homeric Hymns, the extant fragments of other Hesiodic poems (including the *Shield of Herakles*), and those of the Epic Cycle and of the rest of early epic.

By now the day is probably past when it was fashionable to speak of a Boiotian school of poets who produced mainly verse catalogues and, on the other hand, of an Ionian school of heroic epic poetry. Yet most readers of Greek poetry, specialists and nonspecialists alike, still tend to think of its earliest specimens as belonging to different categories: heroic, theogonic, hymnic, didactic, and so forth. This assumption is natural in view of our modern habit of identifying "epic" with "heroic" poetry, but that is the result of the course taken by our literary tradition, which began its development from Homer. Later epic poets took from the *Iliad* and the *Odyssey* certain attitudes and narrative features that seemed most typical of those poems, and a genre evolved that we usually call "epic." And so, in thinking about the Homeric poems, we abstract them from their context within the range of

Greek hexameter poetry. The way is then open for us to make distinctions between other representatives of this poetry. No doubt there are times when these classifications are useful, but they contain a considerable element of the accidental and arbitrary.

In one way, however, they might be justified: by observing that the *Iliad* and the *Odyssey* display characteristics common to a type of poetry that has appeared in a variety of cultures and that C.M. Bowra has described in his book *Heroic Poetry*. Together, perhaps, with the poems of the Epic Cycle, they might seem to fall into a class by themselves. Since my approach is the opposite of Bowra's, it may be instructive to consider the definitions on which he bases his study. Although he is by no means unaware of the affinities between the Homeric epics and the rest of hexameter poetry, what distinguishes heroic poetry for him is above all that "it is anthropocentric in the sense that it celebrates men by showing of what high deeds they are capable. . . . Truly heroic poetry deals with men, and though it may introduce gods into the action, the main interest is in men" (Bowra, 1952, 23). The Homeric Hymns, by contrast, "which tell stories of the gods, stress the inferiority of men" (ibid., 24). Bowra then constructs a genealogy of "primitive narrative poetry":

> At the start is shamanistic poetry in which the chief character is the magician, and magic is the main means of success. This is touched by the new spirit of a man-centered universe which, appearing separately in panegyric and lament, then invades narrative and produces a heroic poetry in which gods and men both take part. This in turn bifurcates into the poetry of gods and the poetry of men. (Ibid., 25)

Besides the derivation of poetry from shamanism, a once-popular theory that has now been generally discredited, the trouble with these statements is that they are too easy. Even what Bowra would consider Greek heroic poetry deals not only with man's achievements but also with his limitations and defines these in large part with reference to the gods. At the other extreme, Bowra is quite right about the emphasis in the Homeric Hymns on human inferiority, but these poems do not merely celebrate the gods by contrast. They are concerned with the relations between gods and men and therefore with showing the nature of humanity. The alleged bifurcation into poetry on two distinct subjects, moreover, ignores what will emerge from the present study as a fundamental characteristic of hexameter poetry: its treatment of stories about both men and gods as fragments in a narrative and thematic continuum, and therefore as reflections of what is essentially a single view of the world. It may be true that heroic poetry represents an identifiable type; I think that Bowra's book, with its impressive range of material, establishes that it does. But Greek heroic poetry, I contend, is also, and just as significantly, part of a broader tradition.

As readers, we disregard this possibility at our peril. The assumption that poems are to be variously classified and distinguished from one another will inevitably guide our perception of them, and if it is a false assumption, if it is not true to the nature of early Greek epic, it will have most unfortunate results. Perhaps readers have in fact allowed their appreciation and understanding to be unnecessarily circumscribed. The Hesiodic poems and the Homeric Hymns have too often been neglected, their wonderful qualities as literary creations eclipsed by comparison with the *Iliad* and the *Odyssey*—a fitting compliment to the latter poems, perhaps, but more than a little unjust to the others. Emphasis on the undeniable differences among these poems has blinded many of us to the more fundamental similarities, and consequently we perhaps do not understand any one of them as well as we might. There have, of course, been scholarly studies that treat certain of the poems together from one point of view or another. But reasons for doing so have not been expressly given, and this activity has not been undertaken in a broadly systematic way. Moreover, although Hesiod and the Homeric Hymns have frequently been paired together, too little thought has been given to what the Hesiodic and the Homeric poems, for example, have in common.

I believe that much can be gained from thinking of early Greek epic as a homogeneous and coherent body of poetry. This book, in fact, originated in the excitement and fascination I felt when, on my first encounter with this poetry as an undergraduate and in subsequent reading and teaching, I found that I could draw significant and provocative connections between passages in various poems.

Meter is not an artificial or arbitrary means of lumping together poems that might otherwise have few similarities. In this case it genuinely serves to define a poetic type. As much careful scholarship in the last fifty years has shown, the composers of all these poems drew on a store of inherited formulaic phrases that, whatever their origin, had gradually accumulated for use in dactylic hexameter verse. Common diction makes the recurrence of themes and ideas from poem to poem natural—indeed, nearly inevitable. The meter also gives us a clue to another normative influence on the poetry, for it implies a specific manner of performance on certain occasions. Now as we shall find, there was actually a variety of circumstances under which hexameter poetry could be performed, but within limits. And it seems fair to assume that poetry intended to be heard on certain types of occasions would have developed its own norms or conventions, as Greek tragedy or epinician choral poetry did later on.

Here we must consider what is meant by *conventions*. Any utterance, if it is to be intelligible, must conform to certain rules understood at some level of consciousness by both speaker and audience. Poetry is no exception. Even poems that seem to require the greatest effort of interpretation and comprehension, such as those written in our own time, fulfill expectations about how poetry works that their audience has developed through experience of reading or listening. Diverse recent theories, moreover, have suggested that poetry, as a construct of language, communicates by means of fundamental codes and structures. I should make it clear, however, that my concern here is different, and that I have not been influenced by any of these theories, of which my knowledge is, anyway, limited.

There is another and more perceptible order of convention that has characterized poetry of different periods that has been particularly stylized. Hexameter poetry is of this type, and the reason, I believe, in addition to meter, diction, and occasion of performance, is its public character. It played a vitally important role in contemporary Greek society, and it reached its audience (which consisted of virtually all members of that society) through oral performance rather than written texts. Under these conditions there was no room for obscurity. Everything had to be easily and immediately intelligible, and conventions served this purpose.

My interest, then, is in the more overt kinds of conventions—that is, in the characteristics, ideas, attitudes, and concerns that all the poems share. What seems to be most important about this poetry is that it was a means of coming to know and of explaining the world and man's place in it: the history and arrangement of the physical world; the course of divine and human history; the conditions that govern men's relations with the gods and with each other; and the significance and value of human civilization and social institutions. Poetic conventions, as vehicles of meaning, furthered this aim in crucial ways and thus enabled the poetry to present a coherent worldview. But because our own culture differs from that of archaic Greece in attitudes and ways of thinking, we must make a conscious effort to understand hexameter poetry— we must *educate* ourselves, so to speak, in its prevailing modes of expression. The original audience's responses were conditioned by the cultural environment and ingrained by long habit of hearing just this type of poetry. But even at this distance we can gain insight, if not complete comprehension, if we try, and a study of conventions is part of this enterprise. Through it we may come to understand what the very existence of hexameter poetry meant for its contemporaries, and what must have been the significance for them of being present at a performance.

I must make clear a limitation of this topic, however. I have spoken of the coherence of hexameter poetry, and I believe with justice. Yet to claim that it constitutes an autonomous poetic genre would perhaps go beyond what the evidence justifies. Many of the formal characteristics and the ideas that will be discussed here as its conventions have parallels in lyric poetry and especially in Pindar. Whether hexameter poetry influenced the lyric that survives, or whether both forms were related in origin, shared essentially the same diction, and then underwent parallel but distinct development, cannot be known. I suspect that the truth is a mixture of the two. At any rate, since the same cultural traditions lie behind both lyric and hexameter poetry, they would both naturally reflect the same ways of thinking. To be complete, therefore, this study would probably have to present a poetics of all of archaic literature (one can also find parallels to certain features of hexameter poetry outside of lyric—in Aeschylus, for example, and Herodotus). That would be an unwieldy and hopelessly ambitious project. But hexameter poetry is much more uniform than lyric, which contains such a miscellany of forms and ideas that it is barely a meaningful category at all. Consequently, what I have called conventions appear more consistently and clearly in hexameter poetry than anywhere else. Despite some overlapping with other forms, then, it seems valid and fruitful to study hexameter poetry as a unified whole.

Any discussion of the typical and traditional characteristics of this poetry, however, risks encountering resistance by some readers who might think that such an approach devalued the poems as artistic creations. That would be an unfortunate misunderstanding, and I should like to head it off at the outset. The danger that it might arise seems due to the course that classical scholarship in this area has taken in the last fifty years or so. Because of what has often appeared a loveless treatment of this poetry in studies of oral formulaic techniques, and especially because the results of such studies have often made composition by those techniques sound automatic and involuntary, many scholars have insisted on the poet's creativity and the uniqueness of each text. This is an understandable and highly laudable reaction. But the result has been that the question of the individual poet's originality as against the influence of tradition has long plagued Homeric studies in particular. The issue is highly charged emotionally, involving, as it seems to, our feeling for the poetry. But how important is it really? Is the opposition it implies genuine or merely the product of a romantic obsession with individual poetic genius at the expense of the text? What matters, surely, is the quality of the poem that confronts us, not the character or the mind or the biography of the poet, even if we could know them (and the composers of our hexameter texts are so shadowy to us that we cannot even put names to all of them). But how are we to read these poems? By what standards should we value them?

The ultimate aim of the oral-formular theory is—or ought to be—to answer these questions by advancing our understanding of the nature of this poetry. Opinions differ, however, on how to assess its results, and there is consequently an unfortunate division in classical studies. On the one hand we learn about formulas and related phenomena; on the other, we read the poems with enjoyment and admiration. Reconciling these activities is the most difficult, and yet the most important, problem that confronts classical scholars in their studies of early hexameter poetry. Attempts have been made, of course, though not as many as there ought to have been; but we are still far from a solution.

Broadly speaking, there are three possible responses to the oral-formular theory. First, one might ignore it—an irresponsible course, because the theory is so well supported and explains so well obvious characteristics of our texts. Or one might concede that it does give us much information of a certain type and yet claim that it has no important consequences for our reading of these poems even if they were orally composed, because there is finally little difference between oral and written poetry. We could then treat these poems just as we would any other poetic texts. Good arguments can be made for this position, and some writers have adopted it with excellent results. My practice in this book will doubtless be found at several points to have something in common with it. This approach has the indispensible virtue of stressing literary appreciation of the poetry. Its weakness, however, is that it makes no use of what the oral-formular theory can tell us, and because it sacrifices this potential advantage, it will never be entirely satisfactory. It leaves the rift in classical studies unbridged and apparently unbridgeable.

So I favor a third approach: to consider the poems as literature *through* their generic aspects. As for the latter, I have in mind not so much the formulaic diction in itself as what it implies about the poetry—that it is highly traditional and highly stylized in nature, so that there ought to exist a comprehensive unity among individual poems in other respects besides language. Here too we shall be entering a relatively neglected area, although there have been, especially of late, some noteworthy exceptions. Most studies of what is typical in hexameter poetry, that is, have concentrated on the meter and the diction, so that attention has generally focused on phrases, single lines, or small groups of lines. This tendency is natural and proper, for it has been necessary to gather specific information. But although much undoubtedly remains to be discovered in this area, enough has been learned that it is now possible to examine conventions on a larger scale. Certain of these, of course, have long received attention—for example, "type-scenes" and narrative patterns, or "themes"—but mainly in regard to their utility to the poet as he composes. Although my interests here are much broader than these features, I do discuss some examples of them also, but as ways of expressing meaning—a function that I think they can have, at least sometimes, along with their practical use. I cannot claim that this study will definitively solve the problem of bringing the technical knowledge to bear on our reading of the poetry, but I hope that it will point toward a fruitful line of approach.

Such an undertaking involves no sacrifice whatever of our sense of the literary qualities of these poems. On the contrary, it will help us toward a more accurate understanding of them, and a more just appreciation of the enormous achievement they represent—an achievement by individual poets, but poets within a particular culture, and so at the same time an achievement by a society as well. There may be properties that all poems, no matter where and when they were composed, share; but a given poem should also be read and judged against the background of the tradition of which it forms a part. If it should be feared that attention to typical elements reduces these works to a uniform level of mediocrity and blots out from view the unique qualities of each one, I would answer that such a worry implies a naive preconception about the nature of literary conventions in general. Conventions are not rigid rules, and conventional ideas are not the same as platitudes. A truly creative artist will not be enslaved by conventions, but will "use" them. That verb, however, should not be taken in this instance to imply consciously premeditated exploitation (as Virgil and Milton later deliberately manipulated the conventions of heroic epic). For the hexameter poets these conventions were more a language than an artistic device, a means of expression made almost instinctive by training and habit. Yet an understanding of them offers scope for interpretation—indeed, ought to be its basis. What we need to appreciate is how a conventional element occurs within a specific context in relation to other such elements, how its generic meaning, which made it intelligible to the audience, is applied to the poet's concerns within a particular passage or poem. The breadth of variation possible within the range of conventions is obvious from a mere glance at our poems. In each we can find one feature after another that is thoroughly typical, yet each is an unmistakably individual composition. Most of them are fine poems, and several are works of profound genius. But their quality stems from what the poets made of the raw material that lay to their hands.

That these conventions exist is shown by the recurrence from poem to poem of certain formal properties and concepts, the latter often expressed in the same or similar diction. This assertion will be documented in the body of this book. Instead of brushing conventions aside through a misguided fear of neglecting the poets' individuality, why not try to understand them and make positive use of that knowledge in our reading? Only then can we really do justice to the poems and—yes—to their creators' originality. Otherwise we risk misreading and incomprehension. One passage after another in this poetry has been branded by scholars as interpolated or has been scorned as an inartistic blemish, when an informed and sympathetic reading would have revealed its true value. In other cases, the meaning of a phrase or a line that seems obscure to us but would have been understood by the original audience can be recovered if we consider it within the wider context of hexameter poetry as a whole. What, for example, does it mean when the Muses, in their epiphany described by Hesiod in the *Theogony* (line 26), call shepherds "mere bellies"? Behind that phrase are complex ideas about humanity and the value of social organization, and we need to understand them in order to appreciate how Hesiod makes them part of the statement about poetry with which he begins his poem. Or, to give a slightly different example, we shall never understand what the Muses say to Hesiod about their powers, or what Dēmodokos tells Odysseus about his art in Book 22 of the *Odyssey,* if we simply refer these statements to Hesiod's or Homer's alleged claims to originality rather than viewing them as belonging to a coherent conception of poetry that emerges from a comparison of all our texts with each other.

I have not tried, of course, to discuss every feature that might be called a convention. I have only selected those that seem to me most interesting as revealing essential qualities of the poetry. Nor have I tried to give thorough interpretations of any single work, although by citing many examples for the purpose of illustrating what I have to say, I hope that I have at least conveyed something of the flavor of this poetry. If a remark here or there sheds new light on a passage or a poem, as I believe it might, so much the better. But I would like this book, as its final result, to enable the reader to return to the poetry with a comprehensive and useful perspective on it, and to appreciate it better for him- or herself.

So many complex questions vex the study of early hexameter poetry that one can scarcely make a statement about it without adding qualifications or without having made up one's mind about certain problems, each of which admits a variety of solutions. In fact, I have already touched on one or two of them above. It seems fair to list here the opinions to which I have come on some of these matters. I discuss a few of them more fully, though not at all exhaustively, later on. But for the most part I must ask the reader to be content with these dogmatic statements of opinion, since proper treatment of any of these subjects would have required a separate volume in itself. I would like simply to make plain the assumptions on which I have worked, although as far as I am aware only the first and fourth, and perhaps the third, of the following positions have affected what I have written.

1. On the question of the integrity of the Homeric poems, I am a unitarian. I believe that each poem was shaped by a single artist according to a coherent design. Whether the same poet composed both seems to me a question that is neither answerable nor important. Some minor passages in each poem may be later interpolations; but their effect on the overall plan of the work is negligible, and they would not be much missed. I would not be greatly disturbed, for instance, if Book 10 of the *Iliad* and some parts of Book 11 of the *Odyssey* (the "catalogue of heroines" and the punishment of the great sinners) turned out to be post-Homeric, although I would prefer not to judge the question. On the other hand, I am convinced, as I indicate in Chapter 6, that the end of Book 23 and all of the final book of the *Odyssey* are genuine and important parts of that poem. I also think that Book 9 of the *Iliad* is genuine. As for the Hesiodic poems, I do not believe that they are riddled with interpolations or rhapsodic expansions, as some scholars have thought. A few individual lines are probably spurious, and the ending of the *Theogony* is a problem (as is the "Days" section of the *Works and Days*); but most episodes and extended passages seem to me genuine. For arguments on specific passages, the reader can consult the splendid editions of Hesiod by M. L. West.

2. As I wrote, I had the following chronological scheme in mind. The *Iliad* is the earliest of our poems. It was followed at no great interval by the *Odyssey*. The Hesiodic poems are somewhat later, and of these the *Theogony* seems earlier than the *Works and Days*. The longer Homeric Hymns probably were composed over the period from the late seventh century B.C. to the middle or third quarter of the sixth, although the *Hymn to Aphrodite,* generally thought

the oldest, may be as early as Hesiod's time (the latest of the long hymns is apparently the *Hymn to Hermes*). I see no secure way of dating any of the hymns precisely, however. Where the poems of the Epic Cycle, the *Catalogue of Women,* and the *Shield of Herakles* fit into this framework remains an open question as far as I can tell. I do not think, however, that my discussion depends on the question of dates, except that in Chapter 6 I consider the *Odyssey* a later poem than the *Iliad* (although the argument made there could just as well apply to the *Odyssey*'s relation to the tradition that eventually found its way into the *Iliad*) and the *Hymn to Hermes* later than the *Odyssey* (a view that probably no one would dispute). In general, I have ignored chronology. Too often the (suspected) temporal priority of one poem over another has been taken to imply its influence on the supposedly later composition. This is to ignore the strong possibility that what the two works have in common is a generic characteristic, and to focus on individual poets at the sacrifice of any notion of conventions—a symptom of our tendency to fragment this body of poetry in thinking about it. Hexameter poetry belonged to a remarkably stable tradition; and for that reason, if we seek to study its typical elements, the dating of individual poems is of small importance.

Perhaps this dismissal of chronology can be explained, and made to seem less cavalier, by referring to Richard Janko's recent study, *Homer, Hesiod, and the Hymns: Diachronic Development in Epic Diction* (1982). If his findings are accepted in full (and I have some reservations about the interpretations of his data, though I cannot speak about his statistical method), they can instruct us about the development of the hexameter tradition and its language, the dates of the various poems, and their geographical origins. That would be a great gain. But what might such information tell us about the substance of the poems themselves? Something, no doubt, though not as much as we would like to know.[1] For the changes in morphology and diction that Janko finds, though they may be significant, are small compared with the overall stability of the tradition. A "diachronic" approach, which emphasizes differences among poems, needs to be supplemented by a "synchronic" study of their common elements, which is no less valid. That is what I shall undertake here.

3. In harmony with my attitude toward chronology, I am highly skeptical of tidy schemes of the development of ideas and intellectual capabilities from Homer through Hesiod and on into lyric poetry and beyond—claims, that is, that Homer did not have one concept or another, which first appears in rudimentary form in Hesiod, is developed in the lyric poets, and comes to fruition in the classical period. The prejudices and assumptions on which such theories are based will not stand up to examination. These constructs are not in principle irreconcilable with the idea of conventions, however, and nothing in this book depends on whether my opinion on this matter is valid, except in one respect. Perhaps partly under the influence of these theories, *early* has been

taken, distressingly often, to imply "primitive," "naive," and "crude." I, on the contrary, consider this poetry sophisticated and profound, both in the ideas and feelings it conveys and in its artistry.

4. *Generic* does not imply "empty of meaning." It is quite possible for the same element in a poem to be both functional and expressive.

5. I think it possible that the Homeric poems, the *Theogony* and the *Works and Days,* and perhaps one or two of the Homeric Hymns, were orally composed. But whether they were, or whether, on the other hand, they were composed in writing or dictated, is another question whose importance should not be exaggerated. For one thing, the terms in which it has usually been posed need clarification. To most classical scholars, *orally composed* means "composed during performance" in the process envisioned by the theory of Milman Parry and Albert Lord. But as Ruth Finnegan has recently pointed out in her book *Oral Poetry,* that is only one of the possible meanings of this imprecise term. Poems can be classed as "oral," she says, in regard to the manner of their composition, the means by which they are transmitted, or their "actualisation in performance."[2] Now the surviving examples of Greek hexameter poetry exhibit certain features that, as has been fairly well established, originated as aids to oral improvisation during performance. We should bear in mind, however, the possibility that any given text evolved in a much more complex fashion than as the record of a single performance, especially since writing was certainly known in Greece by the time any of the extant poems were composed.

Perhaps it is possible to tell whether a particular poem was orally composed in performance, and for some purposes it would be useful to know this—for instance, in considering questions of textual transmission. But the consequences for the understanding and appreciation of the poetry itself are not great. Although the way in which formulaic diction, for example, is used may vary from poem to poem, the end result—the character of the poems—if writing played some role in their creation, is probably not much different from what it would have been if the poets' method was purely oral. For as Finnegan also observes, the distinction between "oral" and "written" poetry is not absolute, as has so commonly been assumed in the case of Greek poetry. The two categories often overlap significantly in manner of composition, in transmission, and in nature (1977, 132, 84, 160–68). There is, however, one aspect of the "orality" of Greek hexameter poetry that *is* important and about which we can be reasonably certain: that however it was composed, it reached its audience through oral performance. The significant opposition, then, is not between "oral" and "written" but between poetry heard in public by members of a group and poetry read by individuals in solitude. This antithesis does not set hexameter poetry off from most of the rest of Greek poetry. But the fact that these particular poems were experienced in performance has left its mark on their character, and that is my interest here. I have tried everywhere to explore the implications of this fact. It is crucial to our reading of the poems and basic to the whole subject of conventions.

I came across Finnegan's book only after I had completed the manuscript of the present work. I have added references below to some of her conclusions that seemed most pertinent to my discussion. But more generally I have found in her book confirmation of my understanding of Greek hexameter poetry from a broader perspective than my own—broader both because of her use of comparative material from various cultures and because of her knowledge of the methods and literature of sociology. Although she refers only to the *Iliad* and the *Odyssey* among Greek texts, her work bears out my arguments, I think, by its demonstration that oral poetry (by any definition of *oral*) is produced not just in "primitive" societies but also in the most advanced and is therefore not necessarily archaic or inartistic or the mindless expression of a collective unconscious; in its emphasis on performance and on conventions as forces that "both constrain and express human imagination and artistic action"; and in its suggestion that we should think, not of literature and society as distinct, but instead of "literature *in* society"—"literature ... conceived as social action by *people* rather than as a static entity in its own right." [3]

This book is addressed to classical scholars in the first instance. The uncertainties and controversies that beset its subject have necessitated some detail in treating various aspects of the poetry, and because the discussion is based so heavily on the Greek texts, I have quoted freely from them. The notes in particular, which are intended to provide documentation, support, or refinements of the points made in the body of the book, are intended primarily for specialists.

I have tried as well, however, to make the book accessible to those who know no Greek, and I hope that it might serve the nonspecialist acquainted mainly with the Homeric epics by bringing to his or her notice other poems that deserve to be better known and by providing an introduction to the nature of hexameter poetry in general. I have therefore given literal translations of all the Greek quoted (these, as will be obvious, make no pretense to literary merit), and I have transliterated words and phrases where I thought it important to know that the diction in one passage resembles that in another. I have presupposed in such readers an acquaintance with the poems in translation, or a readiness to read them in translation while using this book. Because I have written with the nonspecialist also in mind, the classicist may find facts mentioned occasionally that are already familiar; but I hope that other things here will seem worthy of attention.

Above all, I hope that this book will convey to every reader the pleasure in these poems and the respect for them that have come to me in the writing of it.

▣ Abbreviations ▣

Books of the *Iliad* are referred to in upper-case roman numerals, books of the *Odyssey* in lower-case roman numerals. Thus, XVIII. 53 = *Iliad* Book 18, line 53, and xviii.53 = *Odyssey* Book 18, line 53.

Theog. = Hesiod's *Theogony*
W.D. = Hesiod's *Works and Days*
Aspis = [Hesiod's] *Shield of Herakles*
The other Hesiodic fragments are referred to by the numbers given them in the edition of Merkelbach and West (1967).
fr. = fragment; frr. = fragments. Thus, Hesiod fr. 25.17–33 = lines 17–33 of Hesiod fragment 25.
h. Dem. = the *Homeric Hymn to Demeter* (no. 2 in the manuscript collection of the hymns)
h. Apollo = the *Homeric Hymn to Apollo* (no. 3)
h. Hermes = the *Homeric Hymn to Hermes* (no. 4)
h. Aphr. = the *Homeric Hymn to Aphrodite* (no. 5)
The other, shorter Homeric Hymns are referred to by number alone.
Allen or Allen V (for fragments of the Epic Cycle) = volume 5 of the *Oxford Classical Text* of Homer (edited by Thomas W. Allen, 1946)
K (for other epic fragments) = G. Kinkel, *Epicorum Graecorum Fragmenta* (1877)
W (for fragments of lyric poetry) = M. L. West, ed., *Iambi et Elegi Graeci* (1971)
PMG = D. L. Page, ed., *Poetae Melici Graeci* (1962)
L–P = E. Lobel and D. L. Page, eds., *Poetarum Lesbiorum Fragmenta* (1955)
R.-E. = Pauly-Wissowa, *Real-Encyclopädie der classischen Altertumswissenschaft* (Stuttgart: J. B. Metzler, 1894–)
Abbreviations of other ancient authors and texts are those of the *Oxford Classical Dictionary*, 2d ed. (Oxford: Clarendon Press, 1970).

▣ Note on Transliterations ▣

Greek words and phrases have been transliterated exactly. With proper names my practice has been less strict; in them I have used the English *y* for the Greek *upsilon*. For the most familiar names, and the names of later Greek authors, where consistency would have amounted to pedantry, I have used the Latinate forms (thus *Achilles* rather than *Akhilleus, Aeschylus* rather than *Aiskhylos*). Long vowels have not been marked in the names of ancient authors or in other familiar proper names, such as those of the major gods and heroes; thus Mētis, but Demeter (rather than Dēmētēr).

1 The Organization of Thought

AT THE START OF THE SIXTH BOOK of the *Odyssey*, the poet introduces his audience to the Phaiakians by giving their history. They once lived in a place called Hypereia near the Kyklōpes, he says. But the Kyklōpes, mightier than they, kept doing them harm, and their king Nausithoos removed them to Skheria, where Alkinoos was now their ruler (vi. 1–14). Kinship further links the Kyklōpes and the Phaiakians: Polyphēmos is Poseidon's son; Alkinoos, the same god's grandson.[1] Yet in important respects the Phaiakians are the utter opposites of the Kyklōpes. They are exceedingly refined city dwellers with a complex social organization, consummate seamen, and scrupulous observers of divine law, particularly as regards the treatment of guests. A single forebear, it seems, can produce offspring who are antithetical to each other in character. So also in the *Theogony*, Pontos begets both Phorkys and Kētō on the one hand and Nēreus on the other (*Theog.* 233–39). Or an ancestor and his descendant might be similarly opposed: Alkinoos's great-grandfather was Eurymedōn, king of the overweening Giants, who "destroyed his presumptuous people, and was himself destroyed (vii. 58–60).[2]

In such cases, genealogy brings opposites into relation to one another. It thus serves as one way of drawing special attention to polar oppositions, which are a basic mode of expression in the poetry we are considering. The Kyklōpes and the Phaiakians together mark the extremes of savagery and civilization in the world through which Odysseus wanders and, by providing limits, define that world. The others whom Odysseus encounters—mortals, monsters, and gods—do not exceed these limits in their character and behavior, though most of them tend toward one pole or the other.[3] The Kyklōpes and Phaiakians, at the extremes, counterbalance one another; each seems necessary to the other, not only for the sake of mutual characterization but also so that, together, they may give shape to what lies between them. The world would be incomplete without either one. In the same way, the daughters of Nēreus represent the sea's beautiful and benign aspects, while the progeny of Phorkys and Kētō show its grim and threatening side (*Theog.* 240–64, 270–336). In conjunction, they describe the sea as a whole. Each group by itself would give only a partial impression.

The geographical relation between the Phaiakians and the Kyklōpes performs a function similar to that of their kinship, but in spatial terms. Their original proximity, like their common descent from Poseidon, aligns them with one another. The peace-loving Phaiakians' removal to Skheria to avoid the Kyklōpes' lawless violence, explicitly connected as it is with the contrast in their characters, specifies that they are corresponding *opposites*. The sequence closeness-separation also suggests that Hypereia and Skheria enclose the world of Odysseus's wanderings, even though the *Odyssey* gives no evidence that these places are literally at opposite ends of that area, but implies at most that they are distant from each other. Yet if we cannot press the hint of geographical symmetry between them, Hypereia and Skheria still represent experiential extremes for Odysseus and thus round off the world of his wanderings, mark it as self-contained and independent.

Physically, as in other respects, this region is separate from the scene of normal human life where Odysseus is at home. At the same time, there are implicit relations between these worlds, consisting of both similarity and opposition, which are just as significant as the boundaries that divide them. The natural opulence that surrounds Kalypsō's cave, for instance, contrasts with the ruggedness of Ithaka (v. 55–75, ix. 21–36, iv. 600–608), just as the goddess contrasts with the mortal Penelope. On the other hand, the lawlessness introduced by the suitors into Odysseus's home resembles that displayed by the Kyklōps Polyphēmos,[4] and the harmonious order that Telemakhos finds in Pylos and Sparta, and that Odysseus restores on Ithaka, approaches, though it can never quite attain, the refinement of life in Skheria.

Self-sufficient, formally distinct from one another yet subtly interrelated, these two worlds in the *Odyssey* together comprise something larger, the inhabited earth. The earth too has a boundary that encloses it and defines its shape—the stream of Ocean. Beyond this, at least according to the *Odyssey*, lies another realm, the "house of Hades," which Odysseus must cross Ocean to reach (x. 508, xi. 13, 157–59). Elysium is also located at "the bounds of the earth" (iv. 563), as are the Islands of the Blessed to which Hesiod's heroes were sent (these islands are also said to be "beside deep-eddying Ocean" [*W.D.* 168–72]).[5] In the *Theogony* (720–25), a vertical rather than a horizontal arrangement is given.[6] Earth is exactly midway between heaven and Tartaros, as distance is measured by the time it takes a bronze anvil to fall. The whole cosmos is symmetrical, framed and given shape by its two extremes.

These examples suggest that early hexameter poetry as a body reflects a view of the world that is uniform not only in its content but also in its structure, the basic principles of which are similarity and antithesis. Each thing must have its polar opposite in order to be complete, and sometimes even in order to be understood, because its place and function are thereby defined.[7] The resulting symmetries, according to this view, create a consistent and intelligible order in the tangible world and in experience. The foregoing examples suggest how pervasive this conception is. A further instance, the story of

Hestia, will illustrate how action and individual character, as well as physical space and the relations between its inhabitants, can be described by antithesis.

According to the *Hymn to Aphrodite,* Hestia was Kronos's first child and again his last, by the plan of Zeus (*h. Aphr.* 22-23). This refers to the story told in the *Theogony,* that Kronos swallowed each of his children as they were born, and finally the stone that was substituted for the infant Zeus. He was then made to disgorge them by Zeus's devising—first the stone, says Hesiod, and then his actual children (*Theog.* 453-97).[8] The hymn follows up the implication of this account: the order in which Kronos vomited up his offspring must have been the reverse of that in which he had swallowed them. Hestia, who was born and swallowed first, was therefore disgorged last. The birth story of the Olympian gods thus consists of two exactly opposite parts that correspond symmetrically, with Hestia providing the outer frame. She herself, as both the oldest and the youngest sibling, holds the two members of an opposition in balance. In a similar way, as the personification of the hearth, she organizes space by her position in the center of the house, surrounded by equal area on all sides.[9] The story of Hestia's birth and rebirth may be connected with the custom of pouring the first and last libations at sacrificial feasts in her honor.[10] But this practice simply shows the same idea on another plane. So that the gods may be duly honored, the feast is given proper form, encompassed by corresponding acts at beginning and end.

The cosmos, its individual constitutents large and small, and the events that occur within it are thus all conceived in essentially the same way. The basis of this manner of viewing things is a particular sense of form as enclosure, wherein antithetical extremes define what lies between them and the whole consists of juxtaposed but interrelated parts. From our point of view this conception of form might be said to function as an aesthetic principle, but it does not appear to have been consciously worked out. It seems instead to have grown naturally out of certain habits of mind, and thus a certain way of thinking about human life and its environment, which are characteristic of the Greeks of the geometric and archaic ages. The world as they represented it has at once extraordinary diversity and an elaborate but clear arrangement of parts. This combination of qualities may seem paradoxical, but in fact only a careful design could accommodate such glorious variety without incoherence.

Besides art, the only evidence for these statements is the literature of these periods. Whatever may be true of developments in art and in other poetic types, hexameter poetry—perhaps because of the normative and conservative force of its tradition—is consistent in the sense of form it displays. In the organization of even the shortest passages and of entire works, indeed, it reflects the same modes of thought, the same idea of intelligible shape, as its subject matter does. The ordering of the poem resembles the shape of the physical world and of action as the poet and his audience conceived them. This identity of form and content is suggestive, and we shall return to it at the end of this chapter. Here, one consequence of it requires attention—that much of the meaning of any of these poems is implicit in its structure. Just as the examples given earlier, which concern very diverse matters, were found to share the same conceptual basis, so in the poems certain structural patterns, though limited in number, can appear in many different kinds of passages, with widely varying effects.

These patterns are well known. But their significance has not always been adequately appreciated, because of an unfortunate tendency to view them negatively—to consider them products of, and ways of offsetting, flaws in artistic technique or logical deficiencies from which men of the archaic age allegedly suffered.[11] The temptation to do so is strong. The Greeks of that time thought in other modes and held other notions of form than did their descendants of the classical period, whose mental habits were much closer to our own. We should always be mindful of these differences; but they do not by themselves imply that this poetry is inferior to later literature or awkwardly composed, although they do make necessary an effort and a sympathy in our reading that were not required of the original audience.

The main question at issue in judging the poetry and, more fundamentally, in evaluating the formal procedures that give it shape, is what conclusions are to be drawn from an often-observed fact. The characteristic style of archaic literature is parataxis, whereby clauses in a sentence are not subordinated one to the other according to their logical relations but are strung together as coordinate and thus as equal in value and importance.[12] The same habit is evident in the arrangement of sentences within passages and in the structure of whole works. Adverse judgments on parataxis go back to ancient times. Aristotle mentions it only to criticize it. Parataxis, or what he calls *lexis eiromenē* ("the strung style"—the metaphor is apparently of beads threaded together on a string), "has no end in itself, except when the subject being treated is finished. It is unpleasant because of its boundlessness." More pleasant and intelligible is the *lexis katestrammenē* ("the knitted style"), because it uses the period, which has "a beginning and end in itself, and an extent that is easily surveyed" (Arist. *Rh.* 3.9, 1409^{a}27-37).[13]

Subsequent descriptions of parataxis have, in effect, simply enlarged upon this basic criticism. It is easy to point out what the paratactic style lacks: subordination to one controlling idea, a carefully observed proportion of the part to the whole, and clearly stated connections between parts.[14] Inferences from the style are then made about the mentality of those who used it, and Homeric or archaic man is usually said to have lacked this or that conceptual ability. In particular, his mind, it is claimed, contemplated one object or idea at a time in isolation from all others, and he had no interest in, and perhaps not even the ability to perceive, the relations between things, no concept of the whole as opposed to the separate constituent parts.[15] As a result of this view of the style and the corresponding state of mind, poems in which parataxis predominates are all too often considered rambling, formless, incoherent, owing what shape they have to the accidents of the poet's mental associations and perhaps also to the circumstances under which they were composed. If that really is their character, our opinion of these poems will necessarily be low, our attitude to them justifiably patronizing. But can this description of them be reconciled with our experience of reading—for example—the *Iliad* or the *Odyssey*? Such a question, it might be answered, implies a subjective response, one conditioned by modern attitudes and literary tastes, whereas the style gives us the basis for an objective judgment. Certainly there is a danger of imposing modern ideas on this poetry, but in the first place, we can never hope to do it justice if we expect too little of it. In the second place, consider the assumptions on which adverse judgments are based. Aristotle's idea of organic unity is clearly implicit in his discussion of the two kinds of style and guides his judgment (see *Poet.* 1450^b21-1451^a6). The paratactic style does not display the qualities that distinguish this kind of unity, but to think that the poetry is therefore limited and inferior is to fall precisely into the error of applying a later and alien standard. Not everyone, of course, has gone to this extreme, and especially not those writers who have done so much to further our understanding of this style. The assumption still seems widespread, however, that the alternative to Aristotelian unity is necessarily formlessness. Perhaps, on the contrary, the paratactic style has virtues of its own and only needs to be appreciated on its own terms. If so, a reevaluation of the style will lead to a better understanding and appreciation of the poetry.

Even though he did not admire it, Aristotle pointed out the essence of parataxis. His understanding of it might be reformulated in this way. Whereas logical subordination implies the exclusion of all that does not bear directly upon the main idea, parataxis is inclusive. Poetry in this style is wonderfully commodious. A single poem can incorporate an astonishing number of very diverse stories, themes, and ideas (the *Works and Days* is a fine example). Moreover, because of its fundamentally additive nature, parataxis makes it possible to treat each topic by itself in turn. The individual phenomenon is thus dwelt on with what seems loving attention. The style, in the service of the thought it reflects, breaks things down into their component parts and treats experience in all its concrete particularity.[16]

At the same time, this mentality *is* able to conceive of a unified whole with a definite shape. For as we observed at the outset, and as Norman Austin has recently argued in detail,[17] the world as depicted in this poetry is not viewed merely as a formless aggregate of parts. The juxtaposition of these parts has its counterpart within the poems in the stringing together of elements of a sentence or passage. But just as areas of the cosmos are felt to be interdependent, so are the various phrases, lines, and groups of lines, large or small. And just as the heavens are balanced by Tartaros and the earth is encircled and given definition by the stream of Ocean, the arrangement of its parts and their interrelations give a sentence, a passage, or a poem a definite design that, as has been said above and as will shortly be illustrated, exemplifies a certain sense of form and thus reflects particular modes of thought.

Form thus holds in balance the sheer abundance of material in this poetry. The paratactic style, moreover, enables the poem to bring things into relation with one another, even to reveal connections that are not at all obvious and thus to compel discoveries.[18] However, because the significant connections are very often not stated explicitly, but are implied by the mere fact of juxtaposition or by other structural relationships, the poems gain tremendously in suggestiveness, subtlety, and complexity. Far from being a hindrance, the style is a powerful means of poetic expression.

If these are the advantages of the style in general, artists on the order of— let us say—a Homer or a Hesiod will use it as a medium with wonderful results. In fact, the literary quality of most of surviving hexameter poetry is considerable. But to appreciate any hexameter poem, even one marked by particular genius, we must consider in general how to read poetry composed in the paratactic style. We need to understand the norm, that is, in order to appreciate its manifestation in a specific work. To discern the form of a poem and grasp its coherence poses problems of interpretation for us, as it most likely did not for the original audience. That is why it is so important for us to recognize the basic structural patterns that give shape to poetry composed paratactically. In discussing these, I may retread some ground familiar to specialists, but there will be, perhaps, an advantage in bringing together in English what is known about them. All too often, however, scholars have been content merely to catalogue them, without sufficiently considering their significance. In what follows, I hope to show what an understanding of form will contribute to a literary appreciation of certain passages (and—in the next chapter—of whole works); and as part of that enterprise, I hope to show what we can learn from form about the ideas and attitudes of the men who composed and listened to these poems.

The simplest, and poetically perhaps the least significant, pattern is the one known as hysteron proteron.[19] When several objects, persons, or events are to be treated, they are first listed and then described in detail, but in reverse order. A small-scale example is III.103-4:

οἴσετε ἄρν', ἕτερον λευκόν, ἑτέρην δὲ μέλαιναν,
Γῇ τε καὶ Ἡελίῳ.

Bring lambs, one white [a], the other black [b],
for Earth [b] and for the Sun [a].

The sequence of the lambs' colors and the respective powers that are to receive them is thus *ABBA*. As is clear in the Greek, the genders follow the same sequence: the white lamb and the Sun are masculine; the black lamb and Earth feminine. This arrangement is so common in Homer that Alexandrian scholars seem to have taken it as a rule (it is not, in fact, invariable).[20] It can occur on a much larger scale than a sentence; Bassett (1920, 48-51), for instance, notes its use in narrative and descriptive passages in Homer. It is also convenient in poetic genealogies, and Hesiod disposes his material this way when circumstances permit.[21] Sometimes a multiple inversion occurs, an interlocking in the form of a chain. In the *Aspis* (ll. 48-56), for instance, the ancestry and strength of Herakles (*a*) are distinguished from those of his half-brother Iphikles (*b*), and clauses characterizing them are strung together in the sequence *ab ba ab ba*.[22] More than two elements can be involved in hysteron proteron, and the resulting structure is more elaborate. After listing the sons of Iapetos in the *Theogony* (Atlas, Menoitios, Prometheus, Epimetheus), Hesiod tells how each ran afoul of Zeus in the order Epimetheus–Menoitios–Atlas–Prometheus (*Theog.* 507-20).[23]

Hysteron proteron is almost purely formal; but even so, it is interesting because it results in an order that is not one of prosaic logic. We would expect, "bring a white lamb for the Sun and a black lamb for Earth." Instead, the thought is broken down into its components, and these are strung together paratactically—but in a definite and (at least when one is accustomed to it) an intelligible sequence. If we consider the poem in performance from the point of view of both poet and audience, we can understand that hysteron proteron actually maintains clarity. Because it makes possible a short preview of all the forthcoming topics, it allows the poet to get his ideas in order before he proceeds to detailed treatment of each, and it lets the audience know what is to come, so that they never lose sight of the overall plan. This advantage is especially important in large sections of narrative. But in passages of any length, hysteron proteron permits the continuity of thought, as Eustathios observed, and in this way too it helps the poet in composing and the audience in comprehension.[24] How foreign this pattern is, however, to those accustomed to experiencing poetry more with the eye than with the ear appears from Eustathios's fullest discussion of it (390), in connection with the passage quoted above, III.103-4. Whereas two of the terms that belong together (the black lamb and Earth) are juxtaposed, he notes, the other two are separated, and he finds this scheme confused and tortuous. Actually, there is hardly any sacrifice of clarity. Once a listener has connected "black" and "Earth," as he must anyway on grounds of religious decorum, he has no choice, on reaching "Sun," but to associate it with "white." In addition, "white" and "Sun" frame the inner elements and give the sentence a satisfying sense of enclosure and completion. Hysteron proteron thus manifests the concept of rounded form that we have found to be characteristic of the content of the poetry. Conscious planning is not at issue here; the poet instinctively shapes his sentence this way.[25]

Occasionally, under the right circumstances and when used by a great artist, hysteron proteron can take on poetic value, as all formal conventions can. Such appears to be the case at xi.170-203, when Odysseus asks his mother's shade how she died and then inquires about the other members of his family. She answers his questions in eactly inverse order, with a symmetry that is rigid even in detail,[26] and the arrangement allows her fate to come as an unexpected and poignant climax to the series: "longing for you, splendid Odysseus, killed me." Again there is no need to speculate whether the poet consciously intended this effect. The structure of the passage reflects compositional habit.[27] It could therefore serve all the more naturally in the expression of deep feeling. The formal and artistic functions do not in principle exclude one another; here they converge in a way that seems splendidly right.

This example of hysteron proteron is unusual, however. Another pattern, related to hysteron proteron but poetically more fruitful, can also be found on the level of the sentence—for example, at XVII.695-96, where Antilokhos receives the news of Patroklos's death:

δὴν δέ μιν ἀμφασίη ἐπέων λάβε, τὼ δέ οἱ ὄσσε
δακρυόφι πλῆσθεν, θαλερὴ δέ οἱ ἔσχετο φωνή.

For a long time speechlessness gripped him, his eyes
were filled with tears, and his strong voice was held fast.

Antilokhos is speechless with grief: the sentence begins and ends with this idea, in a figure known as ring composition. This may be described generally as the repetition, at the end of a passage of exposition or development variable in length, of an idea introduced at the beginning, so that the passage is enclosed within a frame. Often, but not always, a word, a phrase, or even a whole line from the beginning will be repeated at the end. There may be more than one pair of framing members. In that case the elements recur at the end inversely to their sequence at the beginning. This arrangement differs from hysteron proteron only by the presence of a central core within the frame. Structures yielded by ring composition can range from the very simple to the very complex.[28]

Ring composition can have a very wide range of effects. In the sentence quoted above, it seems little more than formal, but it does have some significance. It achieves emphasis, which draws attention to the importance of this moment. The process is being started by which Achilles will learn that Patroklos has been killed. The course of the action, the direction of Achilles' wrath, is about to shift. If Antilokhos is struck dumb by sorrow, what, we wonder, will Achilles' response be?[29] Emphasis is one of the effects also in the following sentence (W.D. 695-97):

ὡραῖος δὲ γυναῖκα τεὸν ποτὶ οἶκον ἄγεσθαι,
μήτε τριηκόντων ἐτέων μάλα πόλλ᾽ ἀπολείπων
μήτ᾽ ἐπιθεὶς μάλα πολλά· γάμος δέ τοι ὥριος οὗτος.

At the right age (hōraios) bring a wife to your home,
when you are neither far short of thirty years
nor much beyond; this is marriage at the right age (hōrios).

The echo of the first word in the sentence near its end stresses the idea of the proper time or season, which is thematically important to the poem as a whole. The chiastic balance of the participial clauses in the central section (μήτε ... μάλα πόλλ᾽ ἀπολείπων / μήτ᾽ ἐπιθεὶς μάλα πολλά: mēte ... mala poll' apoleipōn / mēt' epitheis mala polla) further reinforces this key concept. The outer framing also rounds off this piece of advice and makes it a self-contained whole, before the poet goes on to another but related topic: the right age and qualifications of the wife.

In this short example, then, we can already observe how ring composition is at home in the paratactic style. It marks off separate passages that are juxtaposed, but with continuity between them of theme or idea. So too with longer passages, to which ring composition can also lend a sense of completion. The description of Herakles' shield in the *Aspis,* for example, consists of a series of discrete scenes, several of them enclosed by ring composition. Within the description of the city at peace, the scenes of ease and celebration are framed by lines that summarize the atmosphere of festivity (ll. 272-73, 284-85, with verbal repetition), and the chariot race begins and ends with references to the prize (ll. 305-6, 312-13). The two passages are self-contained units, yet are, at the same time, parts of the overall depiction of the joys that peace brings.

Because its poet is self-conscious about matters of form, the *Aspis* provides some particularly good examples of ring composition's most basic effect, enclosure. Here is a scene of conflict (*Aspis* 168-77):

ἐν δὲ συῶν ἀγέλαι χλούνων ἔσαν ἠδὲ λεόντων
ἐς σφέας δερκομένων, κοτεόντων θ᾽ ἱεμένων τε.
τῶν καὶ ὁμιληδὸν στίχες ἤισαν, οὐδέ νυ τώ γε
οὐδέτεροι τρεέτην, φρῖσσόν γε μὲν αὐχένας ἄμφω.
ἤδη γάρ σφιν ἔκειτο μέγας λῖς, ἀμφὶ δὲ κάπροι
δοιοί, ἀπουράμενοι ψυχάς · κατὰ δέ σφι κελαινὸν
αἷμ᾽ ἀπολείβετ᾽ ἔραζ᾽ · οἳ δ᾽ αὐχένας ἐξεριπόντες
κείατο τεθνηῶτες ὑπὸ βλοσυροῖσι λέουσιν·
τοὶ δ᾽ ἔτι μᾶλλον ἐγειρέσθην κοτέοντε μάχεσθαι,
ἀμφότεροι, χλοῦναί τε σύες χαροποί τε λέοντες.

And on it [the shield] were droves of wild boars and lions
glaring at each other and raging [*koteontōn*] and anxious to fight.
Their rows were moving all together,
and neither side was trembling, but both were bristling their manes.
For already there lay [between them?] a great lion, and on either side of
    him boars,
two of them, bereft of life. Their dark blood
was dripping down to the ground. And they, with necks outstretched,
lay dead beneath fierce lions.

But the two sides were still more aroused to fight, raging [*koteonte*],
the wild boars and the fierce lions.[30]

Although the description is not entirely clear in details, the most likely arrangement is: file(s) of lions (*a*), groups of lion(s) and dead boar (*b*), dead lion (*c*), group of lion(s) and dead boar (*b*), file(s) of boars (*a*).[31] The ring composition of the passage corresponds to this inverse symmetry around a center: details of the scene in the middle (ll. 170-75); an inner frame (ll. 169 and 176, with repetition of participial forms of *koteō*); and then an outer frame (ll. 168 and 177, markedly similar in language). The verbal description, by its form, embodies the composition of the picture that we are to imagine. Both are unified, contained within boundaries. So is the whole shield (ll. 314-15):

> ἀμφὶ δ᾽ ἴτυν ῥέεν Ὠκεανὸς πλήϑοντι ἐοικώς,
> πᾶν δὲ συνεῖχε σάκος πολυδαίδαλον. . . .

Around the rim streamed Ocean as though in flood,
and it enclosed [*suneikhe*] the much-decorated shield.

Suneikhe: Ocean literally "held together" the diverse scenes on the shield, unified them by providing a border. With that verb the poet insists on the function of the frame. Once again there is a correspondence between the poetic pattern and the physical object described, for the whole account of the shield is enclosed by ring composition. The last sentence of this description begins with these words (l. 318):

> ϑαῦμα ἰδεῖν καὶ Ζηνὶ βαρυκτύπῳ. . . .

A wonder to see [*thauma idein*] even for loud-thundering Zeus . . .

These words may well refer, not to the swans and fish that have just been mentioned but to the shield as a whole (see Van Groningen, 1958, 114), and in any case they repeat a phrase that introduces the description in line 140: ϑαῦμα ἰδέσϑαι (*thauma idesthai*). In this use of ring composition on a large scale, the frame holds together all the descriptive passages within it.[32] Surely the idea that the earth was surrounded by the stream of Ocean, ever turning back upon itself in a wide ring, sprang from the same source as the impulse to round off a poetic passage by recurring to the beginning at the end—a feeling for satisfying form.[33]

The feeling of completion that it lends to discrete poetic units makes ring composition particularly useful in marking off whole narratives or their separate stages. In the *Theogony*, Zeus marries and swallows Mētis, and their daughter Athena is eventually born from his head (*Theog.* 886-900, 924-26).

The two events are separated so as to frame the other marriages of Zeus that characterize his reign.[34] A related but slightly more complex effect is achieved in the same poem when the creation and adornment of Pandora is preceded and followed by these lines (*Theog.* 570, 585-86):

αὐτίκα δ' ἀντὶ πυρὸς τεῦξεν κακὸν ἀνθρώποισιν.

Immediately to offset fire he [Zeus] made an evil for men.

αὐτὰρ ἐπεὶ δὴ τεῦξε καλὸν κακὸν ἀντ' ἀγαθοῖο,
ἐξάγαγ' ἔνθα περ ἄλλοι ἔσαν θεοὶ ἠδ' ἄνθρωποι. . . .

But when he had made a beautiful evil to offset the good,
he brought her out where the other gods and men were. . . .

The echo at the end helps to enclose the account of Pandora's origin. Both statements summarize the intervening action—the first prospectively, the second in retrospect—but in such a way that they stress its significance. But in the second the summary occurs in a subordinate clause, and thus, besides effecting closure, it makes a transition to the next part of the narrative.[35]

Because it can have this resumptive effect, ring composition often serves not only to frame coordinate passages but also to insert material such as an anecdote or an explanation within a continuous narrative or argument. The most famous example is the story of how Odysseus got his scar, which is told just as Eurykleia recognizes him by it (xix.392-468). This passage has a double frame, established by verbal repetitions: the inner one (ll. 393-94, 464-66), with its summary of Odysseus's wounding, encloses the story, while the outer one (ll. 392, 467-68), with the repeated statement that Eurykleia recognized the scar, ties the story at start and finish to the main narrative. (See Van Otterlo, 1944, 16-18, and 1948, 10-11.) The list of Nereids in XVIII.37-50 is accommodated in a similar way, and so is the history of Odysseus's bow in xxi.11-41.[36]

Such passages tend to be developed at length and to become almost independent pieces. They have consequently been considered digressions marked as subordinate by ring composition (van Groningen, 1958, 51), or even the inevitable result of the archaic inclination toward narrative and lack of skill in literary construction (van Otterlo, 1944, 38). Such opinions have this much justice: as we have observed, richness of subject matter and fullness of treatment are among the delights of hexameter poetry, testifying as they do to an enormous interest in life's variety. But did a high artistic price have to paid? Because the notion of "unity" that informed these poems was less narrow than our own, *digression* may be a misleading term if it is taken to imply near or total irrelevance. On reflection, all inserted passages of this type will be found to add something to the surrounding context. We can be thankful for

their presence, though they would hardly be missed if they were not there;
and ring composition, in this usage, takes on a more positive value as making
possible a virtue rather than accompanying a vice in order to offset it.

It is, for instance, fitting that the first time Odysseus has been made welcome in his house without the reserve caused by the presence of outsiders,
when he can speak face to face with his wife (though in disguise and still not
with candor), and when he is being tended, as he should be, by an old and
loyal servant, the poet tells us something about his past. The story of his birth
brings home to us his ties with his family. Eurykleia is a link between the past
and the present, for she figures in the story as Odysseus's nurse (xix.401–4).
We learn that Odysseus inherited his talent for trickery from his maternal
grandfather, Autolykos—a talent that he is exercising even at this moment. We
learn how he got his name and what it means, and the scar seems the visible emblem of the pain that the name implies. (Cf. Dimock, 1963, especially p. 57.)
Odysseus, the man who has given and suffered pain and is about to emerge
triumphant, is facing the women who stayed at home and were faithful. The
story almost represents Eurykleia's own recollection of Odysseus's past, although it is told over a longer time than it would take to pass through her
mind when she sees the scar. True, the action is interrupted in a most improbable way, but that has at all periods been literature's advantage over life.
Even here there is a gain, for during this account of the past we wonder
whether Eurykleia's recognition of her master will lead to Penelope's recognition of her husband.

Similarly, with the story of Odysseus's bow (xxi.13–38) we seem to share
Penelope's memory of her husband just as she is evidently about to put
thoughts of his return behind her forever. The bow is also a reminder of a
social relationship that never had a chance to develop, a small instance of the
disruptions in life's normal patterns that have fallen to Odysseus's lot. Iphitos,
the giver of the bow, was killed by Herakles before he and Odysseus could exchange visits as guest-friends. For all Penelope knows Odysseus is likewise lost
for good, her marriage, like that relationship, cut short by death.[37] Even the
catalogue of Nereids in the *Iliad* (XVIII.37–50) is not just ornament. More
will be said of it later, but we can note here that at the onset of Achilles' grief,
when he has learned of Patroklos's death and must cope with failure, guilt,
and mortality, these names evoke his mysterious kinship with the sea and
with divinity. (Cf. J. H. Finley, 1978, 87.) These apparent digressions, then,
really have implicit connections with their surrounding contexts beyond the
explicit formal links made by the framing elements. The simple juxtaposition
of a passage with the adjacent narrative, for which one of the chief means is
ring composition, invites us to make these connections. This is a very important characteristic of the paratactic style. It is the poet's way of expressing
meaning with more subtlety and emotional force than would be possible with
explicit statement.

A difficult passage in the *Theogony* can be explained along similar lines.

With the mention of Kronos's birth in lines 137-38, Hesiod seems to be on the point of telling about the conflict between the Titans and their father, Ouranos:

τοὺς δὲ μέϑ᾽ ὁπλότατος γένετο Κρόνος ἀγκυλομήτης,
δεινότατος παίδων· θαλερὸν δ᾽ ἤχϑηρε τοκῆα.

After them Kronos of crooked counsels was born the youngest,
the most fearsome of the children; and he hated his flourishing father [*deinotatos paidōn, thaleron d'ēkhthēre tokēa*].

Hesiod retards his progress, however, with a description of further children of Gaia and Ouranos, the Kyklōpes and the Hundred-handers (ll. 139-53), whom we would have expected to be listed before Kronos, since he is the youngest of the Titans. Furthermore, since these additional offspring cannot be involved in the story that follows, they seem to be ignored by it. Yet they have been deliberately accommodated in the text. Hesiod returns to the main narrative with these lines (154-58):

ὅσσοι γὰρ Γαίης τε καὶ Οὐρανοῦ ἐξεγένοντο,
δεινότατοι παίδων, σφετέρῳ δ᾽ ἤχϑοντο τοκῆι
ἐξ ἀρχῆς· καὶ τῶν μὲν ὅπως τις πρῶτα γένοιτο,
πάντας ἀποκρύπτασκε, καὶ ἐς φάος οὐκ ἀνίεσκε,
Γαίης ἐν κευθμῶνι. . . .

For as many as were born from Gaia and Ouranos,
the most fearsome of children, were hated by their father [*deinotatoi paidōn, spheteroi d'ēkhthonto tokēi*]
from the beginning; and as each of them was first born
he kept hiding them all back—and he did not allow them into the light—
in a recess of Gaia [Earth] . . . .

Lines 154-55 resume line 138 and contain similar language.[38] This might seem a case of ring composition used to get a narrative back on track after an awkwardly placed digression, and the ingenious suggestion has been made that the passage provides a clue to the evolution of the poem as we have it. To quote West, who adopts this explanation: "When [Hesiod] came to the Titanomachy, and found that the Cyclopes and Hundred-handers had not been prepared for, he inserted 139-53, not realizing the difficulty that this caused in the following narrative."[39] Aside from the questions this raises about how the poem was composed, there is the further difficulty of explaining why Hesiod put the lines where he did, no matter when he did so. Would he have retrieved one blunder by committing another? In that case, if he had the opportunity to revise the poem once, why did he not patch up this passage as well on a later occasion? Before dealing in such hypotheses, let us look at what the passage accomplishes in its present place. We shall find here another instance of the effective use of ring composition.

In lines 139-53, Hesiod introduces in parallel two groups of offspring, each with three members.[40] Each group will later figure in one of the two parts into which Hesiod separates the third stage of the succession story (the progeny of Iapetos, with a lengthy account of Prometheus, intervenes). (See the discussion of the structure of the *Theogony* in Section a of Chapter 2, below.) Zeus frees the Kyklōpes from their bonds beneath the earth after Kronos has been forced to disgorge his children, and in gratitude the Kyklōpes give him thunder and the lightning bolt (ll. 501-6). The Hundred-handers, also released by Zeus, help him in his decisive battle against the Titans (ll. 617-720). The account of the birth of these creatures, who will reappear at key points in the myth, thus anticipates and helps to clarify beforehand the organization of much of the later part of the poem. This structural feature, however, is merely the basis for the main function of this passage, which is, again, one of telling juxtaposition. Just when Kronos is about to triumph over his father, his defeat by his own son Zeus is anticipated, both implicitly, by the mention here of Zeus's future partisans, and explicitly, by the reference in line 141 to the Kyklōpes' gift of the lightning bolt to Zeus (cf. ll. 504-5). Kronos will pay for his deed by falling victim himself to the process that he is starting: that is what lines 139-53 imply by their position. Hesiod thus hints at the real significance of Kronos's overthrow of Ouranos by letting us glimpse the ultimate consequences of that act—not merely Kronos's own punishment, but what is far more important, the ultimate supremacy of Zeus. That is the focus of the *Theogony* as a whole, with its several anticipations of Zeus's victory. Thus the three stages in the succession myth are brought together here, with a preview of the outcome given at the start of the entire sequence.

Hesiod, then, has good reason to interrupt the narrative at this point and to break the chronological order of Gaia's children by Ouranos. Beside these advantages, the difficulties with the passage, which are of a literal nature, seem unimportant. The Kyklōpes and the Hundred-handers have to be considered as separate from the Titans who, led by Kronos, depose Ouranos, although they are born of the same parents as these and despite the language of line 154. But the way their birth is set off from the list of their siblings (ll. 132-38) indicates that Hesiod thought of them as belonging to a different category—as in fact, with their monstrous appearance, they do. By the same token, although they must have been imprisoned by Ouranos, they cannot have been freed along with the Titans by his castration—an easy and natural inference to make when we hear later of their release by Zeus.

Lines 14-29 of the *Hymn to Apollo* provide our final example of a passage inserted by ring composition. In this case the framing sections are several lines long. Addressing Leto, the poet mentions the births of Artemis and Apollo in lines 16-18:

τὴν μὲν [τέκες] ἐν Ὀρτυγίῃ, τὸν δὲ κραναῇ ἐνὶ Δήλῳ,
κεκλιμένη πρὸς μακρὸν ὄρος καὶ Κύνθιον ὄχθον,
ἀγχοτάτω φοίνικος, ὑπ᾽ Ἰνωποῖο ῥεέθροις.

Her [you bore] in Ortygia, him in rocky Delos [*kranaēi eni Dēlōi*],
leaning back [*keklimenē*] against the high mountain and the slope of
    Kynthos,
next to the palm tree beside the streams of Inōpos.

Here Apollo's birth comes in by way of praise of Leto. Lines 25-28 tell of
the same event when the poet fixes on it as the subject of the narrative that is
to follow in celebration of Apollo himself:

ἤ ὥς σε πρῶτον Λητὼ τέκε χάρμα βροτοῖσι,
κλινθεῖσα πρὸς Κύνθου ὄρος κραναῇ ἐνὶ νήσῳ
Δήλῳ ἐν ἀμφιρύτῃ; ἑκάτερθε δὲ κῦμα κελαινὸν
ἐξῄει χέρσονδε λιγυπνοίοις ἀνέμοισιν.

[Shall I tell] how Leto first bore you as a joy to mortals,
as she leaned back [*klintheisa*] against the mountain of Kynthos in the
    rocky island [*kranaēi eni nēsōi*],
in sea-girt Delos? On either side the dark wave
emerged upon the shore, driven by the shrilly blowing winds.

Between these thematically and verbally related passages come lines (19-24),
which say in effect that there are many possible themes for a song in honor of
Apollo.[41] Because the "range of song" has been laid out for him on both the
mainland and the islands, and because mountain peaks and headlands, rivers,
seashores, and harbors "delight" him, a song dealing with any place would
praise him fittingly. This in itself is praise, for it implies that the god's presence
and influence are universal.

 As a whole, this passage is transitional between the opening vignette of
Apollo and Leto on Olympos and the birth narrative, which begins at line 30
with the wanderings of the pregnant and outcast Leto.[42] It is not insignificant,
however; it introduces the idea of Apollo's omnipresence, which is important
to the poem as a whole (lines 22-23 are repeated at 144-45).[43] This example,
however, illustrates how meaning can be suggested not only through the implied connections of the inserted passage to the larger context but also by the
relation of the central part to the framing sections. The duplication is not
mechanical; except for Mount Kynthos, which they have in common, the two
descriptions mention different aspects of the island's landscape and thus complement and balance one another. Together they attribute to Delos all the
natural features listed in lines 22-24 as pleasing to Apollo: a river and the sea-
shore as well as a mountain. The central section lists typical scenes of the god's
activities, and the frame describes a particular place, but one with special

significance. Just as the account of a god's birth reveals the origin of traits and actions that will become peculiar to him, so Delos, the site of Apollo's origin, is a paradigm of all his other haunts, which effectively encompass the whole world. It is thus fitting that Apollo start from there to rule over all mortals (1. 29). So much is implied by the poet's emphasis on places and his arrangement of his ideas.[44]

This passage shows particularly well another effect ring composition often has, more or less markedly. The earlier of the framing sections simply states a theme or themes, with little or no explanation. By the end of the passage, when the same ideas are recapitulated, they are understood more fully, in all their implications, because the development in the middle part has shed new light upon them. Thus the full importance of Delos as a place sacred to Apollo can be appreciated much better at lines 25-28 than in lines 15-18. Perhaps that is why ring composition is so frequent in speeches of advice and argumentation in Homer. A proposition is stated, reasons are given for it, and it is repeated at the end—but with all the weight of the intervening argument behind it. Thus, when Achilles tells Priam to endure, "for you will accomplish nothing by grieving for your son" (XXIV.550), he is repeating what he said in line 524, but with much more rational and emotional force after the intervening account of the jars on Zeus's threshold. As van Otterlo remarks (1944, 43), ring composition is not so much repetition of the beginning at the end of a passage as anticipation of the end at the beginning. It thus helps the poet to develop his thought and the audience to follow it. But it also adds emphasis, finality, and conviction to the ending.

The examples of ring composition considered so far are simple; they all have a single frame, or at most two. But more complex structures are possible, with any number of framing elements grouped concentrically. Penelope's prayer to Artemis for death in xx.61–82 takes this form:[45]

a.   61–62: May Artemis destroy me, shooting (βαλοῦσα, *balousa*) me with an arrow

b.   63–65: or may a whirlwind snatch me away,

c.   66: as when whirlwinds seized the daughters of Pandareos.

d.   67–69: Aphrodite nurtured them when their parents died (i.e., Aphrodite's presence saved them).

e.   70–72: Hera, Artemis, and Athena gave them outstanding gifts.

d.   73–76: When Aphrodite went to ask Zeus that they be married (i.e., Aphrodite's absence led to disaster for them)

c.   77–78: whirlwinds snatched them away.

b.   79: So may the gods make me vanish

a.   80–82: or may Artemis shoot (βάλοι, *baloi*) me, so that I might go beneath the earth with the image of Odysseus in my mind rather than be the wife of a lesser man.

Penelope has awakened after seeing her husband in a dream, near dawn of the day on which she has decided to let the suitors compete for her with the bow. There can be no doubt of her deep feeling, yet her speech is strictly symmetrical. The story of Pandareos's daughters, itself arranged in a ring, is framed within Penlope's wishes, which form inversely symmetrical pairs. As often in prayers, the mythical example offers a precedent, and so is intended to persuade the divinity to do what is asked. This speech is not, however, just a special case of the formality of a prayer. Penelope's (and one can fairly say the poet's) thoughts move naturally in this order, from a longed-for event into the account of a case when something similar happened, and then out of the story by the same stages and so back to the original wishes.

Penelope dwells lovingly on the details of the story, at what might seem excessive length.[46] This is another case of what strikes many readers today as the disproportion typical of archaic poetry. But the impression given in this way, that she is indulging in a wish-fulfilling reverie, is surely psychologically correct in a situation like hers, and the very pattern of the speech keeps the ideas in focus. Moreover, as in some passages examined earlier, the link between the central myth and its surroundings is not merely formal. The marriage of Pandareos's daughters was prevented when the whirlwinds seized them; Penelope wishes to be saved from marriage to one of the suitors in the same way. The parallel, though inexact, is important. Characteristically, the emphasis is on the whirlwinds as the point of formal connection. Marriage is referred to simply as the object of Aphrodite's errand (l. 74). Penelope's case is put side by side with that of the mythical heroines, and it is left to the audience to make this association.

Passages of narrative can also be arranged in elaborate patterns—for example, XVI.364-93, which describes the Trojan retreat from the Greek camp:

- a. 364-67: short weather simile with whirlwind (λαῖλαψ, *lailaps*), describing the noise and confusion of the Trojan retreat

- b. 367-69: Hektor's horses bear him safely away ("Εκτορα δ' ἵπποι / ἔκφερον ὠκύποδες: *Hektora d' hippoi / ekpheron ōkupodes*).

- c. 369-71: Trojans' plight (hemmed in by ditch, chariots broken).

- d. 372-73: Patroklos pursues Trojans, calling out commands to Akhaians.

- e. 373-76: Trojans' dispersal and retreat; noise, dust cloud (ἀέλλη, *aellē*), horses galloping toward city

- d. 377-78: Patroklos pursues Trojans, shouting as he attacks.

- c. 378-79: Trojans' plight (men fall from chariots, chariots are overturned)

  380-383: Patroklos's horses leap ditch; he pursues Hektor.

- b. 383: Hektor's horses bear him safely away (τὸν δ' ἔκφερον ὠκέες ἵπποι: *ton d' ekpheron ōkees hippoi*).[47]

a. 384-93: Developed weather simile with whirlwind (λαῖλαψ, *lailaps*),
    describing noise of Trojan horses in retreat

The symmetry is complete except for the extra description of Patroklos in
lines 380-83. This may belong with lines 378-79, so that it would help balance
lines 369-71 by providing a sharp contrast (the immortal horses leap the
ditch, while the Trojans' horses are trapped by it). But since lines 380-83
focus Patroklos's pursuit on Hektor—a point crucial to the plot—they gain
emphasis if they are felt as standing outside the structure of the passage.

The poet has reached an important moment, when the Trojans' earlier
triumph is canceled by their rout. Here begins Patroklos's pursuit, which will
gradually obsess and then destroy him; here the plot of the whole poem in-
clines toward the goal that will be reached in the twenty-second book. The
striking description, made all the more impressive by its form, marks this
turning point. At the center of the pattern (ll. 373-76), and so accorded particular emphasis, stands the definitive statement of the Trojans' retreat, "back
to the city from the ships and huts." With the exception noted above, attention in the three inner frames alternates regularly among Hektor, the Trojans,
and Patroklos. Against the background of the two armies, the Greek and
Trojan champions stand out—a juxtaposition that hints of fate. The ordering
bcd-dcb gives the description clarity, helps the poet avoid randomness. In
addition, the stress on horses throughout holds together the parts of the narrative by articulating the contrasts in the various characters' situations. The
Trojans' horses impede them, Hektor's save him, but Patroklos has the best
team: Achilles' immortal horses, which take him effortlessly over the ditch
and into the plain—but will not be able to bear him back alive. (Cf. XIX.411-
14.)

The lines in the middle of the structure (373-76) bear a certain relation to
those that comprise the outermost frame (364-67, 384-93). Like the latter,
they mention prominently the noise of the Trojan retreat, and with identical
words in the same metrical position (ll. 366, 373). They also describe a wind-
storm (ἀέλλη, *aellē*), which is "scattered on high beneath the clouds"—apparently a reference to a cloud of dust. But more important is the relation
between the similes that begin and end the passage. The first briefly anticipates the second, and together they give an effect of linear progress toward a
climax that cuts across the circularity of the passage: at first a cloud when
Zeus starts a storm brewing, and then a storm in full spate as Zeus punishes
unrighteous men.[48]

Instances of complete episodes with multiple frames in both the Homeric
and the Hesiodic poems have often been noted.[49] I shall give one further example in order to illustrate an especially skillful use of ring composition by
Hesiod, in which he reveals complex interrelationships among the various parts
of a story and at the same time creates a unified whole. The myth of Pandora, as told in the *Works and Days,* takes this form (*W.D.* 42-105):

   a. 42: the gods have hidden livelihood.

   b. 43–46: otherwise a life of ease and plenty would be possible.

   c. 47–58: Prometheus deceives Zeus [in the sacrific at Mēkonē?] and steals fire.

   d. 59–82: the making of Pandora

   c. 83–89: Zeus deceives Epimetheus.

   b. 90–92: men's prior life was free from toil and disease.

   a. 94–105: Pandora scatters the evils.

This diagram is schematic and does not take account of the complex evolution of thought in lines 47–50, or of the echo in line 95 of line 49. Nevertheless, the relations that it shows are important.

The innermost members (those marked *c* above), which flank the account of Pandora's origin (part *d*), are complementary; one describes an action, the other the corresponding reaction. These three central sections contain the traditional core of the myth, which this version has in common with that given in the *Theogony*.[50] The two outer framing pairs thus give the story its particular significance within this poem. The *b* sections also complement one another. Not only *would* men live at ease if the events related in the story had not taken place; there was actually a time when they *had* this life. But to understand the precise relation between the two descriptions of this state, it is necessary to observe that they employ opposite terms. Lines 43–46 tell what men might *have* (sufficient food, so that they could be idle), whereas lines 90–92 tell what they *lacked* (evils, toil, diseases). Thus, polar opposites, sufficiency and ease as against toil and disease, which are connected by another antithesis, abundance and lack, in conjunction characterize man's lost contentment. This is another case of definition by antithetical extremes. The members of this opposition are separated in a way typical of parataxis, but are balanced by their corresponding places near beginning and end of the ring structure. That livelihood and disease are polar opposites and perform this function is demonstrated by the way the contrast between them, still expressed through abundance and lack, forms part of a consistent pattern of thought in the poem. The golden race (ll. 109–26) resembles pre-Pandoran man.[51] Its members enjoyed abundance of food and freedom from work, and did not suffer illness, for they died "as though overcome by sleep" (l. 116). Hunger and pestilence—*limos* and *loimos* respectively—afflict the unjust city (ll. 242–43), the foil of which, the just city, which is free of hunger (*limos*, l. 230) and blessed by natural plenty (ll. 232–37), also has much in common with the golden race.[52]

Whereas the two *b* sections depict what once was and might still have been, the members of the outermost frame characterize the bleak reality of the present. They do so, however, by means of a similar antithesis: on the one hand, livelihood, and on the other, the evils that result from Pandora's removal of the lid from the jar; and these are again connected by a pair of opposites analogous to "abundance" and "lack": "hide" livelihood (κρύπτειν, 1. 42) and "scatter" evils (σκεδαννύναι, 1. 95; cf. ἀλάληται, 1. 100, and φοιτῶσι, 1. 103, both signifying "be at large").[53] But the sequence of ideas here is the reverse of that in the next frame inward. There the order is "plenty" (ll. 43–46) and then "lack" (ll. 90–92); now it is "hide" (1. 42) and then "scatter" (ll. 94–105). Thus, not only the two outer framing pairs, when set against each other, but also both pairs of adjacent *a* and *b* sections contrast man's earlier life with his present state. The ring composition allows the juxtaposition, and therefore the sharper contrast, of the conditions of ease and hardship, and admits it at both beginning and end of the story, with extra emphasis the result. The great change wrought by Pandora is described all the more graphically, and this effect is important to the myth's expression of man's need to work and to guide his conduct by recognizing the harsh necessities imposed by his situation.[54]

A sequential narrative such as we are used to would have started with the state of things before Pandora and progressed in chronological order through her infliction on mankind to the consequences. Ring composition has the advantages just noticed and also allows the making of Pandora to be stressed as the decisive event by its central position. Pandora in herself is an evil for mankind (κακόν, *kakon*, ll. 57 and 89) who introduces evils (κακά, *kaka*, 1. 91) into human life. Her action in taking the lid off the jar, important though that is, only reveals her character. Her very person embodies the antithesis that the framing sections link together. She is a gift that *contributes* a lack (of woes) and *removes* ease from man's life forever. She *hides* an evil nature beneath a glittering exterior,[55] but when she *manifests* her true quality, livelihood is *hidden* from men. Pandora stands at the heart of concentric rings as an emblem of the human condition. Like Hestia in another sphere, she stands for the unity (in this case the sorry state of mankind) defined by the outermost boundaries.

The various passages examined above (and they might be greatly multiplied) suggest how many possible uses there are for this one basic pattern. It remains to ask how, if one of the basic effects of ring composition is enclosure, a series of passages shaped in this way can be integrated into a larger unity. Here too we shall find that ring composition is actually an aid in composition.

The first ninety-one lines of the *Hymn to Aphrodite* show the poet using ring composition in several ways to move from his introduction into the first incident of the narrative proper. The hymn is barely under way when the poet inserts and treats at length incidental—though not irrelevant—material: a list of the three goddesses over whom Aphrodite has no influence, Athena, Artemis, and Hestia (ll. 8–32).[56] As several writers have remarked, this section is framed by the nearly identical lines 7 and 33, and lines 34–35 summarize lines 1–6 (Aphrodite's universal power, though with the three exceptions now taken into account).[57] Having returned to his point of origin, the poet next describes the goddess's sway even over Zeus (ll. 36-44), and then tells how Zeus made her fall in love with Ankhises (ll. 45-53). Line 53, which follows the statement of Zeus's motives, repeats line 45 with only slight change, in a resumptive use of ring composition. Now, however, Aphrodite's intended lover is named (this prepares for the short description of him in lines 54-55); and more significantly, the intervening lines (46-52) tell how the audience is to view the story that will follow—as the love of an immortal for a mortal. This sets the tone in important ways for the rest of the poem. (See below, pp. 110-11.) Aphrodite sees Ankhises, falls in love with him, and goes to Paphos to prepare for her encounter with him. The description of her adornment is treated in a way that resembles the short account of the god's birth at the beginning of the *Hymn to Apollo:* it is broken in two. The bathing and anointing of Aphrodite by the Graces are followed by only a summary statement that she put on beautiful clothing and jewelry; the poet passes over details in order to get her to Mount Ida (ll. 60-67), and gives them only later, when Ankhises sees her (ll. 86-90). In this instance, there seems no close relation between the framing lines and the intervening passage, as in the *Hymn to Apollo.* But besides rounding off the account of Aphrodite's arrival on Mount Ida and meeting with Ankhises, the ring composition allows another advantage. By postponing a full description of the goddess's appearance, the poet can give it at the dramatically right moment, when her mortal lover first sees her. Since we view her as if through his eyes (and we should notice the emphasis in these lines on the light that gleams from her clothes and jewels), we understand the effect of her splendor on him more vividly.[58] The description of Aphrodite is itself set within a frame. Line 91 resumes line 84 (both start with Ankhises' name), but is also more specific. At first, Ankhises is said to feel wonder, but after what he sees is detailed (as if his eye were passing over her), desire (*eros*) seizes him. Thus we gauge the power of the goddess's beauty.

In extended passages, then, ring composition shapes and delimits subsections and thus aids in the creation of a series of parallel episodes, actions, or ideas. At the same time, it can provide formal transitions or in other ways facilitate a thematic or narrative development between the parts, although as we have seen the implied connections between passages that are simply juxtaposed suffice for this purpose. In these ways, ring composition enables the poet to mark the stages in his plot or argument with particular clarity, but without any loss of a sense of the whole.

The account of the rape of Persephone near the beginning of the *Hymn to Demeter* (ll. 16-39) will illustrate another way in which the use of framing lines can bring various themes or plot events into relation with one another. The interval between Hades' seizure of Persephone and his disappearance with her below ground is enclosed by mentions of her cries for help (ll. 20-21, 38-39). Between these points, the echo in line 27 of line 21 marks out a smaller section. Hades' epithet πολυδέγμων ("he who receives many") at the end of

line 17 recurs at the end of the impressive three-word line 31, and line 32 repeats line 18 exactly. The result is not distinct segments but interlocking rings.
With extraordinary skill the poet interweaves a number of ideas that together
give a vivid impression of the shock and confusion of the rape: Hades' fear-
someness and violence; Persephone's fright, helplessness, and terrible sense of
abandonment; and the treachery of her father, Zeus. Hekate and Helios, who
will figure in the subsequent narrative, are introduced, and at the end of the
passage (l. 39) Demeter enters the action. This is the first time (with only the
minor exception of line 35) that she has been mentioned since the beginning
of the poem (ll. 1 and 4). She thus provides an outer frame, and the story will
continue through her point of view.[59] Although there is thus a formal symmetry between beginning and end and a clearly perceptible order, one has the
impression that the poet's thought keeps circling back to certain key ideas
even while he moves onward with his narrative.

This type of structure has often, and aptly, been likened to a spiral. It can
involve ring composition but need not. It is, however, closely akin to that
pattern. The description in the *Works and Days* of the benefits of justice
(*dikē*) and the damage resulting from violence (*hubris*) has this design (*W.D.*
213-47):

    a.   213-18: *Dikē* and *hubris* contrasted
      1. 213: O Perses, heed *dikē* –
      2. 213: and do not increase *hubris*.
      3. 214-16: *Hubris* is disastrous for rich and poor alike.
      4. 216-18: The path of *dikē* is superior.

    b.   219-24: *Hubris:* the violation of Dikē by unrighteous men

    a.   225-37: *Dikē:* the just city flourishes.

    b.   238-47: *Hubris:* the city of violent men suffers.

This section begins with a summary statement of the two principal ideas,
which occur in hysteron proteron (ll. 213-18). But whereas an extended
hysteron proteron would require that *dikē* be treated next, after line 218,
Hesiod now shifts back to *hubris* (ll. 219-24). Then, instead of telling how
the goddess Dikē takes revenge on violent men for their outrage of her, he
describes the blessings enjoyed by the just city (ll. 225-37). Only then does
he give the contrasting picture of the sufferings of the unjust city (ll. 238-
47). As in another passage arranged in "spiral" form, Hesiod's encomium of
Hekate (*Theog.* 411-52),[60] the treatment accorded these paratactically arranged topics gets progressively longer, and the regular interchange between
dikē and *hubris* stresses the opposition between them. This effect is heightened
by the similarities in language and structure between the antithetical descriptions of the just and the unjust cities in which the entire section culminates.[61]

"Spiral" form appears at its most effective, however, in Achilles' reply to

Odysseus in the embassy scene of the *Iliad* (IX.307-429). This stupendous speech seems to develop only as Achilles' emotions sweep him from one thought to another; but in fact he comes back again and again to the same key ideas, which are all part of his sense of outraged honor and his contempt for Agememnon and the proffered gifts. The circularity of his rhetoric reflects his mental state. He is locked within his rage.

Occasionally "spiral" structure can yield an elaborate pattern, as in the section on sailing in the *Works and Days* (ll. 618-94). What is at first surprising about this passage is that Hesiod gets around to telling what the proper season for navigation is only towards the end, although that is his principal subject here. In fact, he begins by stating what is *not* the suitable time. The manner of this opening follows, of course, from the joining of this section with the one on agriculture by the mention of the Pleiades and Orion in line 619, which means that Hesiod must now start in autumn.[62] But it is also natural to his way of thinking to balance an idea by its polar opposite, even prospectively.[63] Next, Hesiod no sooner advises the launching of the ship in the right season (ll. 631-32) than he recalls his father's unsuccessful mercantile career, returning in line 641 to admonitions for Persēs. What looks like a new beginning (ll. 646-49) is followed by another autobiographical passage, and only then, from line 663 on, does Hesiod give specific advice on navigation.

This state of the text is not to be attributed to interpolation, still less to what some have supposed the prolixity of the Boiotian peasant. It is actually a sign of dexterous composition. The form of the passage is distinctly articulated by the way Hesiod keeps returning at intervals to certain key ideas, which recur in various combinations: the voyage in the proper season, the ship, the cargo, profit, the danger that remains—despite careful planning— because of caprice on the part of the elements or on the part of the gods who control them (ll. 630-32, 641-45, 663-72, 689-94).[64] These "pivotal" groups of lines, which contain the bulk of the practical advice (aside from lines 673-88, where rather slight advice is spun out at length), have a cumulative effect, and an idea touched on in one will be developed more fully in another. But whereas a poet in a different style would have given this advice all together and with economy, here it is broken up, with repetition the inevitable result. There is, of course, a gain in emphasis. What the "pivotal" lines accomplish by their placement, however, is to align with one another the three passages that they enclose (ll. 633-40, 650-62, 673-88). These, in turn, by their implicit interconnections, add persuasive force to the advice. In them, a triangular relationship is set up among the father and each of his two sons. Hesiod's one short venture on the water, which led to his victory in a poetic competition, contrasts sharply with his father's constant sailing, which ended only in commercial failure, and the triumphant associations of Mount Helikon for Hesiod are played off against the unsavory description of Askra in its foothills, where the father was forced to settle. Hesiod's advice is meant to enable Persēs (if he *must* sail) to avoid their father's ill success, as the relation between line 647

("whenever . . . you wish to flee debt and unpleasant hunger") and the iron-
ical lines 637-38 (our father left Asia Minor "not fleeing riches or wealth and
prosperity, but evil poverty, which Zeus gives to men") suggests. And finally,
the complex relationship between Hesiod and Persēs that obtains throughout
the poem can be fully sensed here. Persēs is being urged to be as successful at
trading the produce of his farming as his brother is in another sphere. That is
as much a religious as it is a practical matter, for it requires recognizing and
conforming to the divine ordering of the world. Hence the superiority of
poetry, which puts Hesiod at a level that Persēs will never attain. The poet has
a theoretical knowledge that makes direct experience, with its attendant risks
(as exemplified in part by the father), unnecessary. It is a question of knowing, through the Muses, the intentions of Zeus (1. 661).[65] Without the autobiographical sections, then, and perhaps with the transposition of a few lines,
this passage could be reduced to a more sensible order, but the richness of all
these associations would be lost.[66]

Besides hysteron proteron and ring and "spiral" composition, which are
circular patterns, parallelism of structure can occur as well. This also can produce a symmetrical balance. It is less complex than the other figures, however.
Its function is not to enfold but simply to juxtapose.

The *Shield of Herakles* offers perhaps the most graphic example of parallel
structure in the account of the fight between the Lapiths and the Kentaurs
(*Aspis* 178-90). These opposing groups are described in exactly the same way:
for each, there is a list of the leaders that is introduced by ἀμφί, "around,"
and that is concluded by lines similar in language, syntax, and structure
(ll. 183, 188):

ἀργύρεοι, χρύσεια περὶ χροὶ τεύχε᾿ ἔχοντες

[Lapiths] Silver, with golden armor protecting their flesh

ἀργύρεοι, χρυσέας ἐλάτας ἐν χερσὶν ἔχοντες

[Kentaurs] Silver, with golden pine-clubs in their hands

Here the civilized humans and the wild semibeasts are contrasted by their im-
plements of warfare, and the parallel manner of their description also balances
them each against the other. Only at the end of the passage are the sides said
to be rushing together (ll. 189-90). As if to unite the two separate accounts,
the combatants' respective weapons are again mentioned, but now in a single
half-line.[67] The two groups have not yet come to close quarters, however. On
one side of the picture are the Lapiths, for the poet says that "opposite them
on the other side (ἑτέρωϑεν ἐναντίοι) were gathered the Kentaurs" (1. 184).[68]
Thus the parallelism of the description reproduces the pictorial composition,
so that once again, as elsewhere in this poem, the construction of the passage
corresponds with the scene described. And since these lines directly follow

the circularly arranged passage on the boars and lions in combat, the visual effect of adjacent scenes with contrasting composition is conveyed poetically.[69]

It is natural to organize genealogical material in parallel, and sometimes groups listed this way can be bound together not only by formal links but also by other similarities that the structure emphasizes. In the line of Phorkys and Kētō (*Theog.* 270-336), each series of children is introduced by ἢ δέ ("and she"), which with one exception (ll. 304-8) is followed by the name of a child and the verb ἔτεκε or ἔτικτε ("gave birth to"). The various sections, however, have more in common than this rudimentary formal connection. In several cases, it is unclear to whom *she* refers; but if we adopt what is on other grounds the most likely arrangement (that given in West, 1966, 243-44), we find that each main series ends with the birth of at least one monster associated with an exploit of Herakles (in capital letters below), as will be evident from this diagram:

270-76: Phorkys and Kētō beget the Graiai and the Gorgons.

277-86: Beheaded by Perseus, Medousa gives birth to Khrysaōr and Pēgasos.

287-94: Khrysaōr's son GERYONEUS, KILLED BY HERAKLES (along with ORTHOS and EURYTION).

295-303: Kētō (?) gives birth to Ekhidna.

304-18: Ekhidna gives birth to ORTHOS, KERBEROS, and THE LERNAEAN HYDRA, WHOM HERA RAISED AND HERAKLES KILLED.

319-25: The Hydra (?) gives birth to Khimaira, killed by Bellerophontēs and Pēgasos.

326-32: Khimaira (?) bears to ORTHOS the Sphinx and THE NEMEAN LION, WHOM HERA RAISED AND HERAKLES KILLED.

333-36: Kētō bears to Phorkys the serpent who guards the golden apples of the Hesperides.

References to Herakles slaying one or another of these creatures occur at regular intervals—at the end of the original list of the descendants of Phorkys and Kētō (ll. 287-94) and thereafter at the end of every second group of offspring introduced by the "and she" formula (lines 304-18, 326-32). The whole passage is closed, in ring composition, by another coupling of Phorkys and Kētō,[70] but the intervening material has been arranged in parallel. The point of the references to Herakles that punctuate this genealogy seems to be that the birth of monsters into the world was at least partially offset by the deeds of a champion of order, a son of Zeus.[71]

This passage is a brief example of a form much employed by early hexameter poets, the poetic catalogue. As is clear from the above discussion, this is a series of parallel passages listing or describing people, actions, or objects that have at least one trait in common. The successive entries usually begin with the same word or phrase, and often contain the same kind of information. Their basic organization and the formulaic phrases used in them may thus be similar. A catalogue might, in theory at least, be extended indefinitely, since any number of entries could be tacked on by means of the connecting formula. Whole poems sometimes took this form.

This sounds very dry, and the catalogue may have originated as a way of preserving information in the absence of written documents. The Catalogue of Ships in the *Iliad* is widely believed to be such a poetic record. (E.g., Page, 1959, 118-54.) The original audience would have been deeply interested in these passages, for only through them could knowledge of the past be maintained. But a catalogue need not be dull, even to modern taste. In practice, it could be expanded by narratives that concerned men or gods listed in the course of an entry. Although the items had only loose formal connections, the poet could arrange them according to a coherent scheme so as to bring out other relations and thus convey a certain meaning—as is the case with all paratactic structures. The form is flexible; poets used it in a great variety of contexts, and often with very high artistry. The *Theogony,* for example, is a kind of catalogue with a very skillful disposal of the genealogical items and a definite goal.[72] The wonderful Shield of Achilles in the *Iliad* is formally a catalogue, as is at least part of the description of Herakles' shield (*Aspis* 141-237; after that, the opening formula of the entries is dropped). After their reunion, when Odysseus relates his wanderings and experiences to Penelope, the poet summarizes these in a catalogue (xxiii.310-41). And when Zeus, asking Hera to sleep with him, tells her that no goddess or mortal woman has aroused him as much as she is doing now (XIV.315-28), he tactlessly lists his wife's rivals together with the sons they bore him—in a catalogue.[73]

Very like the catalogue, but used to construct narratives, is a device that van Otterlo has described in detail and called *Ritornellkomposition.*[74] Here successive episodes are introduced by the same or similar formulaic expressions. Each adventure in Books 9 through 12 of the *Odyssey,* for instance, begins with the basic phrase (often elaborated into several lines), "from there we sailed onward . . . ," which is followed by "and we came to. . . ." The episodes are thus linked in parallel.[75] The recurrent refrain picks up the main thread and makes the narrative as a whole easier to follow during performance of the poem. This technique of repetition and resumption also has obvious close affinities (which van Otterlo stresses) with ring and "spiral" composition.

In the general arrangement of all these series of parallel passages, other principles of composition may also be at work. Hesiod's descriptions of the first four of the five ages in the *Works and Days* are parallel in structure and content, but as we observed earlier, they are also rounded off in ring composition. A scheme of ring composition has also been found in Odysseus's wanderings as he recounts them to the Phaiakians.[76]

Narrative can be shaped by another arrangement of parallel passages as well, when like or contrasting scenes are juxtaposed so as to bring out important connections between events. The first book of the *Iliad* provides a wonderful example. This is the order of incidents in I.304-530:

a. The ship is sent to return Khryseis to her father.

b. The heralds take Briseis from Achilles; his complaint to Thetis; her plan to suplicate Zeus

a. Arrival of the ship at Khrysē; propitiation of Apollo; return of the ship to the Greek camp

b. Picture of Achilles in anger, remaining in his hut; Thetis carries out her plan to supplicate Zeus.

The gods' absence of twelve days among the Aithiopians (I.423-27) allows Achilles' interview with his mother and hers with Zeus to be separated by the scene at Khrysē. The structure that results, with the balancing of four episodes, implicitly associates the return of Khryseis with the seizure of Briseis, the appeasement of Apollo's wrath (μῆνις, *mēnis,* I.75) with the growth of Achilles' wrath (μῆνις, *mēnis,* I.1), which thus seems godlike in its intensity and threatened consequences—a first impression that the rest of the poem bears out.[77]

Again, in the third and fourth books of the *Iliad,* preparations for the duel between Paris and Menelaos, the duel itself, and its aftermath (the breaking of the truce) alternate with views of Helen at home, on the wall of Troy, and at home again in her bedchamber with Paris, in a sequence that, as Whitman notes, reenacts the events that caused the war.[78] The positioning of scenes within the city (the place of women and old men in time of war) next to scenes on the battlefield outside the wall is epitomized in advance by Helen's occupation the first time we see her. She is weaving—in Homer, woman's most characteristic activity—but depicting on the cloth "the many struggles of the horse-taming Trojans and the bronze-clad Akhaians, which they suffered for her sake at the hands of Ares" (III.125-28).[79] What she represents is identical with Homer's subject. Her weaving represents the making of Homer's poem.

Weaving is not a bad metaphor for this poetry. The comparison may, in fact, have been built into the Greek language, for the ancients, probably with good reason, seem to have associated one of the words our poets themselves use for "song," ὕμνος (*humnos*), with the verb ὑφαίνειν (*huphainein*), "to weave."[80] It is natural to think of poetic form as something tangible, and to use (as I have) visual metaphors for it. As in a tapestry, the significance of this poetry is in the design. To say this, however, is to raise a question that must be faced now that we have completed our survey of the basic structural patterns. It may seem paradoxical that poetry that, even if it was not orally composed, was disseminated through performance rather than by written texts, should display such pronounced use of formal techniques, and should make of these techniques, moreoever, such a rich and subtle means of poetic expression. One can look at a tapestry, and at the text of a poem on a page, but not at a poem as it is being recited. On the other hand, these patterns can be found in passage after passage—too often for them to be the product of the bookish scholar's imagination. There must be a reason for their presence. But if, as we have claimed, they are essential to the poetry's effect, how, and in what sense, would the audience at an oral performance appreciate the form of the poetry they were hearing? What is the relation between the schematic diagrams we can make on the page and the effect of this poetry?

We can begin our answer by observing that listeners, unlike readers, cannot pause to ponder the significance of a phrase or a line in its context, or turn back pages to understand how an idea or action fits into the larger whole—a passage or the complete work. In order to follow the poem throughout the performance, they must at every moment comprehend each part and simultaneously have a developing sense of the whole. It follows that an orderly arrangement of parts, a clearly marked structure, far from being incongruous with the conditions of performance, is their necessary product.[81] There can be no doubt of this connection where the simplest types of organization are concerned. The utility for both poet and audience of hysteron proteron, of some kinds of parallel construction, and of ring composition with a simple frame has been pointed out above. The same reasoning holds true, however, of the structure of long episodes, of the designs of whole poems, which will be studied in the next chapter, and of passages with multiple framing. To take this last case as an example: ring composition, as we observed earlier, is in some respects an easy and a natural way to organize thought. The poet moves by degrees to the heart of his story or argument and then by the same stages to his conclusion, which restates the beginning with new understanding or persuasiveness. So methodical is the evolution of the passage that the audience could easily follow. The more complicated the subject is, in fact, the more the listeners need to know what stage in the development of plot or ideas they are hearing at each moment, or they will be lost and the poem will fail. The only essential difference between the kinds of ring composition (multiple as opposed to single framing) is in the complexity of the thoughts they can express. And in general, no matter how elaborate the structures that result from them can be, the basic patterns are simple and easily comprehended.

In many passages, the structure could be articulated, and thus made even clearer, by verbal repetitions. Their effects, in turn, may have been reinforced by aspects of performance that we can know nothing about—intonation of voice, gesture (with head and body if the poet was playing the lyre), and the music itself. These things would have guided the listeners' perceptions at some (not necessarily conscious) level of awareness. We must also take into account the capacities of that audience, which our own habits may lead us to underestimate. Not dependent on the written word, accustomed to hearing rather than reading poetry, they may have been able to catch recurrences of phrasing even over long intervals, and with or without this aid to carry the most complicated structures in their heads, just as the poet may have composed and shaped his work mentally.[82]

In fact, it is the idea of artistic convention that ought to guide us most in this uncertain area. Poetic performances must have been common occurrences. Members of the audience with long experience of listening would have been sensitive to the juxtapositions, the balancing of like and contrasting elements, that were the effects of the formal techniques. That, after all, was what mattered; they probably would not have been able to draw diagrams, and they would not have needed to. Such things have their uses, particularly for those, like us, who rely heavily on the written word. But when one becomes used even to reading this poetry, one can develop a sense of its typical forms and what they signify. From the poet's point of view as well, habit must have been crucially important. He arranged his poems according to certain patterns deeply ingrained by the continuous practice of his art. The more completely he had assimilated them, the more subtle would be the ideas he could express and the poetic effects he could convey without danger of losing his audience. He did not need many different patterns. That they were few and simple made for greater clarity; but there was no limit on the ways they could be realized in particular contexts. Like the formulaic diction, then, the formal procedures were a means of communication between poet and audience, because they were common property. Their typicality did not drain them of significance. It was precisely what made them intelligible, gave them their expressive power.

As it happens, there is one piece of evidence to support these arguments, an instance of public discourse, purportedly given verbatim in one of the poems, that displays a careful circular structure. That is Nestor's speech in I.254-84. It begins with a rebuke of Achilles and Agamemnon and ends with advice addressed to each of them in turn. These parts we may ignore, for we are concerned here with the intervening lines (259-74), in which Nestor urges the feuding chiefs to heed him. Clearly the important section of the speech since it lends authority to the advice that follows, it has this arrangement:[83]

a. 259: obey me (ἀλλὰ πίθεσθε, *alla pithesthe*).

b. 260-261:
(1) I was once the comrade (ὡμίλησα, *hōmilēsa*) of men
(2) who were better than you, and
(3) who valued me.

c. 262: I have never seen such men.

d. 263-65: names of the Lapith chiefs

c. 266-68: They were the strongest of men and conquered the mightiest enemy.

b. 269-73:

(1) I was the comrade ($\mu\epsilon\vartheta o\mu\acute{\iota}\lambda\epsilon o\nu$, *methomileon*) of these men and acquitted myself well.

(2) No man now alive could match them in battle, and

(3) they heeded my advice and obeyed my speech.

a. 274: You too obey me ($\grave{\alpha}\lambda\lambda\grave{\alpha}\ \pi\acute{\iota}\vartheta\epsilon\sigma\vartheta\epsilon$, *alla pithesthe*).

Just before this (I. 247-49), Nestor has been introduced as "Nestor of pleasant words, the clear-voiced orator of the Pylians, from whose tongue speech flowed sweeter than honey." The speech that follows is clearly meant to be a model of persuasive eloquence (even though it fails of its purpose in this case), a particularly fine example of the kind of rhetoric that, we are to imagine, Homeric heroes were accustomed to hear and strove to emulate. It thus must stand as an example of ideas systematically ordered so that Nestor's listeners can follow. The passage shows, then, how ring form makes possible clarity of exposition. Most importantly, the poet has presented this speech in verse, and if the audience is to experience it as effective rhetoric, it must be well constructed according to prevailing standards. That is, Homer has imitated forensic convention by means of poetic convention. This transfer was particularly easy because it accorded with conventional ideas: poetry and rhetoric were represented as related arts. (See below, pp. 140-42).

Still, the issue is not simply one of order and clarity. In the foregoing study of the typical structural patterns, it has been claimed that in many passages they bring about subtle poetic effects. But given the circumstances of composition and performance, would a poet be capable of achieving, and the audience of appreciating, such artistry? In regard to the audience, we might reply with one writer that "the human mind is a strange organ, and one which perceives many things without conscious or articulate knowledge of them, and responds to them with emotions necessarily and appropriately vague" (Whitman, 1958, 256). Something similar might be said of the poet as well. But we can supplement this general truth with an answer that applies more specifically to hexameter poetry, one that is implicit in the very idea of convention. Communication by conventional forms of expression, in poetry or any other medium, is so habitual that it becomes almost a reflex and need not involve conscious mental processes. Thus we are not required, and probably ought not, to assume deliberate intent on the poet's part or reflective understanding on the audience's. At the same time, because its modes are part of everyone's mentality, such communication can be sufficiently precise for essential meanings to be conveyed. The audience's response, therefore, need not have been especially vague. Certainly, as we have seen, the structural patterns allowed a rich suggestiveness ruled out by discursive logic, but listeners who thought in these modes would have been sensitive to implicit meanings. As for the poet, there surely was artistry on his part, artistry of a high quality though perhaps different from the way we conceive it. The poet's talent was the ability to express whatever he wanted to in the conventional forms, so that these did not limit him but were part of his language.

It is necessary to be as precise as possible about what the existence of conventions does and does not imply. We should not be misled into making the assumptions that underlie a slightly different reservation about the effect of structural patterns, one that has been raised in regard to the scheme of ring composition found by Whitman in Books 9-12 of the *Odyssey,* but which is general in scope:

> It does not seem likely that the force of the artistic pattern, *qua* artistic pattern, in a traditional oral song would be great enough in itself to cause either the placing or displacing of incidents. I doubt if the artistic pattern is dynamic to this degree and in this way. This is not to deny that such balances of pattern are felt by the singers—we have seen them operative on the level of interlinear connections. . . . But to suppose that such patterns would be the cause of changes of essential idea and meaning may be carrying their influence too far.[84]

As the discussion just above indicates, and as will be argued further in the next chapter, the distinction implied here between artistic technique and traditional methods of composition is meaningless for this poetry. They are virtually identical. Furthermore, we must not think of the structural forms as abstractions with an existence independent of their content. To assert that they are present and are significant does not imply that they served the poet as models, purely aesthetic in value, according to which he shaped his material with inevitable changes of his "essential idea." They were, on the contrary, his mode of expression, inseparable from the meaning, embodying the meaning, and would not have forced changes except insofar as conceptual or linguistic forms can ever be said to influence thought. Of course, the patterns that we have considered are useful poetically and have an aesthetic value. I have called them an artistic convention, and they function as such. But their importance is not limited to that. They are particular manifestations of an entire way of thinking, and their very existence as conventions is explained by that fact. And this mentality was common to poet and audience. That is the primary reason why listeners at a performance would have responded to poetic structure, from which all the other reasons follow.

The relations between things that the paratactic style, by juxtaposition, reveals, consist, as we have seen, of either similarity or contrast. These correspond to what G. E. R. Lloyd has shown to have been the two basic modes of early Greek thought, polarity and analogy.[85] Both are epitomized in the very forms of the poetry. Any structural pattern can *express* either likeness or contrast, or sometimes both at once. But in *shape,* parallelism displays similarity of structure between parts (analogy), and even contrasting sections must have enough in common—for instance, diction or theme—so that they can be aligned with one another. Hysteron proteron, on the other hand, is a polar pattern, and so, essentially, is ring composition with its inverse symmetry of multiple frames, even though the corresponding parts within the structure can be either alike or antithetical.[86]

This identity between the categories of thought and the mode of their poetic expression has exciting implications concerning the nature and function of hexameter poetry. Analogy and polarity determined not only poetic structure but also the early Greeks' conception of the order of the world. And so we return to what we noticed at the outset, that the sense of form exemplified by the shape of the physical world as the poetry depicts it is the same as that displayed by individual passages and indeed whole poems. There is a perfect correspondence between form and content, as in all good poems. But we cannot leave the matter there.

For those who composed it, poetry was a profession, and for those who listened to it, a means of enjoyment. But at the same time, it was a way of knowing the world, for it told of the physical arrangement of the cosmos, of the divine powers that influenced events, and of man's place in the whole scheme. The poem at once exhibited the world's fullness and variety and discovered its essential order. But it also represented that order by virtue of its existence as a pattern in the mind. By embodying the forms of thought habitual to poet and audience, the poem evolved in the course of performance as a model or mental image of the world that it sought to elucidate.

2 The Design of the Poem

HOW DOES THE POET, thinking and composing paratactically, shape his poem? In what sense does he shape it at all? Even if it is granted that individual passages have a clearly defined and recognizable construction, are they integrated into an overall design?

The discussion of certain examples in the preceding chapter (for instance, *h. Aphr.* 1–91) points to an affirmative answer to the last question. This answer can be strengthened by arguments similar to those given for the coherence of individual passages, for the issues here are essentially the same as before. The only difference is one of scale: we are now dealing, not with single lines or groups of just a few lines, but with larger units and their relation to the complete work. As with the part, so with the whole: passages are interrelated to form a larger unity (the entire poem) in much the same ways as elements of a passage are. But the problem of unity is more acute on this level, involving as it does our responses to the poems and the way we judge them as literature. These judgments have not always been admiring.

The nature of parataxis has led some scholars to think of an archaic poem as a mere series of episodes that may be bound together by formal devices but that otherwise have little or no connection with one another. Ring composition, for example, marks off discrete passages and, when used resumptively, makes possible the linking of equivalent sections. It has been considered a symptom of the paratactic style's characteristic disunity or a means of achieving a loose coherence at most.[1] Discussing another pattern, *Ritornellkomposition,* van Otterlo (1944–45, 204–5) concludes that the paratactic style, since it aims at stringing together as much material as possible, rules out a planned structure. He mentions as evidence the remarkable fact that this poetry generally lacks pronounced endings, and also the tendency for the body of the poem to develop beyond the subject announced at the beginning. The first of these characteristics may have another explanation, as we shall see in due course. (See section h of this chapter.) As for the second, no literary artist has ever felt compelled to begin his work with a complete program of what is to come; and though it is true that the hexameter poets, because of the necessities imposed by performance, often anticipated the later development of themes in order to make their poems intelligible to the audience,[2] they could

also, as they proceeded, introduce other material related to the subject announced at the beginning. But these matters are subsidiary to the main argument for disunity, which derives from the character of the style itself. To
that we might reply that as we noted earlier in regard to catalogues, sections
of a poem, though linked in a series, may at the same time be arranged according to a well-defined plan. The formal connections in that case are, precisely,
formal, in service of a more basic design. Nor does the paratactic mentality,
with its disposition to view things successively, necessarily result in the lack
of a controlling theme or a basic thought in a work of archaic literature.[3]
That always exists, though it is liable to be broken down into its components
and not to be stated explicitly. We should not, moreover, imagine that the
poet's interest in the particulars of his material tempts him into wandering
from his original direction.[4] As we have observed, this concentration on the
individual aspect is complemented, in this mode of thought, by an equally
important sense of the unity of the whole.

The whole question of design is complicated by the way this poetry seems
to have been composed—either orally or (if writing played a role) at least
according to the habits of oral composition. Any of these poems may be to
some degree an improvisation, whatever importance we assign the possibility
(which is imponderable) of premeditation or of revision in later performances
or with the aid of a written text. It is difficult, then, to conceive the poet beginning with a detailed plan of the whole work in his head, or with much more
than a general notion of the goal he wanted to reach.[5] This probably holds
true even of any poet who may have composed entirely in writing, for as the
continued use of formulaic diction shows, the fundamental procedures of the
oral poetic tradition persisted in the works we are discussing. The problem is
to know what conclusions to draw. Did the poem simply run away with the
poet? Does the lack of a clearly foreseen design at the start mean that the
process of creation could not have *resulted* in a coherent form by the time
the end was reached? And would such a result have been merely accidental?

Verdenius has argued that the principle of composition in the *Works and
Days,* the Homeric poems, and other archaic poetry is the association of ideas.
Although some general themes connect the parts of each work, it is association, he says, that yields a basic order, yet an order that is dynamic rather
than static.[6] This view recognizes what is doubtless an important phenomenon—the occurrence of subtle verbal, thematic, and conceptual connections
between sentences and passages. Yet the emphasis on mental association as
their cause may be misleading. It implies a more or less random development,
despite the influence of other structural principles that we have observed within the passages and that we shall find in whole poems. There is also a theoretical difficulty: the concept of association may put the case the wrong
way around. Granted, for instance, that the connections between the elements
of *W.D.* 356–82 that Verdenius finds (1960, 349–52), or something like them,
really exist, how can we know that Hesiod's mind, prompted by the language

he uses, is involuntarily progressing from one topic to another? Perhaps association of ideas is simply the appearance that the passage finally gives, whereas Hesiod is actually engaging in a more authentic kind of poetic creation. In lines 354-67, for instance, he seems to be exploring the notions of giving and not giving, showing their various manifestations, putting them in the context of related ideas (stealing, for example), and letting the meanings of various words refract upon one another in order to define the ideas they represent.[7]

Another attempt to grapple with the problem of form, the poet's mentality, and his creative method is the admirably lucid and sensible account recently given by M. L. West (1978, 41-59) of the process by which he imagines the *Works and Days* to have been composed. According to this thesis, Hesiod started with an idea of the course his poem would take ("the prospect") and some independent passages on various topics, already complete in themselves ("heavy units"). He then had to work the latter together with connecting material (here West attributes an important role to association). As his poem grew, Hesiod's "prospect" changed and became more ambitious, so that parts of the poem that seem not directly pertinent to what precedes them are to be explained as points where Hesiod altered course or expanded the scope of his subject.

One can only be grateful for any effort to discover how Hesiod and his fellow poets worked, especially when it is based on a recognition of the differences between archaic and later poetry. But is such a confident reconstruction justified either by the evidence or by its results? There may be some truth in it; Hesiod might have changed his mind as he created or re-created his poem. But whether we can now locate the points at which he did so may be doubted. It is surprising, for instance, to find *W.D.* 265-73 called "a mere dribble of additional thoughts," and to be told that the entire section on farming was "an extension added on to the original plan" (West, 1978, 50, 52). As these examples indicate, such a method of analysis poses a danger. It necessarily ignores relations between parts of the poem that are deeper-rooted and more significant than association of ideas, because it seems to start from the assumption that those do not exist. Interpretation might too easily become simply a matter of detecting the stages in the poem's evolution rather than of understanding and appreciating the text in its present form.[8] That might be a position on which to fall back if the latter kind of interpretation fails to discover coherence in the text, but it should not be allowed to forestall this attempt.

Accounts of the poet's activity such as those by West and Verdenius imply that the only alternative to a clearly preconceived plan on his part is a haphazard, if not entirely random, development of the work. There is another possibility between these extremes. It is true that as he went along the poet apparently felt the desire and found the opportunity to include a large amount of material subsidiary, but not alien, to his main subject. At the same time, he would have had ways of disposing all this material into an intelligible design, methods analogous to those used in the formation of large or small parts of the poem. Like the latter, these must have been conventional. The poet would have applied them, not with conscious deliberation, but out of habit and the reflexes conditioned by an underlying mentality. However diverse and massive his raw material, then, he will have arranged it systematically, yet not according to any mental or written outline but *as he composed the poem.* [9] By this argument form retains significance, demands our attention.

What, then, were these methods? The poet's task was not simply to join together neighboring blocks of poetry by providing formal transitions. He did that, of course; but the surviving poems show other, less obvious but more expressive organizational patterns as well. In some cases, whole poems were arranged in ring composition. [10] But in nearly all the poems, ideas or episodes that appear in different and often widely separated parts are connected with each other by means of two intimately related kinds of repetition. First, the recurrence of words, phrases, whole lines, or even groups of lines stresses important ideas and clarifies the overall form of the poem, as several scholars have noted. [11] Second, certain patterns of action or event might be repeated, often but not necessarily with echoes in phrasing, so that the poem becomes a balanced design of similar and contrasting elements. In both categories, well-known features of oral poetry are involved (formulaic diction, typical scenes, and the like). These are, of course, aids to the poet in composition, the "building blocks" of his poem. But the generic nature of the language and of some types of episode should not blind us to the significance their use can have in certain contexts. These functions, far from excluding one another, are complementary and inseparable.

There is no need to argue here that composition by formula is not necessarily automatic but is subject to the poet's control, as Whitman and, more recently, Austin have done. [12] I am sympathetic to that approach; but whatever the truth of that matter may be, the present discussion does not have to depend on the poet's conscious artistry. We need only reflect that if, under particular metrical conditions, there is usually only one way of expressing a given idea (that is, by a particular formula), then the repetition of the formula indicates the recurrence of that idea. This statement, I am aware, simplifies a vastly complicated subject, but it seems essentially true and provides at least a working assumption. One way in which it might be justified in detail may be found in the studies of Michael Nagler (1967, 1975). From this point of view, the conventional nature of the formula helps in conveying meaning, for this diction is the language shared by poet and audience. The repetition of a formulaic phrase or line brings again to the listeners' minds the underlying thought, which is itself related to a shared conceptual pattern (what Nagler calls the "preverbal Gestalt"). Repetitions thus can be very expressive, but the extent to which this power is exploited varies from one instance to another. Within a poem, recurrent formulae have little or no discernible significance in some cases, while in others they have a considerable amount.

Analogous to the formulae are typical scenes, "themes" as described by Albert Lord (1951; 1960, 68-98), and even larger conventional sequences such as occur in the battle scenes of the *Iliad* studied by Fenik (1968). These are natural ways of organizing a narrative. How useful they were has been strikingly demonstrated by Mary Louise Lord (1967), who has found in the *Hymn to Demeter* a sequence—composed of the central character's withdrawal, devastation in his absence, and his return—that resembles the one on which the plot of the *Iliad* is based.[13] Much other work has been done in this area, with illuminating results.[14] In speaking above of recurrent motifs and patterns of action, I have had in mind partly such typical arrangements of plot, as well as others that are at least not demonstrably generic. But even the most clearly typical pattern can be expressive. There is, on the one hand, what Albert Lord (1960, 148) calls the "supra-meaning" of a theme, the meaning that has accrued to it in the poet's mind from all the other occasions on which he has used it, and in the audience's minds from all the other contexts in which they have heard it used. But in a particular poem too, at least at certain points, such sequences can convey meaning,[15] and these cases are important for our purposes. Sometimes it is less profitable to recognize a sequence as traditional than to ask why it is developed in a certain context. It can often best be understood in relation to similar patterns elsewhere in the poem.

Narrative patterns and motifs are frequently repeated with the same formulaic diction, and in such cases their function overlaps that of the recurrent formulae. Charles Segal, who has demonstrated the significance of a theme that runs through the *Iliad* and who also draws on Nagler's theories, well describes the reciprocal relationship between language and plot: "the parallels in the narrative situation . . . evoke the formulaic repetitions; and, conversely, the repetitions allow the parallels (or divergences) of situation to clarify and develop" (Segal, 1971, 5-6). This covers many instances of meaningful repetition that we shall find, as the nature of this poetry would lead us to expect. But the two aspects are not wholly interdependent. Formulae do not have to recur in large clusters to be significant, and meaningful structures of like and contrasting motifs and events can take shape in the course of a poem without much repetition of language.

For illustration of these general arguments, let us consider the relation between two episodes in the *Odyssey*. In the fourth book, Telemakhos arrives at Menelaos's palace with Nestor's son Peisistratos. He receives hospitality from Menelaos and later from Helen, who almost overshadows her husband in performing this duty. When they first enter, the visitors marvel at the splendor of the house (iv.42-46). Later, at supper, when Menelaos speaks of Odysseus, Telemakhos weeps, holding his cloak before his face (iv.113-16). But Menelaos notices, and his guest is eventually identified as Odysseus's son. Later, Menelaos tells the story of his wanderings after the Trojan War. In Book 7, Odysseus gazes in wonder at Alkinoos's opulent palace as he enters (vii.84-132; 84-85 are nearly identical to iv.45-46). He is received in the first instance by a woman, Arētē. Later, during meals, Odysseus twice weeps while Dēmodokos sings his deeds at Troy (viii.83-85, 521-31); the first time, he holds his cloak before his face. The second occasion leads to revelation of his identity, and thus to his account of his experiences after the sack of Troy.

In detail, the two scenes differ greatly, but these basic features are unmistakably similar. There is, of course, the risk of subjectivity. But dismiss these scenes as *only* generic, versions of a basic type-scene, and we shall miss an important part of the parallelism between the journeys of the father and the son. We shall also risk ignoring the function of Sparta and Phaiakia as related paradigms of civility and their combined bearing on the situation in Ithaka. And finally we shall miss the contrast between Menelaos's narrative and that of Odysseus, which the similar ordering of events brings into relation with each other. The fact is that the basic sequence is typical, and its realization in these scenes is *both* functional (a way of shaping narrative) *and* meaningful.

To oppose artistry to useful compositional habit is misleading, as was argued earlier, and in regard to this poetry the question of poetic intent is the wrong one to raise. Certainly the good poet will be master of his material, however traditional it is, and will use it creatively. But whatever his intentions are, he arranges that material in ways consonant with his own and his listeners' modes of thought. It will be natural for him and his audience to feel similarities and contrasts between sections of a poem. Repeated formulae and motifs are not deliberately inserted pointers to these relations, but rather reflexes of them. But the argument made here—that the poem can have a coherent form that is expressive of meaning despite the lack of detailed planning by the poet before he began to compose—will find its best support from an examination of the designs of particular poems. In addition, although such a study cannot aim at exhaustive interpretation, it should give an idea of how poems of very different character could be produced with recourse to just a few basic structural techniques.

a. THE *THEOGONY*

Several writers have asserted that all the parts of this poem fall into a pattern of ring composition, with the Prometheus episode (and thus treatment of the problem of relations between gods and men) prominently in the center; but their classifications of the passages that precede and follow seem too general to be very useful.[16] It is possible, however, to find three pairs of framing episodes at beginning and end (the Prometheus story no longer being considered at the center of the whole poem), as follows:

a.   1-115: proemium
b.   116-210: the first gods, birth of Titans; first stage of succession story

   c. 211–32: offspring of Night

d–1. 233–336: offspring of Pontos, including list of Nereids

d–2. 337–70: offspring of Okeanos, including list of Okeanids

e–1. 371–403: marriages of other Titans, ending with episode of Styx

e–2. 404–52: marriages of other Titans, ending with description of Hekatē

f–1. 453–506: marriage of Rheia and Kronos; second stage of succession story begun

   g. 507–616: offspring of Iapetos, including Prometheus episode

f–2. 617–720: battle with Titans; second stage of succession story ended

   c. 721–819: description of Tartaros

   b. 820–80: battle with Typhoeus: Zeus's last enemy

   a. 881–?929: Zeus is made king of the gods and divides honors; his union with Mētis (a final threat averted, so that he is permanently established); his other marriages

It is true that the fight with Typhoeus (the second *b* section) bears some strong resemblances to the Titanomachy (*f*-2) and that the description of Tartaros (the second *c* section) acts as a bridge between these episodes. Similarly, the line of Night (the first *c* section) is related by contrast to that of Pontos (*d-1*).[17] But the sections devoted to Night and Typhoeus function one way in their immediate surroundings and another in the design of the poem as a whole.

The passages that compose the frames (*a, b,* and *c*) bear implications, direct or indirect, for Zeus's rule. Night and her progeny are linked with the account of Tartaros (*c*) by her own reappearance there with her children Sleep and Death. The relation between these sections shows that although dread as well as beneficent powers exist in the cosmos, they have their allotted subterranean place and their allotted times to be at large in the world above. But we only learn of this arrangement late in the poem, and the positioning of the Tartaros passage after the Titanomachy associates control over these powers with the ordering of the world under Zeus. Tartaros must have been inhabited before the incarceration of the Titans, of course, but the structure of the poem induces us to ignore this fact and makes the function of Tartaros in the cosmic design seem pertinent to Zeus's rule.[18] This impression is strengthened by another, more subtle connection between the sections on Night and Tartaros, that "the train of thought . . . [in lines 782–93] reproduces that in the list of the progeny of Eris (226–32)."[19] The later passage tells how the gods deal with quarrels and false oaths among themselves. Strife (Eris) is at work even among the gods, but her influence can be contained by an orderly process that is part of the new Olympian dispensation. For Styx too, we now discover, is in Tartaros as "the great oath of the gods"—an honor she has from Zeus (1. 400; cf. ll. 805-6). And finally, it is at least suggestive that in the *Enuma Elish,* the Babylonian creation epic with which the *Theogony* has close parallels, the episode that occupies the position in the succession story analogous to that of the Tartaros passage is Marduk's ordering of the natural elements.[20]

The episode of Typhoeus corresponds with the section on the births of the earliest gods and of the Titans (*b*) because Typhoeus is the last, as the earlier passage described the first, of Gaia's offspring (1. 821).[21] He is also the last to be born who is not either a mortal human being or an anthropomorphic divinity, and he thus rounds off the cosmic process of generation that precedes the cycle of births under the Olympian gods by which the world takes its final form. Most important of all, though the succession story reaches its end only with Zeus's swallowing of Mētis (ll. 886-900), the series of physical struggles for supremacy, which began with the Titans' overthrow of Ouranos, is concluded here. The contrast between these balancing episodes is all-important. Ouranos was emasculated and deposed by Kronos, but Zeus defeats the monster that threatens to supplant him and to rule over gods and men (ll. 836-38).

Although the genealogy of Gaia provides a suitable frame for the bulk of the poem, the *Theogony* begins and ends emphatically with the present time, the world order under Zeus (*a*). The Muses furnish a direct link: their birth is narrated in full in the proemium (ll. 53-67) and recalled in summary form at the close (ll. 915-17). More generally, the marriages and children of Zeus (aside from the traditional unions with Demeter, Leto, and Hera) characterize his rule.[22] The proemium depicts one central aspect of this dispensation, its effect on human life through the Muses and their gifts of poetry and eloquence.

At the center of the framing sections are placed, not one passage, but three groups of passages that, though self-contained, show a progress that culminates in Zeus's victory. The families of Pontos and Okeanos (sections *d-1* and *d-2*) have in common a long list of daughters. The former also contains an anticipation of Zeus's kingship: Pēgasos is said (ll. 285-86) to live in Zeus's house and to bring him thunder and lightning, which, as Hesiod has told us and will repeat (ll. 141, 501-6), are forged by the Kyklōpes. Each of the next pair of passages (*e-1* and *e-2*) ends by singling out a particular goddess. The descriptions of Styx and Hekatē give similar accounts of Zeus's division of provinces among the gods (ll. 392-96, 421-28). Hekatē's story, in fact, illustrates how Zeus fulfilled his promise to deprive no god of the honors he or she had enjoyed under the Titans. Styx's children, moreover, live with Zeus (ll. 383-88, 401) as Pēgasos does, and their names, like his possession of the thunderbolt, reflect the force by which he wins and retains the supreme power: Zēlos (Glory), Nikē (Victory), Kratos (Might), and Biē (Force). On the other hand, the role that Zeus assigns to Styx herself—to be "the great oath of the gods" —exemplifies the enlightenment and civilization that his rule brings. Only after these anticipations, which stress the significance of the event, is Zeus actually born. Now the second stage in the succession story is reached, but this is divided into two parts by the passage on the children of Iapetos (sections *f-1, g,* and *f-2*), much as lines 139-53 interrupt the first episode of the story and, in the third stage, the description of Tartaros separates Zeus's battles with the Titans and with Typhoeus. As we observed in Chapter 1, the relationship among lines 139-53, 501-6, and 617-720 articulates this design. The line of Iapetos, with the crucial Prometheus episode, is thus framed by the narrative of the struggle with the Titans. Just as Zeus is deposing Kronos, Hesiod suspends his progress and jumps ahead to a time when Zeus is already in control. The central part complements the frame. Not only does his treatment of Iapetos's sons show Zeus defeating and punishing those who defy him in the same way as he overcomes the Titans;[23] but also Zeus defeats the Titans by force and Prometheus by intelligence.[24] These are his two essential qualities.

Through the relation of the framing passages to one another and through the grouping of the sections that fall within them, then, the structure of the poem stresses the supremacy of Zeus and its meaning. At the same time, the material is organized according to the families of the various gods and powers, on clearly discernible principles. (For these, see West, 1966, 37-39.) With triumphant thoroughness, Hesiod has assimilated cosmogony and divine genealogy with the myth of succession to the kingship over the gods. Every passage has its appropriate place in the poem with reference to both schemes at once. Even the family of Iapetos, the position of which has sometimes been thought to show a tension between these two aspects of Hesiod's subject,[25] bears, as we have seen, an important relation to the succession story and fits into the genealogical system as the last member of the series of the Titans' marriages and progeny.

Hesiod's point lies precisely in this combination and is illustrated by the structure that the poem assumes while achieving it. Amid all the diversity of being in the world, the great overarching fact is Zeus's sovereignty, and in particular his intelligent ordering of what before had been the scene of violence. The circular plan allows Hesiod to begin with the world as it is under Zeus, to look back to the ultimate origin of things (ll. 115-22), and then to work back to the present time. But the progress is not entirely linear even in the body of the poem. There are leaps backward and forward in time, and also recurrent references to Zeus's reign. These refer specifically to the two aspects that we have seen exemplified by the cases of Hekatē and of Styx's children: his kingship and might (ll. 71-73, 285-86, 402-3, 458, 503-6; cf. 883, 886), and his distribution of prerogatives, or τιμαί (*timai*), among the gods, which is a particular manifestation of his intelligence (ll. 73-74, 348, 391-96, 421-28; details of the actual division, which is summarily mentioned in line 885, thus do not have to be given). The intertwining of present and past in these ways connects the account of origins with the order that ultimately results, so that each event is shown to be significant, not in itself, but by virtue of its place in

the progress toward the world in which we now find ourselves. The future, by
implication, is accounted for as well. Zeus assures the permanence of his rule
by warding off threats to it. So, although further differentiation in the world
is possible through continued unions of gods with each other and with mortals
(as in the last part of our text of the *Theogony* and the continuation of that
poem, whether planned by Hesiod or not, in the *Catalogue of Women*), the
arrangement of the world will remain essentially unchanged. Hesiod, in effect,
is reproducing the subject of the Muses' song, which they taught him (ll. 32,
38): "the things that are and will be and were before."

The circularity of the ring pattern, however, is offset by a straightforward
development of the succession story. Recurrent patterns of plot and language
of the kind discussed earlier relate its three phases by similarity and contrast.
Cosmic history begins with unchanging elements such as Earth and Night, and
ends with lasting order. But in between comes process through time.

There is, first, a progression from the raw violence of Ouranos through the
deceit of Kronos to the intelligence of Zeus, which is emphasized by formular
language. Ouranos's physical power is represented by his genitals, μήδεα
(*mēdea*, l. 180). Zeus's understanding is expressed by a formula that uses the
same word, but in an entirely different sense: Ζεὺς ἄφθιτα μήδεα εἰδώς,
"Zeus who knows unwaning *counsels*" (*mēdea*, e.g., ll. 545, 550, 561—all
from Zeus's battle of wits with Prometheus).[26] In a usage of the related verb,
Ouranos is said to have "contrived" outrageous deeds (μήσατο, *mēsato*,
ll. 166, 172). Kronos, who castrates him by Gaia's "evil, deceitful contrivance"
(δολίην κακὴν ... τέχνην, *doliēn kakēn ... tekhnēn*, l. 160), receives the epithet ἀγκυλομήτης (*ankulomētēs*, ll. 167, 473, 495), which apparently meant
to Hesiod "him of the crooked counsels."[27] Zeus, by contrast, is μητιόεις
(*mētioeis*), "the counsellor"—an epithet given him when his birth is finally
mentioned (l. 457). Just after this, by planning (ll. 465, 496) although with
Gaia's advice, he will force Kronos to disgorge the children he has swallowed.
Zeus's intelligence includes cunning and deceit but is not limited to them. He
outwits Kronos, Prometheus (who also receives the epithet *ankulomētēs* in
l. 546),[28] and Mētis herself, who personifies intelligence (ll. 889-90). His
swallowing of her, so that she should always advise him (l. 900), justifies his
epithet *mētioeis* retrospectively. All of these are conventional expressions;
Zeus and Prometheus, for instance, get the same epithets in the *Works and
Days*, where there is again a contest of intelligence but no question of a larger
design in the use of this diction (*W.D.* 48, 51). But the recurrence of these
words and phrases in the *Theogony* is so persistent and patterned that Hesiod
must surely be manipulating their sounds and meanings.

Motifs are also repeated, so that the phases of the story follow a similar
plan. A pattern of expectation is thus created, which is then thwarted by the
victory of Zeus. The basic sequence is that the father wrongs his children and
is then supplanted by one of his sons. Ouranos imprisons his children in Earth,
their mother, as they are born. By an analogous act, Kronos swallows each of

his children. But Zeus remains safe because he forestalls the birth of the threatening son by swallowing the pregnant mother, Mētis. Kronos and Zeus are both motivated by the information, supplied by Gaia and Ouranos, that their sons will be mightier than they and will depose them; there are strong similarities in phrasing between lines 461-65 and 891-94. In each case, the decisive act of swallowing is expressed by the phrase "put (it, her) in his belly" (ἐὴν ἐσκάτθετο νηδύν, *heēn eskattheto nēdun*, ll. 487, 890). Ouranos is castrated, and Aphrodite is born from his severed genitals. Kronos is forced to vomit up his children—their second birth, according to the *Hymn to Aphrodite* (see p. 3 above).[29] From Zeus's head is born Athena—but not the son who would have overthrown him.

What is the point of these parallels? It is not enough to say, as one excellent study does, that "the many formulaic correspondences between the story of Kronos' attempting to swallow Zeus and Zeus' swallowing Metis pregnant with Athene . . . indicate that these are oral variants of one type-scene" (Angier, 1964, 340). They may be exactly that. But why should they occur as part of a pattern of events that befall each of three successive generations? As Solmsen (1949, 26) has observed, it is "the idea of guilt and retribution" that underlies all the similarities and is stressed by them. A curse, in fact, runs through this family. When the drops of Ouranos's blood impregnate Gaia, the Erinyes are born (l. 185). Ouranos gives his children a name that recalls their guilty deed (ll. 207-10: Titans—which Hesiod associates with τιταίνειν, *titainen*, the verb for "to strain, to strive," or perhaps "to stretch out," as Kronos stretched out his hand in violence in line 178); and he promises that there will be vengeance in the future (τίσις, *tisis*, which also seems to be drawn into the wordplay).[30] This is, in effect, the pronouncement of a curse. Accordingly, in the next generation Rheia asks Gaia and Ouranos for a plan by which she might bear Zeus without Kronos's knowledge, and thus (ll. 472-73):[31]

. . . τείσαιτο δ' ἐρινῦς πατρὸς ἑοῖο
παίδων <θ'> οὓς κατέπινε μέγας Κρόνος ἀγκυλομήτης.

. . . so that she might exact payment [*teisaito*, related to *tisis*] for the erinyes of her father
and of the children whom great Kronos of the crooked counsel swallowed.

Shortly afterward, at a critical point in the story, Kronos is described in a marvellously ominous line that at once evokes his deed by naming him as Ouranos's son and foreshadows his fate. Rheia gives the stone that she has substituted for Zeus to her husband (l. 486):[32]

Οὐρανίδη μέγ' ἄνακτι, θεῶν προτέρων βασιλῆι.

to the widely ruling son of Ouranos, king of the former gods.

The sequence could be extended indefinitely, with each son doomed by the curse to repeat the action and suffer the punishment of his father. It ends, however, when Zeus faces the same threats as Ouranos and Kronos but circumvents them. The role of Gaia, who is joined by Ouranos in the phases of the story concerning Kronos and Zeus, binds together the events in all three generations, is decisive in accomplishing Zeus's victory and continued security, and thus stresses the difference between his fortunes and those of his forebears. Her actions in the cases of Ouranos and Kronos help to establish a pattern that is then broken in the third generation. Zeus is freed of the menaces posed by the darker aspects of the past.

In the first two episodes of the story, Gaia helps the son against the father by contriving plans and giving advice. Her role is regularly described by the verb φράζειν (phrasdein, "point out," or, in the middle voice, "devise"), its compounds, and related nouns and adjectives. She "devised [ἐπεφράσσατο, epephrassato] the evil, deceitful ruse" by which Kronos overthrew Ouranos and "showed" (ἐπέφραδε, epephrade) the sickle to her children (ll. 160, 162).[33] Later, now with Ouranos, she at first continues to help Kronos by telling him what fate holds for him, but then she switches loyalties. At Rheia's behest, Gaia and Ouranos "join her in contriving a plan" against Kronos (μῆτιν συμφράσσασθαι, metin sumphrassasthai, l. 471) and "tell" her what is fated (πεφραδέτην, pephradetēn, l. 475). As a result, Kronos is fooled and defeated. He disgorges his children, "tricked by Gaia's very clever suggestion" (Γαίης ἐννεσίῃσι πολυφραδέεσσι δολωθείς, Gaiēs ennesiēisi poluphradeessi dolōtheis, l. 494); and his physical overthrow is assured when the Olympians release the Hundred-handers from Tartaros "by Gaia's cunning advice" (Γαίης φραδμοσύνῃσιν, Gaiēs phradmosunēisin, l. 626). Gaia now helps Zeus get established. The Olympians choose him as their ruler "by Gaia's cunning advice" (Γαίης φραδμοσύνῃσιν, Gaiēs phradmosunēisin, l. 884). But will Zeus now stay in power? She and Ouranos tell Zeus, as they told Kronos, that he is fated to be deposed by his son. According to the precedent she has set, Gaia should now turn against Zeus and contrive the birth and survival of that son.[34] Instead, she remains on Zeus's side, for he swallows Mētis "by the cunning advice of Gaia" and Ouranos (Γαίης φραδμοσύνῃσιν, Gaiēs phradmosunēisin, l. 891; cf. φρασάτην, phrasatēn, l. 892). The same phrase begins the line here as began lines 626 and 884, but the similarity only underscores the change in Gaia's role. It is a sign of the stability of Zeus's position now that he will no longer need Gaia and Ouranos to "help him devise a plan" as Rheia did (μῆτιν συμφράσσασθαι, metin sumphrassasthai, l. 471). He has incorporated Mētis herself, so that she might "counsel with him" (συμφράσσαιτο, sumphrassaito, line 900).

The phrases cited above are all formulaic, but their appearance at key points of the succession story is significant. Whether or not Hesiod placed them deliberately—and it is useless to inquire if he did—their repetition shows that he thought of the myth in terms of its recurrent patterns. These helped in arranging the narrative but also gave it its meaning. As Solmsen has observed, the shape of the story in this poem anticipates the plan of the later tragic trilogy.[35] There could hardly be a more expressive form.

b. THE *ILIAD*

Like the *Theogony,* the *Iliad* is arranged in ring form (though with a far more detailed system of corresponding episodes, according to Whitman's findings), and at the same time shows patterned sequences that give the effect of a linear development in the plot.[36] The latter, of course, help to keep in focus the narrative material of such an immense poem, although they would also have had, for the audience at least, the kind of meaning that was inherent in all traditional themes.[37] But one pattern of events in particular seems to reflect the poem's central concerns. The later books of the *Iliad* progress by a rhythm of significant deaths that are related to one another by a complex of shared motifs. The series culminates in those deaths that are the final consequences of the action, those of Hektor and Achilles, the one explicitly narrated and the other only foreshadowed.[38]

It begins, however, with an episode at first apparently unimportant to the plot, the two parts of which flank Hera's seduction of Zeus. During the fighting in which Poseidon has covertly aided the Greeks, the Trojan Dēiphobos kills Askalaphos, son of Ares (XIII.518–25). The god, says the poet, had not yet learned of his son's death, for he was sitting on Olympos, restrained from the battle by Zeus's command. It is Hera, returning to Olympos after Zeus has awakened and discovered her deception, who—with morbid satisfaction—gives Ares the news. Furious with grief, Ares arms to avenge his son in defiance of Zeus, but is dissuaded by Athena (XV.100–142).

The theme of a god's impotence and unavailing sorrow when faced with the death of a mortal son recurs, and is developed with magnificent pathos, in connection with the fate of Sarpēdōn. Here Zeus knows beforehand of his son's death, considers saving him, and is dissuaded by Hera (XVI.431–61). One of her arguments, the impossibility of saving all the gods' sons at Troy (XVI.444–49), somewhat resembles the reasoning Athena uses on Ares (XV. 139–41). In particular, when Hera says, "for around the great city of Priam are fighting many sons of immortals, in whom you will arouse fierce resentment [if you rescue Sarpēdōn] " (XVI.448–49), the recent case of Askalaphos comes naturally to mind.

Patroklos's death is related to Sarpēdōn's by the structure of the narrative. Fenik has shown how the battle episodes in Book 16, and also to some extent in Book 17, follow the same basic pattern.[39] Significant details in these two books reinforce the general similarity. The killing of Sarpēdōn (XVI.462–81) follows this sequence: Patroklos kills Sarpēdōn's companion Thrasymēlos; Sarpēdōn hurls his spear at Patroklos, misses, and hits Achilles' mortal horse

Pēdasos instead;[40] Sarpēdōn again throws and misses; and Patroklos throws and fatally wounds Sarpēdōn. Later, at the start of his encounter with Hektor that will end with his own death, Patroklos throws a weapon (now a rock), misses, and hits Hektor's charioteer Kebrionēs (XIV.733–39). The considerable differences between these scenes do not disguise the duplication in the later scene of the most important motifs in the earlier one, which are now combined in the actions of Patroklos himself. As he did before, Patroklos first kills his Trojan opponent's companion; but now, doomed, in his turn, like Sarpēdōn, he misses his main target. This detail is the more striking because in duels in the *Iliad* it is usually the eventual *victor* who misses with his first spear-cast.[41] But the implication for Patroklos of this departure from the norm has been established by the death scene of Sarpēdōn, who misses *twice*. These two scenes mark respectively one of the high points of Patroklos's success and the moment when defeat begins to close in on him. Another link between his and Sarpēdōn's deaths is indicated by the fact (observed in Fenik, 1968, 210, 213) that the fighting at this point in the *Iliad* tends to center upon a fallen hero. The three most prominent examples are the battles over the corpses of Sarpēdōn, Kebrionēs, and Patroklos, the last developed at great length in Book 17. Furthermore, the cloud of darkness that oppresses the warriors who fight over Patroklos's body (XVII.366–75) recalls the bloody drops that Zeus pours down when Sarpēdōn is about to die (XVI.459–61).

Sarpēdōn's death is thematically linked with that of Askalaphos, and Patroklos's is associated in turn with Sarpēdōn's. Hektor dooms himself to Achilles' fury when he slays Patroklos, but beyond the causal link there is a stern symmetry in the order of events: Sarpēdōn is killed by Patroklos, Patroklos by Hektor, Hektor by Achilles. In Hektor's fate the earlier ones converge. On the one hand, the motif of helpless divine sorrow reappears. Zeus thinks of saving Hektor as he wanted to spare Sarpēdōn, although there is no blood tie in this case, and Athena checks him with a shorter version of Hera's earlier speech (XXII.166–85; lines 178–81 are identical with XVI.440–43). On the other hand, Hektor's death reenacts Patroklos's—appropriately, for it is Achilles' revenge. Armor provides an explicit link. The blow Apollo deals Patroklos shakes off his armor, which he has borrowed from Achilles, and the helmet rolls in the dust. "Then Zeus gave it to Hektor to wear on his head," says the poet; "his own destruction was near" (XVI.799–800). The armor and Hektor's fate are associated at greater length at XVII.193–214, and just when Hektor suffers the fatal blow from Achilles, we are reminded that he is wearing the arms he took from Patroklos (XXII.322–23). There is presumption in Hektor's assuming the armor of Achilles, a man greater than himself, as Zeus comments in pity (XVII.201–3). And in fact, as Patroklos did before him when he was bearing those same arms, Hektor is carried away by his success and thereby becomes vulnerable in turn.[42]

The relations, formal, thematic, and verbal, between the death scenes of Patroklos and Hektor have been widely recognized but should be summarized here. The weighing of the fates of Hektor and Achilles (XXII.208-13) may be anticipated in truncated form in XVI.658. When he finds himself alone against Achilles, Hektor realizes that the gods have called him deathward, as the poet earlier said they summoned Patroklos (XXII.297, XVI.693). In both scenes, the same order of events attends the slayings. First comes the fatal wound, and then a boast by the victor (XVI.830-42, XXII.331-36). The victim prophesies his killer's doom (XVI.851-54, XXII.358-60). The actual death follows, described in both episodes with the same three lines (XVI.855-57, XXII.361-63). In each case, the victor then addresses the corpse of his victim, dismissing the prediction of his fate (XVI.858-61, XXII.364-66). There is an important contrast, however, between Achilles' indifferent acceptance of death and Hektor's infatuated optimism that shows how far beyond normal human concerns Achilles' grief and rage have carried him, into a realm where foreknowledge of fate, denied to most men, can no longer matter.

Finally, Charles Segal's study *The Theme of the Mutilation of the Corpse in the "Iliad"* shows how the deaths of Sarpēdōn, Patroklos, and Hektor are all bound together by this and subsidiary motifs.[43] The treatment of the corpse becomes of increasing concern in the late books of the poem as the passions aroused grow more savage. The gods must intervene to defend the body from decay and, in two instances, from outrage. Apollo rescues Sarpē-dōn's corpse from the fight that has been raging over it and anoints it with ambrosia (XVI.680). Thetis preserves Patroklos's body, which Achilles in his extremity of grief will keep from burial for a time, with nectar and ambrosia (XIX.38-39), and in a similar way Aphrodite and Apollo protect Hektor's body from corruption and disfigurement by Achilles' maltreatment (XXIII. 184-91, XXIV.18-21; cf. Segal, 1971, 54-55).

Each of these scenes of death is complete and final in itself, and each has its individual pathos. But the similarities that bind them together show that finally there is only one death, though it may take slightly different forms. This death is the common fate of humanity. But in particular these motifs combine to depict what is at issue in the death of the greatest of men, the hero: how the gods can do nothing to save him; how his success is inevitably followed, sooner or later, by failure, because even this kind of man is mortal and limited. There can be no exception, even for the supreme hero. For the series that began with Askalaphos culminates in Hektor's death only within the poem's narrative. It also points beyond the end of the *Iliad* to the death of Achilles. Much more is involved in the foreshadowing of this event as an imminent certainty than the prophecies by Achilles' horses and by Thetis (XIX.404-17, XVIII.94-96). These only make explicit what is implied by the whole sequence of deaths. "Your fate is ready soon after Hektor's," Thetis tells her son. But the connection is somehow as much causal as temporal. Like Hektor, Achilles has slain his enemy, boasted, and received a prophecy of his own death. According to the pattern that has been established, he must die soon. But the poet, as he so often does, gives moving expression to his thought by means of tangible objects. References to the armor lent by Achilles to Patroklos and captured by Hektor and the scenes in which the immortal horses Xanthos and Balios grieve stress the way Achilles' fate closes in on him at least from the time he sends his comrade into battle. The armor and the horses are parallel symbols that express their meaning in similar ways.

The shaking of the helmet from Patroklos's head by Apollo's blow is not only the occasion for an explicit prophecy of Hektor's doom (XVI.800). The defilement of the plume by dust and gore prefigures Achilles' fall: Achilles no longer seems invulnerable, as he has heretofore (XVI.796–99):

πάρος γε μὲν οὐ θέμις ἦεν
ἱππόκομον πήληκα μιαίνεσθαι κονίῃσιν,
ἀλλ' ἀνδρὸς θείοιο κάρη χαρίεν τε μέτωπον
ῥύετ' Ἀχιλλῆος.

Before it was not allowed [themis]
that the helmet plumed with horsehair be defiled [miainesthai] by dust,
but it protected the head and handsome forehead of a godlike [theios]
    man—
Achilles.

Like the helmet, the man it once protected will soon be stained with blood in death, despite his semidivine parentage. Is the epithet "godlike" (theios) in this context merely generic and metrically convenient, or may we feel irony and incongruity in its use? We cannot be sure. At any rate, the fates of three men are determined at this moment. The two deaths to come are foreshadowed as successive consequences of the one that is occurring. Hektor's head will drag in the dust, the dark hair streaming behind it, when Achilles drags his corpse behind the chariot (XXII.401–4). When the horses mourn for Patroklos, they bow their heads; their manes, drooping to the ground, are defiled like the helmet's plume (ἐμιαίνετο, emiaineto, XVII.439).[44] This spectacle prompts Zeus to reflect how cruel is the association of immortal beings with mortals and how wretched man's life is (XVII.441–47). He explicitly mentions Pēleus; but the situation makes us think of Patroklos, and Achilles too is surely drawn into this circle of death and grief. Later, in fact, in a scene that recalls this one, Xanthos again hangs his head and lets his mane fall to the ground as he foretells Achilles' fate (XIX.404–17). This time, defilement is not explicitly mentioned, but XIX.406 is nearly identical to XVII.440.

The horses and the armor alike are emblems of Achilles' relation to divinity, but that relation is ambivalent. On the one hand, these possessions mark him as superior to ordinary mortals, even to the other heroes at Troy. On the other hand, since his ownership of them taints them by contact with mortality, they stress how even he falls short of full divinity. The arms (and presumably the horses also)[45] were a wedding gift to Pēleus from the gods when he married

Thetis—a fact alluded to, significantly, along with Achilles' fate at XVIII.82–93 and also in an earlier passage that is more pertinent here (XVII.194–97):

> ... ὁ δ' ἄμβροτα τεύχεα δῦνε
> Πηλεΐδεω Ἀχιλῆος, ἅ οἱ θεοὶ Οὐρανίωνες
> πατρὶ φίλῳ ἔπορον· ὁ δ' ἄρα ᾧ παιδὶ ὄπασσε
> γηράς· ἀλλ' οὐχ υἱὸς ἐν ἔντεσι πατρὸς ἐγήρα.

> ... and he [Hektor] put on the immortal arms
> of Pēleus's son Achilles, which the gods descended from Ouranos
> gave to his father. And he handed them on to his son
> in his old age [*gēras*]; but in his father's armor the son was not growing
>   old [*egēra*].

The balance of words signifying old age at beginning and end of the last line is eloquent. Unlike Pēleus, Achilles is not growing old wearing his armor—is not to grow old at all. These lines occur as Hektor dons the armor and immediately precede Zeus's prophecy of the Trojan hero's death. So the horses connect Achilles' fate with Patroklos's, and the armor links Hektor with Patroklos and associates Achilles with both of them as mortal and doomed. In Book 22, when he deals the fatal wound to a Hektor still clad in this armor, Achilles seems virtually to be killing himself—especially since we know from Thetis's prophecy in Book 18 that he is in fact sealing his own fate.

This fate looms over the final third of the *Iliad* not only because of explicit prophecies and symbolic anticipation but also by virtue of the pattern of the action. There is good reason to believe that the significant deaths that form a sequence through the later books, by the motifs they express and the circumstances that surround them, would have evoked in the listeners' minds Achilles' own death as they had heard it told in other poems, just as narrative patterns elsewhere in the *Iliad* allude to events of the Trojan story that precede and follow those that form its plot.[46]

Epic accounts of Achilles' death are known from two sources: the last book of the *Odyssey* (xxiv.36–92) and Proklos's summary of the *Aithiopis*, one of the poems of the Epic Cycle (Allen V, 105–6). It appears that the story recapitulated the whole series of deaths in the *Iliad* that was discussed above. Nestor's son Antilokhos—like Patroklos, a special comrade of Achilles[47]—was slain like him by the warrior who was then the main champion on the Trojan side, Memnon. Memnon, in turn, combined the features of both Sarpēdōn (Trojan ally, son of a divinity) and Hektor (his death at Achilles' hands was evidently preceded by a weighing of fates, with the divine mother of each hero begging for her son's life).[48] In several ways Achilles' own death repeated that of Patroklos. He was slain by Apollo and Paris while attacking the city, and similarly Patroklos assaulted the Trojan wall, was driven back by Apollo, and was killed by the same god in conjunction with two mortals. As with

Patroklos, there was a prolonged battle over Achilles' corpse until the Greeks finally carried it off the field. His funeral was celebrated with elaborate games, for which Thetis offered lavish prizes according to one version. Thetis, like Zeus and Ares forced to accept the death of her mortal son, mourned him with her sister Nereids and the Muses.[49]

The accounts of the major heroes' deaths within the *Iliad* contain some specific anticipations of these events, which reinforce the general similarities. The dying Hektor's prophecy of the way Achilles will fall at the hands of Paris and Apollo in the Skaian gate (XXII.359-60) stresses the resemblance which that event will bear to Patroklos's death. When Apollo warns Patroklos to withdraw from the city wall, he indirectly foretells the death of Achilles: "It is not fated that the city of the great-hearted Trojans be sacked by your spear, or by Achilles, who is much greater than you" (XVI.707-9). After Hektor's death, Thetis mourns her son's approaching doom (XXIV.83-86), much as the women of Hector's household lamented him while he still lived (VI.500-502). This is, however, a brief repetition of another scene as well. Hearing from her cave in the depths of the sea Achilles' lament for Patroklos, Thetis cries out and her sisters surround her (XVIII.35-64). They beat their breasts, and "Thetis led off the lament" (Θέτις δ᾽ ἐξῆρχε γόοιο, l. 51); the same formula introduces speeches of mourning for Hektor later on (XXII.430, XXIV.747, 761). In tears, Thetis and her sisters then emerge from the sea and go to Achilles (XVIII.65-72). Thetis takes her son's head in her hands, in the same stylized gesture of mourning that Andromakhē will make with Hektor (XXIV.724; cf. Griffin, 1980, 27-28). Surely in this scene Thetis and her sisters enact in advance their uncanny emergence from the sea to mourn the dead Achilles that so frightened the other Greeks and that was described in both the *Aithiopis* and the *Odyssey*.

On the basis of the remarkable similarities between the Iliadic and the non-Iliadic episodes, scholars have argued either that the *Aithiopis* influenced the *Iliad* or vice versa.[50] But the question of influence and of the relative dates of the two poems is not very important. If the *Aithiopis* was the earlier, the *Iliad* was alluding to a poem that the audience probably knew. If the chronology was the reverse, the audience surely would have known the story of Achilles' death from epic versions that found their way eventually into the *Aithiopis* and the *Odyssey*. Our argument is unaffected whichever alternative is true. More probably, however, literary influence is not at issue here (and anyway the question cannot now be resolved). We seem to be dealing with a number of generic themes connected with the killing of a major hero that were used piecemeal in several scenes of the *Iliad* and were brought together most completely in the epic story of Achilles' death reflected in our sources.[51] But it is precisely their typicality that makes them intelligible and enables the poet to put them to such profoundly expressive use, to deploy them in a sequence that clearly demands completion, so that the truly climactic death can overshadow the last six books of the poem without needing to be narrated directly or foretold circumstantially. The *Iliad* derives wonderful effects from the resonances that run through it from the whole mass of other poems that must have been in the air, and with the death of Achilles the poet plays on his audience's associations most movingly. He gives us the feeling of fate. Because it can be known in advance, the death is fixed and inevitable. Just as important as the simple fact of anticipation, however, is the sequence that events are to follow, which is prescribed by tradition but—for that very reason— significant. Against the background of the other heroes' deaths that are its forerunners, Achilles' death takes on coherence. That it must conform to a set pattern makes us sense a grimly beautiful order in events that is the shape of Necessity itself. Under these conditions, even the best of men is fallible, mortal, and doomed.[52]

These deaths are finally all the same. Each hero, as he kills and is killed, advances a process and falls victim to it. These men reach the height of human greatness in acts that turn out to be self-destructive.

c. THE *ODYSSEY*

No one familiar with Whitman's study of Homer needs to be told that the design of the *Odyssey* is far different from that of the *Iliad*.[53] It is dangerous, however, to draw conclusions from this difference, as Whitman does, about the dates or even the relative chronology of the two poems. The contrast is more a matter of literary propriety than of prevailing aesthetic fashions. The *Odyssey*'s structure is as perfectly fitted as the *Iliad*'s to its own subject and tone.

The poem falls almost exactly into two parts of twelve books each. The division into books, though it may be late, corresponds in most cases with natural pauses in the story and is a fairly safe guide to narrative units. We do not have to rely entirely on it, however. Counting lines gives an idea of the amount of time required for performance, and variation in the time devoted to different episodes or groups of episodes yields varying degrees of emphasis in orally performed poetry. It is a remarkable fact that the first twelve books are only slightly more than 300 lines longer than the second twelve—a negligible difference in a poem of more than 12,000 lines.[54] Conditioned by Dante and Tennyson, we think of Odysseus as The Wanderer. But for fully half of this poem he is on Ithaka. His arrival, his experiences and actions there, are therefore just as important to the poem as his earlier wanderings and Telemakhos's journey.[55] In many ways, as we shall see, the first twelve books are preparation for the second twelve. The *Odyssey* is less concerned with travel than with a homecoming and all that that implies: a man's restoration to his family and to the symbols of his own identity, and the affirmation of the values of human society in the reconstruction of domestic order.

A sign of the poem's emphasis on the homecoming is that the wanderings are narrated in Books 9–12 as already past, and only the last two stages, Kalypsō and the Phaiakians, are recounted as they occur. Even with the Kalypsō episode, the poet picks up the thread of the story when Odysseus is about to leave the goddess and his long sojourn with her is ending. Kalypsō and the Phaiakians enclose Odysseus's acount of his experiences. This begins with the most remote episode—the Kikones—and the narrative proceeds, by way of Kalypsō at the end (xii.447-50), back to Odysseus's present situation at Alkinoos's court. The treatment of time here is the same as in the *Theogony,* which begins in the present order of the world under Zeus, juxtaposes with it the very first gods, and ends back in Zeus's reign. In the *Odyssey* just as in the *Theogony,* the past is recalled not so much for its intrinsic interest as for the sake of the poem's present time. The *Odyssey* focuses on the dramatically right moment of its hero's homecoming, and its action is the long process of the return. That is complete only after Odysseus defeats the suitors, when Athena makes a settlement between Odysseus and his opponents at the very end (xxiv.546-48). But it is significant that Odysseus's actual arrival on Ithaka takes place very near the center of the poem (xiii.88-121).

The *Odyssey* divides further into six parts of four books each. Among these smaller segments there is less equality of length, though only two groups (Books 5-8 and 21-24) vary significantly from the rest.[56] Still, a distinct break in the plot follows every four books, so that the plan is roughly this:

a.   1–4: Situation on Ithaka; Telemakhos's journey, with scenes in Pylos and Sparta

b.   5–8: Odysseus's arrival at Skheria and his reception by the Phaiakians

c.   9–12: Odysseus's narrative of his wanderings

a.   13–16: Return of Odysseus and Telemakhos to Ithaka and their meeting. Action centers on Eumaios's hut.

b.   17–20: Odysseus's house; disguised as a beggar, Odysseus tests the loyalty of various people in his home and bides his time until he can act.

c.   21–24: Killing of the suitors; Odysseus is reinstated at home and in Ithakan society.

The result of these divisions is that the poem is laid out in parallel segments of approximately equal importance (parataxis once again). We are thus invited to make connections between the segments. Most of the action of the first four books follows from Athena's visit to Ithaka after a divine council in Book 1. At the beginning of Book 5, another council on Olympos, in which Athena again protests against the gods' neglect of Odysseus, leads to the dispatch of Hermes to Kalypsō and so to the main events of Books 5-8. This arrangement is practically indistinguishable from the convention, well known in the Homeric epics, by which parallel and simultaneous actions (cf. i.81-95) are described as if they happened consecutively.[57] The unique characteristic here is the duplication of the divine council, but that is probably the result of the scale on which the poet is working. The second scene appears necessary to resume the main thread of the story after so long an interval since the first scene and to maintain that clarity of exposition that was indispensable to poetry composed for performance. But the duplication also has the effect of stressing the relations between events widely scattered in space, and especially between the experiences of Odysseus and Telemakhos. Both travel, although Telemakhos, under Athena's protection, has a fair voyage, and Odysseus is shipwrecked off the Phaiakians' coast by Poseidon. Both are received with civility and entertained lavishly; we have already noticed parallels in particular between the scenes in the palaces of Menelaos and Alkinoos. But there is also one enormous difference, intimately connected with the poem's major concerns. Odysseus, in Books 5-8, takes the decisive step on the way back to Ithaka when he leaves Kalypsō, whereas Telemakhos leaves Ithaka to go out into the world. Athena sends him to make a name for himself as well as for news of his father (i.93-95). Odysseus, who has roamed the world and gained an incomparable reputation, wants to get to only one place on earth—the island that Telemakhos temporarily forsakes. The contrast between mature experience and aspiring young manhood is thus reinforced by structural means. Yet Telemakhos's journey remains a minor theme that throws Odysseus's yearning and his homecoming into relief.

The son is left at the farthest extent of his travels, Sparta, and the father on the threshold of the familiar world, Skheria, while the account of Odysseus's earlier wanderings (Books 9-12) puts the events of the preceding books, and the action that is to come, into the context of the past and, by exploring a part of the world that is dominated by forces beyond man's control, shows what is at issue in Odysseus's homecoming, the value of civilization itself. Then, with Odysseus now on Ithaka, Books 13-16 and 17-20 represent two distinct stages in the plot (as the change of focus from Eumaios's hut to Odysseus's house indicates). But throughout both sections Odysseus engages in the planning and the testing of others that lead to his success in the final four books.

Within each half of the poem, then, the rhythm is the same: the third section caps the first two and brings to an end the movement that they initiate. The poem thus consists of two parallel sequences, each of three parts. But— again in a way typical of parataxis—there are also important relations between these two halves that are governed by a well-defined balance. The symmetry here is not inverted but progressive. That is, the first, second, and third segments in the second half are related respectively to the first, second, and third segments in the first half. The two main aspects of the plot, at first developed separately, are united in Books 13-16 when Odysseus and Telemakhos converge on Eumaios's hut,[58] but this is a separate organizational device. The connections of Books 13-16 with Books 1-4 are especially pronounced. In Book 15, Telemakhos departs from Sparta, where the poet left him in the fourth book. The suitors conspire to ambush Telemakhos near the end of Book 4 (iv.663-72, 778-86, 842-47); in Book 16 they find that their plan has failed and are forced for the time being to give up thoughts of murdering him. Having failed to get definite news of Odysseus, Telemakhos returns home—to find his father already there. After observing with envy the harmony of two households, he must face the chaos in his own house; but he will now help to set it right, although he cannot yet know this. The middle sections of the poem's two halves (Books 5-8, 17-20) show Odysseus, his identity unknown, received in a royal house, where a woman gives him hospitality. In the first instance, he is genuinely shipwrecked. In the second, though his beggar's guise is assumed, he is still an outcast—in his own home. This is a measure of the obstacles that he must overcome after he has reached Ithaka, whereas the Phaiakians have received him hospitably and Alkinoos has even offered him a place in society as his son-in-law. The opulent decorum that surrounds Alkinoos is a foil to the suitors' wasteful riot. Finally, Odysseus's recapitulation to Penelope of the story he told the Phaiakians (xxiii.310-43) formally links the two third sections, and the relation between these two parts of the poem is perhaps most important of all. In Skheria, Odysseus tells his name as preface to the narrative of his past exploits (ix.19-20); on Ithaka, he reveals his identity as he embarks on an achievement that unfolds in the present. All those earlier deeds and triumphs of survival, with which the victory over the suitors is associated structurally, have led up to this moment, which is the culmination of Odysseus's heroic career. His true test was not to reach home— Agamemnon did that but still was murdered—but to regain his rightful place and thereby to reclaim for civilization territory that had been lost to chaos.[59] This achievement demands of Odysseus, to a greater degree and in combination, the qualities that the wanderings evoked singly: courage, strength, cunning, and self-control. At the same time, we know the importance of this final triumph because of the wanderings. They have demonstrated the value of home.

So much—and it is a considerable amount—can be inferred simply from the placing of the various units of the narrative. But although its sections are laid out in series, the *Odyssey* is unified, and its main concerns are articulated, by recurring themes and sequences of action. It is impossible to do anything like justice here to the number of these patterns and the wonderful complexity of the design that results.[60] One example might indicate the possibilities for interpretation: feasting. As part of scenes of hospitality and of sacrifice, it expresses men's relations with each other and with the gods.

The *Odyssey* is full of scenes of feasting, and this is a typical sequence if there ever was one. It thus provides a good test of whether generic elements are capable of expressing meaning. In this case, a positive answer has already been given by Whitman, who asks in connection with the first book, "who can miss the sharp dramatic contrast between the feast spread by Telemakhos for Athena-Mentes and that enjoyed simultaneously at the other side of the hall by the suitors, and all in the space of twenty-two lines?"[61] This scene, however, merely adumbrates the contrast between the norm of decorum in eating and its violation, which permeates the *Odyssey* in various guises. The norm is firmly established by Telemakhos's reception at Pylos (during a sacrifice) and at Sparta (during a wedding feast), and by the elaborate entertainment offered Odysseus by the Phaiakians. On the other hand, the Kyklōps's treatment of Odysseus in the ninth book is a parody of a scene of hospitality. The themes appear in the proper order: the meal, the inquiry about the guest's name, and the bestowing of a guest gift, ξεινήϊον (*xeinēïon*). But Polyphēmos eats Odysseus's men, gets a false name from the stranger (in keeping with his own transgression of accepted conduct), and promises, as his *xeinēïon*, or guest gift, to eat Odysseus last (ix.369-70). This travesty of civilized modes of conduct not only characterizes the Kyklōps and places him within the broader opposition between nature and culture. It is also a religious offense. To Odysseus's reminder that Zeus is the protector of strangers and suppliants, the Kyklōps replies that he and his kind pay no heed to Zeus and the other gods (ix.269-78).

When Odysseus's men eat the cattle of the Sun, their preparations for the meal are described through the usual formulae of feasting and sacrifice (xii. 353-65). But two departures from the norm, especially striking because they are mentioned at just those points in the typical sequence where the customary actions should come, are ominous. The sailors do not have barley to sprinkle on the cattle before the slaughter but must use leaves instead. And for lack of wine, they have to pour libations to the gods with water.[62] This is a meal that should not be eaten, and the ritual is flawed—a sign that, as we are told at the beginning of the poem (i.7), these men perish by their own folly.[63]

Like the Kyklōpes and Odysseus's sailors, the suitors eat the wrong things in ways that travesty social and religious norms. Feasting is their commonest activity, but it lacks the solemn purpose it should have. More than gluttony is involved, however; they are consuming Odysseus's property, literally. The suitors "are violently devouring Odysseus's house," complains Telemakhos to the Ithakans in assembly (κατέδουσι βιαίως / οἶκον Ὀδυσσῆος, ii.237-38); Antinoos himself has used similar language in the same scene (ii.123). "My house is being eaten," Telemakhos says to Menelaos (ἐσθίεταί μοι οἶκος, iv. 318). He tells Athena that the suitors "are wasting the house" (τρύχουσι δὲ οἶκον, i.248). Hesiod uses the same verb of drones consuming the labor of bees (*W.D.* 305). The house, with the storeroom at its heart, and the wealth it contains are in the *Odyssey* the owner's substance, and not just metaphorically. They define what he is, in both his familial and social roles.[64] What the suitors do, in consuming Odysseus's substance, is not much different from Polyphē-mos's cannibalism. Like him, they outrage the gods by mistreating a stranger and a beggar (xvii.468-87). As he did, Ktēsippos gives Odysseus a parody of a guest gift, the cow's hoof that he hurls at the apparent beggar and that he calls a *xeinēïon* (xx.292-98). It is not only in the world of his roaming that Odysseus must confront violence unrestrained by law. The thematic connection with that other world comments on the suitors' conduct, but in order to point up the magnitude of the final and greatest obstacle to Odysseus's homecoming.

The suitors, like Odysseus's companions, bring destruction on themselves by their wrongful eating; and the Kyklōps episode only anticipates Odysseus's revenge. As he outwitted Polyphēmos by giving a false name to match his adversary's burlesque of civilized behavior, he now plays a deadly variation on the suitors' parody of the same norm. The banquet he prepares for them is their own slaughter; the accompanying music is the sound, not of the lyre, but of the bowstring (xx.392-94, xxi.428-30). Fittingly, the ringleader Antinoos is shot through the gullet as he is lifting the wine cup to his lips, and he kicks over the laden table in his death agony (xxii.8-21). We are not to feel this death as pathetic or to question the violence of Odysseus's vengeance. He meets the suitors on their own terms, matches their disorder for the sake of restoring order. He can do so safely because he knows the value of law and custom, and understands the limits beyond which he cannot go (cf. xxii.407-16). Ultimately, the theme of feasting glorifies the poem's hero by revealing his mettle, his ability to rise to any occasion.

The *Iliad*'s circular form gives it an effect of concentration and implies a sense of the limits on even those human lives distinguished by great achievements. Even the events that will occur after the poem's end but are foreshadowed in the later books will follow a pattern that has been—at least poetically—preordained. The *Odyssey* moves to triumph, the joy of reunion, and final reconciliation, and then stops. There is no need for the poem to continue. We know that after Odysseus has paid his debt to Poseidon and made his last return to Ithaka, life will go on in peace and contentment, of which the earlier vicissitudes have demonstrated the value. The *Odyssey* could be extended, but its open form accords with the sense of life it conveys. Structurally, as in so many other ways, this poem is the *Iliad*'s perfect complement.

d. THE *WORKS AND DAYS*

The structure of the *Works and Days* deserves, and has received,[65] detailed study, for in this poem, perhaps more than in any of the others discussed here, meaning is implicit in the form. The essential point for our purpose, however, is that although there is some large-scale framing, the basic principle of composition is the juxtaposing of discrete sections. The important connections between these parts are to be found, not in the formal transitions (which are in some cases—such as line 42—vestigial), but in recurrences of important ideas that are often stressed by verbal echoes. There is an obvious analogy with the

Odyssey in this respect. The *Works and Days* lacks a progressing plot, however, although its ostensible occasion is the poet's quarrel with his brother.[66]
This poem is more concerned with presenting principles and doctrine, and depends on the development of ideas. Yet it is suggestive rather than rationally
argumentative. Hesiod lets his thought play over various ideas—never casually
or aimlessly, but in a way that, although nondiscursive, brings out their interrelations. Drawing as it does the most basic concerns of human life into the
exhortation to work, the *Works and Days* is a fine example of the subtlety
and emotional persuasiveness of which the paratactic style is capable.

As we observed in the preceding chapter, the adjacent sections devoted to
agriculture (ll. 383–617) and to sailing in order to trade the produce (ll. 618–
94) are connected by means of the temporal indications in lines 615 and 619–
20. The subjects of these sections, which are clearly complementary,[67] are
juxtaposed as early as lines 45–46—an indication that they are conceptually
related and a small sign, perhaps, that the poem's development is not random.
On either side of the poem's didactic core appear passages of advice on various
topics (ll. 327–82, 695–764) that correspond and function as a frame.[68] They
supplement the sections between them by treating the details of life that do
not come under the headings of farming or sailing, and thus by providing a
background for those activities. The *Days* section (ll. 765–828) falls outside
this ring but should not be considered spurious for that reason.[69] If genuine,
it complements the advice on agriculture. It is similarly concerned with the
right time for each action (with the addition, in polar fashion, of the wrong
time), but according to the days of the month rather than the months and
seasons of the year.

There remains the long hortatory section (ll. 1–326) that precedes the advice proper. Overall, this part is also held together by ring composition: the
important words and themes of lines 1–41 reappear in lines 306–26, but now
with new clarity and force because of the intervening lines.[70] If we discount
the *Days* as an appendage (but a relevant and useful one), the poem divides
into two principal self-enclosed portions, placed side by side.[71] The design is
then as follows:

1. Exhortation (ll. 1–326)
    a. 1–10: opening invocation
    b. 11–41: the two Erides; Persēs warned against the evil Eris
    c. 42–105: Prometheus / Pandora myth
    d. 106–201: the Five Ages
    e. 202–12: fable of the Hawk and the Nightingale
    f. 213–92: the two paths (216–18, 288–92); advantages of *dikē*, dan-
        gers of *hubris*
    g. 293–326: concluding admonitions (with echoes of 1–41)

 2. Advice (327–764)

   a. 327–82: miscellaneous advice

   b. 383–617: agriculture

   c. 618–94: sailing

   a. 695–764: miscellaneous advice

 3. The *Days* (765–828)

The important question is how the two major sections (1 and 2) are related.

Marcel Detienne (1963, Chapters 4 and 5) has shown that this poem attributes a religious value to agricultural work, as the Greeks did generally. The earlier part of the poem makes this connection by exploring the affinities between justice and work, and the agricultural advice, which has notoriously little practical value, would be almost meaningless without it. Hesiod begins by showing how work is the basis for stable relations within human society and—because history has taken a certain course and we are in the Iron Age— between mankind and the gods. The farming section, for its part, demonstrates by example that something positive can be made of conditions in the present, although it never loses touch with the hard realities of life on Greek soil.[72]

More specifically, thematic repetitions bind these parts of the poem together and implicitly establish this relation between them. In considering these, we move from paraphrase to trying to appreciate the poetry itself. Among the admonitions that precede the agricultural instructions, for example, the injunction against dishonoring an aged father on pain of punishment by Zeus (ll. 331–34) is especially forceful because this is one of the crimes for which Zeus will destroy the iron race (ll. 185–87; note the similar phrasing in ll. 332 and 186). Similarly, the warning to sacrifice to the gods (ἔρδειν, *erdein*) in order to get prosperity (ll. 336–41) appears against the background of lines 134–39, where Zeus is said to have hidden away the silver race in anger because they did not perform sacrifices (ἔρδειν, *erdein*) on the gods' altars, "which is the rightful custom for men in their different dwelling places." These are just details, but they are symptomatic of the complex system of thematic interconnections in this poem; and they also show, incidentally, how the miscellaneous advice in lines 327–82 is integrated into the general design.

A more significant relationship between the major sections appears in lines 397–98:

$$\text{ἐργάζευ, νήπιε Πέρση,}$$
$$\text{ἔργα τά τ' ἀνθρώποισι θεοὶ διετεκμήραντο.}$$

Foolish Perses, perform
the [agricultural] tasks, which the gods have portioned out [*dietekmēranto*] to men.

In the story of Prometheus and Pandora, Hesiod has shown how the gods hid livelihood from men and why the work that he is about to describe here is man's lot. The gods have assigned it (*dietekmēranto*), he says in line 398, and uses the same verb as he did when telling how Zeus assigns punishment to the unjust city (τεκμαίρεται, *tekmairetai*, 1. 239) but does not assign warfare to the just city (οὐδὲ . . . τεκμαίρεται, *oude . . . tekmairetai*, ll. 228-29). Hesiod's conception of the moral order in the world is epitomized in these three uses of the verb. Lines 397-98 recall both what Hesiod has said about why men must work and what is involved in choosing whether to submit to this necessity or to try (vainly) to defy it. Similarly, as was noted earlier, farming and seafaring are alluded to together in lines 45-46, just as they are later dealt with contiguously. But the former passage describes the conditions that might have been if the gods had not hidden livelihood (l. 45):

αἶψά κε πηδάλιον μὲν ὑπὲρ καπνοῦ καταθεῖο.

. . . you would soon put your rudder [*pēdalion*] over the fire [*huper kapnou*].

In the later advice on sailing, Hesiod is telling how to cope with things as they are, and the verbal reminiscence in line 629 drives home the contrast:

πηδάλιον δ᾽ εὐεργὲς ὑπὲρ καπνοῦ κρεμάσασθαι.

[in late autumn] hang the well-made rudder [*pēdalion*] over the fire [*huper kapnou*].

The difference in the moods of the verbs in the two lines is the difference between the expression of an unfulfilled condition and a command. Rather than almost continuous ease, there is now only seasonal release from certain tasks. Men might have been free simultaneously from both farming and sailing. As it is, the land must be worked when the weather prevents navigation (ll. 622-23). We know why this is; the stories of Pandora and the Five Ages have told us.

Like the poem as a whole, the first main division (ll. 1-326) is constructed of parts arranged paratactically but subtly connected with each other. This is perhaps the most astonishing passage in all our corpus of hexameter poetry. Although Hesiod has scarcely bothered to relate its various sections explicitly, there is such thematic density that the whole is unified by patterns of richly suggestive likenesses and contrast. The structure of the passage can be viewed in a number of ways. The basic principle, however, is once again the repetition of key ideas.

The story of Prometheus and Pandora, for instance, is often considered to be concerned with the necessity for work, and so it is. But it also represents the complementary idea of the relations between men and gods, which will

come to be expressed as justice. You are proud of yourself for stealing fire,
Zeus tells Prometheus; but (1. 56)—

σοί τ' αὐτῷ μέγα πῆμα καὶ ἀνδράσιν ἐσσομένοισιν.

[your deed will be] a great misfortune for you yourself [*soi autōi*] and for
men to come.

Later, when urging the rulers to give "straight" judgments, Hesiod warns
them (ll. 265-66):

οἳ αὐτῷ κακὰ τεύχει ἀνὴρ ἄλλῳ κακὰ τεύχων,
ἡ δὲ κακὴ βουλὴ τῷ βουλεύσαντι κακίστη.

The man who contrives evils for another contrives evils for himself [*hoi
autōi*],
and an evil plot is worst for the plotter.

The story of Prometheus illustrates this truth, for although Hesiod does not
mention his punishment explicitly in this poem, the audience surely would
think of it.[73] The later lines, moreover, immediately follow the warning that
an entire people can be made to atone for the unrighteousness of its ruler
(ll. 260-61, themselves related to ll. 240-41). Mankind as a whole has suffered
for the individual misdeed of Prometheus (admittedly done in their behalf,
but still an affront to Zeus). The myth of Prometheus thus sets the pattern
for what can go wrong in human society, when men ignore or try to avoid
the work the gods have ordained for them and commit injustice instead.

The idea that the evil deed most harms the transgressor crops up elsewhere
also, and in different guises. The man who swears a false oath "is uncurably
deluded" (νήκεστον ἀασθῇ, *nēkeston aasthēi,* 1. 283). Evil profits are "equal
to ruin" (ἶσ' ἄτῃσι, *īs' atēisi,* line 352—we observe another link between the
gnomic advice and the rest of the poem). And right after this the seizure of
another's goods is paradoxically called "the giver of death" (1. 356), with a
grim play on the verb of giving in the preceding lines.

Sometimes a theme will be touched on lightly at first, and then developed
fully in a later section. In lines 216-18, the figure of two roads is used to depict the superiority of justice over violence, and this is followed by the statement—clearly proverbial because it has Homeric parallels (XVII.32, XX.198)
—that the fool recognizes the truth only after he has suffered. The same sequence recurs in lines 287-97, where Hesiod develops the figure of the contrasting roads in greater detail[74] and now applies the idea of the proverb to
Persēs, whom he urges not to be the hopeless kind of man who neither has
understanding himself nor pays attention to one who does. Actually, this
latter motif started with the Prometheus story. Epimetheus, who accepted
Pandora despite his brother's warning, "when he had evil, realized it" (or

"gained understanding," l. 89).[75] From the mythical situation that provides the archetype for so much in human life to the immediate case of these two brothers, the issues are the same: work or idleness, justice or violence.[76]

One final sequence will show how work fits in with these moral ideas. At the beginning of the poem, Hesiod tells his brother (ll. 30-32):

ὥρη γάρ τ᾽ ὀλίγη πέλεται νεικέων τ᾽ ἀγορέων τε
ᾧ τινι μὴ βίος ἔνδον ἐπηετανὸς κατάκειται
ὡραῖος, τὸν γαῖα φέρει, Δημήτερος ἀκτήν.

That man has little concern for quarrels and speeches
for whom sufficient livelihood is not stored up within
in due season, which the earth bears, Demeter's grain.

This follows the injunction not to let the evil Eris or Strife turn Persēs away from work and toward legal quarrels. The same idea, but with the command expressed positively, recurs in lines 299-302:

ἐργάζευ, Πέρση, δῖον γένος, ὄφρα σε Λιμὸς
ἐχθαίρῃ, φιλέῃ δέ σ᾽ ἐυστέφανος Δημήτηρ
αἰδοίη, βιότου δὲ τεὴν πιμπλῇσι καλιήν·
Λιμὸς γάρ τοι πάμπαν ἀεργῷ σύμφορος ἀνδρί.

Work, Persēs, divinely born, so that Hunger [*Limos*]
hates you, but fair-garlanded Demeter, the dread one,
loves you and fills your storehouse with livelihood;
for Hunger [*Limos*] in every way befits a lazy man.

These passages belong to the system of correspondences that establish the ring composition in this first part of the poem, but the ideas they express, and other, related ideas, are basic to the whole section. Hunger (*limos*), whose absence (as we observed earlier) characterized human life before Pandora's advent and in the Golden Age, and distinguishes the just city even today (l. 230), afflicts the unjust city (l. 243). The connection between hunger and strife is very close. In the *Theogony*, Limos is the son of Eris (*Theog.* 227)—the same Eris "delighting in evil" (κακόχαρτος, *kakokhartos*, *W.D.* 28) who threatens to make Persēs neglect work for lawsuits and the rulers' crooked judgments. An almost identical power, "jealousy" (ζῆλος, *zēlos*), which will mark the Iron Age when it is inclining toward destruction, receives the same epithet later on (κακόχαρτος, *kakokhartos*, ll. 195-96). There is thus no separating the concepts of work and rightful action, or their opposites, idleness and violence. The former pair leads to prosperity and other men's esteem, the latter to debt and the contempt of others.

These examples could be multiplied many times over. Such repetitions perform a structural function, to be sure, but by their interweaving they also, and more importantly, create a fine poetic texture. Hesiod seems to return to his basic ideas in different contexts in order to clarify them, define them, examine them in different lights.[77] The repetitions and the paratactic style are reciprocal in their effect. Recurrent ideas link and relate passages that appear merely strung together. At the same time, the paratactic order of the passages makes it possible for each of these ideas to be raised in connection with a great variety of different topics, so that all its implications can be explored in concrete detail. To read the *Works and Days* is to experience through the poetic form, as the original audience must have experienced it, Hesiod's understanding of the world: that there is an order in human life beneath all the surface variety, an order imposed by external necessity but based on a few values that are at issue in the most humble undertakings as in the most grand. For the individual and for his society, the action that fulfills that order is work.

e. THE *SHIELD OF HERAKLES (ASPIS)*

"I wish he had never designed it! May he never design such another, who stored up that belt in his art!" Odysseus's awed response in the *Odyssey* to Herakles' baldric (xi.613-14) could serve as an aesthetic comment on the same hero's shield in the *Aspis*. Yet the bizarreness of the description and its obvious inferiority to its counterpart in the eighteenth book of the *Iliad* should not blind us to its author's evident purpose.

Enclosed by ring composition and set within the account of Herakles's battle with Kyknos (see above, p. 10), the description of the shield makes an implicit comment on the surrounding narrative. The Shield of Achilles performs a similar function within its poem. But whereas it widens the scope of the *Iliad* by putting warfare into context as one of various human activities, the scenes displayed on Herakles's shield represent in great detail the horror of war itself and thus by implication condemn its wanton violence. The descriptions of these scenes, like the sections of the *Works and Days,* follow one another paratactically, but here the parts are not linked by thematic repetition. Instead, the description as a whole conveys its meaning by the mere placement of episodes.

The poet works from the center of the shield to its rim, and so the figure in the middle of the sculptural composition does not occupy the central place in the passage. Poetic and artistic forms, which the author tries in other respects to assimilate to one another, diverge here, evidently because he has other concerns that override his desire to imitate visual effects. At the center of the poetic account lie three scenes of gods (ll. 191-206), which stand out from the five scenes that precede and the five that follow them. In these flanking parts there is a general progression from monstrous personifications of war and violence through strife in the animal world to warfare among mankind.[78]

Over the head of the serpent[79] in the first picture hovers Eris (ll. 147-50),

who in the *Iliad* (IV.439-45) is one of the spirits of war—in fact, Ares' sister
and companion. Then comes a group of beings who personify aspects of
battle (ll. 154-55). If the disputed lines 156-60 are genuine, Eris herself reappears here.[80] In any case, two of the monsters certainly represented—Phonos
(Murder) and Androktasiē (Manslaughter)—are children of Eris in Hesiod
(*Theog.* 228; cf. xi.612), so that her spirit at least pervades this scene. Twelve
snakes' heads, which add to the hideous atmosphere (ll. 161-67), are followed
by the first scene of conflict (ll. 168-77). This battle is entirely between animals (boars and lions). Next (ll. 178-90) appears the fight between the
Lapiths and the Kentaurs—that is, between humans and semibeasts who represent respectively civilization and nature. (See above, pp. 24-25.) This scene is
thus transitional between warfare among animals and the warfare among men
that will be depicted. The central representations of gods interrupt the sequence. These are followed by another transitional scene (ll. 207-15): a
harbor, with fish fleeing dolphins (animal, predatory violence again),[81] but
also a human figure, a fisherman (man preying on beasts). The succeeding
mythological scene (ll. 216-37) shows a different kind of violence, that between mankind and monsters. Perseus, victorious after his killing of Medousa,
is nevertheless being pursued by the other Gorgons. With the scene of the city
at war (ll. 237-70), the series reaches its climax in the representation of strife
solely among men. The Kēres here may recall the single Kēr of line 156, if
that is genuine. It is fair to say, at any rate, that with their presence here
along with the Fates and Darkness of Death (Akhlys), the personifications of
war's horrors, which resemble those that appeared at the beginning of the description, have now been placed in the setting in which they affect humanity.
Then the city at peace (ll. 270-313) is depicted not for its own sake but as a
foil to the preceding scene in order to stress the ghastliness of war. The fish
that flee the swans in the stream of Ocean (l. 317) touch lightly once again on
the theme of natural violence and by recalling the fish in the harbor (ll. 207-
12) round off the part of the description that follows the divine scenes.[82]

Cumulatively, then, the pictures on the shield make an implicit statement
about war. It is monstrous, irrational, an activity proper to beasts in which
man also engages. His civilization incorporates nature: with the joys of the
feast and with constructive work on the land coexists savage force.

The scenes in the middle of the description reiterate this contradiction on
the divine level and bring the implications of the shield to bear on the poem's
main narrative. Two warlike gods, Athena and Ares, are pictured in full
panoply (ll. 191-200). Then appears a scene of dancing and song on Olympos
(ll. 201-6), which forms the divine counterpart to the festivities in the city at
peace and which is similarly a foil to martial ferocity (here the character and
activities of Ares and Athena).[83] Thus the gods' nature contains the same
ambivalence between the extremes of peaceful festivity and violence. The
same two warrior divinities, later in the poem, will champion the mortal combatants Herakles and Kyknos. On the shield Athena appears with the aegis that

she will shake when she stands beside Herakles in his chariot (ll. 343–44). Ares is accompanied by Deimos (Fear) and Phobos (Flight) in lines 195–96. These are his squires in Homer (XV.119), of course, but in this poem the same pair will tend Ares after Herakles has wounded him (ll. 463–66).

The images on the shield, then, reflect the encounter that is about to take place. Herakles will face Ares' son Kyknos and then the war-god himself, carrying a shield that exposes the grotesque ugliness of war. It might seem therefore that his triumph over Ares is all the more splendid, the defeat of the monstrous and irrational in behalf of culture, and in part this is true. But the case is not that simple. If Herakles' shield comments on war in general, it comments on its owner's particular actions within this poem, and its message rigorously excludes the notion of heroic glory. That this champion of order, this "defender from harm" (ἀρῆς ἀλκτήρ, l. 128), defeats Ares by violence extends the paradox implied by the pictures on the shield. The value of his exploit is questioned even in the act of narration. The grim reality of violence can never be altered: momentary victory is the most that can be gained. For Herakles wounded Ares once before, at Pylos (ll. 359–67). In the Iliadic version (V.395–402), it is Hades whom Herakles wounded on that occasion, and the duplication, in the *Aspis,* of Ares as the victim seems pointed. Now as then, Ares will recover: war is irrepressible.

The composer of the *Aspis* may have imitated the Homeric Shield of Achilles, but if so, he used what he appropriated in his own way. The poem's execution is not worthy of the underlying conception, but even in this case we can observe how naturally the archaic poets expressed meaning through simple juxtaposition, and how much even a mediocre poet could accomplish in this way.[84]

f. THE *HYMN TO APOLLO*

The structure of the Homeric Hymns seems regulated in many respects by the formal conventions of hymnic poetry.[85] Yet within that framework there is room for much diversity, as the extant poems show—evidently because individual poets manipulated hymnic conventions to suit their own purposes without ever breaking with them altogether. The hymns, and particularly the narratives that form the bulk of the four longest ones, also reflect the same habits of composition we have found in the examples above.[86] To discuss each of these poems would add little to what has been said. The *Hymn to Apollo,* however, presents special problems and raises in a particularly clear way the question of what constitutes unity in early Greek poetry. For the last 200 years most scholars have regarded this hymn, not as a single work, but either as two separate poems clumsily patched together or as an original poem with a later (and inferior) continuation. According to both versions of this separatist hypothesis, the two parts are distinct because they honor

Apollo under different guises, the first as the god of Delos, the second as the god of Delphi.[87] Much spurious religious history, including a rivalry between these two cult centers, has been manufactured out of thin air to prove that Apollo could not have been associated with both places in the same poem at the time when the "Delian" hymn was allegedly composed. In fact, there is no valid external evidence for the separatist view.[88] And if we consider the hymn from the point of view of its form—form as determined not only by hymnic conventions but especially by the conventional compositional methods discussed here—we shall find it a unified piece by the standards of archaic hexameter poetry, and one of no slight merit at that. The poem, like so many others, achieves a balance of complementary elements by means of recurrent themes and narrative patterns.[89]

Although those who would divide the poem into two separate compositions have not entirely agreed in locating the end of the "Delian" hymn (or as much as remains after the supposed junction with the "Pythian" hymn), most have put it after lines 177-78. The phrase "I shall not cease praising Apollo" has commonly been thought to resemble the formulas of farewell to the god that close most of the hymns in our collection. In a recent article, however, Andrew Miller has pointed out formidable obstacles to this view, and has argued persuasively that the lines instead signal the poet's intention to continue singing Apollo, that the conventional leave-taking is indeed present (ll. 166-76) but is directed to the Delian maidens rather than to the god, and that lines 165-78 are thus a passage of transition back to the main subject (celebration of Apollo) from a subsidiary theme, the description of the Delian festival.[90] We would therefore expect the poet to begin again in lines 179 ff. on the course interrupted, after line 146, by the passage on the festival. And that is what happens. The list of places under Apollo's sway in lines 179-81 resumes the list of the god's haunts in lines 140-46. Both passages end with Delos and are addressed to Apollo in the second person. But the later passage complements the earlier one, for it specifies particular places, whereas lines 140-46, besides Delos and its mountain Kynthos, enumerate only natural features that could be anywhere.

These passages are transitional in two senses. First, they frame and help to insert the description of the Delian festival. The earlier passage, a priamel that sets off Delos as the place most pleasing to Apollo (l. 146), leads by an easy glide into that scene (l. 147).[91] Through lines 179-81, the poet returns after his farewell to the Delian maidens from what is formally subsidiary material to the main task of praising Apollo. Second, the two passages help effect the transition between major parts of that program. On the one hand, they round off the birth narrative. As we noticed earlier in connection with lines 14-29 (pp. 14-16, above), Delos incorporates all the natural features mentioned there and again in lines 144-45. An important motif of the narrative just ended is thus recapitulated in lines 140-46. The places named in lines 179-81, moreover, are all in the East, in Asia Minor (except for Delos). They thus evoke once again the scene of the pregnant Leto's wandering, just when the essence of the birth story and Apollo's relation to Delos are restated with finality (ll. 178, 181). On the other hand, as many writers have noticed, lines 144-45 essentially repeat lines 22-23; but the effect is not just closure. When it first occurs in the poem, the idea that all places delight Apollo is linked to the poet's choice of subject (l. 19). Lines 140-46, and hence also lines 179-81, have the same association: selection of a new topic in praise of Apollo now that the program announced in lines 25-29 (narrative of the god's birth) has, strictly speaking, been fulfilled. Lines 140-46, with their reminiscence of the earlier choice of theme, indicate that the poet plans to go on with his song. Transition to the new topic is then interrupted by the account of the Delian festival, after which follow an explicit statement of intent to continue (ll. 177-78) and a passage renewing the "choice of theme" idea. Although it will not be complete until line 215, the transition is aided by the naming of Delphi in line 183. This place will be the focus of the new theme in praise of Apollo, the foundation of the Delphic sanctuary—a theme that Miller regards as "ultimately the poet's real focus of interest in the Hymn," to which the birth narrative and other material have been preliminary.[92]

The hymn as a whole thus falls into two main sections, with the division occurring between lines 181 and 182.[93] The partition is carefully marked not only by the function of lines 179-81 but also by the switch from direct address of Apollo to description of him in the third person.[94] This arrangement, typical of parataxis, is entirely appropriate within a unified hymn. I doubt that either of the major sections ever existed as an independent poem. As I hope to show, they are, on the contrary, necessary to one another.

In many ways, the description of the Delian festival is unique and non-traditional. Yet it is accommodated in the larger design by conventional means —through a pair of balanced framing passages (ll. 140-46, 179-81). This procedure does not imply that this splendid passage is irrelevant or an accidental digression, though it is unexpected. The scene completes the birth story with an account of the recurring human activity that commemorates the divine event, and thus appropriately postpones the shift in theme begun in lines 140-46.[95] It also has an important place in the scheme of the whole poem as one of a pair of festive scenes. The second scene on Olympos (ll. 186-206), which also depicts music and dancing, but among the gods, balances it and provides a divine perspective upon it. In particular, the subject of the Muses' song (ll. 189-93) qualifies the appearance of immortality that the brilliance of the festival casts upon the Ionians gathered on Delos (ll. 151-52)—a fact that Kakridis noted long ago and used to argue for the unity of the hymn.[96] These scenes straddle the boundary between the two main parts of the hymn and help connect them.

The paratactically placed major sections are linked by other shared motifs and narrative patterns, and complement each other. Both, for example, begin with scenes on Olympos (ll. 1-13, 186-206).[97] On each occasion, Apollo's entrance into Zeus's house causes a stir among the other gods, and he then takes his proper place in their midst. His parents' joy as they watch him at the end of the second scene (ll. 204-6) recalls Leto sitting beside Zeus at the beginning of the poem (1. 5) and her pride—there also described at the end of the scene—in her son's prowess and might (ll. 12-13). There are obvious differences between the two scenes; but these are also important as showing how the passages complement one another by representing opposed aspects of Apollo's nature, dreadful on the one hand and festive on the other. Many scholars have thought that these scenes belong to a type of description that often follows narratives of divine births, the newborn god's first entrance onto Olympos, or at least that they were influenced by such set pieces.[98] It is probably better, however, to consider them accounts of Apollo's typical activities, as the often-cited parallel of Hymn 27 suggests. There Apollo's sister Artemis is depicted as hunting with the bow. A graphic description of the cries of beasts, the trembling of the mountains, and the shuddering of earth and sea illustrates the goddess's awesome power. When she has had her fill of the hunt, Artemis unstrings her bow, goes to her brother's sanctuary at Delphi, hangs up bow and quiver, and leads the dance of the Muses and the Graces. The obvious resemblances here to the two Olympian scenes in the *Hymn to Apollo* do not mean that one poem influenced the other, or that the same poet composed both. The conclusion to be drawn does not concern these matters at all, except that the analogy with Hymn 27 weakens the hypothesis, adopted by some Analysts, that the second Olympos scene was modeled on the first. Rather, we are dealing with conventional elements, and the poet of the *Hymn to Apollo* has made individual use of an apparently typical sequence —archery (originally in hunting), followed by dance and song.[99] He has divided two themes that illustrate antithetic traits and thus in combination depict the nature of Apollo (or Artemis), and he has used each in a scene that initiates a major segment of his poem.[100] Consequently, the two main narratives of the hymn are aligned with one another, and this effect is surely an indication that the whole poem has a coherent design.

In both sections of the poem, the poet effects the transition from the opening vignette to the narrative proper in essentially the same way—with two questions, similarly phrased, of which one suggests the wealth of potential themes for praising Apollo and the second indicates the choice of one theme. Thus line 207 repeats line 19, and lines 214 and 25 resemble each other. In the later passage, an enumeration of places dear to Apollo ought strictly to intervene in lines 208-13 between the two questions. But since the poet has used two such lists shortly before, he here substitutes allusions to stories in which Apollo figured as suitor to mortal women and that show a different side of his nature from those celebrated directly in the hymn. Whatever the precise form of these tales may have been, they share one feature with the founding of the Delphic oracle: the journeying of the god, a motif that is, as we shall now see, important to the poem as a whole (note ἔκιες, l. 209, and compare ἔβης, l. 215; both verbs mean "you went").

Correspondences between the narratives in each section of the hymn have long been recognized.[101] In particular, Leto's search for a place to give birth resembles Apollo's wandering to find a site for his oracle. We might go further and observe that there are three journeys in the poem (the third being Apollo's voyage in the form of a dolphin on the deck of the Cretans' ship) that are interrelated in two ways. First, Leto's reception by Delos contrasts with Telphousa's attempt to get rid of Apollo by deceiving him,[102] and in its results (the institution of a cult, enrichment at pilgrims' expense of those who conform to the god's wishes) resembles the accommodation that Apollo makes with the Cretan sailors. Second, the description of all three journeys involves a list of places visited or passed by (ll. 30–46, 216–43, 409–39, the first two at the beginning of each story). Each list follows a definite order, and together they complement one another. Leto begins in Crete, proceeds to Athens and Euboia, and from there goes clockwise around the edge of the Aegean until she reaches Karpathos (that is, she comes almost full circle back to Crete). She then cuts into the middle of the sea to Naxos and Paros, and finally arrives at Delos in the center of the Cyclades.[103] On his first expedition in the "Pythian" section Apollo goes from Olympos to Pieria, then to Iolkos, down the length of Euboia as far as Kalkhis, where he crosses the Euripos, and through Boiotia, eventually reaching Delphi. That is, he proceeds southeast as far as Kalkhis, and then generally westward. Later, he takes the Cretans west from Cape Malea, then northwest along the western coast of the Peloponnesos, and finally eastward in the Gulf of Corinth to Krisa. This route is semicircular, like that of the journey from Olympos, and also has Delphi as its goal, but the compass directions it follows are just the reverse of that one. Together, the three lists include nearly all of Greece: the coasts and islands of the Aegean, the eastern part of the mainland north of the Gulf of Corinth, and the Peloponnesos. In general, the hexameter poets seem to have been fond of geographical catalogues,[104] but here a familiar feature is put to good use. This poet manages to draw into his stories landmarks familiar to a traveler almost anywhere in Greece, and thus to associate them, however faintly, with the origins of the two most important centers of Apollo's cult. The three catalogues in conjunction bear out the statement in line 20 that "Everywhere, Phoibos, the range of song is laid out for you." All places delight Apollo. The passages that express this idea we have called transitional, and that is their formal function. But it is characteristic of the paratactic style that such transitional passages should convey what the geographical catalogues show to be an important idea, one that balances the poem's concentration on Delos and Delphi as the places most closely associated with Apollo. This god is at once local and universal.[105]

From this point of view, there is no difficulty, as some have felt there is, in conceiving a poem that includes a description of the Delian festival being performed elsewhere than on that island, and there is nothing inappropriate in the treatment of two different cult centers in the same hymn.[106] In fact, the duality in Apollo's nature—the way he is prominently connected with two particular places and at home everywhere—is reflected within the poem by the gathering of worshippers from various localities at Delos and Delphi (ll. 58, 147, 539—all with a form of the verb ἀγείρειν, "to assemble"). The Delian festival is specifically Ionian, but the homes of those who converge on the island represent a considerable part of the area covered by Leto in her wanderings.[107] Delphi is truly international, for as Apollo says when he founds the sanctuary (ll. 290-91), men will come to consult the oracle from the islands, from "Europe" (here, northern Greece),[108] and from the Peloponnesos—that is, from the three principle divisions of Greece that are included respectively in the three geographical catalogues.

The two parts of the hymn are further connected by similarities in the founding of the two temples and in the blessings that Apollo's cult will confer on the places that receive it. Lines 287-93 (= 247-53) and 535-37 correspond to lines 56-60 and 80-81, with repetitions in phrasing. Apollo will establish a temple in each place "to be an oracle of men." Worshippers who throng both sanctuaries will bring hecatombs, so that Delos and Delphi, naturally poor, will feed their inhabitants "from other men's hands" (ll. 59-60; cf. ll. 535-37). This ubiquitous god adopts places that are out of the way, neglected by the other gods because of their poverty, and transforms them by his cult into crowded and opulent centers of worship.[109] As token of this magic change, Delos blossoms with gold when Apollo is born.

Finally, the two parts of the hymn are complementary because together they depict the three activities that the newborn Apollo claims as his own in lines 131-32—music, archery, and prophecy. This is a standard argument of those who defend the integrity of the hymn: Apollo's oracular nature receives full attention only in the second part, which is therefore necessary for complete celebration of the god. What has not been adequately emphasized is the way the plan of the poem is based on these motifs. In the first place, in the hymn taken as a whole the scenes that illustrate Apollo's association with the bow and the lyre are placed in chiastic order: archery on Olympos (ll. 1-13)—music on earth (the Delian festival)—music on Olympos (ll. 188-206)—archery on earth (the killing of the Python). There is, however, another musical performance in the poem, and this will lead to our second point. Near the end, Apollo and the Cretans go in procession from Krisa to Delphi, the god playing the lyre and his new priests singing the "Iēpaiēon" (ll. 513-19). This song is identified with the paean, which was sacred to Apollo (ll. 518-19). The poem's original audience would surely have associated the whole passage with the Pythian festival. According to several ancient sources, until the early sixth century this festival consisted of a kitharodic contest—the singing of paeans with lyre accompaniment.[110] The hymn thus seems to present the Cretans' procession to their new home, which was the first worship of Apollo by mortals at Delphi, as the *aition,* or tale of the origin of the festival.

This allusion both reminds the audience of the Pythian counterpart to the festival on Delos and balances the reference in line 81 to an oracle on that island. Admittedly, what independent evidence there is for the existence of a Delian oracle is tenuous and late;[111] and to judge from the silence on the matter in the rest of the hymn, prophecy must never have been very important on Delos. But if we take that bare allusion at face value, the two parts of the hymn present a further symmetry of complementary elements. In connection with Delos, the poet alludes briefly to an oracle and emphasizes musical performance at the festival. In connection with Delphi, he alludes to music, again set at a festival, and stresses the oracle. It is fitting that both activities be engaged in at each cult center, for both are characteristic of Apollo. But the way they are developed at length only in successive parts of the poem shows once again how interdependent these parts are.

As a whole, then, the *Hymn to Apollo* seems a balanced and intelligible composition. Some attention must also be given to the structure of its parts, since that has figured in the debate over unity. The organizational features of the first, "Delian" section are well known and need be listed only briefly. The story of the god's birth is framed by the repetition in lines 125-26 of lines 12-13, and the astonishment of the goddesses in lines 134-35 at Apollo's movement (whether from or upon the earth is uncertain) recalls the response of the gods to Apollo's appearance in Zeus's house (ll. 1-4). The description of the Delian festival is inserted in the ways discussed above. That it is related to the preceding narrative as well as to the second scene on Olympos hardly needs pointing out.[112]

The form of this section has been widely—and deservedly—admired.[113] The second part has frequently been criticized as loose and amorphous by contrast. This judgment seems unfair. Critics have pointed to the sharp break between halves of the narrative in lines 387-88. Yet what could be more typical of the paratactic style than just this sort of division, and what more natural than that, having founded his sanctuary, Apollo should populate it with officials? As for the separation of the parts of the Telphousa episode, which also has attracted unfavorable comment, that is just one sign of the elaborate ring composition by which the whole section is shaped. This is the pattern:

a.   182-206: music at Delphi and on Olympos; Apollo goes to Delphi playing the lyre, which gives forth a lovely sound (185). On Olympos he plays his lyre "taking fine high strides" (καλὰ καὶ ὕψι βιβάς, *kala kai hupsi bibas,* 202).

b.   216-43: journey in quest of site for oracle; geographical catalogue

c.   244-76: Apollo encounters Telphousa; she deceives him.

d. 277-99: Apollo goes to Delphi and builds his temple.

e. 300-307:
  1. Apollo shoots the Python
  2. who used to harm men and their flocks (302-4),
  3. and once, receiving him from Hera, she raised (305)
  4. Typhaon, "a horrible and baneful affliction for mortals" (306),
  5. whom Hera bore in anger at Zeus (307).

f. 308-48: Account of Hera's rivalry with Zeus: circumstances leading to the birth of Typhaon

e. 349-62:
  5. Hera bore him (349-51),
  4. Typhaon, "a horrible and baneful affliction for mortals" (352 repeats 306).
  3. Hera took him to the Python, and she received him (353-54).
  2. He used to harm men, and she (the Python) killed whomever she met (line 355 repeats the phrasing of 302-3),
  1. until Apollo shot her (description of her death, ll. 357-62).

d. 363-74: last stage in establishing sanctuary at Delphi:
  1. visitors who bring hecatombs will now be safe from the Python (366 repeats 289);
  2. Delphi receives the name Pytho (371-74).

c. 375-87: Apollo punishes Telphousa.

b. 388-512: Apollo brings Cretans to Krisa; geographical catalogue

a. 513-19: music at Delphi; Apollo goes with Cretans to Delphi playing the lyre, and his playing is lovely (515; cf. 185). He marches "with fine high strides" (καλὰ καὶ ὕψι βιβάς, *kala kai hupsi bibas*, l. 516).

Lines 520-46 fall outside the ring as a sort of epilogue, and there is more narrative material in lines 388-512 than is indicated in the diagram. With these exceptions (which seem minor), the symmetry is remarkably thoroughgoing.[114]

This section is not diffuse and aimless, but highly organized; and the hypothesis of a poetaster who composed a bumbling sequel to a hymn to the Delian Apollo becomes less acceptable the more one considers this form. The "Pythian" section is a fine example of a conventional mode of composition. If we look for unusual elements, they are to be found in the "Delian" section instead, especially in the description of the festival, which is in every way remarkable. Even this, however, is worked into the poem by normal organizational methods; and there is no reason to believe that the same poet—a master of his medium—could not have composed both sections, or that the two kinds of structure could not have coexisted in the same hymn. Each is well suited to its subject matter.

It is necessary to look beyond formal differences and recognize that the second section is not inferior to the first in quality. We can appreciate that it is good in its own way by observing what the ring composition enables the poet to express. The actions in the earlier passages marked *b, c,* and *d* above find their culmination in the corresponding later passages, *d, c,* and *b.* In each of the latter, Apollo or his place of worship receives an epithet to commemorate the occasion: Pytho (ll. 371-74), Telphousios (ll. 385-87), and Delpheios (the altar at Krisa, ll. 495-96).

The story of Typhaon is introduced within the framework of the Python episode. Here, as has sometimes been observed, there is another link with the first section of the hymn. Hera's jealousy when Leto is about to bear to Zeus "a blameless and mighty son" (ll. 100-101) corresponds to her anger at Zeus because he has given birth to Athena by himself rather than in partnership with her, his wife (ll. 323-25). Now Apollo, whose birth Hera tried to obstruct, overcomes a monster who was Hera's ally in another dispute with Zeus involving childbirth. Hera's quarrel with her husband and her plot against him are given special prominence by their place at the center of the structure. The episode that they initiate is clearly part of the succession myth; Hera prays to Gaia, Ouranos, and the Titans (the two earlier generations in that myth) that she bear a son "apart from Zeus, in no way inferior to him in strength, but let him be mightier, by as much as wide-seeing Zeus was mightier than Kronos" (ll. 334-39). Typhaon threatens to depose Zeus and rule in his stead, as in the *Theogony.* In that poem, Zeus's victory over him preserves order in the world. The same must be implied here, even though the hymn does not explicitly mention Typhaon's defeat or its importance. Typhaon is at least said to have harmed men (l. 355), and the whole story was surely a familiar one. The enfolding of this episode within the account of Apollo's killing of the Python relates these two stories to each other, especially since in line 355 the same language is used of Typhaon's injuries to men as is used earlier of the Python's (ll. 302-3).[115] Like Zeus, Apollo rids the world of a monster and preserves mankind—specifically the pilgrims to Delphi—from her ravages. This parallel says much about Apollo's nature. He is on the side of order and against the monstrous and violent forces with which Hera, to satisfy her jealousy, aligns herself.[116]

The passages that comprise the outermost frame balance Apollo's journeys to Delphi and Olympos with his procession to Delphi at the head of the Cretan sailors. The god's lyre playing, described in similar language in the two passages, provides the common element. This section of the hymn thus begins with Apollo's habitual, timeless activity in the neighborhood of Delphi and ends with the completion of his action in time (the foundation of his sanctuary) that inaugurated it. At the outset, moreover, is described Apollo's festivity on Olympos among the other gods, and at the end, the origin in time of the celebration by mortals is told that, like the festival on Delos, mirrors it. The second Olympos scene, then, at once is part of the frame that encloses the

"Pythian" section of the poem and, since it is related to elements in the "Delian" section, is transitional when its function in the entire hymn is considered.

The connections between the two main parts, appreciated in their full significance, show that the *Hymn to Apollo* is a unified whole and, furthermore, a first-rate specimen of paratactic composition. Separatists, however, have noticed a number of these connections, but have claimed them as proof that the "Pythian" part was modeled on the "Delian." Their argument has two serious weaknesses. First, verbal repetitions in themselves do not prove that one passage imitates another. Enough is now known about the traditional diction of hexameter poetry to suggest that repetitions are the result of the use at several points of conventional phrasing (and, as I have argued above, they can signal the recurrence of underlying ideas and motifs). Second, how can one adequately prove which was the model and which the imitation? In fact, M. L. West, while maintaining the separatist position, has recently suggested that the traditional view of the relation between the hymn's two parts should be reversed: that the "Pythian" section was the original poem and the "Delian" the later expansion composed under its influence.[117] I do not find his arguments compelling, but that they can be made at all illustrates the problem. Ultimately, postulating influence and determining its direction is no less subjective than interpreting the hymn as a coherent work. The integrity of the poem, on the other hand, is a more economical and productive hypothesis than the complex, though wonderfully ingenious, Analytical theories about how our present text evolved. Those will have their uses if other approaches fail. But meanwhile we should try to understand what we have before us, discarding as best we can preconceptions about poetic unity that are not applicable here.

But in case the reader cleaves to the Analytical position, or in case it should someday be vindicated by evidence stronger than what has been so far advanced, an intermediate stance can be taken. Suppose, for the sake of argument, that the hymn is composite. At some date, someone, whether the composer of one of the sections or a third poet, joined the two parts together. He did so by methods that were deeply traditional, and he forged a new and intelligible unity by the standards prevailing in hexameter poetry, with the "Pythian" section, by those same standards, a worthy partner to the "Delian" (here I remain opposed to the Analysts). These are the important points for the present purposes.

g. THE *CATALOGUE OF WOMEN*

A poetic catalogue is, as we have seen, a series of passages that need be connected only by the most rudimentary of devices. Enough survives of the Hesiodic *Catalogue of Women,* however, to show that a poem with an intelligible arrangement of parts could be produced even in this form. The *Catalogue* was essentially a genealogical work, and the most recent evidence confirms that it was (in West's words) "a systematic exposition of the great genealogies of Greek mythology, and principally the descendants of Deucalion, Io, Atlas, and Pelasgus" (1963, 758). Each of these families was associated principally with one or two regions, and by collecting heroic pedigrees the poem could also present substantially the geography of the known world. (See Merkelbach, 1968a.) Many of these genealogies in addition shared one important characteristic: to judge from the introduction to the poem, they particularly included mortal women who had borne children to gods.[118] Enough of these women were introduced by the formula ἢ οἵη (*ē hoiē*, "or such a one as . . .") for the *Catalogue* to have been known in antiquity also as the *Ēhoiai*.[119]

Furthermore, the poem moved through time from Deukalion to the Trojan War. Attention was evidently directed several times to that event as the culmination of the whole process of marriages and births of heroes; for the genealogical scheme, by which a particular family would be followed through several generations before the next one was treated, involved leaps ahead and then backward in time. Thus, the fragment (23a), apparently from early in the poem, that deals with the family of Thestios gives particular details about the children his granddaughter Klytaimēstra bore to Agamemnon: the sacrifice of Iphigeneia (Iphimēdē in the fragment), the murder of Agamemnon, and Orestes' matricidal revenge. In this way the fragment brackets many of the important events surrounding the Trojan War. Then, much later, Tyndareus, Klytaimēstra's father, evidently found a place himself among the descendants of Atlas, and his daughters were again mentioned, but now with emphasis on the adulteries of Timandra, Klytaimēstra, and Helen (frr. 175-76). The births of Agamemnon and Menelaos were recorded later still (fr. 195.1-7). References to Troy occur in other fragments as well, and one can observe the generation of those who fought there taking shape—for example, Nestor and his son Antilokhos (frr. 33, 35), Sarpēdōn (fr. 141.14 ff.), and Tēlephos (fr. 165.8 ff.).[120]

No doubt this emphasis on the Trojan War was built into the sagas that provided the material for the *Catalogue*. But this poem gives the war particular significance as marking the end of an age characterized in the opening lines as one in which gods and men had common feasts (fr. 1.6-7)—that is, lived on familiar terms with one another (we shall see the significance of this motif in the next chapter). The war itself is treated in a fragment, clearly from near the end of the poem, which seems to say that Zeus brought it on in order to effect a definitive separation of gods from men (fr. 204.95-103).[121] The Trojan War thus divides the contemporary state of humanity from a time distinguished by the achievements of men whose ancestry was semidivine and whose powers were extraordinary, and the poem must have conveyed by implication a sense of diminution, of lesser possibilities for men of the present.

The *Catalogue of Women*, then, sought to make sense of the world in several ways: physically, in regard to geography; by organizing an enormous volume of heroic saga, which was what the audience knew of their past; but above all by depicting history as coherent and purposeful, perhaps with the ultimate intention (as in the myth of the Five Ages in the *Works and Days*) of explaining the present with reference to a past era—the Age of Heroes—now decisively closed.

h. THE POEMS AND THE LARGER UNITY

At some time the *Catalogue of Women* was added to the *Theogony* as its sequel (*Theog.* 1021-22 and Hesiod fr. 1.1-2). We do not know whether Hesiod himself composed the *Catalogue* and, if so, whether from the outset he conceived of the two poems as related.[122] Other possibilities are that a later rhapsode joined the two independent Hesiodic works or that one of Hesiod's successors extended the *Theogony* with additional genealogical material of his own composing.[123] We do not even know exactly where Hesiod ended the *Theogony* proper if the poem was originally an independent piece. These are interesting questions, but we shall never know the answers. The important and suggestive fact is that the two poems were joined at all. It reminds us that the *Theogony*, coherent though its design is, told only a part of the world's history and could always be continued, and that, conversely, the *Catalogue* presupposed the gods' births and the establishment of Zeus as supreme ruler, regardless of whether it was composed specifically with Hesiod's *Theogony* in mind. It was natural to join these two poems. In combination, they related human to divine history, and thus told the story of the entire world from the origin of the physical universe and of the first gods down through the Trojan War, by way of marriages among the gods, the unions of goddesses with mortal men (*Theog.* 965-1020), and the unions of gods with mortal women (the *Catalogue of Women*).

The Epic Cycle presents a parallel case. Some of its poems were linked with the *Iliad* and the *Odyssey* to form a continuous history of the Trojan War, from its ultimate origin on the divine plane to the fates in its aftermath of the various heroes who survived the fighting. As in the *Catalogue of Women*, the war was explained as the result of a plan of Zeus, though the Cycle attributed different motives to him (*Kypria* fr. 1 Allen V). But the range of the Cycle was broader than this one war. It included poems about the two assaults on Thebes, which Hesiod names as the other setting, besides Troy, of the heroes' battles and deaths (*W.D.* 161-65). The collection thus took in a considerable amount of human history. But because Thebes was sacked before the Trojan War, the period covered by the cycle ended with the fall of Troy and the heroes' subsequent homecomings. Up to that point, the Cycle seems to have aimed at comprehensiveness. For it began with a theogony, the union of Gaia and Ouranos and other stories of gods, and included a titanomachy.[124] Here too, human history was set in context as a continuation of cosmic and

divine history; and the Cycle treated essentially the same subject as the combined Hesiodic *Theogony* and *Catalogue,* though in a different style (consecutive narrative rather than catalogue) and in more detail.

The events surrounding the Trojan War provided a fitting conclusion to
this span of time because with the return of the last Greek leader, Odysseus,
the Heroic Age, with its dangers and achievements and its particular outlook
on life, came to an end. This conception of the war's historical significance is
implicit in our *Odyssey.* We observed earlier that the structure of this poem is
"open," in contrast to the *Iliad*'s circularity. That is because in the *Iliad* life is
circumscribed by a sense of the finality of death, whereas the *Odyssey* is a
poem of reunions and continued life for those who deserve them. The *Odyssey* thus trails off into life as we, the common run of humanity, know it. This
poem makes an appropriate transition from the heroic world because its hero,
who has distinguished himself among the foremost by his deeds, still values
most of all, and finally attains, the tranquillity and decorum of ordinary life.
Hesiod takes a gloomy view of the men who succeeded the heroes, the race
of iron to which he belongs; but the poet of the *Odyssey* teaches the worth
of life in the present and holds out hope for justice in a well-regulated society.
Yet amid this reassurance, there is here, as perhaps in the *Catalogue of Women,* also knowledge that the price of stability is a lessening of human stature,
a sense that

> the odds is gone,
> And there is nothing left remarkable
> Beneath the visiting moon.[125]

It is difficult to imagine, in fact, what heroic epic could have stood as sequel
to the *Odyssey*—unless it be the bizarre, and certainly late, *Telegonia.*[126] Even
that poem offers an interesting demonstration that the heroic standards were
incompatible with the post-Odyssean world of humanity. For it transports
Telemakhos, Penelope, and Telegonos, the remnants of the heroic world after
Odysseus's death, back to the scene of Odysseus's exploits and seals them off
from ordinary mortal life, leaving them in the state of immortal stasis that he
rejected. Independent though the *Odyssey* originally was, then, its place in
the Epic Cycle was foreshadowed by its form and underlying attitudes.

No doubt the poems of the Cycle were inferior to the *Iliad* and the *Odyssey*,
and they may well have been later, at least in the versions from which our
fragments and the information transmitted by Proklos derive.[127] But if we
disregard the *Telegonia,* the stories the others recounted must in essentials
have been much older and must have received poetic treatment from a very
early time.[128] These stories were sufficiently interrelated and together presented a coherent enough scheme (despite contradictions in some details)
that the potential for joining the poems that incorporated them must always
have existed, no matter how late the actual formation of the Epic Cycle was.

The Hesiodic poems and the Cycle are examples of a characteristic of early hexameter works generally. They were at once autonomous and parts of a larger whole. As a group, they reflected the unity of their material and brought out the common elements latent in it (attitudes, values, notions about the physical world and the gods and about the history of mankind). The coherence in this body of poetry did not arise primarily because individual poems might be particular realizations of a limited number of themes that formed the singers' repertoire or because one poem might often allude to episodes developed more fully in another.[129] These things are not so much causes as manifestations of this unity. The point is rather that each poem, because it treated a part of a fundamentally homogeneous mass of stories, was a fragment in a poetic continuum. Hence the rarity in hexameter poetry of epilogues or any sort of emphatic ending.[130] None of these poems is truly finished, though its design might be a satisfying whole. All might be extended. Even in cases where literal linkage is difficult to conceive, for instance between the *Works and Days* and poems on heroic subjects, we can envision clusters of works that were parallel with each other and presented complementary, and in the end not irreconcilable, views of life. A poem called the *Ornithomanteia,* in fact, may at some date have been attached to the end of the *Works and Days.*[131] The paths of song intersect, branch off, run parallel to one another, but together they form a network. Thus, when the author of the *Hymn to Apollo* says that the range of song in praise of the god has been laid down everywhere (*h. Apollo* 20), he is stating not merely what he will show in this case to be a geographical fact but also a fundamental truth about the poetry he composes. Intelligible in themselves, these poems, even the immense *Iliad* and *Odyssey,* are nevertheless parts of *one* poem.

It was never necessary, however, actually to join any two or more of these poems together, or to perform them sequentially. The audience had a sense of the integrity of all the poetry and understood the continuities between stories. For no performance took place in a vacuum, and from constant listening, the audience knew many other poems. Each time they heard one poem, they experienced it in itself and at the same time in the context of all the others they had heard. They knew its place in the overall structure, and that broadened its meaning for them.[132]

This participation of the individual poem in a larger unity is identical with the way distinct and self-contained passages were fused together into a whole poem. And just as, within a poem, the structural relations between sentences or passages disclosed how events or concepts were connected, so the links between poems, potential or actual, showed a coherent pattern in the history of the entire cosmos and the order in the resulting arrangement of the world. By virtue of revealing form on the smallest and on the largest scale, poetry was an act of discovery and learning.

3 The Gifts of the Gods

IN THE SCHEME OF THINGS envisioned by hexameter poetry, man is only one of several kinds of being, and the world does not exist for his sake. The *Theogony* does not even mention the creation of men. They appear suddenly as the passive beneficiaries, and ultimately the victims, of Prometheus's attempt to outwit Zeus. Although many forces active in the world impinge—with good effect or ill—on human life, mankind holds a subordinate place in a larger order. Such, at least, is the strict cosmological view, and its influence helps account for the sense of limits on human aspirations and conduct that was the magnificent achievement of archaic Greek thought. In the succeeding age, as the writings of Thucydides and Euripides make plain, a very different, anthropocentric view, though it encouraged enormous progress, also led men to acts of arrogance as they tried to manipulate the world around them. In our own time too we have experienced the exhilaration and the disasters that attend man's asserting his predominance in the world. Perhaps we have never been in so good a position to appreciate the wisdom of archaic Greece.

At the same time, both poet and audience naturally had a particular interest in man, and their concern with the other aspects of the world order depended in good part on how far these affected human life. How else could they be understood? Many of the powers mentioned in the *Theogony*, for example, such as the children of Night or the offspring of Themis (*Theog.* 211-32, 901-6), are intelligible mainly insofar as they are part of human experience, even though their existence is conceived as completely independent of mankind.[1] The implicit theme of the whole work, in fact, is the evolution of an order under which men can live, moderately well if not in ideal happiness; and all of these poems in one way or another are concerned with man, even when they seem to be talking about something else. We might say that they present two perspectives on the world simultaneously: man's own, determined by and limited to what he knows, and a broader view that belongs to the gods with their more complete knowledge and is only conceivable by man through cosmological speculation. But when these viewpoints conflict, the second always overrides the first and proves more accurate.

What, then, is man's place in the world, and—almost the same question— what is his nature? The poets try to gain and express an understanding of these things in polar fashion, by showing what man is not. He is not, on the one hand, a beast; for as Hesiod explains (*W.D.* 276-80), animals eat each other, but Zeus has given man the basis for organized society—*dikē*, legal procedure and by implication the just judgments that ought to result from it.[2] This distinction is not always so tidy or so easily maintained, however. Culture is artificial, and nature and culture interpenetrate in complex ways. Man can approach bestial savagery—when judgment is based on physical might, for instance, as in Hesiod's fable of the hawk and the nightingale (*W.D.* 202-12),[3] or when men go to war, as many of the animal similes in the *Iliad* and the description of Herakles' shield in the *Aspis* imply.[4] Yet the distinction between man and beast is never entirely blurred. It is always reasserted, with renewed appreciation of its importance, just when it most seriously threatens to break down. Although the bestial element in man can never be eradicated, it can be controlled; and in this way the qualities peculiar to men are revealed and given full range. On the other hand, men are not gods. Again, they have something of divine nature within themselves, and under certain circumstances or by dint of extraordinary achievements they may seem godlike; but the appearance is only temporary, the difference absolute and never forgotten altogether.

Two episodes that befall Odysseus on his wanderings, so alike that they seem almost doublets of each other, illustrate these opposing pulls on mankind. Kirkē threatens to turn Odysseus into a beast, and Kalypsō offers to make him divine. For Odysseus, who yearns only for home, both possibilities are equally dead ends. The *Odyssey,* as we have observed, conveys a feeling of reconciliation with human conditions, and its hero is comfortable with them. Other poems take a more gloomy view. Distinguished from the beasts but ever threatening to fall to their level, like the gods but subject to necessities from which they are free, mankind occupies a strange intermediate position and is not entirely at home in the world. That being human is neither the one thing nor the other underlies the whole dilemma of that state and explains why man's life is complex while gods and animals, for different reasons, enjoy simplicity.

The attempt to explain the nature of man is therefore tremendously important. Our poets carry out this attempt especially with reference to divinity, and it is mainly with this upper limit on humanity that we shall be concerned here. By portraying the gods, the poets not only disclose the forces that influence human life but also show what men and gods have in common and what holds them apart. They present these insights in many different ways and in a variety of moods. The subject is too vast and complicated to discuss completely, but a few leading ideas can be traced.

Two passages in the *Hymn to Apollo* in combination imply many of these ideas. We remarked earlier that the second scene on Olympos comments on the description of the Delian festival, and we may now examine the specific ways in which it does so. The poet expresses the brilliance of the spectacle on Delos with these words (ll. 151-52 as printed by Allen [1946] with the almost certain emendations of the unintelligible manuscript readings):

φαίη κ᾽ ἀθανάτους καὶ ἀγήρως ἔμμεναι αἰεί,
ὃς τότ᾽ ἐπαντιάσει᾽ ὅτ᾽ Ἰάονες ἀθρόοι εἶεν.

A man who happened to be present then, when the Ionians are gathered
    together,
would say that they are immortal and ageless always.

An enumeration of what this observer might see culminates in the performance of the Delian maidens, who sing this song (ll. 158-61):

αἴ τ᾽ ἐπεὶ ἂρ πρῶτον μὲν Ἀπόλλων᾽ ὑμνήσωσιν,
αὗτις δ᾽ αὖ Λητώ τε καὶ Ἄρτεμιν ἰοχέαιραν,
μνησάμεναι ἀνδρῶν τε παλαιῶν ἠδὲ γυναικῶν
ὕμνον ἀείδουσιν, θέλγουσι δὲ φῦλ᾽ ἀνθρώπων.

When they celebrate [humnēsōsin] first Apollo,
and in second place Leto and Artemis the Archer,
then recollecting [mnēsamenai] men and women of old
they sing a song [humnon], and enchant [thelgousin] the tribes of men.

On Olympos, the Muses also sing of gods and men, but their theme is far different (ll. 189-93):

Μοῦσαι μέν θ᾽ ἅμα πᾶσαι ἀμειβόμεναι ὀπὶ καλῇ
ὑμνεῦσίν ῥα θεῶν δῶρ᾽ ἄμβροτα ἠδ᾽ ἀνθρώπων
τλημοσύνας, ὅσ᾽ ἔχοντες ὑπ᾽ ἀθανάτοισι θεοῖσι
ζώουσ᾽ ἀφραδέες καὶ ἀμήχανοι, οὐδὲ δύνανται
εὑρέμεναι θανάτοιό τ᾽ ἄκος καὶ γήραος ἄλκαρ.

And all the Muses together, alternating with lovely voice,
sing [humneusin] the immortal gifts [dōra] of the gods and men's
acts of endurance [tlēmosunas] of all that they get at the hands of the
    deathless gods
as they live witless and helpless, and cannot
discover a remedy for death and a defense against old age.

Men are not, after all, *athanatoi kai agēroi*, "immortal and ageless," as a visitor to Delos might think (l. 151), but *aphradees kai amēkhanoi*, "witless, and helpless" to find a cure for age and death (l. 192). All four adjectives begin with the negative prefix *a*-, and they form opposing pairs that occupy the same metrical position within the hexameter. (See Kakridis, 1937-38, 105.)

The Delian festival expresses the height of human life. The Ionians' ships and their many possessions display their material wealth, and *kharis,* "grace" (l. 153), is shed over their persons—the aura that surrounds men at moments of transcendant joy or success. The festival is an expression of social community, and at the same time by singing and dancing in praise of Apollo these mortals seem to come into contact with divinity. They even appear to surpass human limits. Yet the hypothetical observer only "would say" that the Ionians are immortal; the form of the statement shows that they are only being compared to gods and allows for the difference.[5] So does the use of this observer as intermediary, for it enables the poet to avoid a direct comparison of men to gods (which would be audacious) and the responsibility for what is made to seem a witness's subjective, momentary impression.[6] In the immediate context, however, these things throw no shadow over the festival; the statement remains a genuine compliment to the Ionians. But the scene on Olympos shortly afterward puts this human attainment into a wider perspective and shows where it falls short. The brilliance of the festival recurs periodically when the Ionians gather, but it is time-bound and not a permanent state (recall *then* in l. 152). Men must grow old and die. The gods, on the other hand, are to be imagined as perpetually youthful and always enjoying the delights exemplified here by their music and dancing. Thoughts of man's plight do not diminish their pleasure; if anything, they increase it by contrast. That this can be the theme of their song shows how carefree and—at least at times of particular festivity—how remote and uncaring the gods can be. Even at its height, then, human life is an imperfect copy of divine life. Together these two scenes create a delicate balance between those consummate moments when men are uplifted by all that is best in their world and the somber realization of the limits that being mortal implies.

There is a similar tension specifically between the subjects of the two songs. After celebrating the divinities associated with the festival in a lyric prelude that serves the same function as hexameter hymns evidently did (see pp. 120-21, below), the Delian maidens sing "the men and women of old" (l. 160). This theme sounds very much like the subject of a heroic epic poem, though this particular song, since it accompanies the dance, will not have been in the epic meter. The main part of this performance, then, celebrates glory from the heroic past—that is, human achievements—whereas the burden of the Muses' song is men's helplessness and insignificance. By telling about great men from the past and perpetuating their fame, poetry enables them to live on after death in the memory of later generations. But this extension of life beyond death, although it is the best a mortal can hope for, is not true immortality. Once again, what the gods enjoy is authentic, and man can attain at most a semblance of it. Mortality distinguishes men from the gods absolutely and is the basis of all the other differences. As the language in the above quotations from the *Hymn to Apollo* implies, it has two related aspects. The encroachment of old age exemplifies man's subjection to time and change while he lives, and death is the ultimate expression of human vulnerability.

The attempt to discover the nature of man in hexameter poetry thus becomes, in very large part, the definition of the value of his life in the face of that weakness, the probing of what it means to be a mortal man as opposed to an immortal god.

The viewpoints of these two "songs-within-the-song" correspond respectively to the possible emphases in the actual poems we are discussing. Man's greatness or his weakness can be stressed according to what seems appropriate at the particular moment. In the first instance men and gods seem close together; the second possibility leads to an acute awareness of the gulf that divides them. No contradiction is felt between these perspectives, and indeed there is none. They are the extremes that define the conditions of man's life. The themes associated with them exist side by side, usually within the same poem, for in true polar fashion they are interdependent. Practically every poem, like the *Hymn to Apollo,* combines the optimistic and the pessimistic view, and makes what it can of the mixture.

This ambivalence reflects the combination of success and failure, good and bad fortune, that makes up a human life. The carefree gods send these vicissitudes to men. "The gifts of the gods"—usually signified by "gift" (δῶρον, δόσις, *dōron, dosis*) or a form of the verb *to give* (διδόναι, *didonai*)—epitomize the human condition and form a motif of central importance in hexameter poetry.[7] The phrase occurs in the summary of the Muses' song (*h. Apollo* 190), but there it can mean either the privileges that the gods enjoy or the fortunes they give men. From its use elsewhere, the latter sense is more likely;[8] but in any case the idea of the gods' gifts to men is clearly implied in line 191 ("all that they get at the hands of the deathless gods"). There too, the Muses use a word of man's plight that indicates the only response he can make to these gifts, good or bad: τλημόσυναι (*tlēmosunai*), "acts of endurance." The verb τλῆναι (*tlēnai,* "endure," with the stem *tlā-* or *tlē-*), its derivatives, and the synonymous ἀνέχομαι (*anekhomai*) appear frequently in hexameter poetry in this connection.

The *Iliad* reaches its resolution by defining the limits on human powers, and the gifts of the gods, the contrast between divine and mortal life, and human endurance are ideas that figure prominently in the final book. Apollo sounds the dominant note early on, when he complains about the excess of Achilles' grief for Patroklos and his mistreatment of Hektor's corpse (XXIV. 46-49). One who loses even a kinsman, he says, mourns and then ceases, "for the Fates have put in men a spirit that endures [τλητὸν . . . θυμόν, *tlēton . . . thumon*]." Pain at the death of others is part of what it means to be mortal. But limits have been set upon it, and that makes human life tolerable, compensates for the inevitability of death. There is thus a decorum to be observed in grief as in all other aspects of life.[9] The necessity and even the very capacity to accept and endure suffering are uniquely human. The gods do not need it, for if anything mars their happiness its effects are temporary. By clinging to his grief and anger, then, Achilles defies mortal limits and invites the gods' anger. "He had better be careful," says Apollo, "lest great though he is, we feel resentment [νεμεσσηθέωμεν, nemessētheōmen] towards him. For in his fury he outrages the senseless earth" (XXIV.53-54). The idea of *nemesis* safeguards restraints on conduct by the threat of the resentment that their transgression would arouse.

Achilles himself finally conforms to these limits when he returns Hektor's body to Priam. The sight of the old and bereft king, by reminding him of his loss of Patroklos and Peleus's plight, brings home to Achilles the community of human suffering. Now he is the one who urges Priam to endure (ἄνσχεο, *anskheo*, from *anekhomai*, XXIV.549). Grief's impotence to change the reality of suffering prompts him to a general reflection on what divides men from gods (XXIV.525-26):

ὡς γὰρ ἐπεκλώσαντο θεοὶ δειλοῖσι βροτοῖσι,
ζώειν ἀχνυμένοις· αὐτοὶ δέ τ᾽ ἀκηδέες εἰσί.

For this is how the gods have spun their fate for wretched mortals,
To live in sorrow [*akhnumenoi*], while they themselves are without care [*akēdees*].

In the *Hymn to Apollo,* the Muses sing with carefree detachment of what men must endure, but to Achilles the insight comes through his own and Priam's pain. It shows a remarkable ability to put his immediate situation in a broader context.

The word that Achilles uses of the gods, ἀκηδέες (*akēdees,* "without cares"), is also applied to divinities by Hesiod, who describes the Muses as having a "carefree spirit" (ἀκηδέα θυμόν, *akēdea thumon, Theog.* 61; contrast man's *tlētos thumos* in XXIV.49, quoted above).[10] The phrase aptly describes these goddesses, who bring "forgetfulness of evils" (*Theog.* 55); but it also fits the gods in general. The same word appears elsewhere to describe exceptional men who enjoy a godlike existence or actual immortality: the men of the Golden Age (*W.D.* 112), the heroes who dwell after death on the Islands of the Blessed (*W.D.* 170), and Herakles on Olympos after his apotheosis (Hesiod fr. 229.7). It is never used with the meaning "without care" in regard to ordinary mortals. But the noun on which the adjective is based, κῆδος (*kēdos*), in the plural can name the "cares" or "afflictions" that men suffer,[11] often by the gods' contriving.[12] Another noun with the similar but less concrete meaning "woe," ὀϊζύς (*oïsdus*), and words related to it, are often used of the human condition, especially in the context of death or when human is contrasted with divine life.[13] There are other words that denote misery—for example, ἄλγος (*algos*), "pain," often used in the plural as a virtual synonym of *kēdea;* πόνος (*ponos*), "toil," sometimes describing human hardship and linked with *oïsdus;*[14] two words for "grief," πένθος (*penthos*) and ἄχος (*akhos,* related to *akhnumenoi* in XXIV.526, quoted above), which are often used in connection with rituals of mourning for the dead. (See Nagy, 1979, 94–102.) But *kēdos* and *oïsdus* will occur, along with *tlēnai* ("endure"), with especial regularity in the passages to be examined below. These are common words in Greek, and their range is by no means restricted to these contexts. Among other usages, however, they serve as particular terms for the human situation.[15]

As Achilles' words indicate, men not only lead different lives from the gods but are also at the gods' mercy. Achilles enlarges on this idea with the figure of the jars on Zeus's threshold, which contain the good and evil gifts he sends to men (XXIV.527–33; the words "gift" and "give" occur four times in these seven lines). Probably (though the Greek here is ambiguous) there are two jars of evils and one of good things, so that misfortune is twice as likely to befall. One point is certain, however: no man gets pure good. Some do get only afflictions, and their life is unrelieved misery. To others Zeus grants a mixture of gifts, and good and bad fortune alternate in their lives. That, and apparently no more, is the best that can happen to any man. For Achilles illustrates his general statements with the examples of Pēleus and Priam (XXIV.534–48), for whom the gods' extraordinary favors brought great suffering in their train.

Epitomizing as they do the possibilities and constraints in human life, the gods' gifts are always equivocal. Not only are they a mixture, but also a man endowed to a remarkable degree with one talent will lack other, complementary gifts necessary to full success. So Poulydamas admonishes Hektor, who, he says, lacks prudence to balance his might in battle (XIII.726–34).[16] Even a single gift can be two-edged: the greater a blessing it is, the more danger it poses. But a man has no choice but to accept what the gods give him. When Hektor blames the Trojan War on Paris's devotion to love and soft pursuits, Paris replies that he should not be reproached for Aphrodite's favors; for a man cannot reject any of the gods' gifts, although he might not choose them of his own will (III.64–66). This excuse is not merely self-serving, as an incident soon afterwards shows (III.389–420). When Aphrodite urges her to go home and sleep with Paris, Helen refuses indignantly. Feeling exploited and degraded, she tries in effect to repudiate the goddess's gifts. Aphrodite warns that her singular favor could turn to equally extreme hatred, and Helen is silenced. Benefit from a god's patronage, and you can be manipulated. Refuse it, and you will be destroyed.

In these instances, the divine gifts are personal endowments, although they also influence what happens to their possessors. More often, as in Achilles' speech, they refer to external circumstances imposed on men. Singers are not to blame for the Argives' calamitous homecomings, Telemakhos tells his mother: "but Zeus is responsible, who gives to each among wretched men as he wishes" (i.347–49). Do not reproach a man for poverty, declares Hesiod, for it is "a gift of the Blessed Ones who live forever" (*W.D.* 717–18). Hesiod's father was one mortal who received it; he migrated to Boiotia, fleeing not wealth but "evil poverty, which Zeus gives to men" (*W.D.* 637–38). Because

Zeus has given you bad luck, "you must endure it [τετλάμεν, *tetlamen*]," Nausikaa tells Odysseus (vi.187-90). In the *Hymn to Demeter,* mortals twice try to console the goddess with the same sentiment (*h. Dem.* 147-48, 216-17), and they particularly stress that the gods' superior power leaves man no choice. "The yoke lies on our necks," says Metaneira.

Pandora—so named because "all who dwell on Olympos gave her as a gift, an affliction for wretched men" (*W.D.* 81-82)[17]—is an emblem of the mixture that men typically receive. Sent to offset a benefit, fire, that men possess against Zeus's will (*Theog.* 570, 585), she is "a beautiful evil." Woman's nature itself is ambivalent also. She consumes man's wealth, but he cannot do without her. A man who does not marry enjoys his property but dies without an heir. But for the man who gets the best wife, evil always balances the good, and one who marries a bad woman has unremitting misery (*Theog.* 602-12). This is a restatement in concrete terms of the alternatives in Achilles' account of the jars of gifts. Many have seen in Hesiod's treatment of Pandora a mark of his misogyny. But this biographical detail, if it is one, pales in importance beside the thematic significance he gives Pandora and womankind in order to further the aim of the Prometheus story in the *Theogony:* to define the position of humanity after men and gods separated.

In a world conditioned by the gods' gifts, life becomes in large part unpredictable. Men can discover rules that provide a relatively safe guide for living, but certainty is impossible. "Different at different times is the intention of aegis-bearing Zeus, and it is hard for mortal men to understand," says Hesiod (*W.D.* 483-84). This sentiment occurs in a passage that tells how plowing at the wrong time usually results in a poor crop but might not if Zeus is favorably disposed. Even in the Iron Age, which by all logic should be utterly blighted, good will be mingled with evils (*W.D.* 179).[18] The Hesiodic examples show that this variety can be to man's benefit (for the converse, see *W.D.* 667-69), but the emphasis is more often on man's vulnerability to unforeseen disaster. Earth nurtures nothing more feeble than man, says Odysseus to Amphinomos (xviii.125-50). In prosperity he cannot conceive of falling victim to misfortune. "But when the blessed gods accomplish baneful things, he bears these also, though involuntarily, with enduring spirit [τετληότι θυμῷ, *tetlēoti thumōi*—cf. Apollo's phrase in XXIV.49]." A man should therefore avoid being led on by good luck to deeds of folly, but should "possess in peace the gifts of the gods, whatever they bestow."

It is not always certain that there are reasons for such reversals of fortune, or when there are, that they could be considered valid by human standards. In some cases misfortunes come to a man merely by divine whim; in others, there is a recognizable design. When there is, the victim sometimes clearly deserves what befalls him, but sometimes he does not, either because he has done nothing to incur it or because the punishment is out of all proportion to the offense. These antithetical views of the gods as guardians of justice and as capricious, and of the world as rational and irrational, coexist in the poems.

Each comes to the fore according to what the poet wants to emphasize about human life in a given passage or in his work as a whole. If the gods are depicted mainly as protectors of morality, then a man and his society fare best by discerning and obeying prescribed rules. When the gods' caprice is stressed, the burden of determining what is right action, of finding order in the world and making conduct suit it, falls more heavily on man. This mixture of conceptions may seem contradictory, but it is not. It is recognizably a reflex of polar thought, and the two sides of the gods, both singly and in combination, express important truths about the nature of divinity. The notion that the gods care for justice expresses a natural human desire to find coherence in things. But it also seems right that the gods should be frivolous and inconsistent. They can afford to act that way, as men cannot, because they never have to endure lasting consequences of anything they do.[19]

Thus it happens that no single poem presents one view of the gods to the exclusion of the other. Some kind of coherence emerges from the most random events, and when the world is made to seem most orderly, there is always an element of uncertainty. Even the *Works and Days,* which expresses deep confidence in the gods' justice, allows, as we have seen, for the arbitrary exercise of divine will. In one way, the reminder that man is always at the mercy of the unexpected is a salutary demonstration of the gods' supremacy. If a man could be assured of success by following a clearly discernible course, he would be primarily in control of his fate and less dependent on the gods. The temptation to forget his place would be great. As it is, there is enough coherence to make obedience to moral prescripts the safest course, and enough uncertainty to remind men that they are subservient.

Men often pay grievously for divine willfulness, however, as the *Iliad* shows. There the continuation of the Trojan War after Menelaos's defeat of Paris in single combat rests on a moral incoherence. Justice would be satisfied by the terms of the oath taken by both sides in Book 3, under which Troy would pay a penalty but survive. But Hera (with Athena) feels personal hatred for the Trojans that was caused, we later learn (XXIV.27-30), by the Judgment of Paris.[20] For this sole reason the war must go on and Troy fall. For his part, Zeus grants Hera the city's destruction casually, though not without protest (IV.1-49). The bargain sealed, however, Hera, with curious inconsequence, impels Zeus to send Athena "to contrive that the Trojans first begin to harm the renowned Akhaians in violation of the oath" (IV.66-67). This Athena manages by Pandaros's wounding of Menelaos. Although the real cause of events has nothing to do with justice, then, the gods still observe the external forms of just procedure. Men may not always get what they deserve, it seems, but they are made to deserve what they get, at least formally. Ultimately, however, the sack of Troy *will* be just after all. Through it punishment will be exacted for Paris's violation of hospitality, which is under Zeus's protection—an offense that the Trojans' breaking of the truce renews.[21] That, at least, will be the *result* of Troy's downfall; but the gods' true *motives,* their primary concerns, are quite different. The gods in the *Iliad* observe moral norms, but in a roundabout, confused, and inefficient way.

The *Odyssey*, on the other hand, with its several theodicies, in the main satisfies our sense of justice. Zeus strikes the dominant note at the outset, when he complains that men blame the gods for their misfortunes but actually suffer "beyond fate" because of their own folly (i.32-34). Yet the paradoxical phrase "beyond fate" seems to acknowledge that short of the point at which men become responsible for their actions, there is a basic randomness in their lot—that not all the gods' gifts are apportioned according to human deserts.[22] Telemakhos's blaming Zeus himself for the Greeks' sufferings after Troy (i.347-49) is therefore no contradiction of Zeus's words but a necessary counterweight to them. Poseidon's persecution of Odysseus, moreover, resembles Hera's role in the *Iliad*, although he eventually is forced to give way. In the *Odyssey* the world contains an irreducible core of irrationality.

If mortals, in contrast to divinity, can hope at best only for mixed fortune, how can they turn the gods' gifts to account so as to lead a good, if not the best conceivable, life? The poems offer a variety of answers, but one common element is the positive aspect of the mixture of gifts. If evil regularly offsets good, the gods also compensate for the hardships they inflict by giving men the means to face them and limit, though not abolish, their effects. To give further examples besides the several already noted: success makes good the necessity for toil when the gods are favorable, as a large part of the *Works and Days* and the encomium of Hekate in the *Theogony* (411-52) demonstrate. Or pleasure can balance the sorrow that mortals by nature must undergo, as with the effect of song according to Hesiod (*Theog.* 98-103). If anyone who feels grief in his "newly suffering spirit [νεοκηδέϊ θυμῷ, *neokēdei thumōi*]" listens to a singer, he immediately forgets his cares (κήδεα, *kēdea*), "for swiftly the goddesses' gifts [δῶρα θεάων, *dōra theaōn*] turn him aside." The analogous talent, political eloquence that soothes quarrels among the citizens, is equally the Muses' gift (δόσις, *dosis*, *Theog.* 93). The concept of the gifts of the gods, in fact, underlies all political and social values in this poetry. Dikē is a goddess in her own right, but Zeus has also given the virtue she represents to men (ἔδωκε, *edōke*, *W.D.* 279). Zeus's second wife is Themis (*Theog.* 901-6), who "both gathers and disperses the assemblies of men" (ii.69). She bears to him the Moirai, or Fates, "who give mortal men good and evil for their possessing" (*Theog.* 905-6),[23] and also the Hōrai: Eunomiē (Observance of Laws), Dikē (Justice or Judicial Process), and Eirēnē (Peace). The randomness in the world threatens chaos, but the organization of men into society, also made possible by the gods, forestalls it. Thus Zeus himself is the rulers' patron. And although, as Hesiod and Homer both declare, one unrighteous man, especially if he is a king, can attract ruin from the gods to an entire people (*W.D.* 240-43, 260-62; XVI.384-93), a just ruler can make life flourish splendidly (xix.106-14; cf. *W.D.* 225-37).

Rules both social and religious in their significance govern relations between individuals, as the *Odyssey* in particular shows. Since human life is frail, it is imperative to receive guests and suppliants kindly, for a man may someday find himself in need of such help. Humaneness is a good that arises from the knowledge of human weakness. That is the point of Odysseus's speeches on vicissitudes when he appears in his own house as a beggar (e.g., xviii.130-50, cited earlier; xix.70-88). Beggars, in fact, are the extreme case that illuminates the suffering to which all mortals are by nature vulnerable. Driving them from place to place, their hunger—expressed as the needs of the belly (*gastēr*)—epitomizes their plight, which is described by words typically applied to the human condition. At xv.341-42, the beggar Odysseus thanks Eumaios for taking him in and relieving him of "wandering and woe [ὀϊζύος, *oïsduos*]." In context, the two nouns seem equivalent (a hendiadys: "the woe of [i.e., consisting in] wandering"). Then Odysseus goes on (xv.343-45):

> πλαγκτοσύνης δ᾽ οὐκ ἔστι κακώτερον ἄλλο βροτοῖσιν·
> ἀλλ᾽ ἕνεκ᾽ οὐλομένης γαστρὸς κακὰ κήδε᾽ ἔχουσιν
> ἀνέρες, ὅν τιν᾽ ἵκηται ἄλη καὶ πῆμα καὶ ἄλγος.

Men have nothing else more evil than wandering.
But because of the accursed belly [*gastēr*] they have evil cares [*kēdea*],
men upon whom come roaming and suffering [*pēma*] and pain [*algos*].

Odysseus has earlier spoken in a similar way to Alkinoos (vii.208-21), who, on first seeing him, has asked if he is a god. I do not look like a god but like a mortal man, replies Odysseus; and besides (ll. 211-15):

> οὕς τινας ὑμεῖς ἴστε μάλιστ᾽ ὀχέοντας ὀϊζύν
> ἀνθρώπων, τοῖσίν κεν ἐν ἄλγεσι ἰσωσαίμην.
> καὶ δ᾽ ἔτι κεν καὶ πλείον᾽ ἐγὼ κακὰ μυθησαίμην,
> ὅσσα γε δὴ ξύμπαντα θεῶν ἰότητι μόγησα.
> ἀλλ᾽ ἐμὲ μὲν δορπῆσαι ἐάσατε κηδόμενόν περ.

Whatever men you know who endure woe [*oïsdun*] especially,
I would make myself their equal in pains [*algea*].
And I would speak of still more evils,
the whole number I have suffered by the will of the gods.
But let me eat dinner, afflicted by care [*kēdomenon*] though I am.

Here there is a clear statement of divinely imposed suffering as a characteristic that distinguishes men from gods. Immediately after these lines, Odysseus says that there is nothing more shameless than the belly (γαστήρ, *gastēr*), which cause a man to forget his other woes, however severe. All that afflicts mankind is concentrated in the belly's needs; and reference to them is a homely and realistic touch that, especially in this context, makes man seem anything but godlike. And finally, it is probably the urgency of hunger and its effects that Achilles has in mind when he says of the man who gets only bad gifts from Zeus that evil βούβρωστις (*boubrōstis*, literally "the eating of cattle," and thus the need for meat and the implied want of it) drives him over the earth (XXIV.532).[24]

Once again, however, the gods balance the affliction they give by requiring men to aid beggars and all strangers. That is why the *Odyssey* can encompass human vulnerability and the gods' concern for justice as intimately related ideas. When Antinoos throws a footstool at the disguised Odysseus, the latter says that the act would be justified in defense of one's own property. "But Antinoos hit me because of my miserable belly [*gastēr*] —the accursed belly, that gives many evils to men" (xvii.473-74). Beggars too may have their avenging deities, he goes on to remind the suitors.

Suffering and its meaning are at the heart of the *Odyssey*. Those characters who have known pain and loss in their own lives are the very ones who, in contrast to the callow suitors, are sympathetic to the misery of others and disposed to help them (hence the poem's kindly portrayal of the humble, like Eumaios). Odysseus preeminently has been condemned by fate to endure many *kēdea* (woes), both during his wanderings (v.206-10, where they are the alternative to the immortality Kalypsō offers him) and on Ithaka after his return (xiii.306-7, where Athena admonishes him to endure—τετλάμεναι, *tetlamenai*—them). In all the *Odyssey*, in fact, the diction particularly descriptive of mankind's situation—*tlēnai, kēdea, oïsdus*—is applied most often to Odysseus and Penelope (a fact that underscores the appropriateness of Odysseus's stock epithet πολύτλας, *polutlas*, "much-enduring").[25] This usage shows how the *Odyssey* guides us to an appreciation of human values by exploring the extremes of the pain involved in being mortal. The order finally achieved by men in collaboration with divinity is worth all the more for being rare and fragile. Once he has accepted and understood suffering, a man might reasonably refuse a painless immortality.[26]

When men do harm each other, they can mitigate the damage by being tractable and forgiving. The exercise of these qualities is also under divine protection, as the passage on the Prayers in Phoinix's speech to Achilles (IX.496-512) shows. But sometimes circumstances of extraordinary urgency demand a more spontaneous compassion between men, and then the gods can be of help only in exposing human limits. The scene between Priam and Achilles near the end of the *Iliad* presents such a moment. The gods, to be sure, make this meeting possible. Zeus commands Achilles to give up Hektor's corpse for ransom, and Hermes conducts Priam to the door of Achilles' hut— but no farther. What occurs inside is something in which the gods can have no part, for the two men are drawn together by an awareness of their shared mortal weakness. The meal that they eat together (XXIV.596-632) celebrates this sense of community. Not only does it draw Priam, who has fasted since Hektor's death, out of the isolation of his grief; it also contrasts strongly with Hera's wish to eat the Trojans raw (IV.34-36), Achilles' desire to eat Hektor's liver raw (XXII.346-48), and Hekabe's longing to do the same to Achilles (XXIV.212-14). The decorum of hospitality protects Achilles from a situation that has made him act with anger of divine intensity and has threatened to brutalize him at the same time.[27] What occurs in this scene can rescue neither Priam nor Achilles from the doom now closing in, but it gives that doom what meaning it can have.

Elsewhere in the *Iliad,* and in other poems on heroic subjects, the emphasis is more on public deeds of strength and courage, and so on men's success rather than their weakness. Yet the heroic standards are themselves predicated on mortality, as Sarpēdōn's speech to Glaukos in XII.310-28 makes clear. The ideal would be immortality; then men could live at ease and heroic achievements would be unheard-of because unnecessary. Such, at least, are the unspoken implications of Sarpēdōn's words.[28] But because men cannot escape death, they fight—whether they win or give to another εὖχος ("what one prays for," but also "a reason for boasting"). Behind this motive is the idea of *kleos,* the fame, especially as preserved in poetry, by which a man tries to perpetuate himself after his physical death. The heroic values, then, like the scene between Priam and Achilles though in a different way, show how men realize the full extent of their capacities, not despite, but because of the necessity of death.

Men are capable of greatness but are ultimately insignificant. The gods create both coherence and arbitrary chaos in the world. The poems do not so much oscillate between these extremes as combine them. Human splendor constantly summons the idea of human limits, and weakness in turn becomes occasion for splendor. There is a similar ambivalence in a kindred matter, the relations between men and gods. On the one hand, the poetry reveals ways in which they draw near one another—the Delian festival, man's conformity to the moral standards set forth in the *Works and Days,* Achilles' prevailing on Zeus to vindicate his outraged honor. But on the other hand the distinction between men and gods—an inevitable consequence of their difference in nature—is carefully drawn, both through the motif of the gods' gifts and in other, related ways as well.

Just as men sometimes meet without the gods on the common ground of their humanity, the gods also, on occasion, close ranks and decide that mortals are not worth their disrupting their own peace and amusements. Apollo's speech when he meets Poseidon on the battlefield at Troy expresses this attitude well (XXI.462-67):

ἐννοσίγαι᾽, οὐκ ἄν με σαόφρονα μυθήσαιο
ἔμμεναι, εἰ δὴ σοί γε βροτῶν ἕνεκα πτολεμίξω
δειλῶν, οἳ φύλλοισιν ἐοικότες ἄλλοτε μέν τε
ζαφλεγέες τελέθουσιν, ἀρούρης καρπὸν ἔδοντες,
ἄλλοτε δὲ φθινύθουσιν ἀκήριοι. ἀλλὰ τάχιστα
παυώμεσθα μάχης· οἱ δ᾽ αὐτοὶ δηριαάσθων.

Earth-shaker, you would say that I am reckless
if I fight with you on account of mortals [brotōn heneka ptolemixō],
the poor wretches, who, like leaves, now
flourish in full vigor, eating the earth's fruits,
and now fade lifeless. But come now
let us cease from battle. Let them fight by themselves.

Apollo's language, of course, recalls Glaukos's speech to Diomēdēs at VI.146-49 and expresses the same basic idea, the transience of mortal life. But the god views humanity from the outside and with a broader perspective. Thus, whereas Glaukos sees existence as a continuous process by which mankind unfailingly renews itself—so that, although an individual's identity may be unimportant, the mass endures—Apollo considers the process itself a sign of insignificance. Why, then, should the gods trouble themselves over men? Once again we are reminded, especially in the last two lines, that struggle and achievement are the responsibility of mortals and no concern of the gods.

Hera expresses the same sentiment as Apollo's after she and Athena have been thwarted in their attempt to defy Zeus and go to the Akhaians' aid (VIII.427-31). "I no longer think we should do battle with Zeus on account of mortals [βροτῶν ἕνεκα πτολεμίζειν, brotōn heneka ptolemisdein]," she says. "Let one of them live and another die, however it chances." The most impressive example, however, occurs in the first book of the *Iliad*, when Hephaistos soothes the quarrel between his parents (I.573-76):

ἦ δὴ λοίγια ἔργα τάδ᾽ ἔσσεται οὐδ᾽ ἔτ᾽ ἀνεκτά,
εἰ δὴ σφὼ ἕνεκα θνητῶν ἐριδαίνετον ὧδε,
ἐν δὲ θεοῖσι κολῳὸν ἐλαύνετον· οὐδέ τι δαιτὸς
ἐσθλῆς ἔσσεται ἦδος, ἐπεὶ τὰ χερείονα νικᾷ.

What pestilential business this will be—intolerable—
if you two engage in strife like this on account of mortals [heneka
    thnētōn]
and prolong this bickering among the gods. There will be
no pleasure in the noble feast, since worse things prevail.

And in fact the gods then settle down to feasting and good cheer. The dissolution of the quarrel on Olympos contrasts strikingly with the fatal consequences of the human dispute recounted earlier in this book. Feasting regulates men's relations with each other and with the gods, but as we shall see presently, it also forms part of visions of the ease and pleasure that the gods enjoy and from which ordinary mortals are excluded. It thus plays a role here in contrasting the gods' lot with men's. So does the singing of the Muses while Apollo plays the lyre, which accompanies this feast (I.603-4). Like the comparable scene in the *Hymn to Apollo*, this interlude of divine festivity follows and balances a human ritual that includes dance and song, and that in the *Iliad* has the solemn purpose of propitiating an angry Apollo (I.472-74).

While depicting distance on the part of the gods, the poems also recount occasions on which they come into contact with mortals and try to forge bonds with them. These meetings are not always happy, however; they some-times reveal disjunctions between human and divine expectations, desires, and behavior. Three of the longer Homeric Hymns in particular describe such incidents.[29] At the end of the *Hymn to Apollo,* the god's new priests view the ruggedness of the land at Delphi and wonder—quite naturally, one would think—how they are to feed themselves. Apollo smiles as he chides men for always making their situations worse by fretting (*h. Apollo* 532-33):

νήπιοι ἄνθρωποι δυστλήμονες οἳ μελεδῶνας
βούλεσθ᾽ ἀργαλέους τε πόνους καὶ στείνεα θυμῷ.

Foolish men, poor enduring ones [*dustlēmones*] , who choose
cares and grievous toils and difficulties in your hearts!

This is a genial application of the serious idea that Zeus enunciates at the beginning of the *Odyssey*—that men foolishly bring sufferings on themselves beyond what is due them. Here the motif underscores the difference between divine omniscience and the narrowness of human vision. In this case good for-tune rather than disaster is imminent; the priests will live on offerings brought by worshippers to the sanctuary. But they could not know this, and their worry was, on human terms, perfectly justified. The word that I have trans-lated "poor enduring ones," *dustlēmones,* may recall men's "acts of endur-ance," *tlēmosunai,* which the Muses have earlier sung (1. 191). In any case, Apollo's words here partially offset the bleak view that the Muses take of human life and thus provide a mean between it and the atmosphere of the Delian festival.

Far different is the situation when Demeter upbraids Metaneira, who has tried (as she thinks) to rescue her son Dēmophon. The goddess expresses the same idea as Apollo, but her tone is one of bitter scorn at mortals who, through their own fault, have lost a great blessing (*h. Dem.* 256-58):[30]

νήϊδες ἄνθρωποι καὶ ἀφράδμονες οὔτ᾽ ἀγαθοῖο
αἶσαν ἐπερχομένου προγνώμεναι οὔτε κακοῖο·
καὶ σὺ γὰρ ἀφραδίῃσι τεῇς μήκιστον ἀάσθης.

Men without knowledge, too stupid [*aphradmones*] to foresee
a portion either of good or of evil as it comes upon you!
For you [Metaneira] have been ruined most terribly [*mēkiston aasthēs*]
     by your own folly [*aphradiēisi*] .

The adjective ἀφράδμονες (aphradmones, literally "lacking wit") in the first line resembles ἀφραδέες (aphradees), which the Muses apply to mortals (h. Apollo 192). Both epithets are used by divinities as they view mortal limits from a superior perspective, and Demeter's comment elaborates the theme of the Muses' song, but with a new twist. Here is a case when, with the help of a goddess, a remedy could have been found for Dēmophon's mortality (h. Dem. 259-61), and Metaneira, not realizing this, ruined the chance irretrievably.

The text stresses Metaneira's ignorant folly: ἀφραδίῃσι . . . ἀάσθης (aphradīeisi . . . aasthēs, "by your folly you have been ruined") in the third line of the quotation repeats the narrator's own ἀφραδίῃσιν (aphradīeisin) from line 243 and ἀάσθη (aasthē) from line 246. But on seeing her son put into the fire, she has reacted as any human mother would. What she thought she saw was a nurse trying to kill the child; what she really saw was a goddess trying to make him immortal. Of course she could not know this, but the goddess has no sympathy with her human error or with her feelings. The episode turns, then, on the disparity between the limited mortal viewpoint and the complete knowledge available only to divinity, a situation for which men are not responsible but from which they are doomed to suffer.

This contrast is symptomatic of the hymn's broader concern with the disjunction between mortal and immortal. The entire part of the narrative set at Eleusis reveals the contradiction in a goddess's forsaking divine society to dwell among men in human disguise, and the inability, finally, of man and god to merge completely. When Keleos's daughters, and later Metaneira, attempt to console Demeter by reminding her that the gods' gifts cannot be avoided (ll. 147-48, 216-17), there is, of course, irony, but of a rather complex kind. It lies partly in the mortals' ignorance of whom they are addressing, and thus in the incongruity of a goddess being offered a piece of limited human wisdom,[31] and partly also in the way the consolation does apply after all to Demeter, and thus sets her circumstances in relief: as a goddess she should not have to accept what the gods inflict, yet Hades, backed by Zeus's authority, has carried off her daughter by force. But in addition something is being shown about Demeter and about the nature of divinity in general. The goddess is being invited to join human society by accepting the compassion that unites men in the face of mortal weakness and suffering. But to admit that she is subject to limits, to accept her situation, is precisely what Demeter, as a goddess, cannot do. Her controlling emotion, on the contrary, is anger (ll. 83, 91, 251, 330, 354), which is proper to an outraged divinity. At Eleusis this anger is muted (though it eventually manifests itself in the destruction of crops), but even there she does not simply accept the way things are. Having lost Persephone to the Underworld, she tries to make a mortal child immortal, evidently to compensate for that loss. (Cf. Rudhardt, 1978, 11.) Her humility in descending to the human state turns out to have been superficial; she really attempts to raise a mortal to her own level. And in that she is frustrated.

Even in disguise, she gives a hint of her divinity. As she enters Keleos's house, her head reaches the roof, and the doorway is filled with an uncanny light (ll. 188-89). After she reveals herself, radiance shines from her again and fills the house as though with lightning (ll. 278-80).[32] This framing of her period of service in a mortal's household stresses that even in her sorrow Demeter does not change her true nature. At the end of this interlude comes a full epiphany, when the goddess appears with an intense and dreadful splendor that Metaneira cannot bear. Whereas earlier the disguised Demeter "sat speechless in mourning for a long time" (l. 198), it is now Metaneira who is "speechless for a long time" after the goddess departs (l. 282; the lines begin with the same two words).

Set against this terrifying radiance are the warmth of the human characters and the sympathy with which the poet portrays their feelings. The point of the divergence between mortal and immortal is clearly marked by four superb, frightening lines that balance Metaneira's love for her son against Demeter's godhead, as if the two were rivals for the child (ll. 251-54):

> τῆ δὲ χολωσαμένη καλλιστέφανος Δημήτηρ
> παῖδα φίλον, τὸν ἀέλπτον ἐνὶ μεγάροισιν ἔτικτε,
> χείρεσσ᾽ ἀθανάτῃσιν ἀπὸ ἕο θῆκε πέδονδε
> ἐξανελοῦσα πυρὸς θυμῷ κοτέσασα μαλ᾽ αἰνῶς.

> In her anger at her [Metaneira], fair-crowned Demeter
> with her *immortal* hands thrust from her to the floor
> the dear baby, *whom Metaneira bore unhoped-for in the halls,*
> taking him out of the fire, dreadfully angry in her heart.

The encounter between the two natures thus shows that the gods are limited as well as men. They lack depth of emotion—that feeling of relatedness with those outside their immediate circle that would express itself in respect and compassion for what others feel and suffer—because they are free of the woes that make these qualities necessary for men. The gods can feel love, but mainly within a selfishly circumscribed range: Demeter grieves for her daughter yet has no thought of Metaneira's feeling for her son. There is never any doubt that immortality is superior to the mortal state—Dēmophon cannot be soothed after Demeter has left him on the floor, for "inferior nurses held him" (l. 291). Still, it is a sign of remarkable artistic tact that in a poem so concerned with death, human qualities are given their due.

In the nature of things, if only because of human shortcomings, the attempt to immortalize Dēmophon must fail. There is, however, a reconciliation of sorts. Men are brought nearer to divinity as a result of Demeter's sojourn among them, for she gives them the Mysteries, which improve the lot of initiates after they die (ll. 480-82). Immortality is still beyond their reach, but the sternness of death is somewhat softened.[33] Further, because he was nursed by a goddess, Dēmophon after death will become a hero and receive "undying honor" in the form of yearly games at his tomb (ll. 263-67). His fate thus lessens the distance between gods and men, but without abolishing it.[34] Presently we shall observe other ways in which hexameter poetry uses the concept of heroes and a heroic age to express simultaneously the capacities of mortals and their limitations.

In the *Hymn to Aphrodite,* the contact between mortal and immortal is sexual. Ankhises has to be tricked into the union. When he sees Aphrodite, he guesses correctly that she is divine, and after promising her an altar and sacrifices, begs her in return for fame among the Trojans, a long and prosperous life, and a flourishing line of descendants (*h. Aphr.* 102-6). Ankhises wants human things, precisely what a mortal ought to desire and no more.

But Aphrodite pursues her aim by denying that she is a goddess. She seduces him by pretending to be a mortal virgin and helpless, and by begging him not to touch her until he has married her. Like Demeter, she tries to meet a mortal on his own terms, and she similarly humiliates herself. As she goes towards Ankhises' bed she lowers her eyes to the ground (l. 156). This gesture, though part of her disguise, is also a sign of her self-abasement; for Demeter lowers her eyes when she takes her seat in Keleos's house—that is, at the corresponding point in that story (*h. Dem.* 194; in both places the same half-line occurs: κατ᾽ ὄμματα καλὰ βαλοῦσα, *kat' ommata kala balousa,* "casting down her eyes"). After the sexual encounter, Aphrodite dresses and resumes her divine appearance. Her epiphany takes the same form—light and increased stature—as the momentary revelation of Demeter's godhead as she enters Keleos's house (ll. 173-74; cf. *h. Dem.* 188-89). Both passages contain the phrase, "her head touched the roof."[35] Ankhises, on awakening, is terrified by the radiance of immortal beauty "such as belongs to fair-garlanded Aphrodite" (l. 175). It is now his turn to cast his eyes aside (l. 182)—a motion that stands in the same relation to Aphrodite's earlier attitude as Metaneira's speechlessness to Demeter's. At this moment of separation after their union, Aphrodite and Ankhises are shown to inhabit spheres of existence that properly are separate.

Now Ankhises is truly a suppliant to Aphrodite, as she pretended to be to him; line 187 is nearly identical to line 131.[36] It is a further sign of his predicament that he now asks the goddess for far less than he did before—for life with vigor if not for life itself. "Do not let me dwell among men, alive but without vitality," he begs (ll. 188-90). "For that man does not have flourishing life [οὐ βιοθάλμιος ἀνήρ] who lies with immortal goddesses." Whatever it is exactly that he fears (impotence, or a situation like Tithōnos's vis-à-vis Eos, as has recently been suggested),[37] the point that concerns us is that union with a goddess, which elsewhere is considered great good fortune,[38] is here viewed under its other aspect—the grave danger it poses for the mortal lover.

For Ankhises, this danger is avoided because he himself is "beloved by the gods" (l. 195), and his whole family is "close to the gods" (ἀγχίϑεοι, *ankhitheoi*, l. 200—a word we shall meet again)—close in beauty, to be sure (l. 201), but also, as the context makes clear, in the sense of enjoying divine favor, for the beauty of Ganymede and Tithōnos attracted divine lovers. Charles Segal has shown that this poem explores a series of oppositions—between death and immortality, the latter represented in turn by Ganymede's immortal youth and Tithōnos's immortal old age; between Olympos and earth; and between the wilds of Mount Ida and the human civilization located in Troy.[39] The case of Ankhises, he says, provides the middle term in all of these. Ankhises couples with the goddess in a natural setting but founds a line of kings among the Trojans. He receives immortality of neither the desirable nor the undesirable kind (that of Ganymede and Tithōnos respectively), but he will perpetuate himself through his descendants (ll. 196-97). This may fall short of what the gods enjoy, but it is an excellent fate *in human terms*. In fact, Ankhises gets essentially what he prudently asked for at the outset (ll. 102-6). It is Aphrodite who finally is dissatisfied and suffers grief. Here the goddess, like the mortal Metaneira and unlike Demeter, is prey to folly and must endure the consequences: "I was greatly deluded [ἀάσϑην, *aasthēn*]," she says in line 253. Thus, whereas the *Hymn to Demeter* emphasizes mortals' inferiority to the gods and shows the positive aspects of their life only by implication, the *Hymn to Aphrodite* affirms human values in the face of what men cannot attain.

In the end, the difference between men and gods can never be overcome, except in the comparatively rare instances when mortals are given immortality. Much of the time, a recognition of this fact leads men and gods to draw back from each other, to remember what is unique and precious in their own condition, and to seek community with their own kind. When a man or god tries to cross the dividing line, he may appear to succeed at first. But the attempt ends in failure and sadness and—for mortals when they have been presumptuous—in disaster; and the line is only redrawn more firmly. In this case too a lesson is pointed about proper boundaries and the necessity of observing them. Time and again, in various terms, the precise location of these boundaries—what is and is not permitted to man and god in the nature of things—is examined in the poems, with the ultimate purpose, evidently, of explaining life as ordinary humanity—the poet and his audience—experiences it. This preoccupation lies behind not only all the passages we have so far examined but also the concept expressed in this poetry of the physical world and of history.

One way the poems depict human life through its polar opposite is to present what we might call paradisal visions. These show a keen awareness that there are happier modes of existence than man's, which are, however, unavailable to ordinary mortals.[40] The life of the gods is the obvious and outstanding example, but there are others. Typically, such visions take one of two forms.

Either places are imagined as actually existing outside the world known to mankind, where only mild weather is known, the earth bears food spontaneously and in abundance, and the inhabitants do not need to labor; or such a life is thought to have been man's lot—in a bygone age.

The *Odyssey* contains a remarkable number of paradisal visions of the former type. The bright serenity of Olympos is remote from the cares of men (vi.41–47), but the world below also contains places that offer immortal ease, such as Kalypsō's cave in its lush natural setting (v.55–75) or Elysium (iv.561–69), to which Menelaos will be translated and which, as we noted earlier, resembles the Hesiodic Islands of the Blessed as well as the environment of the Golden Age. Alkinoos's dwelling displays some attributes of these places. The ageless and immortal dogs, made by Hephaistos of gold and silver, that guard the house, and the golden youths on pedestals within (vii.91–94, 100–102), resemble the golden maidservants who attend Hephaistos in his own house on Olympos (XVIII.417–20). Alkinoos's garden surpasses ordinary ones not only by its abundance and fine arrangement. The trees bear fruit all year around—a motif that appears also in Hesiod's description of the Islands of the Blessed (*W.D.* 172–73)—and Zephyros, the same wind that refreshes dwellers in Elysium (iv.567–68), ripens that fruit (vii.117–21).

All these descriptions serve as foils to Odysseus's fate, and indeed to his desires. In rejecting Kalypsō, Odysseus voluntarily leaves the kind of place that Menelaos will someday have the extraordinary fortune to inhabit, and later he will be similarly anxious to leave Alkinoos. Moreover, he refuses not only divine ease but also immortality itself. In a way, he is simply exercising his characteristic prudence; the dangers of mating with a goddess have been set forth by Kalypsō's own reminders to Hermes of the stories of Oriōn and Iasiōn (v.121–28). But more is involved: Odysseus *wants* to go home. He never really explains this longing. To Kalypsō he concedes that Penelope, being mortal and by now aging, is her inferior in beauty, but says that even so he will undergo any trials in order to get home (v.214–24—some of the most moving lines in the entire *Odyssey*). The most he says on the matter is appended to the description of Ithaka that he gives the Phaiakians. The island is rugged (and so the antithesis of the places that figure in the paradisal visions). But, he says, neither Kirkē nor Kalypsō could persuade him to stay with her, for "nothing is sweeter than one's own land and parents, even if one inhabits an opulent house far away in an alien land" (ix.34–36). This apparent absence of conscious reflection on his motives when the stakes are so high is surprising, but perhaps those motives are impossible to explain. They appear more a matter of Odysseus's instinct as a mortal than anything that can be reasoned. Ithaka and Penelope are his own, and that is sufficient. Like Ankhises he will be satisfied with what most men can reasonably—and safely—expect, and especially so because he has had experience of the contrary.

The descriptions of the land of the Kyklōpes and of the island off its coast (ix.105–41) show with particular clarity how complex are the values associated

with paradisal visions, at least in the *Odyssey*. The Kyklōpes enjoy conditions
that resemble the Hesiodic Golden Age. Because they can rely on the gods to
make vines and cereal crops grow for them, they are free from agricultural
labor. On the nearby island Odysseus sees rich farmland going to waste for
lack of anyone to cultivate it; to the Kyklōpes, who lack ships and shipwrights,
it is inaccessible. But this is no miraculous land. What Odysseus envisons as he
contemplates it is cooperation between the soil's fertility and the farmer's
labor. The crops would be abundant but—in contrast to those in paradisal
places—they would grow, not continuously, but at regular intervals, seasonally
(ὥρια, *hōria,* "in season," l. 131; εἰς ὥρας, *eis hōras,* "in their seasons," l.
135). The island's excellent harbor would make possible another kind of
work—sailing, presumably at least in part to trade the produce of farming.
The poet leaves no doubt that this life of work is preferable from the point
of view of mankind, though he does not slight the attractions of the Kyklōpes'
life. On the one hand, the Kyklōpes have the innocence, if not the moral
righteousness, of the Golden Age. They do not need the ships that would
make intercourse with other peoples possible, or the laws and assemblies that
would promote civil intercourse among themselves. The Kyklōpes are beyond
the categories implied by human civilization, and in this sense Odysseus's
arrival among them represents the intrusion of culture and all its complexities
upon primeval simplicity.[41] On the other hand, we as ordinary humans pass
judgment as Odysseus does on the Kyklōpes' monstrous behavior. Simplicity
has its attractions, but it overlaps with barbarism. In Odysseus's description
of a land crying out for cultivation, we sense the desires of a man who has
been barred by two decades of warfare and wandering from such activity. Hesiod depicts the human condition in the same terms, agriculture and seafaring,
and he too uses the Golden Age as its foil. But although he finds value in
mortal life, he views the Golden Age with nostalgia as straightforwardly good
because he stresses the harshness of life in the present age and the pain of
toiling for a livelihood. Odysseus's account of these contrasting landscapes is
filled with longing for such work.

This appreciation of the humanly possible, which is characteristic of the
Odyssey, is sophisticated and profound. More obvious in their effect are the
corresponding negative tales that warn men not to aspire beyond themselves.
One of these is the story of Tantalos, which seems to have been told in the
Nostoi (fr. 10 Allen).[42] When Zeus offered him whatever he asked for, Tantalos demanded to live in the same way as the gods. Zeus granted his request
but suspended a rock over his head to ensure that he would enjoy nothing of
what he had. Here again, human limits are asserted through the ambivalence
of the gods' gifts.

On the historical view that is the alternative to visions of contemporary
paradises, the state of humanity is defined by the contrast between an age in
the past, when gods and men were close to each other and men shared the
gods' life, and the present time, when they live separately and under different

circumstances from one another.[43] A prominent example is the story of the Five Ages in the *Works and Days*. It ends with the terrible conditions of the race of iron but purports to tell "how the gods and mortal men came into being from the same source" (*W.D.* 108)—that is, had common parentage. Whatever the precise reference may be, the line clearly implies an original closeness between gods and men, expressed in genealogical terms.[44] Then the distance between them gradually widened with each successive age (the race of heroes, which is a possible exception, will be discussed below). The cause was humanity's moral decline. Other stories that tell of this rift assign different reasons, but this one clearly fits the concerns of the *Works and Days*. In the other versions, a definitive separation between gods and men dates from one particular occasion, as in the story of Prometheus in the *Theogony*. This begins with a feast at Mēkonē, when gods and men "reached a settlement" (ἐκρίνοντο, *ekrinonto: Theog.* 535). As several writers have remarked, the same verb is used later in the poem of the Olympians settling the question of prerogatives, *timai,* with the Titans (*Theog.* 882; this settlement is by force, however), and the scholiast on line 535 explains that at Mēkonē it was decided what is a god and what is a man.[45] Prometheus's deception of Zeus is appropriately set at this point of divergence between the two orders of being, for the events it set in motion determined the subsequent conditions of human life. That men had previously lived amid abundance and at leisure is made clear by the corresponding story in the *Works and Days* where, as was observed earlier, the description of life before Pandora resembles that of the Golden Age. In this vision of lost happiness, ease and intimacy with the gods are inseparably linked. The convergence of these two motifs helps explain the terms often used to describe the shared life of gods and men that we shall find in our next examples.

The *Catalogue of Women* sets man's enjoyment of this way of life, not in the remote past, but in the Heroic Age. According to the introduction to the poem, the unions of gods with mortal women (the products of which were the heroes of tradition) were encouraged by the terms of familiarity on which the two orders lived (Hes. fr. 1.6–7):[46]

ξυναὶ γὰρ τότε δαῖτες ἔσαν, ξυνοὶ δὲ θόωκοι
ἀθανάτοις τε θεοῖσι καταθνητοῖς τ᾽ ἀνθρώποις.

[mortal women had intercourse with gods] for then the immortal gods
    and mortal men
feasted together and sat together.

As West (1961, 133) has observed, the conception of this age combines features of the golden and heroic races as these are described in the *Works and Days*. This mixture was made easy, perhaps, by the resemblance of the heroes' life on the Islands of the Blessed to the conditions of the Golden Age.

West's further remark that in the *Catalogue* the common life of gods and men took place before the banquet at Mēkonē recounted in the *Theogony* has caused some confusion, because the genealogies in the *Catalogue* apparently began with Prometheus. Most of the unions would therefore have had to take place *after* gods and men had separated if the poet of the *Catalogue* had had the story of Mēkonē in mind, and that would contradict what the poem's introduction seems to say.[47] In fact, the episode at Mēkonē, the scheme of the Five Ages, and the chronology of the *Catalogue* cannot be reconciled, and they do not need to be. They represent three variants of a basic theme, the original intimacy and the subsequent parting of gods and men.

Far more interesting than chronology is the way in which this intimacy is described in the above quotation—as the habit of feasting together. As an expression of abundance and the pleasure it makes possible, feasting naturally forms part of the paradisal vision, and we observed earlier in this chapter passages in which the gods' feasting contrasted their freedom from care with men's toil. The motif of the common meal appears also in the *Iliad* and the *Odyssey,* but in negative form. That is, these poems sometimes stress the *distance* between gods and men by indicating the *impossibility* of their sharing food with each other on terms of familiarity. In the final book of the *Iliad,* for example, Hermes' departure from Priam at the door to Achilles' hut marks the boundary between the gods' control over men's conduct toward each other and men's responsibility to behave humanely among themselves. Hermes takes his leave with these words (XXIV.462–64):

> ἀλλ' ἤτοι μὲν ἐγὼ πάλιν εἴσομαι, οὐδ' Ἀχιλῆος
> ὀφθαλμοὺς εἴσειμι· νεμεσσητὸν δέ κεν εἴη
> ἀθάνατον θεὸν ὧδε βροτοὺς ἀγαπαζέμεν ἄντην.

> But I am going back now. I will not come
> into Achilles' sight. It would arouse resentment [*nemessēton*]
> for mortals to receive [*agapasdemen*] an immortal god face to face [*antēn*]
>   in that way.

The last sentence is somewhat ambiguous in Greek, but I have given what seems the most likely interpretation. The word translated as "receive" (ἀγαπαζέμεν, *agapasdemen*) seems to mean specifically "to receive as a guest,"[48] and this hospitality, by Homeric custom, would be expressed by a meal (as Achilles in fact shares food with Priam). For a god to enter into this relationship openly and without disguise (ἄντην, *antēn*, "face to face") would arouse *nemesis,* the resentment of Hermes' peers, presumably because partaking of a meal puts the parties on terms of equality, and men must be clearly marked as the gods' inferiors. Thus, the tone of the gods' remoteness from men on which this scene depends is set at the beginning through an inversion of the theme of the shared meal.

It is true that Athena eats with Telemakhos in the first book of the *Odyssey,* and with Telemakhos and Nestor at Pylos in Book 3. But both times she is disguised as a mortal, and although in departing she gives a more than broad hint of her identity, she maintains the pretense throughout the meal itself. Athena obeys the rule in letter if not in spirit. This distinction is not mere sophistry, however. We need to bear in mind the ceremonial nature of the meal in Homeric society and its rigid decorum. We should also compare the case of the Phaiakians, who are mortals more than ordinarily blessed. They are "beloved by the immortals" (vi.203) and "near to the gods" (ἀγχίθεοι, *ankhitheoi,* v.35—like Ankhises and his family in the *Hymn to Aphrodite*). These qualities are consistent with the way the account of Alkinoos's palace fits into the pattern of paradisal visions in the poem. The Phaiakians turn out to be literally "near to the gods," for Alkinoos, when he wonders whether Odysseus is a god in disguise, remarks that such a thing would be unprecedented (vii.201–3):

αἰεὶ γὰρ τὸ πάρος γε θεοὶ φαίνονται ἐναργεῖς
ἡμῖν, εὖτ᾽ ἔρδωμεν ἀγακλειτὰς ἑκατόμβας,
δαίνυνταί τε παρ᾽ ἄμμι καθήμενοι ἔνθα περ ἡμεῖς.

Always before the gods have appeared to us in their own form [*enargeis*],
whenever we sacrifice splendid hekatombs,
and they feast among us, sitting where we sit.

The Phaiakians enjoy the relations with the gods described in the *Catalogue,* as the last line quoted, which mentions both their feasting and their sitting together, shows. The word ἐναργεῖς (*enargeis,* "in their own form" but literally meaning "bright" or "clear") connects with the idea behind Hermes' statement to Priam and provides a contrast with Athena's disguise when she dines with mortals.[49] Later in the *Odyssey* we are told that the gods do visit ordinary men—but in disguise and in order to test whether they are lawful or violent (xvii.483–87). In hearing these lines it is impossible not to remember the Phaiakians' high fortune and how they deserve it.

The Homeric poems know of other mortals also with whom the gods feast —the Aithiopes, who live as the most remote of men at the extremes of both east and west.[50] Their direct access to the gods associates their life with that enjoyed in Elysium and the Islands of the Blessed, which are also located at the boundary of the world, and they provide a particularly fine example of polar thought and the sense of form to which it gives rise. The Aithiopes' dwelling places enclose the world, and their circumstances help depict the state of ordinary men (who inhabit the space between) by contrast. It seems inevitable, given the habits of polar thought, that men's normal experience of the gods' remoteness should have led them to imagine a people like the Aithiopes.

Odysseus himself eats with an undisguised Kalypsō (v.194–200), but this scene, unusual as it is, actually confirms the normal Homeric use of the theme of common meals to emphasize the distance between man and god. Kalypsō gives Odysseus "sustenance to eat and drink, such as mortal men consume," while she herself sits opposite him feasting on nectar and ambrosia. The difference in their food reflects the difference in their natures.[51] Directly after the meal Kalypsō offers Odysseus immortality and he refuses. And so the point where mortal diverges from immortal is located with precision. Kalypsō's island is a paradisal place that contrasts with Ithaka; and that a man and a goddess sit and eat familiarly together stresses its otherworldliness. Odysseus is still mortal, as the food he eats reminds us, but he has reached the limit of what is possible for him in that state. Now he can either accept immortality and continue to live with Kalypsō, feasting presumably on nectar and ambrosia, or return to normal human life where the gulf between men and gods is much wider and where he must face hardship and, ultimately, death. His eating with Kalypsō, understood in the wider thematic context, points up the implications of the choice Odysseus makes.[52]

Hexameter poetry, then, uses the theme of common meals and the inverse of that theme to describe the closeness and the distance that characterize the relations between men and gods.[53] The episode at Mēkonē, though chronologically incompatible with the *Catalogue,* falls within this pattern, for it represents the midpoint between the extreme cases of the possibility and the impossibility of men eating in the company of gods. The separation between these two groups takes place in the context of a feast. Afterward, men still share their meals with the gods, but only indirectly and without sitting with them—by offering sacrifices. And because sacrifice not only is the way mankind continues to communicate with divinity but also commemorates Prometheus's deception of Zeus, it is a reminder of what man has lost and thus a fitting symbol of both his access to and his estrangement from the gods. It is thus a ritual parallel to the figure of Pandora.[54]

It will be obvious that the *Catalogue of Women* presents a very different view of the Heroic Age from the *Iliad* and the *Odyssey,* where men, far from leading a godlike existence, are vulnerable to all the evils that attend mortality. In this case as in others, however, the thematic concerns that unite several representatives of hexameter poetry are more fundamental and matter more than the literal contradictions between them. Here the latter are at least in part a result of differences in narrative perspective. The *Catalogue* looks back on the Heroic Age, from the point of view of the present, as an era completely at an end, and it emphasizes the discontinuities, the qualities that distinguish that time from our own (the word *then* occurs twice in the first six lines of the introduction of the poem). Accordingly, the *Catalogue* imagines the intimacy between gods and men as extending through the Heroic Age in order to focus on the ultimate separation, which comes, as we shall see, with the Trojan War. In the Homeric epics, the outlook is for the most part that of the Heroic Age itself, except at those moments when the poet views his subject from the perspective of his own time; and although the Homeric heroes clearly excel men of the present age and live under different conditions from them, the emphasis is more on the continuities, on what all mortals, of whatever period, have in common. Moreover, even in Homer the gods frequently come into contact with mortals (one of the features that, for the audience, would distance the narrative from their own time). As we have seen, however, on such occasions the gods are usually in disguise, and at critical moments men and gods are each often guided by a recognition of what distinguishes them from the other order of being. Thus the Homeric poems also present the antithesis of proximity and remoteness (the theme of common meals being one of the terms used to signify the latter), but as if these states coexisted, whereas the *Catalogue* treats them as temporally successive. In the end, the difference lies essentially in the means of expressing the same polarity.

Like the *Catalogue of Women,* the description of the race of heroes in the *Works and Days* (*W.D.* 156–73) sharply distinguishes that age from the present as superior. This passage retards the process of mankind's moral deterioration presented by the myth of the Five Ages as a whole, and it seems to be a Greek addition, if not Hesiod's own, to a myth of Near Eastern origin that involved only four ages and had nothing that corresponded to a Heroic Age.[55] As it stands in the *Works and Days,* the story conflates two ways of representing the difference between past and present: moral decay through successive periods and an age of heroes, now ended, that immediately preceded the present. The race of heroes conforms to the moral theme; its members are "juster and better" than men of the bronze race (*W.D.* 158) and—by implication—than men of the iron race as well. They should be imagined as living under the same conditions as men in the Homeric poems, but differ from them in being granted after death the kind of existence that the heroes in the *Catalogue* enjoy while alive. The passage in itself recapitulates the sequence of closeness and separation between men and gods that is implicit in the myth as a whole, somewhat intrusive though it is in that story. The separation was effected by the entire race's destruction in the wars at Thebes and Troy, but while they lived, the heroes were bound to the gods by kinship. Hesiod calls them ἡμίθεοι (*hēmitheoi,* literally "half-gods," *W.D.* 160), a term that implies that they were the products of unions between mortals and immortals. As in the phrase that introduces the story (*W.D.* 108), the relationship between men and gods is expressed biologically, although the gods by this period are men's parents rather than their siblings.

The word *hēmitheoi* is almost entirely absent from the Homeric poems, and although many a warrior at Troy in the *Iliad* has a divine parent (XVI. 448–49), not all do by any means. Once again, however, an apparent divergence in conceptions of the Heroic Age is to be explained by differences in narrative perspective. As West remarks (1978, 191; on *W.D.* 160), the single Homeric use of *hēmitheoi* (XII.23) appears "in a passage where that age is viewed from the distance of the poet's own time," and such moments occur outside the main narrative framework of the *Iliad*. The reason for this usage, as West also indicates, is that the word was the regular collective term for the men of the heroic age, and a collective term implies the ability to see the age as a whole and therefore as in the past. That clearly is the perspective from which the myth of the Five Ages in the *Works and Days* is told. In two of its three other occurrences in extant hexameter poetry, *hēmitheoi* is used of heroes as the subject of heroic epic (*h.* 31.19, 32.19), which by its nature preserves the memory of earlier men. When the poets state and reflect upon this function, they imply a consciousness that they are relating events from the past.

Isolated though it is, the occurrence of *hēmitheoi* in the *Iliad* indicates the poet's awareness of a tradition about the Age of Heroes (which for reasons already suggested he did not use in the bulk of his poem) as a time when a race lived who were subject to death but superior to men of the present because they sprang from unions of divinities with mortals. These liaisons were a consequence of the intimate terms on which men and gods then lived.[56] Such a conception is implicit in Hesiod's account of this age, and it is the very basis of the *Catalogue of Women*. In the *Catalogue*, as in the *Works and Days*, the Heroic Age ended with the Trojan War (the Theban conflicts are not mentioned in this connection in the extant fragments), but this poem attributes the war to Zeus's desire to destroy mankind. The motive for this desire had something to do with the existence and fate of the heroes.[57] It is in this connection, and therefore consistent with its usage elsewhere, that our final instance of *hēmitheoi* occurs. The long fragment in question begins in the midst of a catalogue of Helen's suitors that ends with the oath Tyndareus extracted from them, her marriage to Menelaos, and the birth of their daughter Hermionē. Then, abruptly, comes a mention of dissension among the gods "as a result of strife"; this apparently refers to their division into pro- and anti-Trojan factions. (See Wilamowitz, 1907, 42.) After a reference to "wondrous deeds" meditated by Zeus, which are evidently then specified as warfare, occur the lines that interest us. The text, unfortunately fragmentary, is first given here as it appears in the edition of Merkelbach and West, with only those supplements that seem most certain (Hesiod fr. 204.98–103):

$$\ldots\, \mathrm{\mathring{\eta}\delta\eta\ \delta\grave{\epsilon}\ \gamma\acute{\epsilon}\nu o\varsigma\ \mu\epsilon\rho\acute{o}\pi\omega\nu\ \mathring{\alpha}\nu\vartheta\rho\acute{\omega}\pi\omega\nu}$$

πόλλον ἀϊστῶσαι σπεῦδε, πρ[ό]φασιν μὲν ὀλέσθαι
ψυχὰς ἡμιθέω[ν ....]οισι βροτοῖσι
τέκνα θεῶν μι[...] . [..] ο . [ὀφ] ϑαλμοῖσιν ὁρῶντα,
ἀλλ᾽ οἳ μ[ὲ]ν μάκ[α]ρες κ[......]ν ὡς τὸ πάρος περ
χωρὶς ἀπ᾽ ἀν[ϑ]ρώπων[βίοτον κα]ὶ ἤϑε᾽ ἔχωσιν....

Now he [Zeus] was in a great hurry to obliterate
the race of mortal men in order, as he said,[58]

that the lives of the half-gods [*hēmitheoi*] should be destroyed . . . with
   mortals
the children of the gods . . . seeing with their eyes,
but the blessed ones . . . as in the past
should have their livelihood and dwellings apart from men. . . .

It is clear from the last two lines that Zeus wants to separate gods and men
entirely. But what is his reason? Why in particular does he want to kill off the
hēmitheoi?
   A motive is supplied admirably by the text of lines 99–103 with the supplements proposed by Wilamowitz (the fragment's first editor) and by Rzach:[59]

>   . . . πρ[ό]φασιν μὲν ὀλέσθαι
> ψυχὰς ἡμιθέω[ν ἵνα μὴ δειλ]οῖσι βροτοῖσι
> τέκνα θεῶν μι[γέη]ι [μόρ]ο[ν ὀφ]θαλμοῖσιν ὁρῶντα,
> ἀλλ' οἵ μ[ὲ]ν μάκ[α]ρες κ[αὶ ἐς ὕστερο]ν ὡς τὸ πάρος περ
> χωρὶς ἀπ' ἀν[θ]ρώπων [βίοτον κα]ι ἤθε' ἔχωσιν. . . .

>   . . . in order, as he said,
> that the lives of the *hēmitheoi* should be destroyed,
> so that the children of the gods should not mate[60]
> with wretched mortals, seeing death with their eyes,
> but so that the blessed ones, for the future as in the past,
> should have their livelihood and dwellings apart from men. . . .

Before an explanation can be offered for the passage as a whole, two details
require comment. First, the phrase "children of the gods" in the third line
should be understood as a periphrasis for "the gods."[61] Second, πρόφασιν
μέν in the first line seems at first to imply that the reason Zeus gave was a
mere pretext designed to conceal his true motive. It was this difficulty,
indeed, that made Wilamowitz confess himself unable to interpret the text
that he had so admirably restored.[62] There is no sign, however, that the
fragment anywhere told what Zeus's real reason might have been. It is therefore probably better, as it is legitimate, to understand *prophasis* as "explanation," either in the sense of an expressed genuine motive, or neutrally, with
no judgment implied as to truth or falsehood.[63] With the above supplements,
then, the text suggests that, lying with mortal women, the gods produced
mortal offspring whose deaths they had to watch. In order to spare himself
and the other gods the pain of this experience, Zeus destroyed the *hēmitheoi*
once and for all, stopped the mating of immortals with mortals, and so
brought to a close the period of intimacy between them.
   The heroes' mortality may have been one of the themes that gave meaning
to the whole genealogical process recorded in the *Catalogue*, for it seems to
have been referred to in the introduction. Just after the description of their

feasts with the gods, mortals are said not to have had an equal life-span (fr.
1.8-10), but because only the first half of each line is preserved, it is uncertain with whom they are compared: with each other, with men of the present
age, or with the gods (the text can be restored to yield any of these meanings).[64] Of these, the last possibility would fit best with the text and meaning
suggested above for the crucial lines of fragment 204. Blissful though human
existence at that time seems to have been when viewed nostalgically from the
present, the men and women who enjoyed it were still mortal; and this difference between them and the gods, destined to lead to the sundering of the
two races, would be mentioned right at the beginning of the poem.[65] This
interpretation would be compatible with the apparent meaning of lines 11-13
of fragment 1 (again incomplete), which seem to distinguish two classes of
mortals in the heroic age according to life-span: some lived long (in a state of
youth?), while for others the gods contrived death right away. But (so the un-
expressed thought would have run) all died eventually. On either of the two
alternate possibilities for lines 8-10, however, human mortality would still be
the subject of the passage as a whole (ll. 8-13). Only the details would vary.
The problems raised by fragment 1 thus do not affect our interpretation of
fragment 204.

The vision of the Heroic Age that emerges from these fragments and the
other passages we have examined helps to define the limits on human life by
imagining a time when those limits were considerably broader: when the
necessities of life were provided without toil, and men whose prowess and
achievements far surpassed anything nowadays conceivable enjoyed close relations with the gods.[66] But what is demonstrated equally is that even under
the best possible conditions men and gods are by nature incompatible. The
obstacle to ideal union is that man is fated to die, and the present state of
things, where humanity faces the world alone and unaided, is made to seem
the result of a virtually inevitable process. The remarkable feature of the
Hesiodic fragments, if the view taken of them above is correct, is that they
present the gods' rather than man's perspective on death. In this way they use
a lovely motif that occurs elsewhere in hexameter poetry as well (and consideration of other examples below might make this interpretation of the
fragments seem more plausible). Sometimes even the carefree gods must confront death—not, of course, their own, but the deaths of certain men whom
they would like to save but cannot because they are unable to change what is
fated. In telling of such occasions, the poets look beyond human experience
and, in an extraordinary act of sympathy, imagine what the gods' feelings
must be. Then the gods do not seem uncaringly remote. They sorrow, rather,
at the intransigent barrier that separates them from the mortals they have
been so unfortunate as to love.[67]

A god could easily save a man even from afar, a disguised Athena says to
Telemakhos; "but not even the gods can ward off from a man they love death

which comes to all [?] , whenever the baneful fate of gloomy death takes him" (iii.236-38). Athena is speaking generally here, and therefore dispassionately. But the rule she enunciates causes other gods pain. We have already observed Demeter's futile attempt to make Dēmophon immortal in her grief for Persephone, and (in the foregoing chapter) the impotent sorrow of Ares for Askalaphos and of Zeus for Sarpēdon. The figure of Achilles, however, provides the fullest realization of this theme in the *Iliad*. His story, in fact, encapsulates the polarity of nearness and distance between mortal and immortal, and it does so in the same terms as the *Catalogue*. The wedding of Pēleus and Thetis was an occasion on which the gods and men feasted together.[68] But Thetis did not want this marriage: it has meant only sorrow to her, because her husband and the son she bore him are both mortal. As a divinity, Thetis should be carefree (ἀκηδής, *akēdēs*, to revert once again to Achilles' characterization of the gods). But in Books 18 and 24 of the *Iliad*, the diction generally associated with mortals' woe is applied to her. This paradoxical usage makes the pain she suffers all the more vivid.[69] Weeping, she speaks to Hephaistos of her marriage as follows (XVIII.429-35):

Ἥφαιστ᾽, ἦ ἄρα δή τις, ὅσαι θεαί εἰσ᾽ ἐν Ὀλύμπῳ,
τοσσά δ᾽ ἐνὶ φρεσὶν ᾗσιν ἀνέσχετο κήδεα λυγρά,
ὅσσ᾽ ἐμοὶ ἐκ πασέων Κρονίδης Ζεὺς ἄλγε᾽ ἔδωκεν;
ἐκ μέν μ᾽ ἀλλάων ἁλιάων ἀνδρὶ δάμασσεν,
Αἰακίδῃ Πηλῆϊ, καὶ ἔτλην ἀνέρος εὐνὴν
πολλὰ μάλ᾽ οὐκ ἐθέλουσα. ὁ μὲν δὴ γήραϊ λυγρῷ
κεῖται ἐνὶ μεγάροις ἀρημένος, ἄλλα δέ μοι νῦν.

Hephaistos, of all the goddesses there are on Olympos, has any
endured [*aneskheto*] in her heart so many baneful cares [*kēdea*],
as many as are the pains [*algea*] that Zeus, the son of Kronos, has given
    me above all others?
From among all the daughters of the sea he subjected me to a man,
Pēleus the son of Aiakos, and I endured [*etlēn*] a mortal's bed
very much against my will. He lies in his hall
worn down by baneful old age, and I have other cares now.

Like Ēos with Tithōnos (except that Pēleus will also die), she has had to watch her husband age and decay. Her new sorrow is, of course, the imminent death of her splendid son, Achilles. Near the start of this book, in her prospective enactment of the lament she will deliver when her son actually dies (see p. 50), she calls on her sisters to hear her cares, and the word she uses is again *kēdea* (XVIII.53). Achilles' excellence, his doom to die at Troy, his misery while alive: these are the causes of her grief (XVIII.54-64).

Amid his mourning for Patroklos, Achilles enters into Thetis's feelings. Or perhaps it is more accurate to say that immortal mother and mortal son, the latter now and the former in anticipation, share the same affliction, pain at the death of someone beloved (XVIII.86-90):

αἴθ᾽ ὄφελες σὺ μὲν αὖθι μετ᾽ ἀθανάτης ἁλίῃσι
ναίειν, Πηλεὺς δὲ θνητὴν ἀγαγέσθαι ἄκοιτιν.
νῦν δ᾽ ἵνα καὶ σοὶ πένθος ἐνὶ φρεσὶ μυρίον εἴη
παιδὸς ἀποφθιμένοιο, τὸν οὐχ ὑποδέξεαι αὖτις
οἴκαδε νοστήσαντ᾽. . . .

I wish that you were dwelling there with the immortal sea-goddesses
and that Pēleus had wedded a mortal wife.
But it did not happen in this way, in order that you should have in your
     heart grief [*penthos*] without limit
for the death of your son, whom you will not greet
as he returns home again. . . .

Immediately after this speech, Thetis tells him that his own death will follow Hektor's (XVIII.95-96). Although that means nothing to him when set against his urgent need for vengeance, Achilles has felt, with the imaginative sympathy that he will exercise again with Priam, how burdensome and paradoxical is the situation into which Thetis has been put by contact with mortality. The incongruity of her suffering finds expression also in the final book, when, because of her sorrows (*akhea*), she is ashamed to obey Zeus's summons and join the gods on Olympos (XXIV.90-91). When she does go, Zeus greets her with understanding (XXIV.104-5): "You have come to Olympos, divine Thetis, though afflicted with grief [κηδομένη, *kēdomenē*] and with unforgettable sorrow [πένθος, *penthos*] in your heart." There is a sad tension between the epithet *divine* (literally "goddess"), which stirs associations with the gods' way of life as that is usually conceived, and the anguish that Zeus knows she is undergoing.

In Chapter 2, we noticed that Achilles' horses and the armor that he lends Patroklos—the former probably, and the latter certainly, the gods' gift to Pēleus when he married Thetis—suggest at once his near-divinity and his mortality (see pp. 48-49). As happens to Thetis, the divine nature of these gifts is violated by their association with mortals (Pēleus, Patroklos, and Achilles). The words of Achilles quoted above follow his reference to the armor (XVIII.82-85), for the thought of the arms leads him naturally to the subject of his mother's marriage to Pēleus. Like Thetis, moreover, the horses mourn Achilles' approaching death, which they cannot avert, swift though they are (XIX.404-17).[70] Their earlier and unavailing sorrow for Patroklos has drawn Zeus's pity, which he expresses in a way that describes the predicament of all immortal things touched by human suffering (XVII.443-47):

ἆ δειλώ, τί σφῶϊ δόμεν Πηλῆϊ ἄνακτι
θνητῷ, ὑμεῖς δ᾽ ἐστὸν ἀγήρω τ᾽ ἀθανάτω τε;
ἦ ἵνα δυστήνοισι μετ᾽ ἀνδράσιν ἄλγε᾽ ἔχητον;
οὐ μὲν γάρ τί πού ἐστιν ὀϊζυρώτερον ἀνδρὸς
πάντων ὅσσα τε γαῖαν ἔπι πνείει τε καὶ ἕρπει.

Ah, poor wretches! Why did we give you to the lord Pēleus,
a mortal, while you are ageless and immortal? [71]
Was it so that you should have pains [algea] among miserable men?
Nothing, I think, of all that breathe and move upon the earth
is more woeful [oïsdurōteron] than man.

Woeful—the word that sums up man's condition. In the *Odyssey,* when Odysseus speaks to Amphinomos about the gods' gifts and how a man should use them, he begins with lines practically identical to the last two just quoted. [72] Human vulnerability is thus presented in these two passages from the divine and the mortal points of view respectively. From it Odysseus derives the need for wisdom and self-restraint. Zeus voices the immortals' sadness at man's ephemerality, but expresses another idea as well: that the gods would be better off staying among themselves, for associating with man only brings them into his circle of woe. What is expressed here at length and vividly is the same feeling that was behind Thetis's reluctance to marry a mortal, Achilles' pity for her, and—as I would reconstruct it—Zeus's decision in the *Catalogue* to end the Heroic Age. [73]

The theme of the gods' grief for mortals whom they love is used one other time in the *Iliad,* and with a sophistication that suggests how familiar it must have been. Helen accuses Aphrodite of using her to have vicarious affairs with mortals (III.400-402) and then suggests that the goddess enjoy Paris herself (III.406-9):

ἧσο παρ᾽ αὐτὸν ἰοῦσα, θεῶν δ᾽ ἀπόεικε κελεύθου,
μηδ᾽ ἔτι σοῖσι πόδεσσιν ὑποστρέψειας Ὄλυμπον,
ἀλλ᾽ αἰεὶ περὶ κεῖνον ὀῖζυε καί ἑ φύλασσε,
εἰς ὅ κέ σ᾽ ἢ ἄλοχον ποιήσεται, ἢ ὅ γε δούλην.

Go and take your seat beside him, withdraw from the path of the gods,
and don't traverse Olympos any more.
But constantly suffer woe [oïsdue] for his sake and watch over him,
until he makes you his wife—or his slave.

There is an interesting contrast to be drawn between the injunction here to "go and sit beside him" and the sitting together of gods and men at their common feasts as described at the beginning of the *Catalogue.* There the action was an expression of community, but for Aphrodite in this case it would mean humiliation and "woe." She would be taking man's portion on herself and relinquishing her identity as a goddess by leaving the society of the other immortals, just as Thetis, in a more somber context, feels cut off from the gods by her grief. Helen's taunt reveals how absurd and self-defeating such a step would be.

And yet Aphrodite herself loved and lay with the mortal Ankhises, as the poet of the *Iliad* knows (II.819-21; V.247-48, 311-13; XX.208-9), and as the *Hymn to Aphrodite* recounts in detail. The later poem does more than describe a seduction (though it does that with wonderful deftness) or pay a graceful compliment to a family of rulers in Asia Minor who claimed descent from Aineias (if it does that at all).[74] It is a profound exploration of what mortality implies, from the human point of view (as we found in our consideration of the hymn earlier in this chapter), but also from the divine perspective. In arousing her desire for Ankhises, Zeus is making Aphrodite suffer what she has inflicted on all but three of the other gods—sexual union with mortals. Hereafter he means to make it impossible for her to make this boast (*h. Aphr.* 50-52):

... ὥς ῥα θεοὺς συνέμιξε καταθνητῆσι γυναιξὶ
καί τε καταθνητοὺς υἱεῖς τέκον ἀθανάτοισιν,
ὥς τε θεὰς ἀνέμιξε καταθνητοῖς ἀνθρώποις.

... that she mingled gods with mortal women
and they bore mortal sons to the immortals,
and that she mingled goddesses with mortal men.

This passage shows how close a parallel the *Hymn to Aphrodite* provides to the *Catalogue of Women*. The liaisons mentioned here—of gods with mortal women and of goddesses with mortal men—represent the subjects of the *Catalogue* and of *Theogony*, ll. 963-1020, respectively. The latter section would have acted as a bridge from the *Theogony* proper to the *Catalogue* when the two poems were joined,[75] and within it Thetis's marriage to Pēleus and Aphrodite's affair with Ankhises are mentioned in adjacent entries (*Theog.* 1003-10). Furthermore, one of the leading motifs of the hymn is the idea we have found in fragment 204 from the *Catalogue*. The sting in Aphrodite's power is not simply lust but the way the human partners to these unions, and their sons, are fated to die: the word *mortal* occurs in each of the three lines just quoted and is set against *immortal* in the second line (where, significantly, it qualifies *sons*). Zeus now determines that Aphrodite herself will suffer the pain of loving a mortal and bearing a son to him. Later, speaking of the disgrace into which she has fallen by sleeping with Ankhises, she recalls in terms reminiscent of the above quotation how the other immortals used to dread her (ll. 247-51). But she feels more than shame. Of the son she will bear, she says (*h. Aphr.* 198-99):

τῷ δὲ καὶ Αἰνείας ὄνομ' ἔσσεται, οὕνεκα μ' αἰνὸν
ἔσχεν ἄχος ἕνεκα βροτοῦ ἀνέρος ἔμπεσον εὐνῇ.

His name will be Aineias, for a dreadful [*ainon*]
anguish [*akhos*] has seized me because I entered a mortal man's bed.

The second of these lines resembles XVIII.85,[76] where Achilles describes
Thetis's marriage to Pēleus. The similarity indicates how like hers is Aphrodite's situation. Aphrodite also is doomed to grieve for loss, as she explains
later in the same speech (*h. Aphr.* 241–46):[77]

ἀλλ' εἰ μὲν τοιοῦτος ἐὼν εἶδός τε δέμας τε
ζώοις, ἡμέτερός τε πόσις κεκλημένος εἴης,
οὐκ ἄν ἔπειτά μ' ἄχος πυκινὰς φρένας ἀμφικαλύπτοι.
νῦν δέ σε μὲν τάχα γῆρας ὁμοίιον ἀμφικαλύψει
νηλειές, τό τ' ἔπειτα παρίσταται ἀνθρώποισιν,
οὐλόμενον καματηρόν, ὅ τε στυγέουσι θεοί περ.

But if you were to live on with the same form and appearance as you have
    now,
and if you were to be called my husband,
then anguish [*akhos*] would not enfold [*amphikaluptoi*] my wise mind.
But as it is, old age, which comes to all men [?], will soon enfold [*amphi-
    kalupsei*] you,
inexorable old age, which someday accompanies all men,
baneful, exhausting, hateful to the gods.

Grief closes over the goddess's mind as old age will close over the mortal's
beauty. There could hardly be a clearer statement of the distance between
men and gods, what causes it, and what it means for them both.[78]
    We should not imagine that the gods are permanently scarred by these
brushes with mortality, but at least for a time their pain is sharp. Thus it is
not always true (though often it is) that the gods' emotions are shallow by
comparison with men's. Yet they gain the capacity to feel deeply precisely at
those times when their divine nature is betrayed by excessive involvement
with mankind. And even on such occasions, just as when they feel too little,
the gods appear limited by their immortality—by their strength as men are by
their weakness. They are doomed to live on while the men they love perish.
When the gods sorrow for men, they regret associating with them. Yet in
some ways they cannot do without mankind, and mortals are even more
dependent on the gods. Contact between the two races can never be wholly
successful or satisfying, except in nostalgic dreams of the past or in visions of
unearthly paradises. The poems describe the failures, as well as the successes,
in order to establish by both methods the different qualities of gods and of
men. That in turn sets human life in perspective. Man's existence, as these

poems depict it, is tolerable for all its awkwardness and the suffering it entails. And if men are incapable of the heights of divinity, they can still achieve outstanding successes—sometimes because they have come close to the gods, yet sometimes also because of their very limitations.

4

The Poets on Their Art, I:
The Performance of Hexameter Poetry

IN A SOCIETY THAT, from illiteracy or habit, does not rely on the written word, public discourse is necessarily oral; and perhaps the most important mode of oral communication in Greece of the eighth century B.C., and for several hundred years thereafter, was poetry. Through this medium, ideas outlasted the ephemeral single act of speech and gained a certain permanence. Poetry was the means not simply of promulgating and examining matters that were of common concern in a particular era but also, and more importantly, of maintaining information, concepts, and attitudes through time. Because poetry could perpetuate itself by means of its traditions, it was the record of what a society thought worth preserving about itself. Such written records as may have begun to be kept from, let us say, the seventh century B.C. onward cannot have matched poetry in the scope and rich variety of its subjects. Poetry remained the repository of the society's myths, its understanding of its own history, and the results of speculation about the world. Both narrative and discursive poetry expressed the value of the society's customs and institutions. The very organization of the material in each work, as we observed in the first chapter, reflected and reinforced the mental habits and modes of thought common to all those in the audience. Poetry was, in short, the way men knew their past and coped with the present. Both explicitly and by implication, it conveyed a sense of order and coherence in things and was thus a powerful force for stability. As the society's means of self-expression, it exerted a normative influence within each age and on successive generations.[1]

The typicality of meter, diction, themes, and form was, of course, enormously helpful to the poets in composition, whatever use, if any, they made of writing. But it also reflected, and must have helped to preserve, a uniformity of thought, attitude, and subject matter that was essential if poetry was to perform its important service to the society. As is well known, a poem was valued, not for originality of form or idea, but for how well it embodied the tradition. An individual poet could earn fame, certainly; his talent was judged, however, by how well he exploited the generic elements that he absorbed as part of his craft. A great poet would never feel hindered or confined by these elements, but just the reverse. Thus there could be ample diversity among poems, but it was diversity within the bounds of the typical. Even the *Iliad* and the *Odyssey,* monumental achievements though they are in several senses, represent an expansion or development of the tradition, not a break with it. That they and the Hesiodic poems could both come from that tradition shows what possibilities it offered to poets of genius.

Today, poetic creation has become a solitary activity, and poetry is addressed to a limited and generally elite audience. Whether it has, or even ought to have, a social value is open to debate. Poetry has been displaced from the position it held in one of the formative stages of Western literature; for the generic character of hexameter poetry had the crucial advantage of ensuring its accessibility to all members of society.[2] It was their common possession, which helped bind them to one another. Poetry was thus the shared enterprise of poet and audience, and in several senses. In the first place, the audience as well as the poet seems literally to have played an important role in the shaping of the poem during performances; we shall find evidence for this role later on. Second, the concern of this poetry was, as we have said, the common social and cultural heritage. Not only did poetry exert a unifying influence on its audience, but also its form and substance were held to the traditional and familiar by the need to fulfill the listeners' expectations and thus to avoid bewildering them. And finally, during a performance both the poet and audience partook equally of the mysterious gift of song, which was conceived of as at least partly independent of man. Through poetry men came into contact with the divine. A poem might celebrate a god or the gods, but it also was a way of conveying something of divine knowledge to men. Thus to some extent poetry raised human life above its normal conditions, by purging men of the memory of hardship and sorrow and giving them an intimation of what was outside the usual range of their knowledge and perception. This feeling of transcendence, though temporary, must have knit all the participants into a community for at least as long as the performance lasted. Plato's image for performance (*Ion* 553d–e) of the iron rings stretched in a line from a magnet and linked by its force, although perhaps misleading in its emphasis on the irrationality of poetry, is true in many ways to the notion that Greek society traditionally had of this art.

At the end of *The Singer of Tales,* Albert Lord (1960, 220) well expresses the urgent importance of a poetic tradition to an oral society:

> When we know how a song is built, we know that its building blocks *must* be of great age. For it is of the *necessary* nature of tradition that it seek and maintain stability, that it preserve itself. And this tenacity springs neither from perverseness, nor from an abstract principle of absolute art, but from a desperately compelling conviction that what the tradition is preserving is the very means of attaining life and happiness.

The distinction that Lord goes on to make, however, between literary artistry and the utility of this kind of song may not be absolute, or even ncessary at all. Perhaps it would be better to speak instead of a harmony between aesthetic value and social usefulness. Who would wish to separate these qualities, or to decide which was prior, even if that were possible? Poetry was an *art* that also performed a vital *function* and so enjoyed a privileged public status that it has not had for many centuries. There have, of course, been other eras when poetry played a central role on public occasions; Greek tragedy is a splendid example. But less was at stake then, because other means of transmitting ideas and information were freely available by the fifth century B.C. The difference is one of degree, admittedly, but even more than in succeeding centuries, early hexameter poetry offers us the spectacle of the poet's integration within his society.[3] Despite our own distance from these poems in time and in ways of thinking, by reading them we can overhear a society entertaining itself, and its members communicating to one another what was most valuable in their cultural heritage.

In several ways, however, these general statements must be made more precise. The subject of poetry's place in society has to be approached with caution. One writer, for example, has recently given a salutary warning against assuming automatically that oral poetry faithfully reflects its society:

> The traditional emphasis on the communal and homogeneous nature of non-literate society or the democratic connotations of the term "folklore" might lead one to suppose that oral poetry is always equally shared and approved throughout the society and the poet merely the spokesman of that society (of "the folk"). But so far as its *production* goes this is not always the case. In non-literate as in literate societies, powerful groups of poets can retain their positions in conjunction with religious and political interests, can maintain a monopoly over the production of certain types of poems (usually those which express certain points of view) and in addition rceceive good reward and control the entrance of new recruits to their profession. The *reception* of their openly performed poetry may be in principle more widespread than when the appearance of such poetry can be confined to small numbers of inaccessible or expensive books. But even this contrast can be exaggerated, for official poets sometimes address themselves to restricted audiences (wealthy and powerful patrons at court, or members of particular esoteric groups) and in some cases such poets may not travel far beyond the main political and economic centres of the culture of which they are sometimes taken to be the "representatives."[4]

In various cultures, Finnegan also observes (1977, 242–43), oral poetry either can serve to uphold the social order or can be a force for change. These reservations are true in principle, and we need above all to avoid romantic preconceptions about "the folk." In the specific case of Greek hexameter poetry, however, to judge from the surviving specimens (which are all we have to go by), there were no official court or religious poets. Performances were often given to amuse the wealthy and powerful, certainly, and the values expressed in poems delivered on such occasions would have suited the interests of that class. But this poetry had a much broader public also. As we shall find, it could be performed on a wide variety of occasions, and all classes of society would frequently have had the opportunity to hear it. The attitudes and concerns reflected in the poems must have been those of the people at large as well as of the aristocracy. Greek hexameter poetry, therefore, did transmit a coherent and widely shared set of ideas and social values, without being the exclusive property or the instrument of one particular class.

And yet to make this assertion is not to claim that the poetry accurately reflected contemporary social conditions. In fact, whereas hexameter poetry gives the impression of a stable and homogeneous society, the reality was far different. During the seventh and sixth centuries B.C., while hexameter poetry was still being composed and performed, social conditions changed considerably. Some of these changes are already implied by the *Works and Days,* but they can be traced much more fully in the lyric than in the hexameter poets. Conservative as it was because of its all-pervasive typical characteristics, hexameter poetry, for the most part, may portray a state of society that no longer existed when the works we have were composed, as has been thought to be the case particularly with the Homeric poems.[5] That would not necessarily have diminished, and may even have increased, its contemporary value. By presenting traditional modes of belief and thought, hexameter poetry must have afforded a measure of continuity with the past. In this way it could provide cultural unity to a Greek world now politically fragmented, and could offer its audience an idea of order that they might still try to approximate.[6]

Something was said above, in the Introduction, about the much-debated question of oral as opposed to written composition. Here it is necessary to repeat that, although the fact that writing was known in Greece by the eighth century B.C. makes the existence of written texts theoretically possible, hexameter poetry was still disseminated as it always had been—through performances. The same is evidently true of lyric and choral poetry. It still makes sense, then, to speak of an essentially oral society no matter how much use may have been made of writing in composing and preserving our texts. The audience was conditioned to hear poems rather than to read them, and the poetic art included delivery as well as composition. Thus only when we remember that hexameter poetry was performed can we fully appreciate it. We can begin to gain this appreciation by considering how the poets represent themselves and their art—by examining, that is, the descriptions of poets and of performances within the poems themselves. In this way it will be possible to describe, late in this chapter and in the next, the nature and function of hexameter poetry in its original setting. Perhaps ultimately we shall be able to imagine what it meant to those in the audience to hear a poetic performance.

These poems give the impression that song permeates life. A performance of some kind graces almost every occasion they describe, from the very formal to the casual. On the one hand, song forms part of ceremonies that are religious in nature: funeral games with poetic competition (*W.D.* 654-57), the festival in honor of a god at his cult center (Delos: *h. Apollo* 146-76, Hesiod fr. 357), and the *thrēnos,* or lament for the dead (XXIV.719-76, xxiv.60-62).[7] At the other end of the scale are impromptu performances in informal settings by men who are not professional singers. The *Hymn to Hermes* refers to witty songs improvised by youths at a banquet; to these is compared the extemporaneous song in which Hermes celebrates his own birth as he first tries out the phorminx that he has just invented (*h. Hermes* 55-56). Odysseus mentions to Eumaios similar spontaneous dance and song under the influence of wine (xiv.462-66). Song by nonprofessionals also embellishes work (XVIII.569-72; cf. v.61-62, x.220-23—the latter two examples of singing without instrumental accompaniment). Or it can provide amusement in solitude (IX.185-89, *h. Aphr.* 80).

Between these extremes are the pleasures and festivities of daily life to which performances, generally involving professionals, lend ceremony: the group dance (viii.250-380, *h. Hermes* 481, and perhaps XVIII.590-606), wedding celebrations (XVIII.491-96, *Aspis* 273-80; cf. xxiii.130-51), and the *kōmos,* or revel (*h. Hermes* 481, *Aspis* 281-84).[8] Above all, there is the feast, which, as the *Odyssey* in particular shows, is regularly adorned by a singer with his phorminx (i.150-55, 325-27, iv.15-19—a wedding feast—viii.62-92, 484-520, xvii.269-71; cf. ix.1-11, xxi.430, *h. Hermes* 31, 480).

The performances described are equally diverse in nature.[9] Music, singing, and dancing often appear together, but in varying combinations. The solo dance with the ball by two Phaiakians at viii.370-80 is accompanied by the rhythmic hand clapping of the bystanders. Perhaps we are to understand that Dēmodokos plays his phorminx as well, but without singing. Just before this, he has played this instrument and sung the tale of Ares and Aphrodite, while young men danced silently but perhaps imitatively (viii.250-366).[10] These examples are exceptional in our surviving poetry, however. Far more common is choral song. This is usually, if not always, accompanied by a singer who plays the phorminx, and the singing and dancing of the chorus, when these are not described individually (as in the second Olympian scene in the *Hymn to Apollo*), are commonly indicated by the verb μέλπειν (*melpein*) or the related noun μολπή (*molpē*).[11] Twice a pair of tumblers is said to "lead off" the dance (XVIII.605-6, iv.18-19).[12] The singing of the paean to propitiate Apollo in I.472-74 apparently takes the form of choral song; the performance is twice referred to as *molpē,* whereas ἀείδειν (*aeidein,* "sing") is used when the type and content of the song itself are identified. Rhythmic body movement also accompanies the singing of the paean in *h. Apollo* 513-19, but here in the form of the Cretan sailors' procession from Krisa to Delphi while the god himself leads the way playing the phorminx. The scene in the vineyard on the Shield of Achilles (XVIII.567-72) is rather similar: a boy plays the phorminx and sings a song called *linos,* while young men and girls carry away baskets of the harvested grapes. The word *molpē* indicates that the latter dance, or more probably that they move in time to the music, and also sing—perhaps a refrain to the song. Divine choruses dance and sing hymns in *h.* 19.19-47 and *h.* 27.11-20, and the Delian maidens sing a hymn and then a heroic narrative in *h. Apollo* 158-61, but in none of these is instrumental accompaniment explicitly mentioned (it may well be simply understood, however).[13] The *thrēnos* represents a different kind of performance by a group—an interchange between soloists and the rest of the mourners. In the last book of the *Iliad,* singers "lead off" the lament for Hektor, and the women deliver a moaning refrain (XXIV.719-22); and then, similarly, Andromakhe, Hekabe, and Helen utter solo laments that are followed in each case by the same refrain (XXIV. 723, 746-47, 760-61, 776).[14] The activities of the Muses are archetypes of human dance and song, which are under their patronage. It is therefore not surprising to find them engaging in all the kinds of performance mentioned above. The Muses dance (*Theog.* 3-8), sing while going in procession (*Theog.* 9-21, 68-75), dance while singing (choral song, *Theog.* 63-67), and sing a *thrēnos* for Achilles (xxiv.60-61).

We should think of these types of song as set in lyric meters, however, rather than in dactylic hexameter, which is not a choral or dance rhythm. Even the story of Ares and Aphrodite, recounted in hexameters so that it can be incorporated into the *Odyssey,* must be imagined as sung in a lyric meter, since it accompanies silent dancing.[15] The only performances likely to be in epic meter are the songs on heroic themes by Dēmodokos and by Phēmios in the *Odyssey* and by Achilles in the *Iliad* (IX.185-89), Hermes' celebration of his own birth (*h. Hermes* 54-61), which resembles several Homeric hymns in subject, and the theogony that the same god sings to Apollo (*h. Hermes* 423-33). These correspond to three types of hexameter poem that we possess. But our poems draw into themselves performances of every description, and thereby show song's intimate connection with all aspects of human life. The only important activity from which it is absent, in fact, is warfare.[16] It is as if the essence of every action and every occasion is best expressed by the song that adorns it.

Our concern here, however, is with hexameter poetry specifically; and the poems give us an impression of the circumstances and the manner of their performance. As to the former, we know that there were poetic competitions, for Hesiod won a tripod in a contest at the funeral games of Amphidamas (*W.D.* 654-59). It has been suggested that the poem he performed on that occasion was the *Theogony.*[17] This idea is agreeable, but a composition on a heroic subject would surely have been more suitable.[18] Contests must have been held frequently, and not only at funerals. Religious festivals would have provided another appropriate occasion. Performances of hexameter poetry took place at the Delian festival, for the poet of the *Hymn to Apollo,* and (to judge from lines 169-70) other singers as well, displayed their talents there, perhaps in competition. Some scholars have sought in such gatherings the solution to a difficult problem. The Homeric poems are so carefully constructed and so unified that they must be experienced as wholes to be appreciated. Continuous performance seems necessary to this end, yet the sheer length of the poems would have put such a feat beyond the power of any one singer and would have required an audience with the leisure and inclination to listen for many hours. The festivals at Delos and Mykalē have therefore been suggested as occasions when the poems could have been presented in their entirety by relays of singers, as was evidently done later at the Panathenaea in Athens.[19] On the other hand, Kirk (1962, 274-81) has argued that the *Iliad* took shape in informal settings (houses, taverns, or the marketplace) before popular audiences, and presumably it would have continued to be performed under those conditions. And the evidence provided by the *Odyssey* suggests that heroic epic was at home also as after-dinner entertainment in aristocratic houses. Actually, performances probably took place in all three settings. Thus everyone, at one time or another, would hear them; and the audience of this poetry must have ranged from the common people to the highest level of society.[20] Except, possibly, for rare occasions like festivals, the Homeric poems were probably presented piecemeal. Complete performances may have been given in installments after dinner on successive nights over several weeks, but only aristocrats would have had sufficient time at their disposal to listen. In other settings, individual episodes may often have been selected to fit what time was available. After people had heard enough of these partial performances—and they would have heard each selection many times over—they would have developed a sense of the whole poem. It was simply a matter of habituation, of living with the poetry long enough, as the Greeks of the archaic age plainly did. Conversely, after the *Iliad* and the *Odyssey* became widely known in this way, an audience hearing—for example—the exploits and death of Patroklos would have known where that episode fit in the design of the whole *Iliad,* and their response would have been shaped accordingly.

Their massive scale makes the Homeric epics exceptional. Shorter compositions, on both heroic and other subjects, must have been the usual fare, and these could have been performed in their entirety in the settings mentioned above. The *Theogony* would suit any of those occasions, as would the *Catalogue of Women,* the *Shield of Herakles* (if that was an independent piece in some bard's repertoire), and many of the poems that survive only in fragments. On the other hand, several works represent what we might call the popular substratum of hexameter poetry—the *Margitēs* (which was not purely in hexameters) or the *Precepts of Kheirōn,* for example—and these would surely have appealed more to popular than to aristocratic taste. The *Works and Days,* however, probably does not belong to this class, despite first impressions that tempt modern readers to view it as directed to a local audience of Boiotian peasants, with or without their rulers. The poem's real subject is the material and ethical order of the world and what a man must do to adapt to these conditions if he is to succeed. Hesiod's falling out with Persēs and his admonitions to the rulers are the pretext for this theme, and the agricultural and other practical advice is part of its development. The *Works and Days* can have appealed to a wide audience, although we can only speculate when and where it might have been performed.

The Homeric Hymns—or many of them anyway—seem to owe their existence to their role in poetic performances. Thucydides (3.104) refers to the *Hymn to Apollo* as a προοίμιον (*prooimion,* literally, "that which precedes the path," or *oimē*—the latter being a common term for song), and Pindar (on the most likely interpretation of his lines—*Nem.* 2.1-5, with scholium) indicates that the Homeridae, a school of rhapsodes who originally claimed descent from Homer, began their performances of epic with a *proomion* to Zeus. A number of hymns end with a formula of transition to "another song," and one such formula begins with the poet observing that he has "begun from" a god.[21] One of the shorter hymns to Aphrodite (no. 6) preceded a performance in a poetic competition, for at the end the poet prays to the goddess, "grant that I win the victory in this contest." The two hymns (31 and 32) that conclude with the poet's promise to celebrate *hēmitheoi* certainly introduced heroic epic. The character of these hymns as preludes gives us some insight into the structure of performances, but unfortunately any attempt to be precise about their role can only be speculation. Most scholars today would probably agree that the four long hymns as well as the shorter ones could have had this introductory function.[22] They might, for instance, have served as preludes to full-scale recitations of the Homeric poems; in such a setting the hymn would have been the first of the successive performances by individual rhapsodes.[23] The *Hymn to Apollo* offers a parallel to the sequence "praise of divinity—heroic narrative," and perhaps a clue to its own function, in the lyric performance of the Delian maidens (ll. 158-61). In the next chapter, reasons will be given for considering this internal song a reflection of the actual circumstances of the hymn's performance. There are, however, widely different theories on the relation between the longer and the shorter hymns (whether the one type developed from the other, and if so, which was prior), on the circumstances under which each type was used, and on what kind of poetry it introduced.[24] Whatever the solution to these questions may be, the hymns are a species of hexameter poetry in their own right, and share many basic characteristics with other poems in the same meter, as we have seen. And the important point to be made about their role in performances is that they established a link between poet and audience on the one hand and a god or gods on the other—a connection that was parallel to the singer's own relation with his patrons, the Muses, and that displayed the power that poetry was felt to have of mediating between the divine and the human.

With the hymns we have begun to move from the external circumstances to the way the poems were performed, and we must now consider this latter topic directly. To call a poet or performer a "singer" is to raise the question of his manner of delivery. Poets are always called ἀοιδοί (aoidoi, "singers") in our poems, and in descriptions of hexameter as well as of lyric performances they are usually said to "sing," ἀείδειν (aeidein), and to play the phorminx. Later on, however, at least by the time they had ceased creative activity and only reproduced the poetry of others, rhapsodes seem to have declaimed rather than to have sung, and to have held staffs instead of musical instruments. Some scholars have suggested that the transition between the two kinds of delivery was made in the eighth and seventh centuries B.C.[25] On this thesis, the poetic tradition, conservative as it was, continued to depict the old method. But none of the arguments necessarily outweighs the testimony of the poems themselves; and although the poems display archaizing tendencies in some respects, there is no need to think that their descriptions of performances reflect anything but contemporary practice. Pausanias's statements that Hesiod could not play the phorminx are not based on independent evidence but reflect a questionable inference from Theog. 30–31.[26] There Hesiod says that the Muses gave him a staff of laurel, but that is surely a symbol of inspiration rather than a rhapsode's staff.[27] Verbs meaning "say" or "tell," which are sometimes used in connection with poetic activity, refer primarily to the narrative content of a poem, not to the manner of delivery.[28] Nothing, then, stands in the way of thinking that descriptions of performances mirror the way the audience actually experienced the poems,[29] and there is actually one good reason to do so. As we shall see in the next chapter, these descriptions serve to remind the audience of what it means for them to be listening to a poem, and such a function implies a correspondence between the internal and the actual performance. A disparity between the two would have weakened this effect, though without doing away with it entirely.

It is not necessary, however, to imagine hexameter poems as sung in the way those in lyric meters were, although that should not be ruled out. They may have been delivered in recitative, halfway between speech and singing.[30] The phorminx, in that case, would have been used to set the rhythm, to fill pauses between parts of the poem, to provide emphasis at exciting or critical points, and conceivably even to clarify the structure of a passage by stressing musically the similarities between corresponding phrases and lines.[31] As for this instrument itself, Max Wegner (1968, 2–16), has given an admirable and persuasive account. The normal term for it in Homer, and elsewhere in hexameter poetry, is phorminx, not kithara (which, like lyra and barbiton, would represent a later type). The instrument contemporary with at least the Homeric and Hesiodic poems would have been the one with four strings pictured in geometric vase paintings. Somewhat later, the number of strings was increased to seven, an innovation attributed by Strabo to Terpander, who flourished in the second quarter of the seventh century B.C. The *Hymn to Hermes* assumes this later form; the phorminx that Hermes there ostensibly invents has seven strings (*h. Hermes* 51).

Besides the musical accompaniment and the mode of delivery, a number of other aspects of performance would have colored the audience's experience of the poetry. Among the elements discussed in this connection by Ruth Finnegan (1977, 122-26) are the atmosphere and the demands of the occasion, the performer's relation to the audience, the speed of his delivery, his pauses, rhythmic movements, gestures, and facial expressions, and the amount of "dramatic characterization" he attempts to give to heroes of narrative poetry. We have no direct evidence about such effects, for (as Finnegan also observes), operating as they generally do at a level below the conscious awareness of performer and audience, they would naturally not be mentioned in descriptions of performances. But we must keep them in mind if we are to imagine what performances must have been like. They make all the difference between a live performance experienced by members of a group and the solitary reading of the bare words of a text.

For detailed descriptions of performances we must look to the *Odyssey,* although in some respects we can supplement the information offered there with parallels from other poems. In the *Odyssey,* performances of hexameter poetry follow the main part of a meal, and the diners listen quietly as they drink their wine. The contrast between this kind of entertainment and one that includes dancing may be observed in the opening book. When we first see the suitors, they enter Odysseus's hall and enjoy a feast. Then they sing and dance (the words that describe their activity are μολπή and ὀρχηστύς, *molpē* and *orkhēstus*), following the lead of Phēmios's song and harping (i.150-55). This song is clearly in a lyric meter. The suitors continue to amuse themselves in this way during Telemakhos's conversation with Athena, but after the goddess departs, the character of the performance changes. Phēmios sings the Returns of the Akhaians—surely a hexameter poem—while the suitors "sat listening in silence" (i.325-27).

A line used of Dēmodokos indicates how such a performance might start: ὁ δ᾽ ὁρμηθεὶς θεοῦ ἄρχετο, φαῖνε δ᾽ ἀοιδήν, "setting out, he began from the god, and revealed his song" (viii.499).[32] Dēmodokos either invokes the Muses (as in the opening lines of the *Odyssey* itself and of other poems) or begins with a brief prelude like one of the shorter Homeric Hymns.[33] The latter possibility would not rule out an invocation to the Muse at the outset of the song proper. Another phrase for "he began to sing," though more problematical, perhaps implies something similar: ἀνεβάλλετο . . . ἀείδειν (*aneballeto . . . aeidein,* i.155, xvii.262, viii.266—the last in a melic performance). The main verb may mean no more than "he began";[34] but it may also refer to a prelude (*anabolē*). Those who understand the verb in this sense usually take it to imply the playing of a few preliminary notes on the phorminx to set the pitch and rhythm.[35] Such a prelude is more likely to have been sung than instrumental, however, and it would therefore have been, once again, an invocation or brief praise of a divinity.[36] The wording of viii.499, then, is probably an alternative to this phrase, with essentially the same meaning.

The listeners might be silent while the poet is singing, but they are not wholly passive. They make their contribution to the poem. The singer pauses at convenient places, such as the end of an episode, and then it is up to the audience whether he continues with more of the story. Thus in his song on the quarrel of Odysseus and Achilles, Dēmodokos stops several times. Whenever he does so, the Phaiakians urge him to continue, for "they took delight in his words" (viii.87–92). The span of the audience's attention, their willingness to sit and listen or their restlessness, determines the length of the song, the degree of elaboration or compression of its narrative and themes. Openness to influence of this kind has been recognized as characteristic of oral poetry in general. "The essential element of the occasion of singing that influences the form of the poetry," writes Lord, "is the variety and instability of the audience."[37] Dēmodokos is favored with a singularly stable audience; the Phaiakians are tireless listeners to song (viii.248). In this instance, however, and during his later song on the Trojan Horse, one member of the audience, Odysseus, weeps, and his response prompts Alkinoos to bring the performance to an end.

Besides the formal aspects, inferences can also be drawn about the content of performances. A subject can be chosen either by the listeners' request (viii.492–95), so that here too the audience can play an important role, or by the singer's own impulse—his *noos* (i.347) or *thumos* (viii.45), or the Muse who inspires him (viii.73–74). In asking Dēmodokos to sing the story of the Trojan Horse, Odysseus requests an incident from a larger whole, and this, as was suggested earlier, must have been the character of many an epic performance. Dēmodokos, complying, chooses an appropriate point in the narrative from which to begin, "taking up the tale from the time when" the Greeks had burnt their huts and pretended to leave for home in frustration (ἔνθεν ἑλών, *enthen helōn*, viii.500). In the same way, the poet of the *Odyssey*, in his own exordium, asks his Muse to tell of the matters to which he has just alluded "from some point" (ἁμόθεν, *hamothen*), and in the next line he begins his narrative with an emphatic "then" (ἔνθα, *entha*, i.10–11). At least ostensibly, he is showing us the process by which he settles into his narrative, and he does so in a way that implies a certain attitude towards his material. The story that he is to treat is regarded as a continuum, from which he (or the Muse) will select a segment as material for the present poem. This notion faithfully reflects the idea that individual poems, in aggregate, formed a comprehensive unity, so that they could be and sometimes were linked together. (See Chapter 2, Section h, above.)

The same conception evidently underlies the references in this poetry to a song, and more precisely to its narrative subject, as an οἴμη (*oimē*, viii.74;

cf. *h. Hermes* 451)—a usage that survives in the term *pro-oimion*. Similarly, the poetic art is considered the knowledge of *oimai*, which are presumably all the potential themes for song (viii.481, xxii.347). According to the commonly accepted derivation, this word means "path."[38] If this explanation is correct, the term may be associated with several verbs that imply motion and are used in a faintly metaphorical way to describe poetic creation. When he asks Dēmodokos to alter his subject from the sufferings of the Akhaians to the Wooden Horse, Odysseus says literally "come now and change direction" (μετάβηϑι, *metabethi*, viii.492), and at the end of several Homeric Hymns a stock phrase of transition from praise of a god to the main recitation uses the same verb, μεταβήσομαι (*metabēsomai*, "I shall change course"—e.g., *h. Aphr.* 293). Poetry itself is once spoken of as something that can be trodden: Hesiod says that the Muses "set his foot upon" song (ἐπέβησαν, *epebēsan*, *W.D.* 659). (Cf. xxii.424—with Stanford's note—and xxiii.13, 52.)

The possible subjects for song, then, make up an area that is traversed by paths. This implied image expresses the fundamental unity in the raw material of this poetry. All conceivable poems when combined might cover this entire area—that is, exhaust these subjects; in this way the mass of stories and other topics would be given definite form. Any one poem treats only a part of this material, but presents it in a clear and consecutive order. That is what the notion of a "path" seems to imply, and we can understand this order in two complementary senses. On the one hand, we can refer it to the poem's structure, the paratactic linking of discrete passages that conform in shape to the traditional compositional patterns. On the other hand, there is the kind of ordering of the content that originated in oral composition. As Lord has shown, the elements of a theme are grouped in a typical sequence, and theme follows theme according to the logic of the narrative. The plot of the entire poem, moreover, might be based on a traditional story pattern.[39]

Thus, no matter how small the scale of the performance, the members of the audience would understand what they heard in relation to the larger whole, which was always present to their minds, though not necessarily consciously. From a lifelong habit of listening to such performances, they would know, on each occasion, the place of the episode within the poem, and of the poem within the traditional body of poetry.

Any new song that came to their ears would also find a place within this overall framework. Poetry, as the poems themselves represent it, is thus a living process; it is always being brought up to date by the incorporation of new events as they happen, and these events in turn are given meaning by being put in a historical and artistic context. They can therefore be viewed as part of a coherent human history; in this way they can be understood in retrospect by the actors in them and by subsequent generations. Even the act of fitting accounts of recent occurrences to the requirements of poetic narrative is part of the way in which poetry makes discoveries about life and explains it. For the new story must be told by means of the traditional themes, motifs, and language, so that its outlines are seen to be perfectly familiar. Whatever there may be in it that is new or surprising or perplexing is limited and controlled by the strongly generic character of the narrative medium. And so despite individual variations, the new event turns out to have resemblances and analogies to other events that poetry has made part of the audience's experience.

The first song by Demodokos that Odysseus hears concerns the recent past (viii.72–75):

αὐτὰρ ἐπεὶ πόσιος καὶ ἐδητύος ἐξ ἔρον ἔντο,
Μοῦσ' ἄρ ἀοιδὸν ἀνῆκεν ἀειδέμεναι κλέα ἀνδρῶν,
οἴμης τῆς τότ' ἄρα κλέος οὐρανὸν εὐρὺν ἵκανε
νεῖκος Ὀδυσσῆος καὶ Πηλεΐδεω Ἀχιλῆος.

But when they had put off the desire for food and drink,
the Muse set the bard to singing the fames of men [klea andrōn] ,
from [40] the song-path [oimē] of which the fame [kleos] was then reaching
   the wide heaven,
the quarrel of Odysseus and Pēleus's son Achilles.

The phrase klea andrōn puts this quarrel, an incident purportedly from contemporary life, into the mainstream of epic tradition. If an action is great enough in the achievement it represents or in its consequences, it merits a place, secured for it by poetry, among the deeds of past generations. And audiences evidently enjoy hearing the very latest stories. As Telemakhos tells his mother in connection with another song on a contemporary theme (i.351–52):

τὴν γὰρ ἀοιδὴν μᾶλλον ἐπικλείουσ' ἄνθρωποι,
ἥ τις ἀκουόντεσσι νεωτάτη ἀμφιπέληται.

Men give more fame [epikleiousi] to whatever song
comes newest about the listeners' ears.

Novelty of subject is prized, but not necessarily—or even probably—originality of treatment. A good singer would be one who can assimilate new stories to the traditional techniques, who can break them down into component themes and, on the level of line-by-line composition, retell them in the formulaic diction. The test of his skill is his ability to deliver, on demand, a well-formed and effective song about any subject. His capacity to absorb new themes from other poets explains rationally how it is that in the world of the Odyssey and of hexameter poetry in general, song can "come about" the ears as though it were simply in the air. But we need to respect also the way poetry was originally experienced by both poet and audience: as a numinous presence. This quality could be sensed in the person of the singer himself. It derived from the source and the nature of his gift.

The singer is inspired by the Muses. This relationship implies a certain conception of poetry but needs to be carefully defined.[41] The Muses bestow, in the first instance, the ability to sing, which is referred to as a "divine voice" in this Hesiodic fragment (fr. 310):

Μουσάων, αἵ τ' ἄνδρα πολυφραδέοντα τιθεῖσι
θέσπιον αὐδήεντα

... of the Muses, who make a man very eloquent [or "very wise"],
divinely articulate [thespion audēenta]

The last two words resemble the "divine voice" (αὐδὴν θέσπιν, audēn thespin) that the Muses "breathed into" Hesiod (Theog. 31–32). But the Muses' aid only begins here. Having given a man the capacity for song, they still must help him put it into practice on each occasion by giving him knowledge of the particular subject that he is to treat. So, for example, the Muse "set [Dēmodokos] to singing the fames of men" (viii.73); perhaps in the verb ἀνῆκεν we should understand something of its common meaning, "to release." Similarly, Hesiod, who has previously received the gift of song so that he might sing of past and future, must invoke the Muses afresh before the main part of the performance that has come down to us as his Theogony (ll. 104–15). In this way also we should interpret the invocations that begin the Iliad and the Odyssey.

Begging Odysseus for his life, Phēmios describes his art in this way (xxii. 347–48):

αὐτοδίδακτος δ' εἰμί, θεὸς δέ μοι ἐν φρεσὶν οἴμας
παντοίας ἐνέφυσεν.

I am self-taught [autodidaktos], and in my mind a god planted
the varied song paths [oimai].

It is tempting to find differentiated in the two clauses of this sentence the humanly attained and the divinely inspired aspects of poetry respectively. To the former would correspond the technical skill, such as mastery of the formulae, that makes poetry a craft. The Muses' contribution, on the other hand, would be knowledge of stories, the oimai.[42] It is, however, doubtful that the poets' absorption of the formular technique was a conscious enough process to allow a distinction to be made between form and content. The word autodidaktos, moreover, should not be taken to mean a purely personal acquisition of knowledge that is independent of external aid, as the English phrase "self-taught" would imply, although some scholars have even interpreted it as Homer's own claim to originality as against other poets in the use of the traditional techniques.[43] In this context, autodidaktos is more likely to signify an innate ability exercised spontaneously, without the conscious will.

That is clearly the word's implication when Aeschylus uses it in connection with song. The chorus of the *Agamemnon* describe the way a part of them expresses fear involuntarily, without their conscious knowledge of its cause (*Ag.* 990-94):[44]

τὸν δ᾽ ἄνευ λύρας ὅμως ὑμνῳδεῖ
θρῆνον Ἐρινύος αὐτοδίδακτος ἔσωθεν
θυμός, οὐ τὸ πᾶν ἔχων
ἐλπίδος φίλον θράσος.

But from within, my spirit [*thumos*], self-taught [*autodidaktos*],
sings the lament of the Erinys, the song without a lyre,
for it entirely lacks the cherished confidence inspired by hope.

The *thumos,* the spirited, irrational component of man's inner organization, sings this unmusical song of foreboding independently of the personality as a whole. Here *autodidaktos* means almost the same as "of its own accord."[45] In the Odyssean line also it probably implies the welling up of song from inside the singer, without his deliberate control. The two clauses of Phēmios's sentence thus describe the same thing—song, without distinction between language and content—from rather different, but not irreconcilable, views of its cause.[46] For it makes little difference whether song is referred to an inner source or an external, divine agency. These are simply alternative ways of talking about a talent that depends on something beyond the mortal's conscious intent. Thus Robert Fitzgerald's rendering of "I am *autodidaktos*" is true to the underlying idea: "no one taught me."[47]

It would be carrying this concept of inspiration too far, however, to imagine the poet in the act of creation as being in a state of ecstasy or divine madness. Plato, who for reasons of his own depicted Homer and other poets in this way, has made the idea familiar to us, but our hexameter texts give it no support.[48] Still, they do represent song as something mysterious, and hence often as divine, in origin. At the same time, they occasionally use language that suggests that poetry is a skill that can somehow be acquired.[49] A Hesiodic fragment (fr. 306), for example, describes the singer Linos as παντοίης σοφίης δεδαηκότα, "learned [*dedaēkota*] in every kind of skill [*sophiē*]." Hermes uses similar terms when he gives the phorminx to Apollo (*h. Hermes* 482-88). This instrument must be approached by one who is τέχνῃ καὶ σοφίῃ δεδαημένος, "Learned [*dedaēmenos*] in art [*tekhnē*] and skill [*sophiē*]." It must be played with a gentle touch made possible by familiarity, and it "flees painful laboriousness."[50] Apollo is the ideal recipient of the phorminx. Whatever he wants to know (δαήμεναι, *daēmenai*) is αὐτάγρετον (*autagreton*) for him: he can grasp it for himself, because he has a natural talent for learning this kind of skill (*h. Hermes* 474, 489). (On *autagreton,* see Görgemanns, 1976, 124.) Thus *autagreton,* which shares with *autodidaktos* the prefix "self-", refers, like that word, to an inner, not wholly rational quality. The "learning" of song should therefore not be reduced to the acquisition of a mere technique that can be conveyed by instruction to just anyone. Gods, in fact, can be said to "teach" (διδάσκειν, *didaskein*) song to mortals (*Theog.* 22, *W.D.* 662, viii.488). No contradiction is felt, then, between learning an art and receiving it through inspiration. Especially when we have freed ourselves from thinking of poetic creation as ecstatic, we can understand that skill, arising both from practical experience and from an innate aptitude, is a necessary complement to divine intervention. Gods, after all, would hardly favor with their gifts mortals who were not by nature worthy of them and able to receive them.

Once again, it would be misleading to suggest that the singer acquires through training the technical aspects of his art, whereas the Muses provide him with the content of each song. We know, after all, that composition by theme, which helps to determine content, is part of the oral poet's technique. And, on the other hand, knowledge of formulae and the ability to use them are basic to the capacity for song and ought properly to come under the Muses' patronage. Yet although dexterous handling of the formulaic diction was doubtless part of a song's charm, the hexameter poets appear simply to assume it when they describe their art. They emphasize instead, as the Muses' gift to them, knowledge that no man could possess unaided. The poet's dependence on a divine source for this knowledge is well expressed in the invocation to the Catalogue of Ships in the *Iliad* (II.484–87):

ἔσπετε νῦν μοι, Μοῦσαι Ὀλύμπια δώματ᾽ ἔχουσαι—
ὑμεῖς γὰρ θεαί ἐστε, πάρεστέ τε, ἴστε τε πάντα,
ἡμεῖς δὲ κλέος οἶον ἀκούομεν οὐδέ τι ἴδμεν—
οἵ τινες ἡγεμόνες Δαναῶν καὶ κοίρανοι ἦσαν.

Tell me now, Muses who dwell on Olympos—
for you are goddesses, and are present everywhere,[51] and you know all
     things,
but we hear only the fame [*kleos*] and know nothing—
who were leaders and rulers of the Danaans.

As goddesses and hence outside of time, the Muses are present at all events and have direct knowledge of them. Mortals can hear only the report of what happened in the remote past or what is happening in the present outside the range of their perception. *Kleos,* which came to mean "fame," is literally "that which is heard" (it derives from *kluein,* "to hear"). And yet when the Muses aid the singer and give him knowledge of the truth (an important precondition, as we shall see in the next chapter), his tale takes on the quality of an account by an eyewitness. That is the substance of Odysseus's speech in praise of Dēmodokos, which is perhaps the clearest statement in hexameter poetry of what makes a poem good (viii.487–91):

Δημόδοκ', ἔξοχα δή σε βροτῶν αἰνίζομ' ἀπάντων·
ἢ σέ γε Μοῦσ' ἐδίδαξε, Διὸς πάϊς, ἢ σέ γ' Ἀπόλλων.
λίην γὰρ κατὰ κόσμον Ἀχαιῶν οἶτον ἀείδεις,
ὅσσ' ἔρξαν τ' ἔπαθόν τε καὶ ὅσσ' ἐμόγησαν Ἀχαιοί,
ὥς τέ που ἢ αὐτὸς παρεὼν ἢ ἄλλου ἀκούσας.

Dēmodokos, I admire you above all other mortals;
either the Muse, Zeus's daughter, taught [*edidaxe*] you, or Apollo.
For you sing the fate of the Akhaians very much as is fitting [*kata
    kosmon*],
all the Akhaians' deeds and sufferings and labors,
as if you yourself had been there or had heard it from someone else.

With these words Odysseus pays tribute to the quality of Dēmodokos's inspiration, and he, if anyone, is a competent judge. Himself a participant in the
events at Troy, he can attest that Dēmodokos sings of them "fittingly," *kata
kosmon*—not just in proper sequence, but "accurately," "truly," as the last
line of the quotation demonstrates.[52] Similarly, Odysseus goes on to say that
if the singer can also tell the story of the Wooden Horse truly (*kata moiran*),
he himself will tell all men that a god has favored Dēmodokos with "divine
song" (*thespin aoidēn*: cf. *Theog.* 31-32, Hesiod fr. 310, cited earlier). A
singer in remote Phaiakia could have such accurate knowledge only by divine
aid, and Odysseus's speech shows vividly why the power of song was experienced as something unearthly. Hesiod also undertakes to explain to Persēs
the safe seasons for navigation, even though his own experience of sailing has
been—to say the least—scanty. But he does not need practical knowledge. He
has something better: the Muses' instruction, which enables him to "tell the
mind of Zeus who holds the aegis" (*W.D.* 660-62).

The Sirens, who are, like the Muses, both goddesses and singers, know all
that happens on earth, in both the past and the present. Thus they can tempt
Odysseus with a song like those he will later hear from Dēmodokos—one on
events that occurred in the recent past and far away at Troy (xii.189-91).
Mortal singers also receive, by divine inspiration, the knowledge that the Sirens
possess by themselves, and they share something of the gods' omniscience. In
this way they resemble seers. Like seers, poets can tell "the things that are,
the things that will be, and the things that were in the past." The phrase used
in the *Iliad* of Kalkhas's gift (I.70) describes in Hesiod the Muses' song on
Olympos, and the song they teach him to sing is referred to in nearly identical
terms (*Theog.* 38, 32). Appropriately, Apollo's provinces include both music
and prophecy (*h. Apollo* 131-32).[53]

Its extraordinary qualities mean that song will have a powerful effect on
the listener. The words most frequently used in this connection portray song
as arousing pleasure: τέρπειν (*terpein*), "to give delight"; τέρπεσθαι (*terpesthai*), "to take delight in" a thing or activity; and the noun τέρψις (*terpsis*),

"delight." [54] This pleasure has several forms, however. It manifests itself most basically, but still significantly, as sensual pleasure. In this respect song is akin to love and erotic desire—ἔρος (eros) or ἵμερος (himeros). The Hymn to Hermes stresses this aspect of song especially (ll. 422, 434, 449), but music is linked with the "gifts of Aphrodite" as a typically unwarlike pursuit in the Iliad (III.54) also. [55] Himeros, along with the Graces, lives near the Muses on Olympos (Theog. 64)—the same god who, with Eros, accompanied Aphrodite when she first went among the gods after her birth (Theog. 201). But because of its divine origin, song naturally has the power also to enchant, θέλγειν (thelgein), as, for example, the Delian maidens "enchant [thelgousi] the races of men" by singing the men and women of old (h. Apollo 160–61). Odysseus experiences the magical effect of the Sirens' song, and Kirkē has told him beforehand that they enchant (thelgousin) all who hear them (xii.39–40). Kirkē herself sings at her loom, and the sound entices Odysseus's comrades to her (x.220–31) so that she can work her spell on them with her drugs and her wand. A magic charm, in fact, is an ἐπαοιδή (epaoidē), a "singing over" someone (xix.457, where the charm is used in healing). As these examples indicate, and as we shall have occasion to observe again, so potent is song's magic that it can be a great blessing for men, but also very dangerous.

And finally, according to Hesiod, poetry soothes mental pain. It causes men to forget their sorrows by distracting them with tales about men of former days and about the gods (Theog. 55, 98–103). The Hymn to Hermes shows, in rather a lighthearted way, the exercise of this power. When the conflict between himself and his brother has reached an impasse and threatens to turn violent, [56] Hermes calms Apollo by playing the phorminx and singing a theogony (h. Hermes 416–18). In a speech full of wonder at what he has heard, Apollo asks, "what craft is this, what charm [literally, Muse] against overwhelming cares?" (l. 447). [57] In a more serious capacity, song provides mortals with a means of offsetting the woe that is an inevitable part of their condition. This benefit is a particular application of song's power to delight and to enchant, but it is surely the most important one.

What is the relation of all these kinds of pleasure to the knowledge that poetry also conveys? How is it that Hesiod suggests that song bestows understanding of the world, yet speaks explicitly only of consolation as song's effect? The two are not incompatible, of course; the Sirens promise Odysseus both pleasure and knowledge (xii.188), and Hermes says that the phorminx, when rightly handled, "teaches all sorts of things delightful to the mind" (h. Hermes 484). The former passage in particular has been interpreted as reflecting the archaic Greek's pleasure in knowledge, so that instruction is part of poetry's delight. [58] This explanation, while undoubtedly correct, is perhaps not complete. Many of the amusements with which poetry is associated may strike us as frivolous, and our texts themselves represent it as the antithesis of war and athletic competition, where reputation is won through physical prowess (for example, viii.246–49). Nevertheless, feasting, dancing, and above all song, which accompanies them, compensate for the woes that afflict mankind, blunt their pain. Similarly, the understanding offered by poetry at least partly offsets men's natural ignorance and helplessness. Some poems celebrate (κλείεω, *kleiein*, "spread the *kleos* of," *Theog*. 32, 44, 67, 105) the gods and thus inform men of the divine powers at work in the world. On such knowledge, the successful individual life and the aggregate of those lives—the entire social order—must be based. Heroic poetry perpetuates the *kleos* of outstanding men. It thus preserves the individual's name beyond his own death, and provides succeeding generations with knowledge of human history and with exemplary patterns of conduct. Pleasure and understanding, therefore, have this in common, that they are both ways of extending mortal limits. They may do so in slightly different ways, but as effects of poetry they are practically inseparable. Both as a means of knowing the world and as the epitome of the pleasures that men in community share with one another, poetry is the expression of civilization—that is, of all those values and institutions that save human life from hopelessness and chaos. [59]

This conception of poetry explains the way these poems portray the most imposing figure at a performance, whose presence we have so far taken for granted: the poet. Men who follow this calling are highly respected, and Odysseus explains the reason to the herald by whom he sends Dēmodokos a choice piece of meat (viii.479–81):

πᾶσι γὰρ ἀνϑρώποισιν ἐπιχϑονίοισιν ἀοιδοὶ
τιμῆς ἔμμοροί εἰσι καὶ αἰδοῦς, οὕνεκ' ἄρα σφέας
οἴμας Μοῦσ' ἐδίδαξε, φίλησε δὲ φῦλον ἀοιδῶν.

For in the eyes of all men on earth singers
have a share of honor and reverence, because
the Muse teaches them the paths [*oimai*], and cherishes the race of singers.

The signs of divine favor that the singer bears ensure his value to the community and make him a central figure within it. In a famous passage, Eumaios ranks him (along with the seer, the physician, and the carpenter) as one whom—in contrast to a beggar—a man would voluntarily summon to his home from afar (xvii.382–87). Dēmodokos's name literally means "welcomed by the people [*dēmos*]," [60] and that he must be summoned (presumably from the town) to Alkinoos's palace (viii.43–44) indicates that he is not just a court poet who provides amusement to aristocrats in their idle hours. The existence of contests also implies that poetry is a profession, as does the inclusion of singers with potters, builders, and also with beggars [61] in Hesiod's list of those whom the good Eris spurs to healthy and productive competition (*W.D.* 25–26).

Speaking to the Delian maidens in his own person, the poet of the *Hymn to Apollo* gives a vivid picture of himself and his activity. First, he may be competing formally with other singers at the Delian festival, but even if he is not, it is at least clear from his words that he expects to be measured against them. He asks the Delian maidens to say that he is the "most pleasing" singer who comes to the island, that they delight (τέρπεσθαι, terpesthai) in him the most (ll. 169-70), and that his songs are the best (l. 173). In the second place, he travels (ll. 174-75). Poets must have been itinerant, going from one festival or contest to another in order to display their skill and win reputation, and to whatever towns or wealthy houses would receive them and offer them a livelihood. We find Homer and Hesiod leading this kind of life in the *Contest of Homer and Hesiod* and in the pseudo-Herodotean *Life of Homer*. This wandering was clearly an important means for disseminating poetry, and thus for spreading knowledge of men and events, those of the distant past right down to and including the present. The poet of the *Hymn to Apollo* himself offers to transmit among all men he encounters the Delian maidens' "glory" (*kleos*, l. 174). In fact, he is doing just that in the hymn itself, as well as spreading his own fame by the words he tells them to utter.

The Delian maidens deserve *kleos* by virtue of their skill as performers of poetry; the earlier description of their performance began with the assurance that their *kleos* would never die (*h. Apollo* 156). Apparently they, and (what is more pertinent here) hexameter poets, can achieve the kind of glory that we usually think of as the special reward of the epic hero. The poet of the hymn resembles the hero in having his eye on his future reputation and in imagining what others will say about him.[62] When he tells the maidens how to praise his songs, he uses the verb ἀριστεύειν (*aristeuein*, l. 173) for "be the best," which, along with the related adjective ἄριστος (*aristos*), is one of the catchwords in epic for heroic excellence.[63] Furthermore, in the *Odyssey* a member of the audience, Odysseus, promises to tell all men among whom he travels about Dēmodokos's distinction as an inspired poet (viii.496-98). A song itself can be given *kleos;* Telemakhos says that men "celebrate more" (ἐπικλείουσι, *epikleiousi*, literally "give more *kleos* to," i.351) the newest song. It may be a reflex of this conception of the singer's fame that, as several writers have recently pointed out, ancient biographies of poets depict their subjects as though they were heroes of cult (Nagy, 1979, 301-8) or of epic (Austin, 1975, 248-49). More is involved in this matter than self-promotion by individual poets. One who came into contact with divinity, and through his gift enabled others to do so, might understandably be looked upon as above the level of ordinary men. Another explanation might also be suggested that is not incompatible with this one. There is a reciprocal relation between the song and its subject that is so close that they practically become identical.[64] If a poem is to fulfill its function and confer glory, and hence a kind of immortality, upon those it celebrates, it must earn fame itself by being spread among men. And so the poet, in his striving and achieving, naturally takes on the qualities of his heroes. The moment when these interests intersect and reinforce one another, the medium for furthering them, is the performance.

Small wonder, then, that (as the next chapter will show) the poems often call attention to themselves, their nature and purpose.

The poet of the *Hymn to Apollo* is blind (l. 172). This is evidently not a conventional characteristic of the singer—Phēmios in the *Odyssey* is not blind nor, as far as we know, was Hesiod, although legend has it that Homer was. What would a poet's blindness have meant when it did occur? Guided, perhaps, by Sophocles' depiction of Teiresias, we are accustomed to think of sightlessness in such cases as a sign of superior inner vision.[65] The description of Dēmodokos, however, suggests another meaning, one more pertinent to the concerns of hexameter poetry (viii.62-64):

κῆρυξ δ᾽ ἐγγύθεν ἦλθεν ἄγων ἐρίηρον ἀοιδόν,
τὸν πέρι Μοῦσ᾽ ἐφίλησε, δίδου δ᾽ ἀγαθόν τε κακόν τε ·
ὀφθαλμῶν μὲν ἄμερσε, δίδου δ᾽ ἡδεῖαν ἀοιδήν.

The herald approached, leading the trusty singer,
whom the Muse favored above all, and she gave him both good and ill:
she deprived him of his eyesight, and gave him sweet song.

Song, then, is a divine gift and must therefore, by its nature, be ambivalent; it cannot come as an unmixed blessing. Moreover, like all such gifts that set certain mortals apart from most of their kind, the good fortune it confers can turn to disaster when its power in one way or another proves too strong for mere men. Thus blindness can be a token of the Muses' punishment of a former favorite, as the story of Thamyris shows (II.594-600). Encountering the Muses, he was led by his skill, their gift, to boast that he could surpass even them in song. Angry, they blinded him, took song away from him, and "made him forget" how to play the phorminx. Though usually benevolent to men, the Muses can display jealousy of their privileges like any other gods. The divinities who give have the power also to deprive; and outstanding favor, when abused or scorned, can turn into terrible persecution. In this respect, song is no different from the sexual fascination Aphrodite bestows on Helen (III.413-17). We shall find these same ideas—that the Muses have characteristics typical of all gods and that their gift is ambivalent—in the introduction to Hesiod's *Theogony*, the most remarkable statement by a hexameter poet about the nature and function of his art.

5 The Poets on Their Art, II:

The Introduction to Hesiod's Theogony *and the Self-Reflectiveness of Hexameter Poetry*

IF WE WISH TO DEEPEN OUR UNDERSTANDING of the hexameter poets' conception of their craft and also to appreciate why they so often describe poetic performances, we can do no better than to consider in detail the opening section, or "proem," of the *Theogony* (ll. 1-115). Any student of hexameter poetry—or of Greek poetry in general—will find himself returning again and again to this extraordinary passage. It is a subtle and complex account of what the existence of poetry and its manifestation in particular performances imply for men and their world.

Yet the complexities make understanding difficult: the many repetitions of words and phrases within the passage, for instance, and the unusual autobiographical material in lines 22-35. Hesiod's question to himself in line 35 (the precise meaning of which is uncertain) halts the narrative abruptly, and the next line contains what appears to be a new beginning. From that point on, moreover, Hesiod depicts the Muses as inhabiting Olympos, whereas in the opening lines he put them on Mount Helikon. On these grounds, scholars —especially Analytical critics—for many years could not accept the passage as a unified composition. Today the verbal repetitions do not trouble us much because of what we know about formulaic diction. As for the other features, in 1914 Paul Friedländer went far toward explaining them when he drew attention to the presence of the conventional formal elements of the hymn. He argued that lines 36-115 contain a typical hymn to the Muses, with all the traditional elements succeeding one another in the normal order. Hesiod prefaced this ordinary hymn, however, with lines 1-35, which also display hymnic characteristics but are atypical in content, expressing as they do his individual experience of a poetic vocation.[1] Others have addressed the problem of Hesiod's association of the Muses with the two mountains. It has been suggested that he was trying to reconcile a local cult of these goddesses with the epic tradition that placed them on Olympos[2] or, alternatively, that he was identifying mountain nymphs of Helikon with the Muses of Olympian religion.[3] Both ideas are pure speculation; and they are open to the considerable objection that Hesiod refers to the Muses as Olympian as early as line 25, just when he describes his encounter with them in the foothills of Helikon, so that a sharp distinction between Helikonian and Olympian Muses cannot be maintained.[4] There is, nevertheless, a shift from one mountain to the other as the focus of the Muses' activities; but it is unnecessary to seek an explanation outside the poem. One will be suggested later that has to do with the internal organization and the meaning of the proem itself.

Valuable and humane though his discussion is, Friedländer's solution is unsatisfactory in one important way: it leaves the passage as a whole awkwardly divided into two unrelated parts. (Sharp structural divisions are normal in this poetry, but there should be an overarching unity. Friedländer himself concedes at the outset that Hesiod's thinking was contradictory and the form of his poems imperfect.) More recent writers have followed his approach, studying the formal elements in order, as one of them puts it, "to show that the whole of the proem is an integrated hymn or hymn-complex, with the opening hymn to Hesiod's native Muses of Helicon . . . interrupted upon his consecration as poet by a 'dramatic' hymn to the Olympian Muses."[5] This view has the advantage of discovering unity in the passage, if not complete coherence (the word *interrupted* is somewhat disquieting). It takes for granted, however, the difference in cults of the Muses and depicts this as determining the poetic form. Whether this assumption is necessary to the thesis as a whole is not clear, but it does weaken the argument. Other scholars have examined the passage from the point of view of its structure, and have sought to prove its unity by arguing that its parts are arranged in ring composition.[6]

That Hesiod made sophisticated use of hymnic conventions seems to have been convincingly demonstrated. We can recognize this fact and at the same time take the complementary approach of considering how the various sections of the proem are related to one another. Although the case for a ring pattern in the passage as a whole seems weak, the composition here is unified and coherent. We must pay close attention to the structure in order to demonstrate this unity, but more importantly in order to understand what Hesiod is suggesting about poetry. For this passage offers a wonderful example of how the hexameter poets express meaning through formal techniques.

Let us begin at lines 35 and 36, where Hesiod makes a fresh start in his celebration of the Muses and has been thought to shift from one type of hymn to another. There is undeniably a division here, but Hesiod's interruption of himself and his new beginning are simply a way of moving from his own experience of the Muses (ll. 22-35) to the description of their usual activities on Olympos (ll. 36-52). In fact Hesiod carefully relates these two sections to one another by an interesting use of ring composition. The echo in line 51 of line 37 rounds off the description of the Muses' song on Olympos, so that the divine scene is a self-contained whole juxtaposed with the goddesses' epiphany on Helikon. But an outer frame, which encloses both sections and binds them together, is provided by the repetition of line 25 in line 52 ("the Olympian Muses, daughters of Zeus who wields the aegis"). Moreover, the break in thought after line 35 is not so sharp as might at first appear but is subtly smoothed over. As Hans Schwabl has pointed out, lines 36–39 repeat in inverse order the ideas, and in three instances the phrasing, of lines 31–34.[7] Thus, as the content of these corresponding groups of lines indicates, the song that the Muses enable Hesiod to sing is the same as the one with which they delight Zeus (ll. 32, 38); and that means that Hesiod's performance, which will turn out to be the *Theogony* itself, is a human copy of the often-repeated divine archetype. "Let us begin from the Muses" (l. 36) shows Hesiod carrying out the Muses' injuction to "sing them first and last" (l. 34)—as he has already begun to do in the first line of the poem. Line 36 thus represents less a fresh start than a return to the beginning after Hesiod has finished his account of the Muses' gift to him of poetry. It reminds us that the poem already under way is part of the song they commanded him to sing. The *Theogony* is the product of that visionary experience.

There is a sharper structural division after line 52. Reference to the Muses as Zeus's daughters leads naturally into the narrative of their birth, and we shall later find connections between what precedes and what follows this point. But just as line 52, with line 25, marks off the intervening material as a discrete whole, the next sections are also enclosed by ring composition on a large scale. The motifs of memory and forgetfulness implied by the name of the Muses' mother (Μνημοσύνη, Mnēmosyne, l. 54) and the phrase that describes their own essential nature (λησμοσύνην τε κακῶν, lesmosunēn te kakōn, l. 55) are repeated in inverse order in lines 102–3: ἐπιλήθεται, οὐδέ τι κηδέων / μέμνηται, epilēthetai, oude ti kedeōn / memnētai ("he forgets and in no way remembers his cares"). The Muses' qualities are thus reflected in their effects on men, and formally the story of their birth, the moment that sets the pattern for all subsequent time, is linked with the description of the benefits they confer on mortals through singers. Stress on Zeus's kingship over the gods (ll. 71–74) also prepares for the account of the Muses' favors to mortal rulers (ll. 80–93), who are under his patronage. (See Walcot, 1957, 44.)

According to the design that has emerged so far, the passage consists mainly of two large units juxtaposed (ll. 22–52 and 53–103), each marked off by ring composition and containing internal subdivisions. The opening description of the Muses on Mount Helikon (ll. 1–21) lies outside this pattern, although it obviously leads into their epiphany to Hesiod and balances the section devoted to their singing on Olympos. Lines 104–15, which are similarly isolated, contain Hesiod's direct invocation to the Muses and make the transition to the main part of the *Theogony*. Further aspects of the structure will be evident from the diagram that follows.

In this hymn to the Muses, timeless descriptions of the goddesses' —but in the last case of men's—habitual activities (ll. 1–21, 36–52, 63–67, 80–103) alternate regularly with narratives of specific events in time (ll. 22–35, 53–62, 68–79).[8] The Muses' gift of song to Hesiod was a single instance, which occurred at a particular moment (ποτε, "once," l. 22), of their habitual and

Figure 1. Structure of *Theogony* Proem

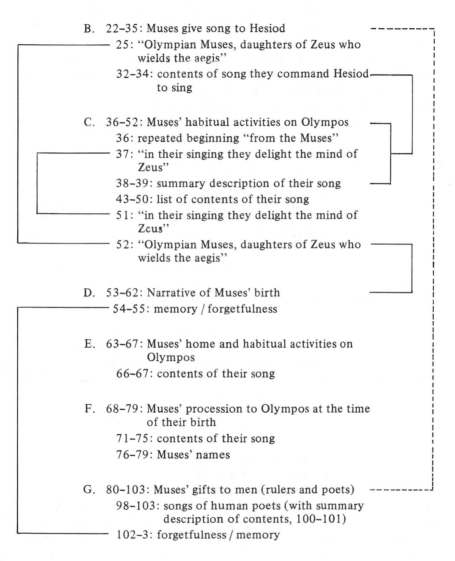

A. 1–21: Muses' habitual activities
    11–21: list of contents of their song

B. 22–35: Muses give song to Hesiod
    25: "Olympian Muses, daughters of Zeus who
       wields the aegis"
    32–34: contents of song they command Hesiod
       to sing

C. 36–52: Muses' habitual activities on Olympos
    36: repeated beginning "from the Muses"
    37: "in their singing they delight the mind of
       Zeus"
    38–39: summary description of their song
    43–50: list of contents of their song
    51: "in their singing they delight the mind of
       Zeus"
    52: "Olympian Muses, daughters of Zeus who
       wields the aegis"

D. 53–62: Narrative of Muses' birth
    54–55: memory / forgetfulness

E. 63–67: Muses' home and habitual activities on
       Olympos
    66–67: contents of their song

F. 68–79: Muses' procession to Olympos at the time
       of their birth
    71–75: contents of their song
    76–79: Muses' names

G. 80–103: Muses' gifts to men (rulers and poets)
    98–103: songs of human poets (with summary
       description of contents, 100–101)
    102–3: forgetfulness / memory

H. 104–15: Hesiod's invocation to the Muses;
       prospective list of contents of
       Theogony

often-repeated activities on the heights of Helikon (ll. 1–21)[9] and on Olympos (ll. 36–52). The time-bound is a copy of the timeless, but both proceed from a single prior event in time that, as the rest of the *Theogony* shows us, came at the end of a long process of cosmic development: the Muses' birth and their procession to Olympos on that occasion (note especially τότε, "then," l. 68). The events surrounding the Muses' birth set the character and ensure the value not only of their subsequent usual occupations on the two mountains and their single encounter with Hesiod but also of their repeated interventions in the world of men—that is, the typical activities of all mortal poets and kings who receive their aid (ll. 80–103). The moment of ultimate origin, which Hesiod recovers in his poem, is particularly sacred and therefore reveals the essential nature of song.[10] In connection with this event Hesiod not only characterizes the Muses explicitly for the first time (ll. 54–55) but also names them (ll. 77–79). Each of these names derives from words and phrases that Hesiod has used earlier in this introduction to describe the Muses' song and dancing.[11] But it is not enough to say merely that the Muses therefore personify the various aspects of song, although that is certainly true. With the transformation of descriptive verbs, nouns, and adjectives into proper names, Hesiod virtually summons these goddesses into existence through language, just when he has told of their birth in anthropomorphic terms. Song turns into the divinities who are its patrons: everything in the poem before this point has been part of this process of conjuring, though we recognize this fact only now. In an act of language that defies time, Hesiod recreates the moment of song's origin.

To some extent, of course, Hesiod is adhering to well-established hymnic norms. The story of a god's birth, which is very common in hymns that have developed sections of narrative, always reveals his character, tells how the behavior that was to become typical of him was initiated, and associates him with the occupations of which he was to become the patron. The Muses' procession to their father's home also represents, though in a somewhat unusual form, a conventional motif in hymnic birth narratives: the newborn divinity's entry into Olympos and into the company of the other gods (See Friedländer, 1966b, 285–86.) More generally, narrative hymns almost by definition present an interplay between typical descriptions and particular actions, and trace both back to their origin in a single, decisive event. In this way the god could be made more accessible to this worshippers, his qualities and powers more immediately apprehended. But recognizing the formal affinities of the proem of the *Theogony* and comparing it with other hymns only shows, in the end, what a startling composition it is. By means of what remain recognizable formal conventions, though he uses them deftly and subtly, Hesiod expresses a profound sense of the nature and importance of poetry.

All sections of the proem except lines 53–62 end with mention of a song (two sung by a human poet, the rest by the Muses) and at least an indication, but in several instances a detailed list, of the contents (ll. 11–21, 32–34, 43–52, 66–67, 71–75, 98–103). The accounts of the Muses' singing form a regular

progression by virtue of the subjects of the songs. First there is divine genealogy that begins with Zeus and the other Olympians and works back (though
with a few exceptions) to the first gods (ll. 11–21). Next comes another
genealogy, this time in chronological order "from the beginning," but with
Zeus–his kingship and might–singled out as a special subject (ll. 43–50).[12]
There follows a celebration of "the ordinances and benevolent ways of all
the immortals" (ll. 63–67)–that is, the order of Olympian society and hence
Zeus's dispensation (and perhaps specifically his division of privileges among
the gods if the "ordinances" refer to that, as West suggests–1966, 178; on
l. 66). And finally, the song at the time of the Muses' birth has as its sole content Zeus in his complementary aspects as wise and all-powerful, with all subsidiary themes pared away (ll. 71–75). This is the original performance, the
paradigm of all subsequent songs, and those are elaborations of it. Zeus, with
or without the genealogical background, is the particular subject of each of
them, and they are all essentially the same song. Their identity is stressed by
thematic and verbal repetitions that link their subjects.[13] The same device
connects with them the song the Muses command Hesiod to sing (l. 33; cf.
ll. 21, 44). And the song for which he finally asks their aid (ll. 104–15) combines the subjects of their performances and uses motifs and phrases from all
the previous descriptions.[14] The Muses' gift to the mortal poet, the Theogony
itself, is the human realization of the divine song.

In this way Hesiod implicitly claims validity for the Theogony as the
medium for transmitting a knowledge of the world that would be the gods'
sole privilege if it were not for the Muses' intervention. The way in which this
knowledge comes to him is all-important. By means of the various song catalogues, Hesiod constructs a hierarchy of relationships: he sings of the Muses,
and the Muses sing of Zeus. In this way Hesiod contrives also to sing of Zeus,
but he can do so only obliquely, by putting this song on the lips of the Muses
as a performance within his own poem. Hesiod cannot know Zeus directly,
and the relation between the divine and human songs that he describes exemplifies the Muses' necessary role as intermediaries between gods and mortals.
The whole proem is a way of enlisting their aid. By setting forth the subject
of the Muses' song, Hesiod makes it accessible to himself. Then, at the end, he
shifts from third-person narrative and description to direct invocation, and
asks the Muses to transfer their song to him and to celebrate the race of the
immortals. Only then can he proceed with his Theogony. The poet's dependence on the Muses expresses the wonderful power of song as the means by
which man achieves contact with the divine, and at the same time–as we shall
observe in more detail presently–song's limitations when possessed by
mortals.[15]

The conception of song implied by the representation of the Muses' performances and by the structure of the proem is more clearly expressed in the
two sections devoted to the Muses' influence upon men (ll. 22–35, 80–103).
Let us first consider the later section, which concerns the public experience

of the Muses' gift. Hesiod treats two categories of men, rulers and poets, whom he clearly thinks of as parallel beneficiaries of the goddesses' favor, even though lines 94-96 may at first seem to distinguish between them.[16] On both, the Muses bestow effective utterance that, in the form either of political discourse[17] or of song, charms and heals. In line 97 (where the thought clearly includes the poets who are about to be described) the voice of the man favored by the Muses is characterized in the same way, and with some of the same words, as is the utterance of the persuasive ruler (ll. 83-84). The phrasing in both places, moreover, echoes the description of the Muses' voices as they sing on Olympos (ll. 39-40). The Muses give each kind of mortal, then, something of their own capacity for lovely speech. In both cases also the effect of this inspired utterance is essentially the same. Poetry soothes its listeners just as, in the civic sphere, eloquence settles quarrels by gentle persuasion. When a man is afflicted with grief, poetry "turns him aside" from it (παρέτραπε, *paretrape,* l. 103), and kings, by using persuasion on the parties to a quarrel (παραιφάμενοι, *paraiphamenoi,* l. 90—literally, "speaking them aside"), accomplish "deeds that turn back" (μετάτροπα, *metatropa,* l. 89). There is a further resemblance between the last lines of both descriptions (ll. 93, 103), both of which mention the Muses' gift (δόσις, *dosis,* δῶρα, *dōra*). Both talents not only bring prestige upon their recipients but also benefit society as a whole. That is why Hesiod can end a description of the homage that the eloquent ruler receives with a summarizing line that embraces humanity in general (l. 93): "such is the Muses' holy gift to men." But poetry no less than eloquence improves the lot of its audience, although it cures different miseries; and by this parallel between king and poet, Hesiod shows how central a role song plays in society.

It has been suggested that the parallel was Hesiod's own invention, and in fact the *Theogony* is the only extant poem in which the Muses are said to aid rulers as well as poets.[18] But if Hesiod did extend the Muses' role, he thereby defined more sharply a concept that seems already to have existed: the fundamental kinship of song and political discourse. Lines 39-40, 83-84, and 97 of the *Theogony,* which play an important role in stressing this similarity, resemble a line in the *Iliad* that describes Nestor's gift of speech (I.249):

τοῦ καὶ ἀπὸ γλώσσης μέλιτος γλυκίων ῥέεν αὐδή.

From his tongue the voice flowed sweeter than honey.

We need to recall the context of this line, as it was discussed in the first chapter (see pp. 29-30, above). Nestor is here presented as the type of the wise and persuasive counsellor, and the line expresses the ideal of eloquence. That the speech he then gives is a model of *poetic* composition is perhaps, though not indisputably, a sign of how closely related the two forms of discourse are. In the second place, Nestor is attempting to pacify the parties to a public quarrel, one of whom, Achilles, claims to have been unjustly injured. The circumstances are generally like those in which Hesiod's kings act (*Theog.* 88-90). In the *Iliad,* the social order threatens to break down (Achilles has just thrown the speaker's staff to the ground), and the consequences of Nestor's failure at mediation show how necessary is the ruler's normally successful use of speech, as Hesiod depicts it, to the functioning of the community.

The parallel between Hesiod's diction and the Iliadic line is well known. The question is, What may we conclude from it? There is no justification for assuming that Hesiod composed his lines with Nestor in mind.[19] The phrasing in both poems seems formulaic and traditional; and if the same diction can appropriately be applied to the utterance of the Muses, the poet, and the orator, that suggests that all three were thought to share the same essential qualities.[20] Still, it could appear that Hesiod extended to poetry phrasing primarily associated with a conventional notion of political eloquence, if another line in the *Iliad* did not suggest a direct link between the two. It may not be mere coincidence that Nestor is once again involved, and here too as a master of speech in a difficult situation: he must make to Agamemnon what he expects will be an unpalatable suggestion. This is how he begins his address (IX.96-99):

ἈΑτρεΐδη κύδιστε, ἄναξ ἀνδρῶν Ἀγάμεμνον,
ἐν σοὶ μὲν λήξω, σέο δ᾽ ἄρξομαι, οὔνεκα πολλῶν
λαῶν ἐσσι ἄναξ καί τοι Ζεὺς ἐγγυάλιξε
σκῆπτρόν τ᾽ ἠδὲ θέμιστας, ἵνα σφίσι βουλεύῃσθα.

Most glorious son of Atreus, Agamemnon king of men,
in you I shall end, from you I shall begin, because
you are lord of many peoples, and Zeus has given you
the scepter and the precedents, so that you might take counsel for them.

This is not servile flattery, although we may not feel that Agamemnon, through his conduct, measures up to the ideal expressed here. Nestor extols the institution of kingship as preface to reminding Agamemnon that one duty of a king is to listen to good advice from subordinates. It is the second line of the quotation, however, that mainly concerns us, for it strikingly resembles the formulaic expressions used in the Homeric Hymns and the proem of the *Theogony* for singing a god first and last, or beginning and ending with him. Nestor, the consummate orator, is speaking *like a poet.* The justification for his use of this diction in addressing a mortal is, of course, that Agamemnon derives his royal authority from Zeus. (Cf. Leaf, 1900-1902, I, 378.) In the *Theogony,* Hesiod presents as his personal experience one line of relationship, the Muses (and Apollo) / singers. Here we are shown, from the standpoint of one deeply involved in the problems raised by the issue of authority, the importance of that other line, which Hesiod only describes: Zeus / kings. Nestor is delivering the political counterpart of a hymn. Like the singer, he is paying homage, through Agamemnon, to the divine protector of human civilization. Once again, the use of the same diction by the speaker in the assembly and the singer shows that they both exercise what is fundamentally the same power—the charm of language.

Nestor is not the only orator whose speech is described in terms that are also appropriate for song. This is how the Trojan elders who sit at the Skaian gate are characterized (III.150-52):

γήραϊ δὴ πολέμοιο πεπαυμένοι, ἀλλ᾽ ἀγορηταὶ
ἐσθλοί, τεττίγεσσιν ἐοικότες, οἵ τε καθ᾽ ὕλην
δενδρέῳ ἐφεζόμενοι ὄπα λειριόεσσαν ἱεῖσι.

Old age had stopped them from war, but they were excellent
speakers in the assembly, like cicadas who sit on a tree
in the wood and send forth a delicate [?] voice [opa leirioessan].

All that remains to them is their voice, now that their physical powers have waned, and they are rather like Tithōnos (h. Aphr. 237). But here the emphasis is on their ability as speakers, and specifically on the fine timbre of their voices, delicate and resounding like those of cicadas.[21] The phrase used in this connection is the very one with which Hesiod describes the sound of the Muses' singing on Olympos: "The house of Zeus their loud-thundering father rejoices at the goddesses' delicate [?] voice [ὀπὶ λειριοέσσῃ, opi leirioessēi] spreading through it" (Theog. 40-42).

These examples show speakers described in language that might also be used of poets. The Hymn to Hermes, by contrast, presents that god as a poet-like figure who uses his talent for the same purpose as kings (according to Hesiod) use persuasion. On the one hand, Hermes invents the phorminx and his son allays cares, just as Hesiod says poetry does. But on the other hand, he uses song to pacify Apollo (h. Hermes 416-18) and thus to settle his own quarrel with his brother, just as kings with their eloquence resolve disputes.

Poetry, then, on Hesiod's account of it and in the traditional view, is public discourse and performs a social function like persuasive speech, though on a different plane. Hesiod stresses this quality by the arrangement of the proem to the Theogony. As several writers have remarked, both the description of kings and poets and Hesiod's meeting with the Muses concern the goddesses' activities in the human world and flank the divine scenes on Olympos.[22] The two sections are parallel, but differ in one significant respect. Hesiod encountered the Muses in a pastoral setting, and poetry, in that initial experience, was a private transaction between one man and his divine patrons. In the later passage, song has an audience and a public setting. There is thus a progression in the course of the proem from the country into the town, from the singer's private experience of his art to the integration of poetry within the community.

Both sections describe an aspect of this art, and neither is complete without the other. This progression takes place through the intervening scenes of the Muses on Olympos, where they sing of Zeus's kingship and his world order, which makes human civilization possible. Above all, these scenes depict the Muses as at home in divine society, and indeed recount their first entry into it.

We can now appreciate the significance of the shift from the Helikonian to the Olympian Muses. Helikon is the place associated particularly with the Muses. There they are alone, although their dancing around Zeus's altar (l. 4) stresses their close relation with their father in the midst of their isolation. It is from Helikon also that they enter the world of men—their meeting with Hesiod took place at the foot of this mountain (l. 23), presumably during one of the processions described in lines 9–21. Such journeys, *from* the peak of Helikon toward mankind, balance their progress, at the time of their birth, *to* Olympos and the company of the immortals. Olympos is the focus of their divinity, the setting for their direct contact with Zeus that guarantees their knowledge of the truth. The complementary relation between the two mountains stresses the Muses' role of mediating between gods and men, an effect that is strengthened by the naming of the Muses as "Olympian" and "daughters of Zeus" just as they are giving song to Hesiod beneath Mount Helikon (l. 25). The placement of these early sections of the proem is also important. Hesiod first shows us the Muses by themselves and then in the act of establishing a relationship with a mortal (himself). He then describes them as singing the same song they gave him, but now on Olympos, and after that he tells the origin of their life there (the birth narrative). The sequence Helikon—Olympos parallels on the divine plane the movement of poetry among mankind from the wilds to the city. In both ways Hesiod shows how the possession of poetry by an individual in isolation is followed by the diffusion of its benefits through the entire community. The proem as a whole suggests that poetry is not simply a private gift. Its possession necessarily entails a movement into society. It is, therefore, a *civilizing* force.

The Muses' address to Hesiod (*Theog.* 26–28), the only direct statement in all the hexameter poems about the nature of poetry, also alludes, among other ideas, to the social value of this art:

ποιμένες ἄγραυλοι, κάκ᾽ ἐλέγχεα, γαστέρες οἶον,
ἴδμεν ψεύδεα πολλὰ λέγειν ἐτύμοισιν ὁμοῖα,
ἴδμεν δ᾽, εὖτ᾽ ἐθέλωμεν, ἀληθέα γηρύσασθαι.

Shepherds who live in the wilds, evil disgraces, mere bellies [*gasteres*],
We know how to say many false things [*pseudea*] that resemble the truth,
and we know how, when we want, to speak true things [*alēthea*].

The first line may represent the divine abuse of mortals typical in scenes of epiphany,[23] but that does not explain the *content* of this reproach. Why do

the Muses call shepherds "mere bellies"? An answer is suggested by Svenbro's
study, with reference to this line, of the way in which the word for "belly,"
gastēr, is used elsewhere in hexameter poetry. He finds that it appears in a
series of oppositions that characterize organized life in society on the one hand
and, on the other, a precarious existence outside, or on the fringe of, civilization. The idea of "the belly" marks the negative term of each pair of opposites
—that is, nonsocial conditions or behavior.[24] With this term of abuse, then,
the Muses are scorning the shepherd's solitary life in nature without benefit
of human community—a meaning that is reinforced by the phrase "shepherds
who live in the wilds" and that fits nicely with the implied opposition between
the foot of Mount Helikon and the city. With the gift of song, the record of
humanity's collective past and the means of knowing the divine world order,
the goddesses furnish men with a foundation for unity among themselves, so
that the scattered shepherds are replaced later in the proem by citizens in the
agora. For the individual, the capacity for song offers an honored place within
the collective whole. But by presenting the change from nature to civilization
as his personal experience, Hesiod makes vivid what the Muses' gift means for
all mankind.

Svenbro's analysis may be extended if we consider the most important of
several passages in the *Odyssey* in which Odysseus speaks of the compulsion
of the belly. Here is part of the speech in which he characterizes himself to
Alkinoos as the most afflicted of mortals (vii.215-21):[25]

> ἀλλ' ἐμὲ μὲν δορπῆσαι ἐάσατε κηδόμενόν περ ·
> οὐ γάρ τι στυγερῇ ἐπὶ γαστέρι κύντερον ἄλλο
> ἔπλετο, ἥ τ' ἐκέλευσεν ἕο μνήσασθαι ἀνάγκη
> καὶ μάλα τειρόμενον καὶ ἐνὶ φρεσὶ πένθος ἔχοντα,
> ὡς καὶ ἐγὼ πένθος μὲν ἔχω φρεσίν, ἡ δὲ μάλ' αἰεὶ
> ἐσθέμεναι κέλεται καὶ πιέμεν, ἐκ δέ με πάντων
> ληθάνει ὅσσ' ἔπαθον, καὶ ἐνιπλησθῆναι ἀνώγει.

But let me have dinner, careworn [*kēdomenon*] though I am.
For nothing is more beastly than the contemptible belly [*gastēr*] ,
which forces a man by necessity to remember [*mnēsasthai*] it,
even when he is very oppressed and has grief [*penthos*] in his heart,
as I now have grief [*penthos*] in my heart, but the belly always
commands me to eat and drink, and makes me forget [*eklēthanei*]
all that I have suffered, and orders that it be filled.

According to these astonishing lines, the belly does precisely what Hesiod says
poetry does! And its effect is described with the same diction. We find here
the same opposition between memory and forgetting—and the same verbs for
both—as in Hesiod's account of the working of song (cf. *Theog.* 102-3, with

Theog. 54–55), and in both cases it is grief (*kēdos, penthos; Theog.* 98, 102) that is forgotten.

But the belly and song are not being equated here. In fact, this passage confirms the opposition between them that we find in the *Theogony.* Hunger and poetry may produce similar *effects,* but in *nature* they are antithetical. Poetry is a benign and valuable possession, and the forgetfulness of woe it causes is part of its more general capacity to delight. The belly is a plague that eclipses all other afflictions simply by causing sharper and more immediate pain (as a lacerated knee would make one forget a headache). Hunger is the greater nuisance because it is recurrent and trivial and yet distracts a man from far more serious troubles. Presumably, however, once his belly was filled, he would be flooded with the memory of his other cares (cf. xii.308–10), and poetry, which would beguile him with the memory of other things, would be necessary to console him. But hunger blocks this healing use of memory. Just before the lines quoted, Odysseus has said that he could recount more sufferings of his own than anyone else (vii.213–14). He will eventually tell his story —after he has been fed.[26] And in general, as we have observed, narrative song also has its normal place after the meal, when the diners' hunger has been satisfied. Song and the belly, then, are the terms of a complementary antithesis; both produce memory and forgetfulness, but they are opposed through what is in each case the object of memory.

They also stand for the opposite states of social organization and its lack in the *Odyssey* as well as in Hesiod. In his speech to Alkinoos, Odysseus presents himself as someone outside society who needs to be taken in and fed, and thus as the antithesis of the poet. For just as meals are in this poem a sign of social decorum and their violation a mark of disorder (see Chapter 2, Section c, above), the poet whose art adorns those feasts epitomizes order, and maltreatment or constraint of him expresses social disintegration. The obvious examples are Dēmodokos, whom the civilized Phaiakian nobles treat with great respect, and Phēmios, who is forced against his will to sing for the unruly suitors on Ithaka (i.154). But there is also the singer mentioned in iii.267–72, whom Agamemnon, departing for Troy, left as guardian of his wife (an attempt to maintain propriety) and whom the adulterous Aigisthos left to starve on a desert island (the overthrow of order).

In Chapter 3 (where we discussed the lines that immediately precede the part of Odysseus's speech quoted above; see pp. 88–89), we observed how hunger is managed by social institutions. In the first place, there is the meal, with its prescribed order and religious observances (libations and so forth), where those with an established place in society share food. But mankind also protects itself against the ferocity of hunger through the interrelated practices of supplication and begging, which are under divine protection. Whereas hunger is the condition, and the bane, of "unaccommodated man," the inviolability of the beggar guarantees that outcasts will be fed and incorporated into society, though in a marginal position. The activities of both poet and beggar center around the meal, where they earn their livelihood. Odysseus, now a guest in Alkinoos's house, sends a piece of meat to Dēmodokos (viii.474–83), and on Ithaka he himself, disguised as a beggar, will solicit food among the feasting suitors. We can now understand why Hesiod lumps beggars and singers together as examples of productive competition (*W.D.* 26). But just as these two figures stand in an antithetical relation to the needs of the belly, the poet's status at the feast is the opposite of the beggar's (though both are sub-ordinate to the diners). The poet is summoned to adorn the meal with his art, and members of the audience give him meat in token of their respect for his divine gift. But it is a duty to feed a beggar, and no one willingly sends for him (xvii.382–87).

The Muses' disdain of shepherds as "mere bellies," then, must be under-stood within a complex of ideas that define the value of social organization, of which poetry is an inseparable part. Svenbro (1976, 46–49) rejects the view of those who understand the goddesses' words as a summons from gross materialism to a life of spiritual achievement. He does so justly for the most part, although it may still be said that a contrast is implied between the un-reflective life that is limited to physical survival and the life led in conscious-ness of how the world is ordered. But the mention of "bellies" implies a further opposition, which is intimately related to the contrast between nature and civilization. As was emphasized in the consideration of "the belly" in Chapter 3, in his speech to Alkinoos, Odysseus replies to the Phaiakian king's question whether the suppliant before him is a god in disguise. He depicts servitude to the belly as the archetypal human woe and thus as emblematic of the afflictions that distinguish men from gods. Similarly, the Muses in the *Theogony* allude by means of "the belly" to the necessities that hem in mortal life, and then go on, in lines 27–28, to describe their own powers. When mor-tals live scattered in the wilds and reduced to "mere bellies," they are very near the state of beasts and as far as they can be from resembling gods. But when they are organized in society and can keep at bay the harsh compulsions of the natural world—when the Muses impart to the poet, and through him to humanity in general, something of their divine knowledge—then men can ful-fill their potential and draw nearer to the gods' level. Without, however, at-taining it; for the distinction between mortality and divinity remains inviolate, and the Muses do not grant the human poet their powers to the same degree as they themselves possess them or in the same straightforward form. Like all mediated things, the gift of song to mortals is of mixed nature, complex.

The Muses speak the truth when they wish, but they can also tell lies that resemble truth. These lines (*Theog.* 27–28) have often been understood as a criticism of heroic epic poetry as deceitful, if charming, and a declaration by Hesiod himself that he, by contrast, will tell the truth. This view is unconvinc-ing, especially because hexameter poetry as a body is so homogeneous in formal characteristics, ideas, and attitudes that a difference on this fundamental matter between two of its main types seems incredible. There is no evidence at all for various poetic schools, which have sometimes been imagined, and they probably did not exist. And to postulate rivalry between the individual poets is to become enmeshed in the fancied biographies of these men and to ignore what Hesiod is saying about poetry itself. Certainly when he implies that his poem resembles what the Muses sing, he claims that it will be authoritative and true. But the Muses' statements should probably be interpreted as describing qualities that every poem potentially has.[27] The same art either can so adorn falsehood as to make it a semblance of truth (a kind of imitation— see Detienne, 1967, 76-77) or can represent the truth without deception. As we shall find, however, the possibilities are perhaps actually more complicated than either of these alternatives by itself would indicate.[28]

Let us consider what kind of truth and what kind of falsehood (in that order) these lines suggest that poetry might convey. The work of several French scholars enables us to understand that "truth" in this context is not simply a faithful detailing of facts, although that is certainly included, but something broader and more significant. Jean-Pierre Vernant has shown that in mythic thought, memory—which is intimately related to the conception of truth—is more than recollection of the past: it is a means of approaching "the essence of being" ("le fond de l'être"), the reality that lies beyond the sensible world. Memory enables a living man to pass freely to that other world and to return. It is, he says, not merely a means of passing over time ("survol du temps") but an escape from time altogether ("évasion hors du temps").[29] This is, as Vernant notes, precisely the aim of the *Theogony*. Memory's daughters, the Muses, sing, and enable the poet to sing, of present and future as well as of the past, and the connection with prophecy is natural and clear.[30] Marcel Detienne has elaborated this view by studying the mythic concept that seems to underlie the etymology of the word used by Hesiod in line 28 for "truth," ἀλήθεια (*alētheia*). The opposite of this word, to judge from its literal meaning, must have been, not falsehood, but λήθη (*lēthē*), "forgetfulness," and there is evidence in surviving literature to support this inference. *Alētheia* personified is thus a mythic doublet of Mnēmosynē, Memory, and the Muses are intimately associated with it.[31] The "truth" that the Muses can speak, then, has the value accorded memory in mythic thought; it is a means of transcending time and of understanding what is stable and coherent and beyond the limits of ordinary experience. This conception explains why poetry was credited with the mysterious power to make contact between men and gods, why its importance was so urgent for individuals and for their whole society. The stakes could hardly have been higher. For *lēthē* is ultimately the oblivion of death, and Memory, the mother of the Muses, is therefore "the force of life."[32] We are now in a better position to appreciate the nature of the delight that is song's effect, and in particular to understand that poetry is not simply an anodyne, as Hesiod's description of it might at first suggest. Poetry does work forgetfulness of the pain and sorrow that are part of being mortal, but it does so by turning its listeners towards a vision of ultimate truths that makes their immediate pains seem trivial by comparison.

In lines 27-28 of the *Theogony,* however, "true things," *alēthea,* are explicitly opposed, not to *lēthē,* but to lies, *pseudea.* This antithesis characterizes a later, more rational way of thinking, where *alētheia* means "truth." According to Detienne (1967, 75-77), these lines represent an intermediate stage between mythic and rational thought. Specifically, in the proem the antithesis "truth / falsehood" seems to overlie the more truly mythic one, "*alētheia / lēthē,*" which is implied by the combination of the play on memory and forgetfulness in lines 54-55 and 102-3, of the Muses' association with Mnēmosynē, and of their claim to *alētheia* as one of their powers. These two antitheses do not exclude one another; they coexist in the *Theogony* and elsewhere in hexameter poetry. On the one hand, the mythic notion of memory helps explain the whole concept of the nature and importance of poetry, as we have just seen. And on the other hand, the capacity of poetry for truth and for falsehood or deception is also a fundamental idea, and one that is not unique to Hesiod. For it appears also, and even more clearly, in the *Odyssey,* as will be evident in the next chapter. What this falsehood is, and how a poem with the authority of divine inspiration can admit it, we must now consider.

In reality, this system of oppositions cannot remain wholly stable. Ambiguity enters, for as Detienne (1967, 69-75) has also shown, between the opposites *alētheia* and *lēthē* there is an intermediate zone where these two powers approach one another. No mortal, neither poet nor king, can possess *alētheia* free of *lēthē,* or can utter truth without an admixture of deception. This situation has a positive aspect. Since in mythic thought, opposites are not contradictory but complementary, the ability to speak the truth implies the ability to deceive as well (Detienne, 1967, 77-78). If conscious deception is at issue, this would seem to apply more to the Muses than to human poets, and to mortals only under certain circumstances (as in the case of Odysseus, which will be discussed in the next chapter). More recently, Pietro Pucci has shown that the ambiguous nature of both political and poetic discourse is reflected in Hesiod's own language. Song, the province of Memory's daughters, works by making men forget. The king who gives straight judgments (*Theog.* 86) settles quarrels by "speaking aside" the disputants (*Theog.* 90), and the poet's art works in a similarly oblique way (*Theog.* 103). Even Hesiod, despite his implicit claim for his poem of privilege and truth, cannot be wholly master of his art; there is no way of knowing whether the song with which the Muses inspire him is authentic truth or falsehood that simulates it.[33] Pucci's argument is based on the ideas not only of Detienne but also of Jacques Derrida, which I find difficult to evaluate. But readers of any theoretical persuasion might all agree that if an absolute reality and a language that corresponds with and describes it exactly, and which thus can only be divine, are assumed to exist (as they must be in the *Theogony*), then human speech at best will always fall short of that divine language, will always contain an element of error or deception. Man therefore cannot know the truth completely or precisely. (For in hexameter poetry there seems to be no conception, as there is in Plato, of the sudden flash of intuitive insight that transcends language and cannot be put into words; the attitude seems to be instead that what cannot be described cannot be known.) The disparity in power of language is of a piece with the disparity in knowledge. As the poet of the *Iliad* says, the Muses as goddesses are present everywhere and know all things; men hear only the *kleos* and can know nothing with certainty (II.485-86). It is with the dependence on the Muses that the possibility of error or delusion enters, except in the rare case when an eyewitness to events is present who can vouch for the truth of the song (as Odysseus bears witness to the authenticity of Dēmodokos's tale about Troy).

The emphasis is usually on the positive value of poetry, its capacity to heal and enhance, and nowhere more so than in the proem to the *Theogony*. Yet even here signs of its ambiguous nature appear, and they show that, as in the account of Dēmodokos's blindness in the *Odyssey,* poetry is presented as a divine gift (cf. *Theog.* 93, 103), with the mixed value typical of all such gifts. [34] The Muses, as we have seen, are no different after all from other divinities; they deal out their favors arbitrarily. The truth or falsehood of the song they give depends ultimately on their own caprice more than on the merits of the recipient, as a phrase in line 28, which has generally drawn little attention, suggests. We know how to speak true things, they say, "whenever we wish"— εὖτ' ἐθέλωμεν (*eut' ethelōmen*). That these words imply the freedom to act arbitrarily that is characteristic of gods is demonstrated by the use of similar phrasing in another passage of the *Theogony* (ll. 429-47), where it recurs with impressive frequency to qualify almost every item in the catalogue of Hekate's benefits to men. She stands beside and aids "whomever she wishes" (ᾧ δ' ἐθέλει, *hōi d' ethelei,* l. 429) in general, and in particular men in the agora (ὅν κ' ἐθέλῃσιν, *hon k'etheleisin,* l. 430), in war and in athletic contests (οἷς κ' ἐθέλῃσι, *hois k'etheleisi,* ll. 432, 439), and so on (see also ll. 443, 446). There is no certain way to win her favor. All a man can do is to call upon her with sacrifice, but the choice of whose prayers to accept is hers (ll. 416-20).

That this most wonderful of all powers granted to humanity conforms to the pattern of divine gifts means that, when measured by his possession of poetry as in other respects, man is shown to occupy a position between god and beast, tending in his capacity for achievement more toward the gods, yet unable to obtain their perfection of knowledge and freedom from care. As an amusement at times of celebration and pleasure, especially the feast, song expresses all that is most decorous in human life and induces forgetfulness of woes. And yet such moments are mere reflections of what the gods enjoy, and the time when men shared their banquets is long past. Song perpetuates the hero's *kleos,* but it is powerless to confer true immortality. It typifies social organization, but that in turn is a response to human vulnerability. Through song, men can discover order in the world, gain knowledge, and reestablish links long broken with the gods. Yet this very degree of power and charm involves dangers (Thamyris, the Sirens, Kirkē), and even in ordinary circumstances, when song is most benign, it remains slightly inauthentic. Poet and audience are always at the mercy of song's divine patronesses. Still, all human things are flawed, and song perhaps less than most. On balance, it offsets the evil that being mortal entails, and brings men joy.

Yet despite the limitations of human speech, the hexameter poets do manage to express, with wonderful precision, man's place in the world, the conditions of his existence, and his very nature, though they often do so with reference to what cannot be directly known or described. Even their language, which because it is so stylized invites us to generalize from the particular man or thing to the typical and thus constantly reminds us of the larger patterns, helps convey these lessons. Their art has the quality that Wallace Stevens calls "acutest speech":

> To say more than human things with human voice,
> That cannot be; to say human things with more
> Than human voice, that, also, cannot be;
> To speak humanly from the height or from the depth
> Of human things, that is acutest speech.[35]

Gods in this poetry never do sing of "human things": their songs do not describe man's condition with the insight and compassion of, let us say, the Achilles of the final book of the *Iliad* (or of the *Iliad*'s poet). On the rare occasions when their songs include the race of men, the gods view it from without—either merely as a part of the larger order of the world (*Theog.* 50) or, unsympathetically, as limited and helpless, in contrast to themselves (the Muses' song on Olympos in the *Hymn to Apollo*). Men, on the other hand, lack the resources to sing with complete authority about "more than human things." But their poetry does speak humanly. It expresses man's potential and his failings, brings him close to the gods and yet is itself subject to mortal limits. Thus song, by its nature, epitomizes precisely what all our surviving poems seek to express about man and the world.

Once we recognize that song was invested with this significance, we can understand why the poems so often become self-reflective, and why they display such self-consciousness on the part of the poets about the nature of their art. Here it is crucial to keep in mind that these poems were themselves performed. Whenever they used poetry as a theme, and in particular whenever they described performances of song, the poets reminded their audience at the moment of singing that they were actually listening to a poem, what were the essential qualities of what they were hearing, and what it meant for them to be hearing it. In what clearer or more economical way could the poem convey its meaning? The songs being described were identical in nature to the one being heard, internal performances mirrored the actual one, and the listeners were made conscious of the kind of knowledge being conveyed and the emotions that the poem should arouse in them. The act of performance itself was therefore significant. While it lasted, poet and audience were knit together in a shared experience: a heightened awareness of what they all had in common as mortals. Not only in its content but also by its very existence, the song that came about their ears gave them some intimation of the numinous world and by placing them in relation to it gave them a sense of the weaknesses and the worth of their humanity. Knowledge of the world, of the gods, and of their own past, the value of their social institutions and of civilized life in general, the splendor of achievement and the limitations of mortality: the song stood for all of these things.

Such must have been the meaning implicit in every performance; it was, after all, a consequence of the conventional notion of poetry. But passages of self-reflection brought this meaning to consciousness. The strength of this effect will have varied from case to case, of course, as will its precise function in the particular poem. But there can be no clearer example of the possibilities it offers for expression than the *Theogony* itself. Why, after all, is a passage devoted to the nature of poetry and the poet's calling prefixed to *this* poem? It gives the background to Hesiod's exercise of his art by recounting how he got it, and his relation with the Muses is his way of claiming, at least overtly, the truth of what he will tell. But his personal pride is not the issue here, or not the main issue. The effect of the proem is to present the *Theogony* itself as an act of mediation between man and god, by which man is granted knowledge that would normally be denied him. The performance of the *Theogony*, moreover, is made to seem the reflection of the Muses' activity on Olympos, so that the radiance of the gods' festivities is shed upon this human occasion, which is suspended above the pain and transience of human experience almost as if it were out of time. And indeed, by means of this poem those in the audience at its performance are put in touch with the origin of things in a way that abolishes all the intervening time between "then" and "now." But this return to origins has the purpose of showing the development, and the value, of Zeus's reign, which in turn guarantees human civilization. And just as the Muses' singing, as part of that order, expresses its very nature, so song among mankind—not just song in general but the *Theogony* in particular, which is at this moment being experienced—together with its allied art, rhetoric, embodies and puts into practice the best attainments of men in community with each other. The effect of a performance of the *Theogony* would have been to induce the listeners to translate the powers at large in the world under Zeus's patronage—Dikē, Themis, and the rest—into their own lives. At the same time, however, the Muses never explicitly promise to convey the truth to Hesiod; and this inconclusiveness in their speech, as well as other, more subtle indications, hints that the *Theogony* will, after all, be a way of speaking humanly about the world and not necessarily an absolutely faithful representation of it. And so the members of the audience are reminded that the poem they are hearing is a symbol of all that is and is not possible for them.

The *Theogony* invites its listeners to measure it against its ideal prototype, the song of the Muses to which it persistently alludes, and to generalize from this comparison about their own condition. The *Hymn to Apollo* creates essentially the same effect, but perhaps more overtly. Here too, divine and mortal life and the difference between them are described by means of the kind of song that typifies each. In this poem, however, the Muses' song on Olympos qualifies the one sung at the human festival by presenting a contrasting theme, as we remarked in Chapter 3 (see pp. 79–82, above). The hymn itself probably corresponds closely to the human song on Delos that it incorporates, for although it could eventually have been performed anywhere,[36] it must have been composed originally for the festival of Apollo on that island. Furthermore, what the Delian maidens sing in lyric meter—praise of the gods followed by stories on heroic themes—is evidently identical in content to the performance in hexameters by the poet of our hymn, so that this poem would have been the first stage in his program. (Cf. Heubeck, 1972, 142 n.18.) The poet ties the hymn to this setting explicitly when he addresses the Delian maidens in his own person. Thus, by describing to his audience the occasion in which they are taking part even as they listen, he draws attention to his poem as the epitome of the festival's meaning—as the expression, that is, of the way those present make contact with divinity and themselves appear godlike. Yet after this splendid description the poet goes on to imagine life on Olympos, and to depict the gods as imagining in turn how bleak the life of mortals is. This is a sobering reflection, but not really inappropriate to the occasion. The larger perspective is necessary here if the poem is faithfully to convey to the listeners what they are experiencing: a celebration that for all its brilliance has limits and cannot fully enable them to cross the gulf between god and man. What the Muses sing is also true. The internal performances thus comment on the poem that includes them.

The other autobiographical passage in Hesiod (*W.D.* 633–62) has no discernible connection with the circumstances of its poem's performance, but in it the poet does use an incident from his career (which he connects in lines 658–69 with his encounter with the Muses on Helikon) to suggest something about the value of his art. Structurally, Hesiod's participation in the singing contest at Khalkis is parallel to the information he gives about his father and to the advice on sailing directed to Persēs. Song is as much a profession as sea travel and trade—and, in fact, is superior. For Hesiod's victory in the competition contrasts with his father's failure at commerce, and the Muses' teaching enables him to give advice without practical experience of the sea. (See pp. 23–24, above.) What is more, he makes a point of saying that he set sail to Khalkis from Aulis, where the Akhaians once spent a winter while they mustered their forces for the expedition against Troy (ll. 651–53). By evoking heroic saga, Hesiod is putting his own compositions—the one he sang at

Khalkis and perhaps also the *Works and Days*—on the same level, placing them within the poetic tradition. And the coincidence of Aulis as his own and the Akhaians' point of departure from the Greek mainland ranks Hesiod's exploit with the Trojan War and gives him something of the aura of the epic hero. His victory over his professional rivals, tangibly commemorated by the tripod that he won and dedicated to the Muses, gives him a claim to *kleos*. Once again we are reminded of the intimate connection between poetry and heroic action and the possibility for the poet to gain renown. The reason is only partly that poetry celebrates extraordinary deeds. In its own right it represents great achievement on a mortal's part, and like warfare it involves the poet in competition with his peers. Thus a passage with heroic resonances can be included even in a poem of nonheroic content like the *Works and Days* to remind the audience that they are hearing something of great value. This apparent digression really adds in this way to the poem's persuasive force.

The most direct of several ways in which heroic epic displays awareness of its function is exemplified by Helen's vision of herself as a poetic heroine when she says to Hektor that the gods gave an evil portion to herself and Paris "so that we may be the subject of song for men to come" (VI.357-58)—a thought that is generalized to include all the Greeks and Trojans in Alkinoos's similar remark in viii.579-80. The realization of the song Helen imagines is the *Iliad*, which bears out the truth of her words even as it records them. With this statement and with her weaving in III.125-28 (which functions in the same way as a "song within the song"), Helen reveals the importance of the transformation of experience into art. Only the possibility that this process will occur gives meaning to suffering that otherwise would seem merely arbitrary, fits it into an intelligible pattern. (Cf. Marg, 1957, 18-19.) Furthermore, poetry itself discovers order in mankind's experience. Once a poem is made of Helen's and Paris's adultery and its consequences, the story will be placed within the poetic tradition, and in the case of hexameter poetry that means within human history. Its connections and similarities with what preceded and followed it will be revealed, and it will become part of the general story that, taken as a whole, teaches what it means to be mortal. But the individual is not submerged by being incorporated into the poetic tradition. Heroic song serves him by spreading his *kleos*, as the *Iliad*, for better or for worse, serves Helen. But the nature of *kleos* is ambivalent; the preservation of a man's fame in poetry keeps something of him alive after death but cannot bestow true immortality. Helen's statement to Hektor, then, jolts the audience out of absorption in the story, reminds its members that they are hearing about men and women of long ago through a performance of poetry. They reflect that the *Iliad* has a serious purpose that it is even now in the process of fulfilling, and that it, like all poems, typifies the issues that it treats: achievement and failure, life and death.

Other Homeric Hymns besides the *Hymn to Apollo* present performances within the poem. In the hymn to Pan (no. 19), this god and the nymphs sing "the blessed gods and great Olympos"—a theogony?—and, as part of that theme, Pan's own birth (ll. 27–47). A similar passage occurs in hymn 27: Artemis, the subject of the poem, together with the Muses and the Graces, sings how Leto bore children who surpassed the other immortals in wisdom and deeds (ll. 18–20). We should imagine a narrative like the birth story in the *Hymn to Apollo*,[37] but one that gives as much prominence to Artemis as to Apollo. In these examples, we may see a combination of two types of hymn: one that essentially describes the god's nature and characteristic activities, and one that narrates a specific incident in his life, often the story of his birth.[38] These types are kept distinct, however: the main part of the poem represents the former type, but the poet can include the latter by putting it into the mouth of the very god being celebrated. But of course this is a subterfuge. The poet is also singing the birth narrative himself. In describing the god's song the poem becomes a reflection of it, and the audience is made to feel that it is participating in an occasion like the one on which the god hymns himself. His worshippers praise the god by imitating him, and that brings them closer to him.[39]

In the *Hymn to Hermes,* the god also sings his own birth, but the body of the hymn itself recounts the same event, with the related story of how the god received his characteristic privileges and attributes. Here, then, the activities of Hermes and of the human poet who celebrates him correspond directly. But this poem differs from all the other examples in that it is an artistic jeu d'esprit that plays on poetic conventions, including the habit of self-reflection. This tone is fully in keeping with the character of the god being praised—Hermes must surely sing just this kind of hymn when he celebrates himself within the poem. But this capacity for parody is also a sign of the remarkable vitality of the poetic tradition.[40]

The poet describes Hermes' invention of the phorminx and hits upon the happy conceit of having Apollo say that before then he and the Muses had engaged in song with only the flute for accompaniment (ll. 450–52). The audience would have caught the incongruity: nowhere else in the extant poems are Apollo and the Muses accompanied by the flute rather than the phorminx. In the first performance with this new instrument, Hermes improvises a hymn on his own birth (ll. 54–61). Later, when he sings a theogony in Apollo's presence (ll. 423–33), he stresses his poetic vocation by honoring Mnēmosynē first, just as Hesiod, in his *Theogony,* gives special praise to the Muses. Mnēmosynē "obtained Maia's son [Hermes] as her portion" (λάχε, *lakhe,* l. 430). This is part of Hermes' general theme, for he sings "how each of the gods obtained his portion" (λάχε, *lakhe,* l. 428). Like Hesiod, Hermes makes himself a character within his own poem in order to stress the divine source of his inspiration. But he is a god himself; and in this way, and in the extravagance of Hermes' claim to be Maia's allotted portion, the whole concept of inspiration becomes the subject of sport.

The hymn implies the affinity between poetry and deceit, for Hermes is not only an inventor but also a thief and a consummate liar. And on the other hand, it also suggests the kinship of song with prophecy. The narrative tells how Apollo obtained the phorminx from Hermes, and it also emphasizes Zeus's gift to Apollo of oracular powers. Playing the instrument is called "inquiring of" it ($(\epsilon\xi)\epsilon\rho\epsilon\epsilon\iota\nu\epsilon\iota\nu$, *(ex)ereeinein*, ll. 483, 487); the same verb is used for men's consultation of Apollo's oracle (line 547).[41] Like prophecy, moreover, the phorminx must be approached in the right way if it is to yield its benefits (ll. 482-88, 543-49).

Even Hermes' exchange of the phorminx for Apollo's cattle may be related to a theme traditional in accounts of mortals who receive a poetic vocation. The closest parallel is the story of Arkhilokhos, whose father sent him to the countryside to bring back a cow for sale in town. As the boy was returning at night with the animal, he met some women who jokingly asked if the cow was for sale and promised him a "worthy price" for it ($\tau\iota\mu\dot{\eta}\nu$ $\dot{\alpha}\xi\dot{\iota}\alpha\nu$, *timēn axian*; cf. *h. Hermes* 437, where Apollo says that the phorminx is "worth [$\dot{\alpha}\nu\tau\dot{\alpha}\xi\iota\alpha$, *antaxia*] fifty cows"). The women and the cow thereupon disappeared, but Arkhilokhos found a lyre at his feet. The inscription in which this story is told dates from around the third century B.C., but there is reason to think that the story itself, or at least its basic motifs, are far older.[42] A similar anecdote was told of Epimenidēs.[43] And there are obvious similarities with the story of Hesiod (in the proem to the *Theogony*), who was pasturing sheep in the country when he encountered the Muses, received from them a token of inspiration (not a phorminx, but a staff of laurel), and evidently abandoned the pastoral life for poetry. In the *Hymn to Hermes,* therefore, Apollo—the patron, together with the Muses, of mortal poets—undergoes his own initiation into song: but at the hands of his thievish half brother.

To replace the phorminx, Hermes invents a second instrument, the syrinx or "Pan's pipes" (ll. 511-12), and the hymn stresses the difference between the several types of song by way of the manner of their accompaniment. The phorminx, used in performances (including those of hexameter poetry) intimately associated with the customs and institutions of human civilization, will be the property of Apollo. Hermes, who is to be the patron of cowherding and related professions (ll. 491-94; cf. *Theog.* 444-47), will have the *syrinx.* This instrument will therefore be at home mainly in pastoral settings and will be used on informal occasions (cf. XVIII.525-26). Thus the issue of prerogatives between the divine brothers is sorted out in a way that defines the modes of performance and the uses of song. And just as in the *Theogony,* song is the point on which civilization is contrasted with nature, except that this hymn also recognizes a rustic and less serious kind of performance. The subject of prophecy is treated in parallel fashion to that of song, again in accordance with a conventional idea—that they are kindred arts. Apollo professes that he cannot reveal Zeus's counsels to Hermes (ll. 533-40) and gives him instead a secondary, rustic means of divination (ll. 550-66)—one that "I practiced," says Apollo, "when I was still a boy in charge of cattle."

The *Hymn to Hermes* charms and amuses with this cheerful use of self-reflective elements. But conventions may be turned to account in a way that is less extreme, but more complex, than parody. A poem can present itself consciously as a response to its tradition, or at least to one branch of it. In such a case, the poet's touch may be dexterous, his manner graceful, but his object is serious beyond mere game-playing. The poem that has this character to a consummate degree is the *Odyssey*.

6   Poetry in the *Odyssey*

IN THE *ILIAD,* Achilles hears the story of his poetic double, a figure out of older tales who committed the folly into which he himself is falling and who suffered the consequences. That is Meleagros, of whom Phoinix tells in the embassy scene of the ninth book. Achilles is so absorbed in his feelings of outraged honor that he brushes aside the implicit warning, but his own story eventually adheres to this and other, related patterns. From this conformity it derives that sense of fate that weighs so heavily upon it. Of course, the meaning of the poem lies only partially in the generic character of its plot. Most readers would find greater significance in Achilles' response to his situation, especially in the later books, when he understands both his past error and the doom that awaits him. But we can fully appreciate the achievement that the *Iliad* represents only by recognizing the interplay in it between the typical and the individual. The poem itself gives us the necessary awareness of its generic background. The story of Meleagros and other such passages—allusions to the Theban saga, for instance, or Nestor's reminiscences—look back to a poetic tradition, just as Helen's anticipation of being the subject of song looks forward to an extension of that tradition which is the *Iliad* itself. Song is barely mentioned in this poem of war; yet the *Iliad* implicitly asserts its place in relation to other poetic narratives. By drawing attention to its artistic context, the poem enables us to take the measure of Achilles.

In the *Odyssey,* when he hears Dēmodokos's songs, Odysseus confronts not simply his double but himself as a hero of poetry as well. Dēmodokos's themes are drawn from an episode in Odysseus's past, the sack of Troy. But although that stage of Odysseus's life is over, his story as a whole is incomplete. His *nostos,* or homecoming, is still developing. It is the *Odyssey.* This poem thus displays consciousness of itself as a continuation of poems dealing with its hero's earlier experiences and the exploits of the other great warriors at Troy. The scenes in which Odysseus hears his own story and weeps imply its claim to be a *necessary* continuation, for they show the need for a conclusion to that story.

The *Odyssey* enormously expands a tendency observable in the *Iliad.* The latter poem defines itself implicitly, through allusion; the *Odyssey* does so not only with the same device, but also by making poetry itself one of its major themes. Thus, more explicitly and more self-consciously than the *Iliad,* the *Odyssey* conveys its meaning by expressing its relation to other poems and by measuring the significance of its subject against theirs. In this case, however, we possess a poem that represents the branch of the tradition and the narrative themes upon which the *Odyssey* comments—the *Iliad* itself. In a remarkable essay, James Redfield (1973) has depicted the *Odyssey* as a response specifically to our *Iliad,* and its poet as "self-consciously an epigonid" who "confronted an obstacle unknown to the poet of the *Iliad:* he was writing in a literary universe already inhabited by a masterpiece" (pp. 145, 146). Hence the artist's preoccupation with his own craft: since the new work had to be original, "its making was accompanied by a certain kind of reflection on the proprieties of poetry."

On this account of events, the *Iliad* was so "definitive" that it ended real creativity in epic poetry. The *Odyssey* would thus represent an early stage in the genre's consequent decline (Redfield, 1973, 142–45). Certainly it is impossible to overrate the *Iliad,* but there is a danger of undervaluing the *Odyssey* by comparison. The poetic self-consciousness displayed by the *Odyssey* differs in intensity rather than quality from that of the *Iliad* and can be found elsewhere in hexameter poetry as well. In what follows I shall treat some of the same subjects as Redfield, but I would like to concentrate first on how and why this poem comments on its own artistic tradition. Suggestions can then be made about the *Odyssey*'s relation to the *Iliad,* but from the standpoint of the internal economy of the text rather than of reconstructed literary history. The *Odyssey* is the supreme example of hexameter poetry's tendency to self-reflection, discussed in the preceding chapter. It contains the most detailed descriptions of poetic performances in all our hexameter texts. What does it gain by its preoccupation with poetry, and by the careful reminders to the audience that it is a poem that should be set into relation with other works?

Part of the answer must be that scenes that include such performances achieve an effect like that of the "play-within-the-play" familiar in drama, especially in Shakespeare. As listeners to the poem (nowadays in imagination, if not in fact) we are induced to consider the relations between the main song and the internal performance. We observe an audience responding, like us, to a poem, and we learn much about its individual members from the modes of their response. In addition, since we are made aware of our own role as hearers, we are led to ask how poetry is related to life.

The major characters of the *Odyssey,* and other characters as well, are defined by their behavior as members of an audience. Their responses to song or other kinds of narrative differ according to their personal relation to the story being recounted.[1] Near the beginning of the poem, Penelope weeps when Phēmios sings the *Homecomings* of the Akhaians. The suitors, by contrast, take pleasure. They, after all, are taking advantage of the most prolonged and difficult of all the homecomings to woo its hero's wife. Telemakhos is tolerant of their attitude and scornful of his mother's, partly because of "his child's impatience with grief" (Redfield, 1973, 152), but partly also because of his own idea of what poetry is. Immature and inexperienced, he cannot conceive that song might bear seriously on one's life as well as provide amusement. He ends his rebuke to his mother with these words (i.356-59):

ἀλλ᾽ εἰς οἶκον ἰοῦσα τὰ σ᾽ αὐτῆς ἔργα κόμιζε,
ἱστόν τ᾽ ἠλακάτην τε, καὶ ἀμφιπόλοισι κέλευε
ἔργον ἐποίχεσθαι· μῦθος δ᾽ ἄνδρεσσι μελήσει
πᾶσι, μάλιστα δ᾽ ἐμοί· τοῦ γὰρ κράτος ἔστ᾽ ἐνὶ οἴκῳ.

But go to your chamber and attend to your own tasks,
the loom and the distaff, and tell the maidservants
to busy themselves about the work. Storytelling [*muthos*] will be men's
  business,
all men's, but mine most of all; for authority in the house belongs to me.

These lines are almost identical to the end of Hektor's speech to Andromakhe in their great scene in the *Iliad* (VI.490-93), except that Hektor names war rather than song as men's concern. The substitution of one for the other is natural because of the obvious connection between them,[2] but both Homeric poems, as we shall see, imply a sharp distinction between those who act and those who merely enjoy tales about action. His claim to a man's prerogatives may be a sign of Telemakhos's approaching maturity. Nevertheless, his too easy assumption of the masculine privilege of hearing stories without first having had personal experience of action marks him as sheltered, as still between child and man. Thus he naturally finds in song no more than superficial pleasure, and considers novelty of theme a sufficient standard of artistic quality, without caring how closely the story corresponds to experience. In this essential immaturity, the suitors, with their sheltered life, resemble him. Telemakhos's expectations of song and his response to it are surely valid as far as they go—they are, after all, implied by the way the hexameter poets conventionally represent their art. But the *Odyssey* as a whole will suggest that poetry has further possibilities as well.

Because song is associated above all with the banquet, it is an important part of hospitality. In asserting to Penelope his supremacy in the house (i.359), Telemakhos claims his right to act as host—that is, to regulate the entertainment offered the suitors. Near the climax of the poem, Telemakhos will again claim authority when he tells his mother that he, and not she, is fit to decide who may try to string Odysseus's bow. There (xxi.350-53) the same four lines recur that were quoted above, but for "storytelling" (*muthos*) is substituted "the bow" (*toxon*). This later passage is thus much closer to Hektor's words to Andromakhe, and it shows that a development has occurred in the plot of the poem and in Telemakhos's character. Telemakhos is concerned not only with the test of the bow. He wants to remove his mother from the hall because of the battle that—as he knows and she does not—is about to take place. In that conflict he will gain the experience lacking before; he will perform deeds and definitively prove his manhood. He has been growing up to this moment throughout the poem. Thus his later self-assertion to his mother has a substance that the earlier one lacked, for there he laid claim to words without the actions to justify and balance them. How to reconcile word and deed is, in fact, one of the basic questions within the poem.

The Phaiakians, though the opposite to the suitors in respect to decorum, share their and Telemakhos's attitude towards song. Lacking direct knowledge of hardship or sorrow, under no obligation for strenuous action, they feel nothing but pleasure at the performances that grace their feasts. Describing his peoples excellence (*aretē*) to Odysseus, Alkinoos says that they are not distinguished boxers or wrestlers but nimble runners and outstanding sailors. Their favorite pastimes are the feast, music, and dancing, and their concerns "changes of clothing, hot baths, and beds" (viii.246–49). The contrast with the heroic standards that guided Odysseus and all his comrades at Troy is obvious.[3]

For his part Odysseus responds to heroic narrative the way Penelope does, and this similarity links them intangibly despite the distance caused by physical separation and later by his disguise. Just as Penelope weeps in the opening book while the suitors take pleasure, Odysseus's tears at Dēmodokos's first song are set against the background of the Phaiakians' delighted entreaties of the bard to continue (viii.87–92). The relation of these two characters to song is central to the whole *Odyssey,* but it is paradoxical. On the conventional view, as presented by Hesiod, the memory induced by poetry should be pleasurable and obliterate grief. Odysseus especially cannot stay away from the memory of his experiences in the Trojan War—he initiates Dēmodokos's second song on this subject—yet for him poetry cannot discharge its proper function. The reason, one suspects, is important to an understanding of the *Odyssey,* but it is not obvious. That "mourning is not sorrow but a constructive response to sorrow, a mastery of experience" (Redfield, 1973, 153), though probably true in general, cannot be the whole explanation here, because weeping does not mitigate the pain of either husband or wife; they are no more reconciled to their hardships after the songs at which they weep than they were before. A more plausible suggestion is that personal involvement in the story abolishes the necessary distance between audience and poem.[4] Odysseus takes pleasure in the tale of Ares and Aphrodite, which separates and contrasts with Dēmodokos's songs on Trojan themes (τέρπετο, *terpeto,* viii.368). Yet why must the narrative be personally neutral? It should gratify Odysseus to hear his deeds celebrated, and the Sirens tempt him with just this kind of song (xii.189–90). Moreover, as we shall see, the memory of their trials does not always cause Odysseus and Penelope pain. Apparently a poem on a subject of close concern to its listeners risks failure (that is, risks producing distress rather than pleasure) as songs on other themes do not; but under certain circumstances it too can succeed.

What, then, are the right conditions? Distance of some kind is probably necessary, but I would suggest that it must be temporal rather than thematic. What Penelope on Ithaka and Odysseus in Phaiakia have in common when they weep is that they are still undergoing their experiences. The ending is in the future and unforeseeable, scarcely even to be hoped for without fear of delusion by self or by others. When a story is over, it can be seen whole, judged as happy or sad, and—it is to be hoped—understood as part of an order in human life.[5] The outcome need not be fortunate. If it is, as with Odysseus and Penelope, so much the better. But in any case, lapse of time by itself creates a measure of objectivity, and an ending of any sort is a settlement; it brings respite and gives perspective upon events. So Eumaios, about to relate his own very mixed experience, proposes to his ragged guest (xv.398–401):[6]

νῶϊ δ' ἐνὶ κλισίῃ πίνοντέ τε δαινυμένω τε
κήδεσιν ἀλλήλων τερπώμεθα λευγαλέοισι,
μνωομένω· μετὰ γάρ τε καὶ ἄλγεσι τέρπεται ἀνήρ,
ὅς τις δὴ μάλα πολλὰ πάθῃ καὶ πόλλ' ἐπαληθῇ.

But let us feast and drink in the hut,
and let us take delight [*terpōmetha*] in each other's sorry woes,
remembering them [*mnōomenō*]. For afterward a man delights [*terpetai*]
    even in pains,
any man who has had many sufferings and has wandered much.

The last line, unknown to Eumaios, describes no one so well as the man he addresses, the disguised Odysseus. These words introduce the swineherd's account of his own history (xv.403–84), which—with the motif of wandering at the mercy of others and its romantic touches (the royal child sold into slavery, the treacherous nurse who is ultimately punished)—matches the lying tales Odysseus tells.[7] Odysseus's experiences as an outcast, real and assumed, correspond to those of the swineherd. And the recalling of the past with delight, which accompanies a meal, makes this scene the rustic analogue of the entertainments in aristocratic houses with their professional singers.

In this sense memory is constructive, and the narrative that embodies it, whether in song or informal anecdote, gives shape to experience and enables men to assimilate it. With this last example we have moved from poetic performance to spoken story—a natural extension, surely, especially since both forms of narrative fulfill the same function with regard to memory. In Odysseus's case particularly the justification for this shift will emerge when we consider how his storytelling is described.

It is, in fact, a scene of spoken and informal storytelling in which all the narratives within the poem culminate. Reunited in the bed that is the token of the stability in their marriage, Odysseus and Penelope recount their trials to one another (xxiii.300–343). Penelope tells of her endurance in the house

while the suitors, on her account, wasted its riches. The story of the *Odyssey*
has been partly hers from the start, although everyone has ignored her claim—
even Odysseus, who would not reveal himself in Book 19 and so admit her to
the plot against the suitors. Through most of the poem, her role has been to
wait passively. But at the decisive moment she has exercised her feminine
qualities to control the time and manner of her reunion with Odysseus, and in
this way she has asserted her rightful place in the action. Thus, whereas Telemakhos earlier dismissed her by saying that narrative (μῦθος, *muthos,* i.358) is
men's affair, she can now enjoy hearing—and telling—stories (μῦθοι, *muthoi,*
xxiii.301). And Odysseus recalls his wanderings, not to Telemakhos or any
male audience, but to Penelope alone. The poem as a whole thus shows the
process by which storytelling becomes this woman's business.

In the immediate context, this is an interlude of rest. Further labor is in
store for Odysseus: the suitors' kinsmen pose a threat, and Poseidon must be
appeased. But the main trials are over and the future, as we know from
Teiresias's prophecy, is assured. This scene anticipates Odysseus's permanent
restoration to his home. Thus he and Penelope, who wept at such stories before, now take delight in telling over what they endured (τερπέσθην, *terpes-
thēn,* xxiii.301; cf. 308). The content of their stories is not happy—they have
had full experience of the human condition, as the diction shows. Penelope
recounts her sufferings and her endurance (ἀνέσχετο, *aneskheto,* l. 302);
Odysseus, the pains he inflicted on others and his own woeful labors (κήδεα,
ὀϊζύς, *kēdea, oïsdus,* lines 306-7). But their experiences can now be viewed
from the perspective of the virtual ending, and past adversity underscores the
value of the final success. This moment of shared retrospect by husband and
wife is their fit reward in this poem of mature and measured joy.

Together, they retell a substantial part of our *Odyssey;* and this recapitulation—in effect, a "poem-within-the-poem"—acts as a reminder of the nature
and purpose of the main narrative. Odysseus's account especially serves this
end. As we observed in the first chapter, the poet repeats in catalogue form
the tale that Odysseus told at length to the Phaiakians. Near the end comes
the Kalypsō episode (xxiii.333-37), the conclusion of which has formed part
of the *Odyssey*'s action (in Book 5), but which was already in the past when
the hero described it at Alkinoos's court (vii.244-46, ix.29-30, xii.447-50).
In addition, Odysseus tells Penelope about his reception by the Phaiakians
(xxiii.338-41), which also is now a completed incident. Thus his story is progressively updated; in the course of the *Odyssey* events narrated as they occur
turn into past experiences, objects of memory. Even before the Phaiakian interlude, Odysseus told his story to other hosts. Aiolos and his sons feasted
him for a month while he recounted the Trojan War and the returns of the
Akhaians (x.14-16). The latter presumably included his own wanderings, but
by that point these would have consisted only of the episodes of the Kikones
and the Kyklōps. The encounter with Aiolos and the reference to his own
narrative on that occasion in their turn form part of the more fully developed—

but not yet finished—story that Odysseus tells the Phaiakians (his reception by Aiolos is, in fact, a highly compressed version of the Phaiakian episode).

By noticing this progressive transformation of the present into the past, and by tracing the change in the attitudes of Odysseus and Penelope towards stories in which they play a role or have a personal interest, we observe the *Odyssey* come into being as a poem and assume a poem's proper function. The *Odyssey*, that is—any part of which would excite sorrow in Odysseus or Penelope until it has completed their story—is transformed at the end into a means of pleasure through memory. Up to this point, there has always been a difference between the internal narratives and the poem in which they are embedded. But here this distance is abolished. The poem and its subject become identical; and the *Odyssey* presents itself as a finished—or nearly finished—work that at this very moment is taking its place among other accounts of past events. It thus suggests the proper mode of the audience's response: delight in its affirmation of continued life through the memory of pain overcome and triumph achieved. For Odysseus and Penelope the memory exercised through narrative, and for the audience the poem that incorporates it, are alike the way of coping with the suffering to which all mortals are by nature exposed.[8]

This evolution does not take place in a vacuum, however. The *Odyssey* defines itself not merely as a poem but also, and simultaneously, as a particular kind of poem: a heroic epic whose subject is a *nostos*, or return. By setting itself within this category and by alluding to related stories, the poem invites its audience to draw comparisons and contrasts with other poems on those themes. Especially because of the differences, the *Odyssey* claims for itself a privileged status as a song that tells a more significant story.

Phēmios's performance in the first book classifies the poem, for Odysseus's wandering after the Trojan War is among the *nostoi* of the Greeks, as Penelope's tears imply. The story of the returns is characterized as λυχρός (*lugros*, "baneful," i.326-27), a fair description of events as Nestor recalls them to Telemakhos: Athena's wrath, the resulting quarrel between the sons of Atreus, and the scattering of the Greeks (iii.130-36: note λυγρὸν . . . νόστον, *lugron . . . noston*, "baneful return," l. 132). Many eventually reached home in safety (iii.180-92). But Menelaos was blown off course to Egypt, where Prōteus—after warning him that he would not be able to listen without tears—told him of the other outstanding examples of suffering on the way home (iv.491-560): Oïlean Ajax and Agamemnon, the only two leaders (as distinguished from common soldiers) who died, and finally Odysseus himself.[9]

When Menelaos hears of him, Odysseus is trapped on Kalypsō's island. But the return of the last of the Akhaians to arrive home, as the *Odyssey* goes on to tell it, will differ in important ways from the other homecomings of which details are given in the poem. Odysseus survives shipwreck to return alive, thanks to his self-restraint—particularly in the episode of the Sun's cattle. Ajax the son of Oïleus was drowned for his arrogance towards the gods (iv.499–511). At home Odysseus defeats usurpers in his house, whereas Aigisthos murdered Agamemnon. From early in the poem onward, the family group of Agamemnon, Klytaimēstra, and Orestes is compared and contrasted with Odysseus, Penelope, and Telemakhos, and the parallel is drawn between Aigisthos and suitors.[10] Agamemnon's fate, recounted to Odysseus in Book 11, shows what Odysseus's own story would be if his wife were not a Penelope, or what might happen despite Penelope if, like Agamemnon and against his warning (xi.454–56), he were to return home undisguised. Like Menelaos, Odysseus will live on in prosperity at home after long wandering, but as we shall see presently, there are important contrasts in the value of what each attains. Nestor as we find him in Book 3 provides the closest parallel to Odysseus's eventual fortune. But it would be impossible to compose a poem about his homecoming, because it was uneventful. Odysseus must win the contentment that simply falls to Nestor's lot, and he does so by performing an act of heroic prowess, revenge on the suitors. His return, unlike those of Nestor and all the other Greeks, is an occasion for winning glory (*kleos*) that will be added to the fame he won at Troy and will be disseminated in song (the *Odyssey*). In varying ways, then, the homecomings of his former comrades shed light by contrast on Odysseus's return, stress its uniqueness. His *nostos* is "baneful" because he has had to wander for ten years, has lost all his men, and finds evils in his house.[11] But his arrival on Ithaka and his victory there, on which the *Odyssey* concentrates, offset (though they cannot cancel) the suffering. The rest of the Akhaians, whose returns would form the subjects of other songs, either perish or fall short of Odysseus's success. But it is not just the quality of the ending that distinguishes the *Odyssey* from other *nostoi*, potential or real. The peculiar blend of extreme hardship with outstanding achievement that characterizes its subject allows the *Odyssey* to depict the strengths as well as the weaknesses of mankind, and thus to show what being mortal means. The *Iliad* has the same purpose but fulfills it in a very different way and arrives at a different vision of human life.

In order to evaluate its subject against other possible themes for song, the *Odyssey* refers not only to other stories of the returns but also to episodes of the Trojan War itself. Although the poet of the *Odyssey* carefully avoids duplicating the narrative of the *Iliad*, a comparison in the attitudes of these poems is instructive. The *Iliad* sheds no false glamor on the war. It depicts all battle as destructive though inevitable; but it also guides us towards a reconciliation with death and all suffering by revealing the peculiarly human virtues that men exercise in the face of these necessities. The *Odyssey*, on the other hand, even as its own hero's story proceeds, presents a view back over the Trojan War from the perspective afforded by a ten-year interval. At that distance, the war appears to represent misery for all participants, which human greatness might not redeem. The *Odyssey* does recognize the heroism displayed at Troy; but as far as this poem is concerned, it remains to be seen whether coherent meaning can emerge from all the grief. That will depend on the outcome of Odysseus's own story. But for most of its length the poem stresses the war's grim effects on men's lives.

When Odysseus weeps at Dēmodokos's two songs about Troy in Book 8, his grief seems stirred partly by the contrast between his former deeds and his outcast state, but partly also by the memory of toil (that memory cannot now be pleasurable, for present and past have not yet taken their place in a finished story). On the second occasion Odysseus's weeping is likened to a woman's lamentation over the corpse of her husband killed fighting for his city, while her captors, taking her into slavery, prod her from behind (viii. 523-31). This closely resembles the fate that Hektor in the *Iliad* foresees for Andromakhe on the day of Troy's fall (VI.447-65).[12] The simile expresses the *Odyssey*'s revaluation of the Trojan War. It shows that the grief of both victors and vanquished is finally the same. For the "baneful" returns are a consequence of the war, the price that the Akhaians must pay for their victory.

Besides its hero himself, the *Odyssey* shows us several of the Greek leaders, living and dead, as the war has left them. Of these, Nestor (who alone excels Odysseus in his talent for survival) is the most content with his present lot. Yet even for him Troy evokes the memory of hardship and of companions lost. Telemakhos would have to stay in Pylos five or six years, he says, to hear the full tale of the Akhaians' suffering (iii.102-17). Nestor has also been touched by personal loss, for his son Antilokhos was killed in the war. At Sparta Peisistratos will share in his table companions' sorrow for those lost on the Trojan expedition by remembering his dead brother (iv.187-88, 199-202).

We first see the palace of Menelaos through Telemakhos's eyes (iv.20-22, 43-48). The ordered festivity and the opulent surroundings provide an enviable contrast with the situation he has left on Ithaka. Thus our first impression is that Menelaos's life sets an exemplary pattern to which Odysseus's lot, if happy, ought to conform. And in fact these men have much in common. Each is married to an outstanding woman. Both have wandered, and narrate their experiences during the poem. They both have received prophecies of their fate and, overcoming obstacles, returned home with riches. Like Odysseus, Menelaos found the situation at home altered from what it was when he left (Agamemnon dead, and the usurper Aigisthos murdered only on the day of his return).[13] These resemblances, however, merely emphasize the more important contrast between the two homecomings. Menelaos's happiness is irretrievably damaged by the war and its aftermath, whereas Odysseus's labors ultimately serve the constructive purpose of making home and family seem all the more precious. Thus memory plays very different roles for each of them.

Because of Agamemnon's fate, says Menelaos, he cannot enjoy the great wealth he brought home. He weeps often for the others who died at Troy on his and Helen's account, but most of all for the vanished Odysseus (iv.78-112). Eventually, he and Helen and their guests all weep in pain at their memories (iv.183-88). After they stop and turn to food, Helen ensures that their grief

will be kept in abeyance for a while by administering a drug that is described
as (iv.221)

νηπενθές τ᾽ ἄχολόν τε, κακῶν ἐπίληθον ἀπάντων.

banishing grief [nē-penthes] and anger, causing forgetfulness [epi-lēthon]
　　of all evils.

Hesiod, as we have observed, uses very similar language concerning the effects
of song (*Theog.* 55, 98-103; see pp. 136, 147-48, above), and in other respects
Helen's talents resemble those of the poet. In the *Iliad* she transmutes events
into art as they happen (III.125-28). Menelaos tells how she imitated the voices
of all the Akhaians' wives (iv.279)—just as the Delian maidens can imitate the
speech of all men (*h. Apollo* 162-64). In her weaving in the *Iliad* and her use
of the potion here, Helen represents the poles of memory and forgetfulness
that characterize poetry.[14] And indeed, after the doctored wine has been
served, she invites Menelaos and the guests to "take delight in stories" (μύθοις
τέρπεσθε, *muthois terpesthe*, iv.239).

　　This association of Helen with the poet, however, only shows how far she
and Menelaos are from being able to enjoy the proper use of memory. If their
experience at Troy were truly finished, a drug would not be necessary. Their
recollections in themselves should arouse delight and banish cares. The stories
they go on to tell show why this is impossible. The role Helen claims for herself in the episode she recounts is designed to demonstrate her continued
loyalty to her husband and the other Greeks while she was at Troy. Menelaos's
account of the Wooden Horse, by contrast, implicitly accuses her of helping
the Trojans even at the very end of the war (iv.240-89). The fall of Troy for
this woman's sake has settled nothing between them. Helen has brought her
guilt back from the war; Menelaos, his suspicion. Civilized though the surface
of their life together may be, they are condemned to an interminable debate
about the past carried on obliquely by means of memories from which
Helen's drug can only temporarily remove the sting.[15]

　　Odysseus and Penelope, by contrast, will share their memories in bed together with delight. The stories told at Sparta already point ahead to Odysseus's ultimate success because they illustrate qualities in him that are essential
to it. Helen's tale shows him practicing his famous guile, and his visit to Troy
in disguise foreshadows the manner of his return to his own house. Menelaos's
anecdote illustrates Odysseus's self-control, which will enable him to resist
the temptation posed by the cattle of the Sun (xi.105). On Ithaka he will
converse with his wife without revealing himself and will even sit by while she
weeps, just as Helen's imitation of the Akhaians' wives failed against him.[16]
For Odysseus alone, the patterns of action set at Troy portend only good.
These anticipations, in such a context, contrast Odysseus's homecoming and
subsequent life with those of Menelaos; the complete reunion that awaits him

and Penelope with the barrier that divides Menelaos and Helen; the contentment that the future ultimately holds for Odysseus, when memory will be a
source of joy, with Menelaos's servitude to the past. Menelaos may in the end
attain immortal ease, but Odysseus, who has declined immortality, will have
the satisfying human life that the other lacks.

As this episode shows, the poem's retrospect upon the Trojan War is important to the portrayal of Odysseus. His character and fate are also set off
sharply by the contrasts between him and the three Akhaians prominent at
Troy whose shades he meets in Book 11. Agamemnon's disastrous homecoming, as we have seen, is in every way the antithesis of Odysseus's successful one. His tale of treachery draws from Odysseus the remark that Atreus's
sons were unlucky in their women. Between themselves the two sisters who
married Menelaos and Agamemnon epitomize all the woe that the expedition
brought upon the Akhaians: Helen, the cause of the war, and Klytaimēstra,
who helped contrive the most terrible *nostos* (xi.436-39).

The other two encounters reveal, by the contrasts they imply, what kind
of hero Odysseus is. Ajax, with his stupendous silence, is frozen in the attitude
of anger and hatred that led to his suicide. It is the adaptable Odysseus who
proposes a reconciliation, and Ajax's contempt, magnificent though it is,
shows why he is dead and Odysseus alive (xi.541-64). This inflexible anger is
traditionally heroic, but it is too often self-defeating. Odysseus, on the other
hand, can adjust his behavior to suit the demands of complex and changing
situations—without, in the end, betraying his sense of his own worth or his
capacity for passion, or in any other way compromising the spirit of the
traditional values. By the time he meets Ajax, we have already received this
impression of him vividly from his conversation with the shade of that other
figure of whom wrath is most characteristic: Achilles (xi.467-540).

In this passage, the hero of the *Odyssey* confronts the hero of the *Iliad*.
The triumphant survivor of the most arduous homecoming meets the greatest
of the warriors who fought at Troy, the most illustrious of the dead. Each
clearly recognizes the essence of the other's nature and the advantage of the
resulting fate. Achilles marvels at Odysseus's presence, and interprets it as his
greatest achievement, but a characteristic one (xi.473-76):

διογενὲς Λαερτιάδη, πολυμήχαν' 'Οδυσσεῦ,
σχέτλιε, τίπτ' ἔτι μεῖζον ἐνὶ φρεσὶ μήσεαι ἔργον;
πῶς ἔτλης Ἀϊδόσδε κατελθέμεν, ἔνθα τε νεκροὶ
ἀφραδέες ναίουσι, βροτῶν εἴδωλα καμόντων;

God-descended son of Laertes, resourceful Odysseus,
Amazing fellow! What still greater deed will you contrive [*mēseai*] in your
   mind?
How did you endure to descend to Hades, where dwell
the witless dead, images of mortals overcome by death?

Achilles pays tribute to Odysseus's talent for improvisation, his craftiness or *mētis,* a quality that (as the *Iliad* shows) he himself lacked in life. Odysseus, in reply, deprecates his arrival among the dead as one of his many afflictions and praises Achilles' lot as enviable (xi.481–86):

οὐ γάρ πω σχεδὸν ἦλθον Ἀχαιΐδος, οὐδέ πω ἀμῆς
γῆς ἐπέβην, ἀλλ᾽ αἰὲν ἔχω κακά· σεῖο δ᾽, Ἀχιλλεῦ,
οὔ τις ἀνὴρ προπάροιθε μακάρτατος οὔτ᾽ ἄρ᾽ ὀπίσσω.
πρὶν μὲν γάρ σε ζωὸν ἐτίομεν ἶσα θεοῖσιν
Ἀργεῖοι, νῦν αὖτε μέγα κρατέεις νεκύεσσιν
ἐνθάδ᾽ ἐών· τῷ μή τι θανὼν ἀκαχίζευ, Ἀχιλλεῦ.

For I have not yet come near Akhaia, nor set foot
upon my soil, but I have misfortunes always. But you, Achilles—
no man before has been more blessed than you, nor will any be in time to
   come.
Before, while you lived, we Argives held you in honor [*etiomen*]
equal to the gods', and now you have great power among the dead
here. So don't be vexed in death, Achilles.

What Achilles achieved in life was the ultimate goal of heroic conduct, god-like honor (*timē*). With his experience of suffering, Odysseus admires that. Achilles, with his knowledge of death, now finds his own fate deficient. And so he gives his famous answer, that he would rather be the servant of a pauper on earth than lord among the dead (xi.488–91). This is the man who chose a short life with glory over a long but obscure life. The heroic standards, as we observed earlier, are predicated upon death; that is at once their virtue and their weakness. The latter is what Achilles now stresses. He still adheres to the values by which he lived, however; even in death he takes pleasure in the news that his son Neoptolemos is continuing the tradition of heroic action and is a worthy successor to his father. But—although this detail, like the whole scene, pays a moving tribute to Achilles—even here we are reminded of the limits of those standards: Achilles survives not personally but only through his son.

   With his reply to Odysseus, then, the "Iliadic" Achilles speaks with an "Odyssean" perspective that qualifies the glory of the deeds performed at Troy. Odysseus envies him because his own story is still developing and the outcome can be reached only with further labor. A final and, in many ways, an admiring judgment can be passed on Achilles' life because it is over; an ending confers certainty. If Odysseus were to die before reaching home, at sea or in a distant, unknown land, his fate would be inferior to that of Achilles, who was killed in battle at the height of his splendor. (Cf. v.306–12.) But Odysseus has the great advantage of being still alive, and the future holds for him not only dangers but also great possibilities now barred to Achilles.

In the end, Odysseus gets both terms of Achilles' choice: a long and tranquil life (predicted by Teiresias) *and* glory.[17] The latter comes to him not only for his deeds at Troy, through songs like those of Dēmodokos, but also for his last exploit, the killing of the suitors. In the final book, the same shades appear as in the earlier Underworld scene—Achilles, Patroklos and Antilokhos, Ajax, and Agamemnon (xxiv.15-22; cf. xi.467-70).[18] This time it is Agamemnon who congratulates Achilles. The great king, who is to be remembered more as the victim of a murderous plot than as the leader of a magnificent army and the sacker of Troy, naturally admires the manner of Achilles' death and funeral. Death overwhelms all other considerations, so that Achilles now receives fair admiration from the man who was his adversary in the story of his wrath.[19] That episode is in the past, its protagonists alive only in memory. The arrival of the suitors' shades signals that another story has only now reached its climax. When Agamemnon hears of their slaughter, he exclaims over Odysseus's happy lot, just as he did over Achilles' (xxiv.36, 192):

ὄλβιε Πηλος υἱέ, θεοῖς ἐπιείκελ' Ἀχιλλεῦ.

Lucky [*olbie*] son of Peleus, godlike Achilles!

ὄλβιε Λαέρταο πάϊ, πολυμήχαν' Ὀδυσσεῦ.

Lucky [*olbie*] son of Laertes, resourceful Odysseus!

Agamemnon goes on to contrast Penelope and Klytaimēstra, who are exact opposites in character and deeds, and thus will be rewarded with opposing reputations preserved for the future in song. Klytaimēstra will get a "hateful song" for her evil deeds (xxiv.199-202), while Penelope's *kleos* for her excellence (*aretē*) will never perish (xxiv.196-98; cf. 193). This is another self-conscious gesture by the poet, for the *Odyssey* condemns and praises both women respectively, thus encompassing both kinds of song. The terms in which Agamemnon honors Penelope are those that can be—and frequently are—applied to male heroism in battle as commemorated by epic poetry. The usage here is not unique, to be sure; the praise of the Delian maidens in the *Hymn to Apollo* is similar. But it does indicate that the *Odyssey*, a heroic poem, is concerned to define and praise not only the excellences evoked by war but also those exercised in peace.[20] The *Iliad*, of course, gives poignant glimpses of peaceful activities, but provides them for the sake of its presentation of the war. When Hektor tells Andromakhe that warfare will be men's concern (VI.492), they part—Andromakhe to tend her weaving and Hektor to fight—in the Skaian gate, on the line that divides the city from the battlefield. There is finally, in the *Iliad*, no reconciling these two spheres. But in the *Odyssey*, the poem of reunion rather than of leave-taking, domestic virtue is given its due, and the woman's excellence complements the man's. Both are equally necessary to the harmony and prosperity of continuing life. In the roles of Odysseus and Penelope, we have another case of polar opposites, each of which is incomplete without the other but which together create a whole. It illustrates what the *Iliad,* for all its magnificence, or any other poem of war, lacks.

Within the *Odyssey,* the case of Agamemnon shows the disaster that can result when the woman betrays her proper role. And in fact the compliment to Penelope comes in by way of Agamemnon's congratulation to Odysseus. It thus implicitly contrasts the latter's survival with his own death. Furthermore, Odysseus's success caps even Achilles' greatness in defeat. If, therefore, Achilles has been luckier than Agamemnon, Odysseus is the most fortunate of all.[21]

Thus the *Odyssey* looks back even as its narrative goes forward. It gathers into itself stories from all stages of the Trojan War[22] and, by implicitly commenting on them, presents its own subject as somehow more vital. Part of this self-definition is the portrayal of Odysseus, which the poet effects in large part by drawing careful distinctions between him and other important figures from the tradition surrounding the war. The differences are based mainly on Odysseus's final success, but this in turn depends heavily on the qualities of his character (as we see particularly in Helen's and Menelaos's recollections of him). Unlike so many others—especially, but not exclusively, Achilles—Odysseus is fit to be the hero of poems not only about warfare but on other themes as well. The aspect of Odysseus most important to the meaning of the poem has yet to be mentioned, however. Just as the poet (so we observed in Chapter 4) can be conceived as a hero, in the *Odyssey* the hero is represented as a poet. In a poem so concerned with the characteristics and uses of poetry, this portrayal is natural; but nowhere else in extant hexameter poetry is the kinship between the two roles made a poetic theme as it is in the *Odyssey.* It must immediately be added that the similarity between Odysseus and a poet remains just that, and never amounts to literal identity. Odysseus speaks; he never sings or plays the phorminx.[23] Yet as passages cited earlier clearly show, spoken and sung narrative share this essential feature; they both involve the use of memory, in a serious, almost magical, sense of the term that far surpasses mere factual recollection. Odysseus also has the skills that most distinguish the poetic art, and he is several times explicitly likened to a poet.

The relation between Odysseus and the poet of the *Odyssey* appears clearly at the beginning of his account of his wanderings, where he takes over the role of narrator, though his words are set in what really are the poet's verses. It is well known that the attack on the city of the Kikonians (ix.39–61) recapitulates the sack of Troy but is told in a flat, summary style that reduces that victory to the level of everyday brutality.[24] This is also the only episode of the wanderings set in the known world. The other adventures thus seem richer, superior to this tale of warfare that has been deliberately stripped of the heroic element and left grimly realistic. This tone in turn implies a comment on Dēmodokos's songs about Troy in the preceding book. They are devalued. Odysseus's story will excel them, just as the poet of the *Odyssey* implies that his poem surpasses those about heroic battle. The wanderings are to Dēmodokos's narratives as the *Odyssey* is to its tradition, and Odysseus, by the terms of this analogy, is a substitute for the poet.

The way Odysseus presents his story resembles a poetic performance. In Book 11 (ll. 330-32), he interrupts himself and stops, just as Demodokos has done (viii.87-92), and like Demodokos he is urged by his audience to continue. At this point he is explicitly compared to a poet for the first time, in the compliment Alkinoos pays him. You don't seem to be a trickster, Alkinoos tells Odysseus (xi.367-69):

σοὶ δ' ἔπι μὲν μορφὴ ἐπέων, ἔνι δὲ φρένες ἐσθλαί,
μῦθον δ' ὡς ὅτ' ἀοιδὸς ἐπισταμένως κατέλεξας,
πάντων 'Αργείων σέο τ' αὐτοῦ κήδεα λυγρά.

But there is comeliness of words upon you, and excellent sense within you.
You have told your story [*muthos*] skillfully as when a singer [*aoidos*]
    does,
Your own and all the Argives' baneful woes [*kēdea*].

Coming from a Phaiakian, a connoisseur of such performances, this is high praise indeed. But the poet himself tells us that Odysseus's tales have entranced the listeners, as song typically does. All were silent, he says, bound by the story's spell (κηληθμός, *kēlēthmos*, xi.333-34, xiii.1-2).

At the very beginning of his narrative, however, Odysseus seems to distinguish himself from a poet. He first describes to Alkinoos the height of enjoyment—a banquet, wine, and a singer's entertainment—and then continues (ix.12-15):

σοὶ δ' ἐμὰ κήδεα θυμὸς ἐπετράπετο στονόεντα
εἴρεσθ', ὄφρ' ἔτι μᾶλλον ὀδυρόμενος στεναχίζω.
τί πρῶτόν τοι ἔπειτα, τί δ' ὑστάτιον καταλέξω;
κήδε' ἐπεί μοι πολλὰ δόσαν θεοὶ οὐρανίωνες.

But your desire has turned to ask about my mournful
afflictions [*kēdea*], so that I groan still more in grief.
Then what shall I recount first, what last?
For the heavenly gods have given me many troubles [*kēdēa*].

These words do not contradict the comparison Alkinoos makes. They can be explained along the lines suggested above. Odysseus is still undergoing the experiences of which he speaks; therefore he *gives* pleasure to the Phaiakians with his tale, but at the cost of pain *to himself*. The emotions that singers feel as they perform are never mentioned in our poems, but they cannot be sad ones. Thus we gauge the difficulty of Odysseus' predicament not only by the effect of memory on him (as we observed earlier) but more specifically by his difference in this detail from the poet as conventionally depicted, whom he otherwise resembles.

On Ithaka, Odysseus continues to give poetlike performances. He tells Eumaios a story of Troy as a gracefully indirect way of asking for a cloak on a chilly night. In keeping with the occasion, he blames the urge to talk on wine, which induces a man to laugh and dance and *sing* (ἀεῖσαι, *aeisai*, xiv. 463-66). Eumaios refers to the story as an αἶνος (*ainos*, xiv.508), a term that may refer to a type of poetry, specifically that of praise.[25] Of course, the disguised Odysseus is really praising himself, and although his tale is fabrication, his self-portrait is utterly faithful to his character. The verbal deceit on which his trick in the story hinges is the talent he is exercising on Eumaios at this very moment, and with equal success. The swineherd understands just what Odysseus intends him to (that the beggar is in need of a cloak), but misses the real point (that the beggar is really Odysseus), which the audience perceives.

Later on, Eumaios tells Penelope that his guest is like a singer (*aoidos*) and would "enchant" her (ϑέλγοιτο, *thelgoito*) as he has "enchanted" him (ἔϑελγε, *ethelge*, xvii.512-21). Eumaios's admiration shows how skillfully he has been deceived. In the second half of the poem Odysseus tells a series of lying stories that are based upon his actual experiences and have certain elements in common with them. Redfield well describes how poetlike his procedure is: "Odysseus is a poet in the bardic style; he works by thematic variation. . . . [He] has a command of the *oimai:* by manipulating his stock he can make . . . an endless stream of novel lying tales."[26] Like truth, deceit is, as we have seen, a power latent in the poetic art. The poet sums up his hero's false tale to Penelope in a line that resembles the Muses' description of their power in Hesiod (xix.203; cf. *Theog.* 27):[27]

ἴσκε ψεύδεα πολλὰ λέγων ἐτύμοισιν ὁμοῖα.

In his speech he made many lies [*pseudea*] into the semblance of true things [*etumoisin*].

It is unnecessary to suppose that this line is an imitation of Hesiod, or vice versa. Odysseus is portrayed by means of what was very likely a traditional conception of the singer's art.

Thus Alkinoos, in likening Odysseus to a poet as opposed to a liar, is too credulous. He makes the right analogy for the wrong reason. Perhaps it is natural for him to do so, for poets would always *claim* to speak the truth. Or perhaps his words should be taken as subtle characterization of the Phaiakians. Secure and prosperous, with no direct experience of danger or adversity (at least until after Odysseus's visit), they need not trouble themselves much about what is true and what false, whereas for men in normal circumstances the question is crucial. Whatever the reason, the rest of the poem exposes

Alkinoos's attitude as naive. We can observe Odysseus in operation, how he gives his lies the appearance of truth; for we have heard his real story in Books 9-12. This "master of truth" (in Detienne's phrase) also has mastery over deceptive falsehood, and knows, more clearly than anyone else, the difference. That is what makes him a successful liar.

Odysseus finally reverts to truthful discourse, when it is safe to do so—in bed with Penelope. Here too are elements typical of a poetic performance. Husband and wife take delight in each other's stories. Moreover, Penelope does not fall asleep until Odysseus has reached the end of the Phaiakian episode (xxiii.308-9). In the same way, Alkinoos has said that he could stay awake until morning listening to Odysseus (xi.375-76; cf. xix.589-90). This is nearly Odysseus's last performance in the poem, and it is the last one that really matters.[28] In this scene we see memory not only restored to its proper function (delight) but also used for what is, from men's if not the gods' point of view, the proper aim of poetry and related arts: to reveal the truth.

This representation of Odysseus as poet has a remarkable parallel in Hermes of the Homeric Hymn to that god. Hermes is a singer; he invents the phorminx and beguiles Apollo with his art. He is also a skilled liar. Some peculiarities of diction, furthermore, associate this god specifically with Odysseus. Twice in the hymn Hermes is given the epithet πολύτροπος (*polutropos,* "of many turnings," *h. Hermes* 13, 439). This word is the quintessential description of Odysseus, referring as it does to both his long wanderings and his wiles (in the hymn it is used purely in the mental sense). It occurs twice in the *Odyssey,* once in the very first line and again at x.330. These are the only occurrences of the epithet in extant hexameter poetry, and all four times it occupies the same place in the line (before the bucolic diaeresis). Because the generic epithet for a hero that commonly occurs in this metrical position is διΐφιλος (*diiphilos,* "dear to Zeus"), Milman Parry recognized *polutropos* in the *Odyssey* as one of the few epithets used in the Homeric poems with a "particularized meaning" (that is, with reference to the context).[29] The adjective is thus so memorable that its application to Hermes in the hymn (which almost certainly postdates the *Odyssey*) must have evoked Odysseus to the audience and likened the god's cunning to his.[30] Again, Hermes is once called πολύμητις (*polumētis,* "very crafty," *h. Hermes* 319). With one exception,[31] this epithet occurs only here outside the Homeric poems, and in the latter it is used exclusively of Odysseus. Let us add Norman Austin's observation (1975, 39-40) that *polumētis* is associated "with Odysseus as a speaker," whereas Achilles, whose name from the standpoint of meter could receive the same epithet, is always called "swift-footed" when his speeches are introduced in the *Iliad.* Similarly, the word occurs in the hymn after Hermes' false but artful denial that he stole Apollo's cattle and refers specifically to his verbal skill (cf. ll. 317-18). The language thus associates Hermes with Odysseus as a glib speaker. But since Hermes, in harmony with a traditional concept, combines his talent for lying with song, and is even represented (playfully) as the archetypal *aoidos,* the evidence of the hymn lends plausibility to the view of Odysseus's portrayal in the *Odyssey* given here. That holds true whether the hymn was composed under the influence of the *Odyssey* or simply makes use of a conventional means of depicting wiliness and versatility (the truth, in fact, is likely to be a combination of these alternatives). The resemblance between Odysseus and Hermes may even be an idea older than the hymn. Relatively late though this poem seems to be, we cannot tell what religious and poetic conceptions lie behind it. Perhaps it is significant, therefore, that according to the *Odyssey* Hermes was the patron of Odysseus's maternal grandfather Autolykos (xix.396-98), from whose character and deeds Odysseus got his name (xix.405-9).[32]

Most of the explicit and suggested analogies between Odysseus and the poet have recently gained fairly wide recognition.[33] The implications of this means of portrayal, for the character of the hero and thus for the poem as a whole, however, still need to be appreciated. In the preceding chapter, we observed that when Alkinoos indirectly asks his guest's identity, Odysseus declines to tell it, but he does describe himself—as a man at the mercy of his own belly and thus as the antithesis of the singer (vii.208-21). When he tells his story later on, after being fed, he resembles a poet, as we have now noticed. We can reconcile these facts by recalling that song and begging are both related—though in antithetical ways—to the needs of the belly. On Ithaka, Odysseus combines these characteristics. Disguised as a beggar, he casts a persuasive spell upon his listeners just as a poet does. His conduct is effective on two planes at once. In order to restore himself as king, he must first insist on his right to be taken into society as a beggar. In order finally to disclose the truth, he uses his gift of words in its other capacity, lying. Warrior and beggar, outcast and king, poet in both complementary senses of liar and divulger of truth, this "man of many turnings" is master of all roles.

This comprehensiveness is what makes Odysseus extraordinary as an epic hero. Everywhere else in the Homeric poems certain outstanding men act, and others—professional singers—spread their fame. On the other hand, singers do not act. Knowledge comes to them not directly, from experience, but through inspiration. Poetry may epitomize all that is best in civilization, but from the point of view of the warrior, whose profession exposes him to savagery and in some ways puts him beyond civilization, it is typically viewed as the occupation of the weak and cowardly.[34] For the most part, reconciling word and deed is as problematical as reconciling war and peace. Odysseus alone both achieves in traditional heroic fashion and tells the story of his own experiences. The accuracy of Dēmodokos's narrative, Odysseus observes, means that Apollo or the Muse has inspired him (viii.488-91). But shortly after delivering this compliment, Odysseus will combine firsthand knowledge with narrative art (Books 9-12). The singer enjoys the mysterious gift of contact with divinity, but he is limited by it too—at least in comparison with an Odysseus. From this difference follows another. Because of the source of his song, the poet cannot know whether he is speaking truth or falsehood. (See pp. 148–49, above). Odysseus has complete control over both.

The point of the similarity between Odysseus and the poet, then, is to stress his excellence in both speech and action. The proper time for each thus becomes an issue in the poem, one that is closely allied to the question of the use of memory and, more generally, the role of poetry itself. The episode of the Sirens raises these matters urgently for Odysseus and poses a problem for an audience seeking to understand the poem. To hear one's own praises sung, as Odysseus in fact does in Phaiakia, and to share the divine knowledge that the Sirens offer, should be among the highest goods. Yet staying to hear their song would have meant death for Odysseus. The explanation is surely that at this point Odysseus must still strive to get home because the story of his wanderings is evolving and the desired end has not been reached. To linger would be to accept an entirely different conclusion, one without a homecoming, and there would be no *Odyssey*.[35] Here, then, and through most of the poem, song and action alternate, as they do in the conception of poetry generally.

Odysseus's situation at Alkinoos's palace is just the reverse of what it was when he sailed past the Sirens. He can go no farther until the Phaiakians send him, and he spends this interlude listening to Dēmodokos's songs and performing himself. But he declines to stay in Phaiakia, where the civilized arts (dance and song among them) replace the action that is their proper complement (viii.246–49). The overrefined Phaiakians provide yet another foil to Odysseus. Ultimately, Phaiakia presents the same temptation as the Sirens, though the personal danger to Odysseus is far less.

While Odysseus is on Ithaka in Books 13–21, words continue to fill the interval of waiting until the right time for him to act. His poetlike deceptions are part of his disguise, however, and so are essential to the plot. Word and deed begin to merge, though they are still distinct. Then, when Odysseus seizes the opportunity for action that his lies have prepared, they unite in perfect balance in the simile that describes him stringing the bow (xxi.406–11):[36]

ὡς ὅτ᾽ ἀνὴρ φόρμιγγος ἐπιστάμενος καὶ ἀοιδῆς
ῥηϊδίως ἐτάνυσσε νέῳ περὶ κόλλοπι χορδήν,
ἅψας ἀμφοτέρωθεν ἐϋστρεφὲς ἔντερον οἰός,
ὣς ἄρ᾽ ἄτερ σπουδῆς τάνυσεν μέγα τόξον Ὀδυσσεύς.
δεξιτερῇ δ᾽ ἄρα χειρὶ λαβὼν πειρήσατο νευρῆς·
ἡ δ᾽ ὑπὸ καλὸν ἄεισε, χελιδόνι εἰκέλη αὐδήν.

As when a man well-versed in the phorminx and in song
effortlessly stretches a string around a new peg,
fastening the flexible sheep gut at both ends,
so without straining Odysseus strung the great bow.
He grasped it and with his right hand he tested the string,
and at his touch it sang [*aeide*] sweetly, with a sound like a swallow's voice.

On the verge of his greatest triumph, the qualities in Odysseus that make it possible are drawn together in one magnificent comparison. All the earlier portrayals of his poetlike talents stand behind these lines and make them seem absolutely appropriate. But here as never before in the poem, Odysseus the poet and Odysseus the warrior are one.

This simile thus attributes to Odysseus at once both of the qualities claimed by Telemakhos in widely separate parts of the poem (i.358, xxi.352): *muthos* and skill with the bow. Effective though it is for depicting Odysseus, however, it creates an incongruity. Song and battle should properly be kept distinct. Their mixture characterizes the ensuing action as well. Song typically accompanies the meal; but now while the suitors eat, the bow will replace the phorminx. That is the burden of Odysseus's grim jest soon after the simile (xxi.428-30). His words recall the poet's own comment at the end of the preceding book (xx.392-94) and anticipate the manner of Antinoos's death (xxii. 8-21). Although they do not make a negative comment on Odysseus's revenge (see Chapter 2, Section c, above), these passages, with the simile, suggest the abnormality of a situation in which the hero must act violently to restore order. But the simile reminds us once again that Odysseus's talents are for peace as well as war, and in this sense it looks ahead to the poem's outcome. Odysseus's later performance to Penelope resolves the incongruity. There the narrative art (if not literally song) regains its place as an enjoyment in time of peace, when success brings respite from toil and struggles can be remembered rather than borne.

The linking of archery with the playing of a stringed instrument has a parallel in the *Hymn to Apollo,* where the god claims these arts as two of his three provinces (*h. Apollo* 131-32) and is depicted as practicing each of them in the second scene on Olympos and the slaying of the Python. The hymn, though undoubtedly later than the *Odyssey,* must surely incorporate a traditional concept of Apollo's characteristics, to which the simile describing Odysseus's action may allude. The contest of the bow and the revenge on the suitors take place on the day of a feast to Apollo (xx.276-78, xxi.258-59, 267-68). In that case, the simile gives us an even greater sense than it otherwise would of Odysseus's uniqueness as a mortal hero. His moment of triumph becomes one of transcendence, for the revelation of his identity has the character of a terrifying epiphany—and appropriately so, since he acts not only in his own interests but also as an agent of divine punishment on the suitors.

The comparison of Odysseus to a poet—and particularly the simile just discussed—recalls by contrast a memorable passage in another poem. At one point in the *Iliad* a hero sings—Achilles himself (IX.186-89):

τὸν δ᾽ εὗρον φρένα τερπόμενον φόρμιγγι λιγείη,
καλῇ δαιδαλέῃ, ἐπὶ δ᾽ ἀργύρεον ζυγὸν ἦεν,

τὴν ἄρετ᾽ ἐξ ἐνάρων πόλιν Ἠετίωνος ὀλέσσας ·
τῇ ὅ γε θυμὸν ἔτερπεν, ἄειδε δ᾽ ἄρα κλέα ἀνδρῶν.

They found him taking delight [*terpomenon*] in his mind with the shrill
   phorminx,
beautiful, cunningly wrought, and upon it was a bridge of silver.
He got it from the spoils when he sacked Ēetiōn's city,
and with it he was delighting [*eterpe*] his heart. He was singing the fames
   of men [*klea andrōn*] .

It is possible to argue that these lines show Achilles combining the talents for
song and action as no other figure in the *Iliad* does, and in fact this is Schadewaldt's opinion.[37] Achilles and Odysseus would then resemble each other.
But the circumstances in Book 9 of the *Iliad* are against that view. Achilles is
singing an epic poem because he has withdrawn from the action of *this* poem.
The theme of his singing evokes the warfare in which even now he should be
engaging. Song is here a substitute for action, and evidently not a satisfactory
one. For Achilles' singing seems to express his continued preoccupation with
battle and his yearning for it, though he will not fight. In the same way, later
in this book he threatens to go home but never does so. Even the history of
his phorminx, with its reminder of one of his exploits, comments ironically
on his position. As he plays it and celebrates the achievements of others, we
reflect that idleness is unnatural for him, that there is only one place for the
exercise of his monumental powers—the battlefield. Achilles cannot reconcile
peace and warfare; this inability is the condition of his life, as his famous
choice of fates shows. Odysseus, on the other hand, both acts and perpetuates
human fame (his own!), as the simile in Book 21 of the *Odyssey* stresses. Outside of his revenge on the suitors, these activities alternate for him, as they do
for Achilles, and as by nature they must; but unlike Achilles he can engage
fully in each at the proper time.[38] As we shall see later on, it may not be mere
coincidence that specific passages in these two poems lead us to contrast their
heroes on the score of their relation to song and action.

That Achilles literally sings whereas Odysseus never does is unimportant.
Odysseus is the one who genuinely combines the characteristics of poet and
warrior. His resemblance to a singer emphasizes, and is based on, a gift he
possesses that (as Hesiod tells us) is closely related to the poetic talent: readiness of speech, a sign of his mental agility. He himself talks at one point
about the place of this gift among human endowments. Rebuking Euryalos
in Phaiakia not long before he tells his own spellbinding story, Odysseus distinguishes between grace of physical appearance and grace of speech together
with the intelligence from which it is inseparable (viii.166-77):

ξεῖν᾽, οὐ καλὸν ἔειπες · ἀτασθάλῳ ἀνδρὶ ἔοικας.
οὕτως οὐ πάντεσσι θεοὶ χαρίεντα διδοῦσιν

ἀνδράσιν, οὔτε φυὴν οὔτ᾽ ἀρ φρένας οὔτ᾽ ἀγορητύν.
ἄλλος μὲν γὰρ εἶδος ἀκιδνότερος πέλει ἀνήρ,
ἀλλὰ θεὸς μορφὴν ἔπεσι στέφει, οἱ δέ τ᾽ ἐς αὐτὸν
τερπόμενοι λεύσσουσιν· ὁ δ᾽ ἀσφαλέως ἀγορεύει
αἰδοῖ μειλιχίῃ, μετὰ δὲ πρέπει ἀγρομένοισιν,
ἐρχόμενον δ᾽ ἀνὰ ἄστυ θεὸν ὣς εἰσορόωσιν.
ἄλλος δ᾽ αὖ εἶδος μὲν ἀλίγκιος ἀθανάτοισιν,
ἀλλ᾽ οὔ οἱ χάρις ἀμφιπεριστέφεται ἐπέεσσιν,
ὡς καὶ σοὶ εἶδος μὲν ἀριπρεπές, οὐδέ κεν ἄλλως
οὐδὲ θεὸς τεύξειε, νόον δ᾽ ἀποφώλιός ἐσσι.

You spoke badly, my friend; you seem to be a foolish man.
That is always the way of it: the gods do not grant pleasing gifts
to all men, not handsomeness or intelligence or speech.
For one man is inferior in outward form,
but a god crowns his appearance with words, and men take delight
in looking upon him. And he speaks unerringly,
with proper reverence that is honey-sweet, and he is prominent among the
    assembled men.
As he walks through the city they look upon him as though he were a god.
But another man is like the gods in appearance,
but grace is not set as a crown about his words.
So it is with you: your appearance is striking, and not even a god
could make it better. But as for intelligence, you are completely lacking in
    sense.

In characterizing the opposite of the type represented by Euryalos, Odysseus, consciously or not, is actually speaking about himself. This passage recalls Antēnōr's comparison in the *Iliad* between Odysseus and Menelaos as orators, where Odysseus's external appearance and comportment (he engaged in no histrionics with the herald's staff) are described as less impressive than his mighty voice and his words, which flew thick and fast "like winter snow" (III.203–24). Appearance is not a reliable guide to character in the case of so complex a person as Odysseus. The mistake others most often make in their dealings with him is to assume that it is—a tendency upon which he himself is always ready to capitalize. This is Euryalos's error. He has insulted Odysseus by remarking that the stranger does not look like a man who excells in contests of strength (viii.158–64). In his reply Odysseus changes the terms of the opposition. He contrasts intelligence and verbal mastery such as he possesses, not with strength, but with mindless good looks. He must do so, of course, in order to call Euryalos handsome but empty-headed (he later makes the same charge in more serious circumstances against the suitor Antinoos, xvii.454). But the shift is made also in order to correct Euryalos's method of judging men and thus, by exposing him as foolish, to repay the insult. It is appropriate furthermore because, in Odysseus's case at least, physical prowess and action are not the opposites of a good mind and fluent speech. He follows his words with an astonishing throw of the discus.

This passage does not make a connection between the verbal art and song, but it does illustrate how the comparison of Odysseus to a poet arises naturally from his ability as a speaker. Examples given in the preceding chapter show that hexameter poetry presents these talents as similar in nature. In particular, several lines here are nearly identical to Hesiod's description of the ruler who is favored by the Muses (*Theog.* 79-93). There is no need to enter the debate over which passage influenced the other.[39] Behind both probably lies a conventional concept of the ideal of eloquence, and in both this is expressed more or less smoothly with formulaic language. It is significant, however, that Hesiod represents the persuasive speaker as the political analogue of the poet, and that the poetlike Odysseus gives a description of eloquence that resembles Hesiod's and clearly applies to himself. Within the *Odyssey* itself an interesting similarity between two lines in the passage quoted above and a line that appears later on implies the connection between poetry and eloquence. Of the ugly man Odysseus says that "a god crowns [*stephei*] his appearance [*morphēn*] with words" (viii.170), whereas a man might look like the immortals "but grace [*kharis*] is not set as a crown [*amphiperistephetai*] about his words" (viii.175). Together these related clauses—the first because of the word *morphē*, the second by its meaning—anticipate the compliment that Alkinoos pays Odysseus immediately before likening him to a singer: σοὶ δ' ἔπι μὲν μορφὴ ἐπέων, "upon you is beauty [*morphē*] of words" (xi.367).[40]

In his rebuke of Euryalos, Odysseus has in mind public discourse, speeches in the marketplace on political or legal issues. Elsewhere, the poem shows him an adept liar. Whether or not they overlap (and they may to some extent), both forms of speech are related to poetry, as the proemium to the *Theogony* demonstrates. Conversely, Odysseus's resemblance to a poet implies his capacity not only for lying but also for effective political speech.

The latter ability is important because it shows that extraordinary though he is, Odysseus's qualities conform to the traditional heroic ideal as presented in the *Iliad* more clearly than in the *Odyssey*, and particularly as one line of Phoinix's speech to Achilles in the embassy scene summarizes it. Pēleus sent him to Troy, says Phoinix, to teach Achilles (IX.443)

μύθων τε ῥητῆρ' ἔμεναι πρηκτῆρά τε ἔργων.

to be a speaker of words and a doer of deeds.

Speaking here means delivering advice in the assembly and involves not only persuasiveness but also good counsel, the intelligence to devise a course of action to meet the situation at hand. The elegant chiasmus or inverse symmetry of the line embodies the balance in abilities that the hero ought to have. This is the word order of the Greek:[41]

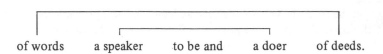

of words   a speaker   to be and   a doer   of deeds.

The *Iliad*'s use of the epithet κυδιάνειρα ("giving glory to men") suggests the same balance between word and deed. It occurs nine times in this poem (and nowhere else in hexameter poetry); in eight of those occurrences it modifes μάχη ("battle"), but once (I.490) it describes ἀγορή ("the assembly"). That the same epithet can be used in connection with two activities indicates that they are thought of as equivalent. If the giving of wise counsel "confers glory on men" as might in battle does, these two kinds of excellence are equal and complementary aspects of the heroic ideal.

Curiously, as Solmsen has remarked, no one in the *Iliad* possesses both talents at once.[42] Sometimes speech is said to replace action in the course of a man's life. Thus good counsel and eloquence characterize old age, when physical powers have waned, as in the case of Nestor (who still fights, to be sure, but without much effect) or the Trojan elders (III.150-52). Or each man of a pair might be distinguished for one quality. Hektor and Poulydamas were born in the same night (obviously a device for contrasting them), but Hektor excelled in warfare, Poulydamas in sound advice (μῦθοι, literally, "words": XVIII.251-52; cf. XIII.726-34). Hektor's failure to follow his comrade's advice leads to his doom. Sometimes, more generally, warriors in the *Iliad* feel a tension between word and deed that they seem unable to reconcile. This happens typically when they find themselves wasting in talk time that should be spent on action (XVI.627-31, XX.200-202, 211-12, 246-58, 430-37). For Odysseus, by contrast, especially when he uses deceit, speech is almost a form of action.

But the character in the *Iliad* who is outstanding in might and tragically lacking in prudent forethought is Achilles. He and Patroklos form a pair analogous to Hektor and Poulydamas. Departing for Troy, Patroklos was warned by his father that although Achilles was the stronger, he himself was the elder of the two and must provide good counsel (XI.785-89; similar is Odysseus's reminder to Achilles of Pēleus's admonition to his son on the same occasion, IX.252-59). Later, Achilles learns to his cost the consequences of rash anger and what it is that he lacks to complement his enormous strength (XVIII.104-6):

ἀλλ᾿ ἧμαι παρὰ νηυσὶν ἐτώσιον ἄχθος ἀρούρης,
τοῖος ἐὼν οἷος οὔ τις ᾿Αχαιῶν χαλκοχιτώνων
ἐν πολέμῳ· ἀγορῇ δέ τ᾿ ἀμείνονές εἰσι καὶ ἄλλοι.

I sit by the ships, a vain burden upon the earth,
such a man as is no one else of the bronze-clad Akhaians—
in warfare: in the assembly [*agorē*], there are others who are better.

The enjambed "in warfare" adds an emphatic qualification to the line that precedes, and "in the assembly," juxtaposed with it, marks a sharp distinction between these spheres of activity which is the truth of things for Achilles.

Once again, then, Achilles provides the strongest contrast with Odysseus. In one episode, the embassy scene in Book 9, the *Iliad* itself reveals how different in nature these two men are by showing the difference in the way they speak. There Odysseus is the first to try to persuade Achilles to return to the fighting (IX.225-306). His speech is a masterpiece of tact and persuasiveness. It presents Agamemnon's formal offer of restitution (ll. 260-99, which essentially repeat Agamemnon's words at IX.121-57). Before and after this "official" section, however, Odysseus makes his plea on more personal grounds, touching just those points on which Achilles is liable to be most sensitive.[43] This speech contains nothing whatever that could be called insincere, but it shows that Odysseus knows his friend's character and has gauged his words by it. Achilles begins his reply by saying that he will speak his mind bluntly, and continues (IX.312-13):

ἐχϑρὸς γάρ μοι κεῖνος ὁμῶς Ἀΐδαο πύλῃσιν
ὅς χ᾽ ἕτερον μὲν κεύϑη ἐνὶ φρεσίν, ἄλλο δὲ εἴπῃ.

For that man is as hateful to me as the gates of Hades
who hides one thing in his mind and speaks another.

He then vents his fury at Agamemnon. There is nothing like the passion of this speech in Odysseus's more meditated style. Achilles can use words as effectively as Odysseus, but he uses them differently. Although his rhetoric derives tremendous power from its directness, and although it may make us sympathetic to him at this moment, it gives no evidence of the tact and the thought for the consequences of one's words that are necessary when men deal with one another and are therefore essential if society is to function. It was, after all, in the assembly that Achilles began his quarrel with Agamemnon. Odysseus's suppleness of speech reflects the suppleness of his character; Achilles' language matches his passionate rigidity.[44]

In expressing his hatred of the insincere speaker, Achilles can hardly be criticizing Odysseus; he is simply giving the reason for his own directness. Yet we know from the *Odyssey* that Odysseus is a man who *will*, when necessary, "hide one thing in his mind and speak another," although he never uses deceit for ignoble purposes. His willingness to compromise when the goal is right is a mark of his intelligence and the reason for his success. Achilles would never use deceit—or even tact when that got in the way of his painful honesty. And so he isolates himself from others. Both men achieve greatness, each in his own way. Achilles does so by refusing to compromise, but he pays the price. Odysseus is the hero of relatedness to others; Achilles, the hero of isolation.

Gregory Nagy has recently argued that the Homeric poems show evidence of a rivalry within the poetic tradition between Achilles and Odysseus; the former's claim to be "best of the Akhaians" is based on his might; the latter's, on his cleverness.[45] The *Odyssey* we possess goes further, however, and depicts Odysseus as endowed with both qualities together (though admittedly not Achilles' degree of strength). In this poem (xiv.491) the Odysseus who fought at Troy is said (by himself, when in disguise) to have been outstanding in counsel (βουλευέμεν, *bouleuemen*) and in battle (μάχεσθαι, *makhesthai*). The comparison of Odysseus to a singer when he stretches the bow and plucks its string, by yoking together two normally incompatible sides of life, perfectly expresses the balance in his character. Not long afterward, Athena encourages him in his fight against the suitors by reminding him how he demonstrated his abilities at Troy (xxii.226-32). She mentions both the number of men he killed in battle and his stratagem (βουλή, *boulē*)—the Wooden Horse—by which the city was finally taken.[46]

We inevitably compare the heroes of these two great epics, and there is every justification for doing so. It is very likely that the *Odyssey*'s audience was intended from the start to make such a comparison and that an intelligent response to the poem requires it. After all, the *Odyssey* defines its position in relation to other poems through allusions to their stories and by directly portraying heroes who figure in them, including Achilles. Characterization of Odysseus by reference to the greatest warrior who fought and died at Troy is part of this poetic process. The *Odyssey*, however, is probably a response not merely to the heroic tradition that was expressed in our *Iliad* among other poems, but specifically to the *Iliad* itself. To view the *Odyssey* as commenting on the *Iliad*, and therefore to claim a relation between their heroes, we need only assume what most scholars who are in any degree unitarians would probably accept: that the *Odyssey* was the later poem and that its composer knew the *Iliad*.

As public speaker, counsellor, liar, and poet, Odysseus displays a quick intelligence and the ability to manipulate situations by means of language. At Troy and at home he shows skill and valor in combat. Achilles, by comparison, is one-sided. Therefore, *on the* Iliad*'s own terms,* Odysseus, not Achilles, fulfills the ideal of the epic hero.

So, at least, the *Odyssey* implicitly alleges. I am not suggesting, nor, I I think, did the poet of the *Odyssey* intend seriously to assert, that the *Odyssey* is a better poem than the *Iliad* or Odysseus a greater hero than Achilles. We need not concern ourselves with the truth of this claim, but only with the fact that it is made at all. It is a device for conveying the poem's meaning. By means of it the poet stresses the important point about Odysseus: that he is more rounded and versatile than even the most illustrious of the other heroes, well adapted to the conditions of peace as well as of warfare. Thus the *Odyssey* signals to us that it is a poem, not about failure and death, but about triumph and continued life on the best of mortal terms as the reward for toil. The *Iliad* shows man succumbing to his limits; the *Odyssey*, without ever losing sight of those limits, reveals how much man can accomplish within them. By commenting upon the earlier poem, the *Odyssey* fills out the *Iliad*'s intense but narrow view of life and is in this respect, as in the others noted when we compared their structures, the perfect complement to the *Iliad*.

What we observe in the relation between the two poems is a tradition at work. On the reading offered here, the *Odyssey* shows no sign of decay, but rather the vigorous creativity that is spurred by previous works of art. We should not be deceived into thinking the poet of the *Odyssey* either presumptuous or at the end of his resources because he emphasizes the differences between his own and other works, particularly the *Iliad*. Rivalry there may have been between him and his predecessors—we know how important competition was to poetry at that time and for much of Greek history—but it was the productive Eris that Hesiod praises. To admire the *Odyssey*, we are not required to depreciate the *Iliad* or its hero. In fact, it would be pleasant, though not, of course, necessary for our argument, to think that the same man, having composed the *Iliad*, later achieved the perspective on his own work and the fullness of vision to produce the *Odyssey* as well. Only together do the two poems offer a comprehensive view of human life.

There is a considerable element of sophisticated sport in the *Odyssey*'s deft use of ideas conventionally associated with song. But the poem works its wonderful enchantment by combining this lightness of heart with the most serious of purposes. It thus perfectly embodies the conception of its art that it presents. For in the society of which it was an institution, song aimed at giving pleasure and yet illustrated man's understanding of himself in his world. Nothing less is at issue when poetry becomes its own theme in the *Odyssey*. References to the subjects of other songs emphasize by contrast that Odysseus's story contains the broadest experience and—in the end—the highest fulfillment possible for man. Odysseus is similarly distinguished from other heroes and at the same time is characterized in his own right. In the series of oppositions that he unites within himself, we recognize the polarizing habit of paratactic thought: the use of opposite extremes to define what lies between them, and the concomitant sense that both elements of the opposition are necessary for completion. The creation of a literary character in this antithetical mode is not surprising, but it is unparalleled. Yet only an Odysseus could be depicted in this fashion, for he is the most complete of all heroes. The antitheses that define his nature can all be subsumed under the great opposition between word and action, which are brought into an ideal complementary relationship by the symmetry in the line from Phoinix's speech quoted earlier. That opposition in turn is held in balance by the portrayal of Odysseus as the poet's own double. This characterization of the hero is an aspect of the *Odyssey*'s general concern with the function of song, by which the poet shows what is at stake in the story he tells. The poem's movement from the pain to the pleasure aroused by memory parallels the development of the narrative from chaos to restored order—or rather, is one with it, because the capacity of song to fulfill its proper role is a token of civilized stability.

In all these ways, the *Odyssey* draws attention to itself as a poem in the process of being completed. No matter how familiar we are with this poem or how assured we are of its outcome, we undergo the same experience on every successive encounter with it: we witness its development. The text is like a coiled spring; an energy is latent in it that is released every time one of us even reads it today. But when the poem was publicly performed, when there was a genuine correspondence between the songs within the narrative and the actual song, the *Odyssey,* the members of the audience must have felt all the more that they were part of an act of creation with tremendous import for them all. For there came into being, on each occasion, an artistic semblance of the order that the narrative taught them to value.

7 Epilogue

AT THE END OF THE *PARADISO*, when his sight is allowed to pierce the eternal Light and reach the Trinity itself, Dante describes his vision with an extraordinary metaphor:

> In its depth I saw ingathered, bound by love in one
> single volume, that which is dispersed in leaves
> throughout the universe: substance and accidents and
> their relations, as though fused together in such a way
> that what I tell is but a simple light.
> *(Paradiso* 33.85–90, translated by Charles S. Singleton, 1975)

Dante's comparison of divine unity to the shape of a book when he has reached the climax of his spiritual progress reflects his self-consciousness as a literary artist and emphasizes his sense of his poem's purpose. These lines consummate the wonderful integration he achieves of the poem with its subject. The form of the *Divine Comedy* enacts the order of the world that emanates (though imperfectly) from the center of that eternal Light. And Dante has made the reading of books (*Inferno,* canto 5) and the creation of poetry (*Purgatorio,* cantos 24 and 26), including his own, part of the issue of love and salvation. For him, literature is not on the fringes of life but at its center; and the poet is an appropriate figure for the soul's exploration of its own depths and heights.

Yet the metaphor of the book is a comparison and only approximates what it describes. And the book itself, a man-made object, is merely a copy of that unattainable divine perfection. Dante himself knows this. Before recounting his vision, he says that speech cannot describe it nor memory retain it, and he likens the dispersal of his impressions to the scattering of the leaves on which the Cumaean Sibyl's prophecies were inscribed (*Paradiso,* 33.55–66). Still, the making of a book puts the pages in order, though the coherence thus achieved remains but a semblance of the divine unity. Thus Dante expresses at once the power and the limitation of human discourse and knowledge, and so of poetry itself.

The book is a tangible artifact, and for Dante, accustomed as he was to the use of writing, it was a natural token for what he was trying to convey. Greek hexameter poetry, although it was set down in written texts sooner or later, was experienced primarily by hearing rather than by sight. But the artists in that tradition made of the poem what Dante made of the book: a representation of an entire view of the world and man's place in it. The poem's form corresponded to its audience's shared modes of thought and their conception of the physical cosmos. By the nature of the poet's gift, the poem demonstrated how far human capacities could be extended; but at the same time it served as a reminder of the crucial difference between man and god. Not just in the words of the text and its subject matter, but more generally through its very existence, its creation and re-creation in performance, the poem expressed the values and normative beliefs of a whole society. The poem *was* its subject, in all its delight and its wisdom.

▣ Notes ▣

INTRODUCTION

1. Wrongly interpreted, it could also have bad effects. It might encourage us to envision different schools of poetry in different places, with geographically determined idiosyncracies emphasized at the expense of the far more important common tradition. At several points, moreover, Janko asserts that one poem imitates another. He is properly cautious about this approach, which has often been recklessly applied, and he sets forth well-conceived principles for determining influence and its direction (1982, 225–28). But he considers only two explanations for similarities between passages in two different poems: either that one of these texts imitates the other, or that they have a common source in a particular poem now lost to us (in the latter case no inferences could be drawn about the chronological relation between the two poems in question). But there is a third possible explanation: the influence of the tradition as a whole, which happens to manifest itself to us in two extant poems. These might use inherited diction wholly independently and with different degrees of success. I think this the most prudent position in view of the state of our knowledge. So little survives of hexameter poetry relative to what must have been composed that alleging direct influence of a particular text upon another is hazardous even when the assumptions being made are clearly understood. To do so is to schematize a corpus of poetry whose original order cannot now be known.

2. Finnegan (1977), 17–24. Cf. also p. 71 and—for an explicit critique of the Parry/Lord theory—pp. 69–72.

3. See especially Finnegan (1977), 88–89, 269–70 (the quotations in the text are from the latter pages).

1. THE ORGANIZATION OF THOUGHT

1. Polyphemos: i.71–73, ix.529; Alkinoos: vii.56–63. On the geographical and familial connections between the Kyklōpes and the Phaiakians, see Clay (1980), who makes the attractive, if speculative, suggestion that the Phaiakians' original home was the island that lies off the coast of the Kyklōpes' land (ix.116–41). Cf. also Segal (1962), 33–34.

2. On the engendering by Night and Erebos of their respective opposites, Day and Aither (*Theog.* 124–25), see Fraenkel (1960), 317–19, and Philippson (1966), 663.

3. Some qualifications are in order, however: 1. The visit to the dead in Book 11 is here left out of account, since that involves a place outside the

world defined by Ocean. 2. The Kyklōpes and Phaiakians do not correspond formally in the scheme of ring composition that Whitman (1958, 288) finds in the order of the wanderings, but they are carefully opposed in other ways. 3. Skylla surpasses the Kyklōps in monstrosity, but essentially repeats his cannibalism and does not have enough in common with the Phaiakians to be suitable as a foil to them. 4. The opposition between Phaiakians and Kyklōpes is not absolute. Civilization and barbarity interpenetrate, both in this case (cf. Kirk, 1970, 162-71, and Clay, 1980, 263-64) and elsewhere in the *Odyssey* (e.g., the Laistrygonians, who are cannibals but possess social organization). But that only means that classes of beings contain *within themselves* antithetical qualities by which their characters are defined (cf. the case of Hestia below). Thus, just as Alkinoos has the Giants in his ancestry, the ambience of the Kyklōpes resembles the Hesiodic Golden Age (see below, pp. 97-98). The opposition between savagery and culture, though manifested in complex ways, is important to the poem and essentially straightforward; and the contrast between the Kyklōpes and the Phaiakians (which I have stated in the text in simple form for clarity) is genuine.

4. For a specific thematic connection between the suitors and Polyphēmos, see Chapter 2, Section c.

5. Note the use in both places of the same expression: (ἐς) πείρατα γαίης.

6. Note the parallelism of expression in these lines (especially if line 721 is retained, as in West's text [1966], but not in Solmsen's [1970]). Both the vertical and the horizontal schemes describe essentially the same thing. As West (1966, 339, on *Theog.* 622) observes, "no sharp distinction is drawn between regions outside and below the inhabited world. The essential fact about these areas is that they are beyond man's ken."

7. Cf. Philippson (1966), 673, on Tartaros in the *Theogony:* "Der Glanz der olympischen Welt ist für den Griechen nur fassbar durch seine polare Gegenwelt. . . ."

8. Hestia's place as the eldest is implied by *Theog.* 454, where she is named first in the list of Kronos's children (so Solmsen, 1960, 2-3).

9. For the significance of Hestia as expressing ideas of space, see Vernant (1965), 97-143.

10. *h.* 29.4-6. Cf. Allen, Halliday, and Sykes (1936), 354, and Solmsen (1960), 2, n. 3.

11. E.g., van Otterlo (1944), 36, 38; van Groningen (1958), 99. These authors are not unsympathetic toward the poetry itself, however, and I have found their work of great help.

12. The standard description of *parataxis* is Hermann Fraenkel's admirable paper (1960, 40-96). Cf. also Perry (1937) and Notopoulos (1949).

13. Aristotle's criticism was anticipated by Plato (*Phdr.* 264c), who used similar criteria of form. For discussion, see Notopoulos (1949), 4, 6.

14. E.g., Fraenkel (1960), especially 50-51, 94 (but he also does justice to an advantage of the style; see note 18, below).

15. Perhaps the clearest and fullest statement of this position is by Perry (1937). Notopoulos, even though he rightly argues that we cannot judge Archaic poetry by Aristotelian standards of "organic unity," also describes the paratactic mind as limited in these ways (1949, 13-14). Moreover, he finds the origin of paratactic style in the conditions of oral composition; the style, in turn, produced the mentality (see especially pp. 15-16). This explanation rests on debatable assumptions about the oral nature of Homeric poetry, and in any case it is more likely that the mentality was prior and the style reflects

it. The circumstances of oral composition—and more generally of oral performance—may well have exerted an influence, but that was surely secondary. Our main concerns should be a way of thinking and of conceiving the world, and how the poetry expresses it. Notopoulos's view makes these things unimportant, the effect rather than the cause. On the impossibility of reducing the differences between the paratactic and periodic styles to the difference between oral and written literature, see Greene (1951), 31-32.

16. The same tendency toward concreteness can be observed in another respect as well. Although some early hexameter poems contain more abstract language than others, there is distinctly less in this poetry as a whole than in later literature. See Sellschopp (1934), 88-105, and Blusch (1970), 45-53.

17. Austin (1975), 81-129. On parataxis as affording a sense of the whole, see Fraenkel (1960), 69, and Notopoulos (1964), 59. As the latter well says, parataxis reflects "the splendid capacity of the early Greek mind to see things separately and as a whole" (this seems a revision of his earlier view—see note 15, above).

18. Cf. Fraenkel (1960), 51: "andrerseits kann die Reihung seine Auffassung und Phantasie anregen und leiten, gerade das Gleichartige und Zusammengehörige in Darstellungsketten zu schildern, *oder auch in schweifender Kühnheit die geheimen Verbindungen zwischen den verschiedenen Bereichen des Daseins aufzudecken*" (emphasis added).

19. An excellent treatment of this figure is in Bassett (1938), 120-28. See also his earlier article on this subject (1920).

20. These scholars apparently athetized an entire passage of the *Iliad* (XV.56-77) because it does not conform to this arrangement. On this, and for other references to hysteron proteron in ancient commentators and in Cicero and Pliny, see Bassett (1920), 56, and (1938), 120-21, 124-25.

21. E.g., *W.D.* 11-19 (good Eris—bad Eris—bad Eris—good Eris); fr. 64.15-18. But the figure is not as common in the *Theogony* as might be expected, because other considerations also influence the order (on these see West, 1966, 38). In *Theog.* 233-336, for instance, the genealogies of Pontos's children are given in the order in which the children are first listed (ll. 233-39). This is probably the result of a desire to contrast Nēreus with the progeny of Night (see especially ll. 229 and 233).

22. Lines 55-56 are usually thought to have been added to the *Aspis* to make the passage end with Herakles, so that the fight with Kyknos and the description of the shield could be attached (Wilamowitz, 1905, 121; more elaborate excisions in Schwartz, 1960, 464). But by essentially repeating the information in line 48, they would round off the passage. For other arguments for retaining the lines see Russo (1965), 85-86. Excision, in any case, would not seriously affect the point made here; the series would simply be shortened. For examples of multiple inversion in the *Iliad*, see Bassett (1920), 42.

23. Prometheus is reserved for the end because of the narrative that will follow. But the result is a framing effect: Epimetheus (ll. 511-14) before, and Prometheus (ll. 521 ff.) after, Menoitios and Atlas. Cf. Nicolai (1964), 207.

24. Eustathios 339, 24 (on II.761-70). These advantages are emphasized by Bassett (1920), 42.

25. Cf. Bassett (1938), 124: "The Homeric hysteron proteron is not a rhetorical figure, but the unstudied, intuitive expression of intimate human discourse." This says succinctly what I shall argue at the end of this chapter about all of the structural patterns examined here. But the potential for poetic effect is not, for this reason, ruled out.

26. For instance, when she denies that her death had natural causes (xi. 198–201), Antikleia reverses the order of her son's questions in lines 172–73.

27. On hysteron proteron in questions and answers in the *Odyssey*, see Bassett (1920), 45–46. But there are also cases in Homer where the answers follow the order of the questions: e.g., ii.28–47, xi.397–411, VI.374–89. If our passage had taken this form, then, that would not have been surprising; but the feeling it conveys would have been blunted.

28. The basic treatments of ring composition are von Otterlo (1944 and 1948) and van Groningen (1958), 51–56.

29. The same lines at iv.704–5 mark Penelope's reaction when she learns that Telemakhos has gone to Pylos and that the suitors are plotting to kill him.

30. I have borrowed some phrases of this translation from Evelyn-White (1914), 233.

31. Evelyn-White's translation implies this order. For a totally different arrangement, which, however, seems unjustified by the text, see Myres (1941), 26–27.

32. The Shield of Achilles in the *Iliad* also is bordered by the stream of Ocean (XVIII.607–8), but the poet does not stress its function as a frame. This description shows far less self-consciousness in its design than the *Aspis* (and so is not as useful for the present purposes), but it is all the more subtle. It provides, in fact, a wonderful example of how much can be expressed through the relations among the various elements in the kind of complex pattern of ring composition that will be examined below. For the symmetries between the scenes, see Sheppard (1922), 6–7, Myres (1930), 517–25—whose scheme is perhaps overwrought—and the particularly fine treatment in Marg (1957), 26–28. The material of the shield also calls for some comment here. Hephaistos makes it of five layers (XVIII.481). Later, when Aineias's spear pierces it, we find that the two outer layers, front and back, are of bronze. Within them are two of tin, and at the center is one of gold (XX.269–72). This shows how naturally these poets thought in rounded, inversely symmetrical structures, even at the cost, here, of giving an arrangement of metals that Leaf (1900–1902, 368) calls "absurd, for the gold is hidden away in the middle, where it would be neither useful nor ornamental." Practicality, of course, is irrelevant. The poet at this moment needs to name the metals of which the shield is composed and simply does so according to a scheme that is thoroughly habitual with him.

33. Another long passage of exposition framed with similar effect is the advice on farming in the *Works and Days*. Progressing through the year from one autumn to the next, this section both begins and ends with mention of the Pleiades' setting as the time for plowing (*W.D.* 383–84, 615–17). The form seems to embody the cyclical nature of time as that is measured by the regular recurrence of constellations in the heavens and of tasks on the land. For more details on the organization of this section, see West (1978), 253. Note how the ending also provides a point of departure for a new passage, the advice on sailing, which starts with another reference to the Pleiades' setting and to Orion (l. 619; cf. l. 615). This is the same phenomenon as that observed earlier in Chapter 1 in connection with *W.D.* 695–97, and it shows again how enclosed, paratactically placed sections can be linked.

34. Cf. the story of the five ages in the *Works and Days*, where the similarity of the heroes' afterlife with the conditions of the Golden Age (with lines 172–73 echoing 117–18) sets the first four periods apart as complete, past,

and superior to the present era of iron. Contrast *W.D.* 570–86, discussed immediately below. There is a similar result of ring composition in xix.1–52, as described by Whitman (1958), 253: ". . . the effect is to give an extraordinary finality to the scene which preceded, to make it shine with the enclosed inviolability of a perfect circle, so that, however sequential it may be in the plot, it seems like a thing apart." For clarity I have here simplified a complex scheme in the story of the five ages; for details see Walcot (1961), 4–7, Vernant (1965), 19–47, and Nagy (1979), 155–61.

35. This passage is noted by van Otterlo (1944), 22, as an example of what he calls "die rekapitulierend-anaphorische Verbindung" and considers to be only related to ring composition. But the distinction, if any, is unimportant.

36. Nereids–XVIII.37–50: inner, enclosing frame, ll. 38 and 49; outer, "transitional" frame, ll. 37 and 50. Odysseus's bow–xxi.11–41: this passage has multiple enclosing frames (ll. 14 and 37, 13 and 38, 11 and 41), and lines 8 and 42 connect it with the main narrative (for further details, see van Otterlo, 1948, 24–26). Cf. the insertion of Theoklymenos's genealogy into the narrative, xv.222–23, 256–58. A "transitional" frame can suffice by itself, without an enclosing frame within it. In the seventh book of the *Odyssey*, for instance, lines 56–57 lead into, and lines 61–62 return from, the ancestry of Periboia.

37. Further aspects of the bow's significance are suggested by Segal (1962), 50.

38. Lines 138 and 155, though verbally and acoustically similar, are not identical. The adjective "most fearsome" (*deinotatos*) is transferred in line 155 from Kronos to all the offspring of Ouranos and Gaia, and the verb is changed not only from one stem to a related one but from active to passive (*ēkhthēre, ēkhthonto*). The latter change is necessary to lead to Ouranos's treatment of his children, but the result is that the lines complement each other by telling of hatred on both sides (Kronos and Ouranos). Lines 139–53 make the transition between these framing lines: the Kyklōpes and the Hundred-handers were dreadful in appearance, and in fact (ll. 154–56) all the children were fearsome and were hated by their father (this is West's explanation of γάρ, "for," in l. 154–1966, 213).

39. West (1966), 206. Cf. van Groningen (1958), 273–75. This explanation practically assumes a written text (which West thinks probable anyway), although revision in subsequent performances is also conceivable. It is difficult, however, to see how lines 139–53 were an afterthought unless, as West suggests, lines 155–56 were added at the same time. If we think away the allegedly later lines, so that 157 follows 154 immediately, a possible arrangement results ("for as many as were born from Gaia and Ouranos, he kept hiding them all back"), but it involves some sacrifice of clarity. The statement that Ouranos put away his children in earth *as each was born* would be lost. More important, Ouranos's treatment of his children would lack a motive (this is supplied by ll. 155–56). Recently, Solmsen (1982, 4–5) has adopted the same hypothesis as West does, and has suggested that line 154, as part of the original text, was replaced by "a new beginning" (now lost) when lines 139–53 and 155–56 were inserted. Just how the complicated mixture of old and new versions coalesced into the text we now have is not clear. It is easy enough to summon the specters of rhapsodes and lost lines, but the whole hypothesis becomes ungainly. It also does not help us to understand what we have before us. As it stands, the text shows well-attested compositional techniques: not only ring composition, but also an extended hysteron proteron:

a. Kronos's hatred of his father (l. 138); *b.* Ouranos's hatred of his children (l. 155); *b.* Ouranos's treatment of his children (ll. 156–59); *a.* Kronos's revenge on his father (ll. 159–210). In any case, the important question is not *when* lines 139–53 were added, but *why* they were put precisely where they were, whether they are part of the poem's "original" version or an afterthought.

40. This attempt at parallelism probably explains the form of the wretched line 153 (cf. l. 146).

41. So Càssola (1975), 488 (on l. 20).

42. I take it that lines 14–18 are in place here and that all of lines 1–29 is genuine. See Càssola (1975), 485–87 (on ll. 1–13 and 14–18). The passage used to be considered a patchwork of original and interpolated groups of lines. See, e.g., Bethe (1931), 13–18, and Jacoby (1933), 723–30; and for the opposite view even by those who take a separatist position on the question of the unity of the hymn as a whole, Drerup (1937), 113–14, and Deubner (1938), 263–64. Lines 1–13 have their difficulties, but these are not insurmountable; and there is no convincing reason to excise lines 14–18.

43. For further discussion of this idea, and its other manifestations in the narrative sections of this poem, see section f of Chapter 2.

44. On this passage, see most recently Janko (1981), 17–18. If one considers it solely from the point of view of hymnic conventions, one is bound to find "awkwardness" in it, as he does. But the presence of the "awkward" elements can be accounted for, and a more positive appreciation of the lines can be gained, if they are recognized as an example of a subtle use of a normal compositional pattern. Miller, on the other hand (1977, 22–30), explains the poet's "apparently bizarre procedure" as a deliberate rhetorical tactic (in a way different from, but compatible with, my view).

45. Although Penelope's speech continues after line 82, the prayer itself ends there, and the rest need not concern us. On this prayer, see van Otterlo (1948), 22, who notes only the correspondences between lines 79 and 61 and lines 66 and 77 (the latter pair used to incorporate what he calls a "digression" on the daughters of Pandareos).

46. This is not an argument that the mythical section was added later. Furthermore, not an interpolator's clumsiness (cf. Stanford, 1967, II, 344), but the fact that lines 66–78 are a developed narrative section, explains why Artemis is referred to in the third person in line 71. This in turn influences the reference to her, again in the third person, in line 80.

47. That τόν in line 383 refers to Hektor is guaranteed by the recurrence of this line at XVI.866.

48. Commentators have long noted the relation between the first of the similes in the present passage (XVI.364–65) and the earlier XVI.297–302. Moulton (1977, 33–38), however, aligns XVI.384–93, at the end of our passage, with the other two similes. In sequence, he says, all three similes "emphasize the important role of Patroklos and the Myrmidons in restoring the Greeks' initiative" (cf. also Scott, 1974, 113–14). So XVI.364–65 and 384–93 evidently both form part of a large sequence and frame and articulate the description of the Trojans' retreat. It will be evident, I hope, that the passage as a whole (XVI.364–93) is too well integrated into its context, and too important for the plot of the entire poem, to be an interpolation. For the problems that some have thought that it raises, see Moulton (1977, 33–38). These are minor; but two points related to the closing simile (XVI.384–93) might be singled out as illustrating my own disagreement with a major strain in traditional scholarship. First, the resemblances to Hesiod in lines 387–88 prove

nothing about date or authorship, for they can be explained as an independent use of conventional diction and concepts by two poets. Second, the moral coloring of the comparison as a whole is not necessarily a sign of late composition. It might be "a reflex of later conditions which, by an inadvertence common in Homer, has been allowed to slip into a simile" (Dodds, 1951, 32). Or, if one feels uneasy—as I do—at the dating of concepts with such certainty, one might say that the poet, for the purpose of developing the simile, has drawn on a moral outlook with which he was familiar but which he chose to exclude from the main body of his poem for the sake of his portrayal of the gods there (see pp. 86–87).

49. E.g., for Homer, Whitman (1958), Chapters 11 and 12; for Hesiod, Walcot (1957, 1958, 1961), West (1966), 356–58, on the description of Tartaros in the *Theogony*, and the different view of the same passage by Northrup (1979), especially p. 34.

50. See Blusch (1970), 94–95. In what follows, I am endebted in several ways to his excellent discussion of Hesiod's treatment of the story.

51. Specifically, line 91 resembles line 113 (cf. also 115), and 103 contrasts with 118.

52. With line 231, cf. 115; and with line 237, cf. 117.

53. This polarity is pointed out by Blusch (1970), 101–3.

54. A new interpretation of this episode has been given by Neitzel (1976), who suggests that what Pandora scatters by opening the jar is not evils but the livelihood stored within it (that is, $\beta\iota o\nu$, and not, as has traditionally been thought, $\kappa\alpha\kappa\alpha$, is to be supplied as object of $\dot{\epsilon}\sigma\kappa\dot{\epsilon}\delta\alpha\sigma\epsilon$ in line 95). I have followed the usual interpretation, which still seems to me more plausible. Neitzel's view would affect my discussion of the structure only partially. The scheme of ring composition would remain—Neitzel himself (p. 400) finds similarities between lines 42–49 and 90–95—as would the polarity, in the outermost frame, between scattering and hiding. However, both members of that frame would now express lack, the balance with the adjacent *b* frame would be lost, and the contrast between lines 90–92 and 94–105 would be blurred.

55. For the theme of concealment in this story, see Beye (1972), 32.

56. This section implicitly praises Aphrodite: there are only three exceptions to her power. They in turn have to be praised so that Aphrodite will seem ineffective only under extraordinary circumstances. This, of course, prepares for lines 36ff.: nothing else escapes her, and she leads even the mind of Zeus astray. Mention of the three goddesses is thus another case of definition by the boundary (in this case to show how much that boundary encompasses). On this section and on lines 1–44 in general and their relation to the main narrative of the hymn, see Janko (1981), 19, and especially Smith (1981b), 32–38.

57. E.g., van Otterlo (1948), 73; Kamerbeek (1967), 394; Porter (1949), 261–62, who also notes the resumptive effect of line 53 (lines 45–52 are, however, too important to be called a digression, as he does).

58. This has now been pointed out by Smith (1981b), 44–45.

59. Demeter and Persephone are thus treated in hysteron proteron in lines 1–40. Lines 1–15 show a similar interlocking technique, though with less formal framing. The motifs come in this order: *a.* Demeter—*b.* Persephone—*c.* the rape—*d.* Zeus's plan—*a.* Demeter (absent)—*e.* the flowers—*d.* Zeus's plan—*e.* the narcissus—*c.* the rape. This is not random; the themes build up to the climax in lines 15–18, and all that is involved in the seizure there described is made progressively more specific.

60. Hekate's honors among the gods (*a*) alternate with those she receives

from men and her benefits to them in return (*b*): *a. Theog.* 411-15; *b.* 416-20; *a.* 421-28; *b.* 429-47; *a.* 448-52. So van Groningen (1958), 89-90. Summary statements of these topics (411-15, 416-20) are followed by their fuller development in the same order, so that, as van Groningen well says, the ideas seem to come in waves, and to spread themselves more widely with each occurrence. Whereas in *W.D.* 213-47 the form contrasts the two main topics, in the praise of Hekate the effect is complementarity. Hesiod stresses that Hekate is honored by *both* gods *and* men; her influence pervades the entire universe. At the same time, this passage has an enclosed form. Lines 448-52 recapitulate the summary statement in 411-15, and lines 421-28, with their important reference to Zeus's defeat of the Titans and his division of provinces among the gods, are emphasized by their central position. But the overall effect is more a regular interchange of topics; thus, whereas the end echoes the beginning (ll. 415, 449), it also looks back to the middle section (ll. 448, 426). To treat the passage as *solely* an example of ring composition (van Otterlo, 1948, 77-78, Walcot, 1958, 12) is slightly misleading.

61. For these similarities, and on the structure of the whole passage, see Sellschopp (1934), 119, and Nicolai (1964), 57-60, especially 58. My view is closer to Sellschopp's. Walcot (1966, 82) finds a still different arrangement, but it leaves lines 219-24 out of account. The passage might also be broken down into two sections: (1) lines 213-18, enclosed by hysteron proteron, and (2) lines 219-47, with passages on the unjust city (ll. 219-24, 238-47) framing the one on the just city (ll. 225-37). But the most prominent feature of the second part, the parallelism between lines 225-37 and 238-47, works against this, and any framing effect that might be felt is subdued.

62. See note 33, above.

63. This polar relation can be observed specifically in the contrast between the παντοῖοι ἄνεμοι ("fickle winds") of line 621 and the εὐκρινέες αὖραι ("regular breezes") of line 670.

64. The distribution of these motifs is as follows:

> 630-32: seasonable voyage (ὡραῖος πλόος, *hōraios ploos*), launching of ship, loading of cargo, profit (κέρδος, *kerdos*);
>
> 641-45: works in their season (ἔργα ὡραῖα, *erga hōraia*), size of ship, size of cargo, profit (κέρδος, *kerdos*), caprice of the winds;
>
> 663-72: seasonable voyage (ὡραῖος πλόος, *hōraios ploos*), caprice of the gods, launching of ship, loading of cargo;
>
> 689-94: size of cargo, the right time (καιρός, *kairos*).

65. On the relation between Hesiod and Persēs as typifying that between poet and laborer, cf. Detienne (1963), 44-48.

66. Cf. West (1978), 55-56. After describing the continuity between the pieces of advice Hesiod gives, he concludes, "the autobiographical passages are of course authentic, but they do interrupt this coherent argument, and appear as a superimposed layer." This illustrates the difference in outlook between these poets and modern readers, and the danger, if we ignore easily recognized habits of composition, of embracing too readily theories of interpolation or of the later addition of passages. On West's argument about the composition of the *Works and Days*, see pp. 35-36. Even if his view of this passage is right, it does not replace interpretation of the text as it stands. The questions become: Why did Hesiod feel that the autobiographical passages could come where he put them? How did he work them in, and what do they add?

For another view of the structure of this passage, see Nicolai (1964), 123-

34, who briefly observes the contrast between Hesiod's victory and his father's failure (pp. 131–32). He regards the two autobiographical passages as forming Hesiod's *sphragis* (a dangerously pseudotechnical term)—the guarantee of the poet's identity and so of the quality of the poem. These sections disturb the structure of the passage, he says. On this view, lines 641–45 become merely a transitional section that at once connects and interrupts the personal material (see especially pp. 125, 127, 130). The passage has far more interesting qualities than this analysis uncovers.

67. Because the two groups are distinguished by their weapons in lines 189–90, εἵματ(α), the reading advocated by Russo (1965, 121), should not be adopted in line 183, but rather the better-attested τεύχε(α).

68. Here again Myres (1941), 27, gives a different arrangement, which the language of line 184 would seem to rule out.

69. This does not mean that the poet was describing an actual shield (I do not think he was: see Russo, 1965, 22–29), but only that he was trying to give his description a visual quality.

70. Note especially lines 270 and 336. Cf. van Otterlo (1948), 77. The apples of the Hesperides are also connected with Herakles.

71. The killing of Khimaira by Bellerophontēs and Pēgasos (l. 325) links the passage on her birth with the first series of descendants of Phorkys and Kētō, where Pēgasos is born (ll. 280–81). Similarly, the children of Ekhidna and Khimaira are connected through Orthos (l. 309) with Khrysaōr's son Geryoneus (cf. especially ll. 293–94).

72. See the discussion of the form of the *Theogony* in Section a of Chapter 2.

73. On the poetic uses of catalogues in Homer and other hexameter works, and for further examples, see Edwards (1980), especially pp. 97–103.

74. Van Otterlo (1944–45). Several of the examples he gives are discussed by Edwards (1980), 101–3, as catalogues. The difference is actually very slight (see, for example, the next note).

75. There is a similar device in *h. Apollo* 216–387, the account of the journey to find a site for his oracle (ll. 229 = 239 = 277, and l. 222 is similar to these). This passage is actually a geographical *catalogue*.

76. Whitman (1958), 288; J. H. Finley (1978), 76. The visit to the dead of Book 11 is at the center. Whitman's arrangement, based on the length of treatment given the various incidents, is not entirely satisfactory. If one counts Kirkē only as preceding the *nekyia,* as Finley does (even though visits to her and Elpēnōr's death and burial frame it), the six adventures on either side of that central episode correspond symmetically in related pairs.

77. This example and the next may seem to belong more with "spiral" composition. I have treated them as showing parallel structure because there is less a sense of recurrence to the same ideas, with fuller development each time, than simple juxtaposition in order to establish likenesses and contrasts. Still, the two patterns are formally similar; and the Hesiodic passage on the just and unjust cities, which ends with two contrasting parallel sections, may be considered on the borderline between the two classes. The important point, in any case, is not so much how we are to categorize a particular passage— opinions on that may differ in many instances—as that we recognize the influence of conventional formal principles and what this can tell us, in each instance, concerning the way the poet thought about his material.

78. Whitman (1958), 268. In both examples given here, the juxtaposed scenes are part of adjacent frames in large-scale ring composition, according to Whitman's scheme. But they also work together in the immediate context.

79. The anticipation of the structure of the later narrative here resembles the use of the Kyklōpes and Hundred-handers in *Theog.* 139–53, discussed above.

80. Cf. Bacchyl. 5.9–10: ὑφάνας ὕμνον; also Bacchyl. 19.8, Pind. *Nem.* 4.44, 94. See Wunsch in *R.-E.* 9, 140–42 (s.v. *Hymnos*), and Diehl (1940), 89.

81. The argument here bears some similarity with that of Notopoulos (1949–cf. his later article, 1964, 45–65, especially 51–54), but there are differences. Notopoulos takes it as certain that the Homeric poems, and the rest of early hexameter poetry, were orally composed, whereas, for my purposes, that question is unimportant by comparison with the fact that they were performed. Second, Notopoulos is concerned mainly with the practical effects of the circumstance of oral composition on the poem (among them the attitudes and capacities of the audience); I try to consider the poetic process from the audience's point of view as well. Finally, whereas I argue that the structural patterns enable poet and audience to keep the overall design of the work in focus, Notopoulos denies that they can have any sense of the whole: "the whole only exists as an *arrière pensée* which both the poet and his audience share as a context for the immediate tectonic plasticity of the episode" (1949, 15). For repetition and parallelism as an aid to comprehension of oral poetry, see Finnegan (1977), 126–33. She correctly warns against trying to identify a style that is peculiar to oral poetry: these same features, she observes, can be found in written literature, which itself may be recited aloud.

82. Compare Havelock (1963), 127–28, on the "oral acoustic intelligence" of the Greeks, and his Chapter 9, "The Psychology of the Poetic Performance." His discussion, highly speculative though it is, attempts to understand the nature of a poetic performance and the audience's conditioning by having heard poetry so often.

83. Most of the correspondences are noted by van Otterlo (1948), 16, but he uses the speech only as an example of ring composition used to introduce a "digression" that serves as an example of the conduct being advised—an accurate observation, as far as it goes.

84. Lord (1960), 168. It should be noted that he is reacting to Whitman's comparison of the design of the poems to the decoration on Geometric vases. Whatever the validity of that analogy may be—and I have deliberately stayed clear of it—the essential point is that these compositional forms are not empty "artistic patterns," as Lord interprets Whitman as considering them, but vehicles of expression as well.

85. Lloyd (1966). Cf. also—with special reference to the *Theogony*— Philippson (1966), 685–87.

86. On hysteron proteron as a polar figure, see Whitman (1958), 254, who also sees ring composition as a balance of identical elements and not as polar in shape.

2. THE DESIGN OF THE POEM

1. On the connection of ring composition with parataxis, see Fraenkel (1960), 71–74; van Otterlo (1944), 39–41; and—with a different perspective— Notopoulos (1951), 98–99.

2. See Van Groningen (1958), 62–69.

3. For the opposite view, see Fraenkel (1960), 82–83.

4. Les auteurs grecs archaïques sont même des hommes qui s'intéressent passionnément à leur matière et celle-ci les emporte souvent dans une direction imprévue ou paradoxale. Elle les seduit aux digressions, à un éloignement de plus en plus prononcé de la direction primaire, à un ordre arbitraire, inspiré par des associations momentanées; elle se prête volontiers à des extensions successives et ne se complaît guère à des limites trop définies. La littérature grecque préclassique nous fait assister très souvent à cette lutte entre une matière tentaculaire et des procédés limitateurs. Et c'est un de ses charmes. (Van Groningen, 1958, 99). The last sentence does its author credit, but I think that the charms of this poetry differ from, and surpass, what he finds.

5. The use of notes or an outline, for composition or revision, has sometimes been suggested for Homer (e.g., Greene, 1951, 30–31), but it would be a mistake to base an argument for coherent design on so unverifiable a hypothesis—one that, moreover, Greene derives from the unity he senses in the Homeric poems. We would simply be arguing in circles.

6. Verdenius (1960, 1962) and (1972) 259–60. The idea is not original to him, but he has exploited it with particular thoroughness.

7. On Hesiod's manipulation of certain words in different contexts in order to define them, see Claus (1977); and for other criticism of the emphasis on association, see Nicolai (1964), 78, 184.

8. This is not the inevitable result of West's argument, although he himself writes as if it were (1978, 42–43). As I have indicated several times in the first chapter, one might argue that by whatever process it evolved, the final text is coherent, and proceed from there. After all, if Hesiod, as he went along or in subsequent revision, did add a given section, he must have felt that it was appropriate to do so, and the audience would have been able to perceive how the passage fit into the whole work. In that case, why inquire into the stages of composition, even if the poet has left "signs of his changed mind" in the text, as West maintains Hesiod did? The exercise has only secondary interest.

9. This argument holds whether we are to consider our written texts as records of single performances or (as West supposes) as the results of composition and revision over extended periods. It also avoids the objections that West (1978, 42) raises after (rightly) rejecting mere paraphrases of poems such as the *Works and Days:* "But it is a mistake simply to discuss the relationships between the parts as if the author either had from the start a clear conception of the shape of the whole, and designed each part to play a particular role within the whole, or knew exactly which things he wished to say in his poem and simply had to arrange them in a satisfactory order." The alternative to West's view is not deliberate aristry guided by conscious planning, as I hope the results of Chapter 1 show.

Since I have taken issue rather sharply with West on these matters, this is a good place to say how much I admire and have benefited from his excellent editions of Hesiod. It is natural to express disagreements, because these concern specifics; it is less easy to acknowledge how much a book has generally stimulated one's thinking and increased one's understanding.

10. The *Iliad,* according to Whitman (1958), Chapter 11. For the plan of the *Theogony,* see my discussion in section a of this chapter. The *Nostoi* might also be included here. To judge from Proklos's summary (Allen V, 108–9), the poem apparently started with the disagreement of Agamemnon and Menelaos over the voyage home, and ended with Agamemnon's murder, Orestes' revenge, and Menelaos's homecoming. For this and other symmetries

in the plot, see Monro (1901), 379–80, and (with some caution) Bethe (1922), 277–79.

11. E.g., van Groningen (1958), 91–93; on Hesiod, Sellschopp (1934), 106–22, and Angier (1964); on the *Hymn to Aphrodite*, Porter (1949), especially 257–62. Notopoulos (1951), 89–95, discusses repetitions as devices for providing continuity in narrative poems and thus for counteracting the interruptions that attended oral composition (or, we might add, oral performance). They may well have had this utilitarian function as well as serving, in at least some cases, as vehicles of meaning. Notopoulos enters the latter area when he considers the use of repetitions for characterization (pp. 95–97).

12. Whitman (1958), 108–15; Austin (1975), 11–80. Vivante (1982) has recently put the whole matter in a different light. His remarks on style, "not as a manner of saying things but as at once a way of perceiving, conceiving, expressing" (p. 57), are particularly welcome. To speak of the poet's intention is, I think, to approach the question the wrong way around. Both Vivante and Austin, however, are more dismissive of Milman Parry's work (1971) than I would be.

13. Cf. A. B. Lord (1960), 186–97.

14. E.g., A. B. Lord (1960), 89–91, Minton (1960), Nagler (1974), 131–66.

15. This is well argued by Whitman (1958), 250–52.

16. Walcot (1956), 205–6, (1966), xiii. His categories seem artificial: he finds, on either side of the Prometheus story, "two dramatic episodes set round a less dynamic passage of description." The arrangement of Bradley (1966, 42–47) also uses very general categories (first gods, last gods, Zeus's allies and enemies), lumps Zeus's birth and the Prometheus episode together at the center of the poem, and works only because he follows Mazon (1928) in rejecting the entire Tartaros passage.

17. See Chapter 1, n. 21, and Detienne (1967), 48–49.

18. Cf. Philippson (1966), 673.

19. West (1966), 357, after Schwenn (1934), 28. The latter uses this fact to argue against authenticity of the Tartaros passage, the former (more plausibly) to defend it.

20. See Walcot (1966), 45–46.

21. I consider the Typhoeus episode authentic. For an able defense of the passage, see West (1966), 379–83.

22. The last part of the *Theogony* seems to me authentic at least to line 929 (the births of Athena and Hephaistos). Solmsen (1949, 67–68) rejects the Mētis episode and the birth of Athena for these reasons: (1) "Pindar does not seem to know Mētis as Zeus' (first) wife but gives this position to Themis" (here he follows Wilamowitz). But why can Pindar not have selected among several current versions, or have changed the traditional story to suit his own purposes? See further West (1966), 406. For a discussion of the relation between Mētis and Themis, which suggests that *both* goddesses are crucial parts of Zeus's rule, see Detienne and Vernant (1979), 107–9. Cf. Brown (1952), 133–34. (2) Zeus giving birth to Athena out of his own head is inconsistent with Mētis as her mother. But Zeus has swallowed Mētis! (3) "Athena as daughter of Zeus and Wisdom smacks suspiciously of later allegorical or semi-allegorical theology." How does it differ from Themis as the mother of the Hōrai and Moirai, for example? West, on the other hand, divides genuine from spurious Hesiod at line 900 (1966, 398–99), although he says that lines 901–29, "even if not worded by Hesiod, correspond fairly closely to his intentions." Of his four arguments the first two ("structural" and "historical") do

not affect anything before line 929. Third is his "stylistic" argument: that after line 900, the material "is set out in a homogeneously bare and character-less style which seems to aim at according approximately equal space to each item." But this is a simple and typical catalogue style, which seeks to organize a large volume of material in parallel and with economy. Calling the author of the passage "the registrar poet" does not obscure this fact. The fourth, "lin-guistic" argument has been met by Edwards (1971), 198–99. Note that of the phrases for marriage and birth cited by West as unparalleled in the rest of the *Theogony,* only two occur before line 929, each of them only once (ll. 921, 923), and both in connection with the marriage to Hera—slender grounds on which to reject the entire passage.

23. Menoitios's punishment, in fact, resembles that of the Titans (Zeus strikes him with a thunderbolt and sends him to Erebos, *Theog.* 514–16).

24. Cf. Philippson (1966), 671–72. On the position of the Prometheus episode in the structure of the *Theogony,* see Vernant (1981b), 66–67.

25. E.g., Robert (1966), 166, van Groningen (1958), 264–66.

26. On this expression, see Nagy (1974), 265–78: it combines the two meanings of μήδεα (*mēdea*), so that "Zeus must have unfailing genitals and unfailing knowledge by virtue of having replaced Ouranos and Kronos respec-tively as supreme ruler" (p. 275).

27. See West (1966), 158 (on *Theog.* 18). If the epithet originally meant "with the curved sickle," then it would be a persistent reminder of Kronos's mutilation of his father, for which he too is fated to suffer. But we cannot be sure that Hesiod's audience would have been aware of such wordplay, if it existed.

28. *Mētis* without qualification is also attributed to Prometheus—by Zeus himself, line 559 (cf. also l. 616). But on the Prometheus episode as "a struggle between two kinds of Mētis," see Brown (1952), 132–33.

29. Could there also be a pun in ἤμησε (*ēmēse,* "cut off," literally, "reaped," l. 181) and ἐξήμεσσε (*exēmesse,* "vomited," l. 497)? Note that the like-sounding syllables occupy the same metrical position in each line.

30. See West (1966), 225–26, on lines 209 and 210. There is, of course, a problem in the quantity of the *i* in the first syllable of *tisis* (especially after the lengthening of the first *i* in *titainein* for the sake of the etymology), but it does not preclude a punning wordplay.

31. I follow in line 473 the reading adopted by West, and his interpreta-tion (1966, 296).

32. The patronymic recurs just below in line 502, where it describes the Kyklōpes and, by recalling the context of their birth, stresses their role in the succession story. It occurs nowhere else in extant Hesiod. In Homer it has a different form and is used only once of the Titans (V.898). Otherwise it refers to the Olympians. See West (1966), 301 (on *Theog.* 486).

33. For reading ἐπεφράσσατο in line 160, see West (1966), 215. It has the advantage of sounding like the form of the same but uncompounded verb in line 162.

34. Gaia has given birth to Typhoeus, but he has already been defeated. Whether or not she meant to beget an enemy for Zeus (as Hera does in the variant of this story in *h. Apollo* 307–52), Hesiod does not say. Perhaps he deliberately suppressed this aspect of the myth in order to put the myth to new use.

35. Solmsen (1949), 21, 26. He does not go into detail, but comparison with Aeschylus's *Oresteia* is instructive. There too, a pattern of crime and

revenge is established, and repeated motifs stress the similarities between stages of the story. Apollo orders Orestes to kill his mother and Aigisthos in the same way, and with the same snare, as in their murder of Agamemnon (*Cho.* 274, 556–59). And in the event, Orestes appears with the bodies of his victims and the robe with which they trapped his father just as, at the same point in the *Agamemnon*, Klytaiméstra appeared with the bodies of Agamemnon and Kassandra, and (probably) with the robe. Finally, the whole sequence is cut short by a change of role—on the part of the Erinyes. These goddesses do not alter their nature or their essential function but are made to stop their independent pursuit of the guilty and to abandon their one-sided view of retributive justice. They are incorporated into the new order, and their power is put in its service, much as Gaia ensures the stability of Zeus's reign by continuing to help him rather than prolonging the retributive pattern. Aeschylus, in fact, exploited the similarity in form between the divine succession myth as it appears in Hesiod and the plot he fashioned for the *Oresteia*. He used the succession myth as a paradigm for the human events of his trilogy. See *Ag.* 168–75 and—on what follows here—see Clay (1969), especially pp. 7–9. The reference in *Ag.* 172–73 to Zeus as τριακτήρ, "thrower in the third wrestling match," though it primarily applies to his overthrow of Kronos, also alludes, by wordplay, to his victory in a conflict that extended through three generations. This idea is related to persistent references in the trilogy to the number three, associated with Zeus Sōtér ("The Savior"), to whom the third libation at a feast was poured. Just as Zeus established order in the third generation of the divine family, so the hope is expressed (and finally fulfilled) that an end to violence will emerge in the third generation of the house of Atreus (e.g., *Cho.* 1065–76).

36. For some of these sequences, see the works cited in note 14, above. Whitman's scheme of ring composition (1958) may seem too detailed to some, but Bowra (1930, 14–17) points out inverse symmetry between the first three and the last three books of the poem.

37. Cf. A. B. Lord (1960), 91, on arming scenes in the *Iliad:* "The 'ornamental' theme is a signal and mark, both 'ritualistic' and artistic, of the role of the hero."

38. For a treatment—though in less detail than is given here and with different conclusions—of the deaths of Sarpédōn, Patroklos, and Hektor as forming a structural pattern and as anticipating the death of Achilles, see Leinieks (1973).

39. Fenik (1968), 190–218, especially 209. In fairness, I should point out that Fenik would probably not accept the conclusions I draw.

40. This detail may provide a further connection between the deaths of Sarpédōn and Patroklos, for Leinieks (1973, 103) suggests that Pédasos "is, in effect, a symbol of Patroklos' mortality." Cf. Wilson (1974), 386. One might go further and say that Pédasos evokes the idea of Achilles' mortality as well, just as other details of Sarpédōn's and Patroklos's deaths do. The situation of the immortal horses when they are yoked with Pédasos is similar to their position with regard to their mortal owners Péleus and Achilles, and Thetis stands in the same relation to her mortal husband Péleus. See the discussion later in this section and on pp. 107–9, below.

41. Fenik (1968), 145–46. The only other exception he mentions is XXI. 161–83, which is atypical in other respects as well. On pp. 146 and 204, Fenik says that Patroklos aims at Sarpédōn and misses when he kills Thrasymélos; but nothing in XVI.462–65 indicates that, and XVI.430 does not necessarily imply it.

42. XVI.684–91, XVIII.310–13. Cf. Fenik (1968), 211–12. Note the placing of the lines in Book 16—just after the removal of Sarpēdōn's body to Lykia. As soon as Sarpēdōn's fate is concluded, Patroklos's becomes the focus of attention—a juxtaposition that further associates these two heroes.

43. Segal (1971). See especially pp. 19, 21, 28, 37, 41–43.

44. This similarity is noted also by Wilson (1974), 386–87. He points out that possession of these divine gifts is inappropriate for lesser mortals than Achilles and turns out to be disastrous for them. But he recognizes no ambivalence in Achilles' own situation: "His closeness to Thetis and the clear knowledge he gets from her puts him in a category above the other heroes and makes him more properly the owner of the immortal horses than even Peleus. Achilles alone can understand and live on familiar terms with the divine. . . . Peleus is now old and abandoned, and for him the gifts of the gods are bitterly ironic. But for Achilles, who is proof against irony, they are the natural accoutrements of greatness" (p. 389). I would say, rather, that Achilles is the most painfully exposed of anyone in the *Iliad* to the ironies involved in human life and its contacts with the divine.

45. The horses are gifts from the gods to Pēleus (XVI.381, 867, XVII.443), but we are never told on what occasion he received them. For the suggestion that they were wedding gifts, see Wilson (1974), 385.

46. See Whitman (1958), 139–42, 268–70.

47. Patroklos and Antilokhos appear together as Achilles' companions in the Underworld in identical Homeric lines, xi.468 and xxiv.16, and in Polygnotos's painting at Delphi (Paus. 10.30.3).

48. That this scene was included in the *Aithiopis* is generally agreed, even though the evidence (for which see Schadewaldt, 1951, 160) is indirect.

49. In the *Aithiopis*, Ēōs succeeded in obtaining immortality for Memnon, and Thetis translated Achilles after his death to the White Island. This may be one of the differences in outlook between the Epic Cycle and the *Iliad* (where all mortals must die, whatever their parentage) that throws into relief the latter poem's greatness (so Griffin, 1977, 42–43), or it may be later embroidery on a much older story whose poetic treatment reached its final form after our *Iliad* did. But for an explanation that makes both the hero's death and his immortality part of a traditional pattern, see Nagy (1979), 165–73, 205–7. In any case, it is clear that the *Iliad*'s prediction of Achilles' death is borne out by what we find in Book 24 of the *Odyssey*, and that is sufficient for our purposes. (On the question of the authenticity of the last book of the *Odyssey*, see note 8 to Chapter 6, below.)

50. Priority of the *Aithiopis* (or at least the tradition it reflects): Schadewaldt (1951), 155–202, Clark and Coulson (1978). Influence in the opposite direction: Monro (1901), 357–62, Webster (1964), 251, 274 (but see also p. 252). For a judicious weighing of the evidence and probabilities, see Fenik (1968), 231–40. In the present state of our knowledge, the argument for neither side can be entirely convincing. What matters is that these stories are part of a common poetic stock and include conventional themes. My argument is that the *Iliad* puts these themes to work artistically.

51. So Fenik (1968), 231–40. Cf. Notopoulos (1964), 34–35.

52. The form that Achilles' death is to take may also be foreshadowed by the story of Meleagros (IX.527–99). Although for obvious reasons Phoinix suppresses mention of Meleagros's death, the *Iliad*'s audience might have thought of accounts of it that they had heard in other poems. Meleagros was killed *by Apollo* in the battle against the Kourētes (Hesiod frr. 25.12–13,

280.1–2; cf. Paus. 10.31.3). This is not incompatible with Althaia's curse—the manner of Meleagros's death might have fulfilled it.

53. Whitman (1958), Chapter 12, especially p. 290. Whitman does find ring composition in certain episodes, but not in the *Odyssey* as a whole. For another study of circular form in episodes (those that comprise the "Telemachy") and in larger blocks, see Bertman (1966). His procedure seems questionable in some details; the descriptions he gives of some elements that are said to correspond make them sound more alike than they really are. I cannot agree with his attempt (pp. 18–19, 25) to represent the plan of the whole *Odyssey* as ring composition.

54. If one were to use Notopoulos's calculations for the speed of performance (1964, 4–6), which might give at least a rough idea, this difference translates into about half an hour in the performance of each half of the poem—surely an imperceptible disparity.

55. Odysseus's last day on Skheria, his final meal there and his leave-taking of the Phaiakians are included in Book 13. But they are part of his homecoming and are dealt with summarily in about seventy lines. For additional reasons to include them in the second half of the poem, see Thornton (1970), 122–23.

56. These are the numbers of lines: Books 1–4: 2222; 5–8: 1757; 9–12: 2233; 13–16; 2011; 17–20: 2032; 21–24: 1855. For these figures (used for a different purpose) see Thornton (1970), xiii–xiv; and for the division of the poem into six unified groups, see her pp. 121–24 (I would go beyond her discussion in finding structural correspondences between these groups—see below). She maintains, as I shall also argue, that there is a thematic unity that transcends these subdivisions. For her this is provided by constant variations on the related ideas of concealment and disclosure. But there are also other complex patterns of action and idea, a number of which she herself points out in other chapters.

57. See J. H. Finley (1978), 170. The sequence of events has been a point of controversy between Analysts and unitarians, but it conforms to a compositional norm: Bassett (1938), 122, cites it as an example of hysteron proteron. Page (1955), 70–71, uses the duplication of the divine council to support his Analytical position. But though unparalleled, this feature is not surprising. To us it may seem a clumsy and transparent device, but its use is intelligible when viewed against the background of poetic conventions. Once again, we judge this poetry by our standards and presuppositions at our own peril.

58. For an appreciation of the skill with which this interweaving is accomplished, see Page (1955), 66–68.

59. As we shall see in Chapter 6, the victory over the suitors is represented as surpassing not only Odysseus's own earlier exploits but also the achievements of all the other heroes of the Trojan story.

60. These patterns have been studied especially by Thornton (1970) and Fenik (1974).

61. Whitman (1958), 251. For guest-friendship (of which feasting is a part) as illustrating how "ornamentation with variety and contrast is the principle of composition" often in the *Odyssey*, see Thornton (1970), 38–46.

62. For these features, contrast iii.441–42 and 459–60 with this passage.

63. I find that Vidal-Naquet (1981, 88) has also commented on this.

64. Cf. M. I. Finley (1978), 57–58: "The authoritarian household, the *oikos*, was the centre around which life was organized, from which flowed not only the satisfaction of material needs, including security, but ethical

norms and values, duties, obligations and responsibilities, social relationships, and relations with the gods." For the suitors eating Odysseus's possessions, see also i.250-51, ii.203, xvi.431, xxi.332, xxiii.9.

65. E.g. Friedländer (1966a), 226-28, Wilamowitz (1928), 132-34, van Groningen (1958), 283-303, Walcot (1961), Kumaniecki (1963), Nicolai (1964), as well as Verdenius (1960, 1962) and West (1978, 41-59).

66. Even this is alluded to sporadically and is difficult to reconstruct coherently; and if we could do so, we probably would gain very little in the way of understanding the poem. See van Groningen (1957), Gagarin (1974), Wilamowitz (1928), 134-36, 142-45, West (1978), 33-40.

67. Cf. Nicolai (1964), 123-24. The text gives little support to his claim of an opposition between these activities, despite Hesiod's professedly low opinion of sailing.

68. This is noted by Walcot (1961), 8, and Nicolai (1964), 177, among others. The correspondences between these gnomic passages (despite their obvious differences) yield a detailed pattern of ring composition. The advice in both passages falls under the same general headings, and the order in which these categories appear in the later passage is the reverse of their sequence in the first. Thus, in the earlier passage come (*a*) injunctions on relations with the gods (crimes to be avoided and sacrifices, ll. 327-41), (*b*) injunctions on relations with other men (ll. 342-72), and (*c*) advice on the family (ll. 373-80). In the second passage appear (*c*) advice on the family (matrimony, ll. 695-705; ll. 703-5 recall ll. 373-75), (*b*) advice on relations with other men (ll. 707-23; banqueting is mentioned in ll. 722-23 as well as in l. 342), and (*a*) advice on relations with the gods, now in the form of taboos (ll. 724-59; ll. 724-26 recall ll. 336-41). The later section begins with the theme of the proper time (l. 695, which picks up l. 694), and the earlier section ends with it (l. 382, which means "do every task in its proper sequence"–Sinclair, 1932, 41). The indication of time in line 383 then picks up this notion. These gnomic passages are therefore not random, as they might at first sight appear (e.g., West, 1978, 45, 51, who says that in the earlier passage Hesiod is "free-wheeling").

69. See the discussion in West (1978), 346-50, and the admirable elucidation of the form of the passage by van Groningen (1958), 291-93.

70. These echoes are noted by Skafte Jensen (1966), 23-24, who draws different conclusions. They are worth listing here: ll. 299-301 and 307 correspond to 31-32; ll. 312-13 correspond to 21-24; ll. 315-16 correspond to 27-34; ll. 325-26 correspond to 6.

71. The division between the two major sections has been variously located by different writers. But a strong argument in favor of putting it after line 326 is that then ring composition encloses both sections.

72. Cf. Beye (1972), 37: Hesiod "has managed in the central portion of his poem to find a positive stance to take toward the inexorable rhythm of his life, to have converted necessity into choice."

73. Hesiod himself stresses Prometheus's punishment in the *Theogony* (ll. 521-25, 614-16). It may be implied in *W.D.* 105 (cf. *Theog.* 613).

74. If lines 213-92 are considered a unit, as in the diagram given in the text, the lines containing this figure will frame it. They stand in the same relation to each other as the similes that frame XVI.364-93 (discussed in Chapter 1): a brief anticipation at the beginning, and full development at the end.

75. For ἐνόησε, cf. the same verb in lines 286, 293, and 296. In line 286, σοὶ δ' ἐγὼ ἐσθλὰ νοέων is ambiguous. West (1978, 229) apparently takes it

as "I am saying this because I am well disposed toward you." But as Wilamo-witz (1928, 74) and Mazon (1928, 97) note, it could just as well mean "I am telling you good things, knowing them myself." The latter seems more likely, in view of lines 293–97.

76. The figure of the roads shifts significance slightly from its earlier to its later occurrence. At first, it expresses the choice between violence (*hubris*) and righteousness (*dikē*), whereas later the choice is between *kakotēs* and *aretē* (ll. 287, 289), which are, as West explains, "inferior and superior standing in society, determined principally by material prosperity" (1978, 229, on ll. 287–92). Cf. Wilamowitz (1928), 74. But the similar image associates these two pairs of opposite concepts, and they are related—to judge from the context surrounding the later passage—as cause to effect. The righteous man prospers, and so receives *aretē*. *Kakotēs* will in the end be the violent man's lot.

77. Cf. Sellschopp (1934), 118: "Das, was in diesem Stil nur einmal auf-blitzt, hat noch keine festen Umrisse; und der Dichter, der das empfindet, wird den leitenden Gedanken auch immer wieder möglichst mit denselben Worten hervorheben, ja, er wird dies in seiner Komposition berücksichtigen und eine bewusste Technik daraus machen." How conscious a technique it is, of course, we cannot know—and we do not need to.

78. That there is a principle by which the scenes are ordered is denied by van Groningen (1958), 117–18, but maintained by van der Valk (1966). The view presented here goes much farther than the latter's, however. For a rather similar progression in the Shield of Achilles from city to countryside, and thus an interplay between nature and civilization, see Marg (1957), 26.

79. On the reading in line 144, see Russo (1965), 108–9, and Cook (1937), 205–6.

80. Lines 156–59 are nearly identical to XVIII.535–38. See Russo (1965), 113–15, Solmsen (1965), and Lynn-George (1978), all of whom reject the lines in the *Aspis,* and van der Valk (1953), 271, who defends them (on rather weak grounds).

81. Despite the textual problems in these lines, the nature of the scene as a whole is made clear by the simile in XXI.22–24, which offers a close parallel (it is cited by Russo, 1965, 129–30).

82. Editors and translators tend to play down the force of ἐκλονέοντο in line 317, but this verb's normal meaning in epic is "drive (or, in the passive, 'be driven') in panic."

83. See H. Fraenkel (1973), 110.

84. I have been influenced by, but differ slightly from, Fraenkel's brief but illuminating treatment of the *Aspis* (1973, 109–12). See especially p. 110: "The defeat of a violent robber, who is a son of 'War' (Ares), by the greater warrior Heracles, who achieves peace and security for men and gods, serves as a framework within which the full horror of war and mortal combat is represented. This is the real theme."

85. I have found Friedländer (1966b) and Minton (1970) to be the most valuable treatments of these.

86. One might note, for instance, how the narrative in the *Hymn to Demeter* falls into two parts, which are joined by lines 301–4, and how thematic repetitions between parts are used to show how Demeter turns the tables on Zeus after the rape of her daughter. While Hades was carrying off Persephone, Zeus sat "apart from the gods" (νόσφιν ... θεῶν ἀπάνευθε, *nosphin ... theōn apaneuthe,* ll. 27–28) in his temple, receiving sacrifices

from men. In lines 302-4, Demeter sits "apart from all the gods" in her new temple in Eleusis (μακάρων ἀπὸ νόσφιν ἀπάντων, *makarōn apo nosphin hapantōn*) and, by blighting the earth, makes it impossible for the gods to get sacrifices. When she got information about her daughter from Helios, "more severe and more horrible" grief came over her (αἰνότερον καὶ κύντερον, *ainoteron kai kunteron*, l. 90). Now she makes the year "most severe and most horrible" (αἰνότατον . . . καὶ κύντατον, *ainotaton . . . kai kuntaton*, ll. 305-6). See also Schwabl (1969) on hymn 19 (to Pan)—though I am not entirely in accord with his approach.

87. For bibliography and a review of the question of unity, see Drerup (1937), 81-99, and Miller (1979), 173-76.

88. On what has been adduced as objective evidence for separation of the two parts, see Drerup (1937), 99-107, who reaches the same negative conclusion. To his discussion the following points might be added. Heubeck (1966) convincingly explains Thucydides' use of passages from the hymn at 3.104 against Jacoby's ingenious interpretation (1933, 689-93). There can be no reference to the First Sacred War in lines 542-43 of the hymn, if there was such a war (strong reasons for doubting that there was have been advanced by Robertson, 1978; but see the reply by G. Lehmann in *Historia* 29 [1980]: 242-46). The purpose of the war was allegedly to punish misdeeds by the Krisaians, not by the Delphic priests. For skepticism on attribution of the hymn to Kynaithos, see Burkert (1979). His dating of the hymn to Polykrates' dedication of Rhēnaia (pp. 58-62), if correct (I pass no judgment), does not settle the question of unity, as he recognizes. As for the hymn's internal features, the evidence of language and meter provides no support for the separatist view; see Porter (1951), 33, and Hoekstra (1969), 21-38. The differences between the two sections in regard to formular repetitions and the names and epithets given to Apollo found by Frolíková (1963) seem based on rather crude criteria. If they exist, they tend to show what the observance of the digamma (itself not a reliable guide on the question of unity) indicates: that the Pythian section contains a larger amount of traditional diction. This difference does not necessarily imply divided authorship; it may just as easily result from (for example) differences in the poet's intention and in subject matter (see Miller, 1977, 115-16, and 1979, 175, n.6). The Delian part contains a strikingly untraditional passage (ll. 140-81), and it is here that Hoekstra has noted a concentration of late features in the diction (1969, 26). We shall find that in structure also the Pythian section conforms more strictly to the norms described in this and the preceding chapter.

Janko's recent book (1982), which appeared after this chapter was written, may seem at last to provide objective (i.e., statistically quantified) proof of disunity (the main discussion of the hymn is in Chapters 5 and 6, pp. 99-132). If the "Delian" section dates from ca. 655 B.C. and the "Pythian" section from the opening decades of the sixth century B.C. (p. 93), the hymn cannot be single composition. But the latter date is based on the presumed historical evidence (see above), the traditional arguments for which Janko accepts uncritically; and his whole view relies on this chronology more than might at first appear. It happens that his linguistic data for the "Pythian" section are widely scattered, instead of clustering at a particular stage in the development of epic diction (see especially his table on p. 74). In only two of his criteria does the diction seem as advanced as it should be to conform to the accepted date; the other seven reflect much earlier stages. To explain these results, since this section "can in fact be dated reliably [i.e., on historical grounds] to the early sixth century" (p. 77), Janko invokes the difficult and nebulous concept of "false archaism" (pp. 76–79; cf. p. 132). There is a disquieting appearance, at least, of circularity here. Janko's further argument, on the basis of phrasing in the parallel passages, that the "Phythian" section is dependent on the "Delian" (pp. 109–12), seems to me inconclusive. And his reconstruction of the circumstances under which the two hymns might have been amalgamated (pp. 112–15), though it dovetails with Burkert's suggestion (see above), is very hard to credit. Janko has made an important contribution to the debate, but he has not settled it.

89. Arguments for unity on the basis of structure have been given by Heubeck (1972) and Webster (1975), 90. The latter considers the poem "a very skillful composition in the Homeric manner of balancing and contrasting themes." The work of both authors can be supplemented, as I shall try to do here. On the relevant hymnic conventions, see Minton (1970), 364, n. 13, and 376–77. The *Hymn to Apollo* as a whole is, in his terms, a conflation of two types of hymn—a "hymn-complex," in which the "Pythian" part is "descriptive" but also completes the "theogonic" pattern begun in the "Delian" section. (I do not think that Janko's similar study [1981] shows the hymn to be a disunity, especially since he seems to regard the Analytical position as axiomatic.) In his detailed treatment of this poem, Miller (1977) has made an impressive case for unity from the standpoint of hymnic, and more generally of encomiastic, conventions. My own approach is rather different, but I am glad to find that our views converge on some fundamental points.

90. Miller (1979), especially pp. 181–82 (an expansion of an argument made in his dissertation, 1977, 59–63). Cf. Heubeck (1972), 138–40.

91. Cf. Miller (1977), 53. The sequence of verb tenses in lines 140–45 (aorist, imperfect, and present) may also mark this passage as transitional between narrative and timeless description; it is the reverse of the order in lines 1–13 (so Heubeck, 1972, 136–37). But perhaps all the verbs in both passages should be considered timeless (see West, 1966, 155, on *Theog.* 6; his suggestion, which other scholars have tended to dismiss, merits more serious consideration than it has received). See note 9 to Chapter 5, below. For a different view of lines 1–13 and 140–45, see Janko (1981), 17 and 18 respectively.

92. Miller (1977), 69. On the relation between lines 140–46 and 179–81, see his remarks on p. 64 and Baltes (1981), 28–30. The latter notices that the passages frame the scene on Delos but does not appreciate their full complexity.

93. Miller (1977), 14, puts the division between lines 206 and 207. But although I prefer the earlier location, as I indicate below, I recognize the affinity of the second scene on Olympos—which he would include in the first part of the hymn—with the Delian festival. Miller, in turn, calls the divine scene "a second proem" to the next section of the poem (p. 69).

94. Cf. Baltes (1981), 30–31. This shift has not gone unnoticed by Analysts, who have used it as proof of disruption in the beginning of the "Pythian" hymn. But in fact it presents no problem for the unitarian view. Direct address of a god is appropriate to summary descriptions of the god's nature and powers or of an incident that reveals these. It brings the god more vividly into relation with his worshippers. The third person is more convenient—and conventional—for extended descriptive or narrative passages. Similar shifts in verb persons occur between lines 19–29 and 30ff. (the lack of transition here is also exploited by Analysts, but see Miller 1977, 30–31) and between lines 139 and 140 (from third to second person). Precisely the same interchanges

occur in the second part of the hymn, in the catalogue of places through which Apollo passes in quest of a site for his oracle (ll. 216-387). These can be as abrupt as the one between lines 181-182. A speech of Apollo is introduced by a verb in the second person (l. 246); it is followed by lines of third-person narrative (ll. 254ff.). Cf. also lines 275-76 and 277.

95. For the sequence "priamel–description of festival" and its relation to the conventions of hymnic form, see Janko (1981), 18. An understanding of the norm shows what deft use this poet makes of the conventions within which he works.

96. Kakridis (1937-38); cf. Heubeck (1972), 143-44. On the contrast between the two scenes, see Chapter 3, pp. 79-82.

97. More precisely, the second part begins with Apollo going to Delphi and then to Olympos (ll. 182-87). This journey then leads into the scene among the gods (a similar journey may be presupposed by lines 1-13). It also anticipates Apollo's later quest for a site for his oracle, which takes him on the reverse course from Olympos to Delphi. The adumbration in lines 182-85 of the narrative to come is a sure sign that the poet is not meandering but knows precisely where he is headed.

98. E.g., Jacoby (1933), 728, Deubner (1938), and—more recently— Forderer (1971), 137.

99. For this sequence, see also Hymn 19 and *h. Aphr.* 18-19.

100. The technique here is rather like the use, noted earlier, of the divine councils in *Odyssey* 1 and 5. But I would not accept Forderer's elaborate explanation of the connection between the hymn's two scenes on Olympos (1971, 137), which founders on αὐτίκα in line 188. For an interesting application of Hymn 27, and I.44-52 and 601-4, to the first Olympian scene, see Miller (1977), 5-9. The Homeric example, in fact, illustrates the division of the motifs of archery and festivity into widely separated passages (Miller holds that both themes are implied in the first scene of *h. Apollo,* which represents the transition between them).

101. E.g., Baumeister (1860), 106. Even Gemoll, who was skeptical, allowed the parallel between Leto's and Apollo's wanderings (1886, 113). For a list of correspondences, and a good example of what separatists make of them (a matter that will be dealt with below), see van Groningen (1958), 318-19.

102. This has now been pointed out by Baltes (1981), 34, n.44.

103. For details, see Wilamowitz (1920), 444-46. He was briefly anticipated by Baumeister (1860), 125.

104. E.g., the Γῆς Περίοδος ("Circuit of the Earth") in the *Catalogue of Women* (Hesiod frr. 150-56).

105. In his recent article—which appeared after this chapter was completed —Baltes (1981) also discusses the interrelation of these catalogues and argues that it supports the unitarian position. He also treats lines 179-87 in the same connection (it is not clear, however, in what sense lines 182-87 may be said to be part of a geographical catalogue). Although many of the specifics of his argument seem questionable, on p. 42 he briefly gets at the points made at greater length here: that these catalogues complement one another and reinforce lines 250-51.

106. Cf. Miller (1977), 116, n.8. Nagy (1979, 6-7) argues that this (unified) hymn reflects "the fusion of two traditions about Apollo, the Delian and the Pythian," which "implies a corresponding social fusion of two distinct audiences"—i.e., a trend towards Panhellenism.

107. Lines 162–64 seem to imply an international gathering on Delos, but since their meaning is obscure, this cannot be pressed. Also, though there appears to be a lacuna between lines 81 and 82, Apollo's pervasiveness and his special connection with Delos are clearly expressed even by the text in its present state.

108. See Allen, Halliday, and Sykes (1936), 240 (on l. 251).

109. Cf. lines 53–55. Whatever the meaning of the ritual at Onkhēstos may have been, mention of it and the episode of Telphousa are both connected with this theme, and that explains their presence in the poem. Poseidon and Telphousa both enjoy what Apollo does not have: cult centers in places on the main road that are frequented by horse-drawn wagons (ll. 231–38, 261–66). These shrines contrast sharply with Delphi, but it glorifies Apollo all the more that he does not simply find a place for his own worship that is left over after the more desirable sites have been occupied, but works such a splendid transformation.

110. Strabo 421, Paus. 10.7.2–8, hypothesis to Pindar, *Pythians*. On the paean, see Diehl (1940), 109–12.

111. See Allen, Halliday, and Sykes (1936), 212–13; Càssola (1975, 88) also accepts the existence of a Delian oracle. A comprehensive review of what evidence there is has been made by Bruneau (1970), 142–61. He concludes that there was no oracle on Delos in historical times, but allows that there is an allusion to such an oracle in the *Hymn to Apollo* that may reflect a very ancient institution defunct by the archaic age. Allusions to the oracle in later writers such as Virgil and Ovid would then be explained as a literary fiction backed by "Homeric" authority. All that is necessary for the present discussion, however, is that line 81 of the hymn be granted its apparent meaning. Whether or not the allusion to the oracle is historically faithful is unimportant here, for we are concerned only with the way it functions within the hymn. For a different view, see Miller (1977), 40–41.

112. Niles (1979) has seen ring composition in the "Delian" section, but I am skeptical. Categories such as "opening formula" and "closing formula" (and lines 177–78 are not that anyway), "question" and "answer," are hardly reliable pointers to correspondences between passages.

113. See especially the fine appreciation by Jacoby (1933), 733–34.

114. Observation of ring composition in this section has generally been limited to lines 300–362. See van Otterlo (1948), 72–73, and van Groningen (1958), 54–55. Miller (1977, 97–98) notices in addition the place of the Telphousa episode in this form.

115. This transfer of language seems designed to connect the two episodes, or at least indicates that the poet thought of them as related. He then compensated for it with line 356. The result is not the smoothest of transitions, but the references are clear because in Greek the two monsters are of different genders. There is no reason to suspect disruption of the text. See van Groningen (1958), 54–55.

116. On the implicit characterization of the Python by association with Typhaon and through him with Hera, see Miller (1977), 82–86. It seems that the myths of Zeus and Typhaon and of Apollo and the Python are doublets, perhaps cognate variants of a single prototype (both being originally combat myths concerned with the attack of the forces of disorder upon the forces of order), and that the Telphousa myth is in turn related to the Python myth. See Fontenrose (1959), 77–93, 373–74, 391–93, 465–66. If that is true, it will help us appreciate the way the poet has balanced and interrelated the three

episodes. He may well not have been aware of their kinship, but he has re-created it poetically.

117. West (1975), disputed by Janko (1982), 109–12, who, in deciding for the priority of the "Delian" section, avoids most of his predecessors' fallacies. But I do not think that his arguments amount to proof of imitation by the poet of the "Pythian" section.

118. Hesiod fr. 1.4–5. The genealogies evidently were not strictly organized on this basis, but this feature was important enough to have been singled out in the introduction as a unifying motif of the poem.

119. On the use of this formula, see West (1963), 759.

120. What I have said here is based on the order of the fragments in the edition of Merkelbach and West (1967), which seems a well-justified reconstruction. Note also how the poem keeps recurring to Herakles, who provides a motif parallel to that of the Trojan War. Another daughter of Thestios was Althaia, mother of Dēianeira; and Herakles' death was thus recounted soon after Agamemnon's (fr. 25.17–33; after Thestios's line, furthermore, came that of Porthaōn, fr. 26—a descendant of whom was Iolē). Then near the end of the *Catalogue* Herakles' birth was narrated directly after those of Agamemnon and Menelaos (fr. 195).

121. The text is mutilated, but this much is clear from lines 102–3 of the fragment. See pp. 104–6.

122. In this case, parts of the poem recognizably later than Hesiod (e.g., the story of Kyrēnē or the *Aspis*) would be subsequent expansions.

123. For various theories, see Schwartz (1960), 435–36, Merkelbach (1968a), 132–33, and West (1966), 48–50 (West's conclusion depends partly on his view of authorship in the last part of the *Theogony;* see note 22, above).

124. *Theogony:* Photios, summary of Proklos, Allen V, 96–97. For the *Titanomachy,* see Allen V, 110–11.

125. Shakespeare, *Antony and Cleopatra,* IV.xv.66–68.

126. Late because its author Eugammon was from Kyrēnē, which was founded only ca. 630 B.C. Of course, the story could be older, but that is hard to credit in this case.

127. On the inferiority of the cyclic poems, see Griffin (1977), who, however, quite properly avoids conclusions about chronology.

128. This is clear from references to other stories (surely told in epic poems) in the *Iliad* (e.g., to Theban sagas) and the *Odyssey* (e.g., to other stories of the returns).

129. For example, the *Theogony* briefly lists goddesses who bore children to mortals. The *Hymn to Aphrodite* tells the story of one of these at length, and Thetis in the *Iliad* shows a similar expansion of the same theme (both goddesses are mentioned in *Theog.* 1006–7 and 1008–10). Again, the same story (e.g., that of Typhaon, or Typhoeus) might appear in two poems—perhaps in different versions according to the requirements of the particular context, but still recognizably the same.

130. See Van Groningen (1958), 70–76. The Homeric Hymns, with their closing farewells to the god and promises of "another song," are only slight exceptions, for this manner of ending implies that further poetry is to come. Van Groningen also notes how each poem is part of a larger whole and attributes this quality to the circumstances of oral recitation (pp. 64, 71). These circumstances may have been a factor, but the cause seems to have been broader, part of the very nature and outlook of this poetry.

131. *Scholia vetera* on *W.D.* 828. See West on that line (1978, 364), who

believes that the *Ornithomanteia* was an extension to the *Works and Days* by Hesiod himself. Whether or not that is true does not affect the point made here.

132. Notopoulos (1951), 99, seems to have something similar in mind when he speaks of "the intimate tie that binds both the audience and the poet to their material. The present involves a feeling of the past, a perspective, a tradition." Cf. his earlier article (1949, 20-22). But his approach and his idea of the kind of unity in this poetry and of how it was achieved are all rather different from mine. For the integration of stories into a coherent system as a characteristic of mythic thinking, see Rudhardt (1978), 1-2. Presumably his remarks could be extended to the texts that incorporated these stories, despite the obvious differences between myth and literary narrative. If so, that would give us further perspective on aspects of the audience's mentality that helped determine their response to a performance. At least, his general description of the coherence of myths sounds very much like what we have found in regard to the Epic Cycle and the *Theogony* and *Catalogue of Women*.

3. THE GIFTS OF THE GODS

1. Some of the conditions embodied by Night's children—strife, false oaths, and so forth—can exist among the gods (*Theog.* 775-806), but are most fully realized in the world of men. Others, such as death, are unknown to the gods.

2. Here and elsewhere I have used the term *justice* as the equivalent of the Greek *dikē* despite Gagarin's contention (1973) that in Hesiod the word means "legal process" or "settlement" and that the abstract concept of *justice* is lacking. This surely is an extreme view. See Claus (1977) and Dickie (1978).

3. Various interpretations of this fable have been given, but I adhere to the most widely accepted one in view of *W.D.* 189, 192, and 276-78.

4. On this theme in the *Iliad,* see Redfield (1975), especially pp. 183-203. For the *Aspis,* see Chapter 2, Section e.

5. The expression "(you / someone) (would / would not) say" always indicates the existence of a gap between a subjective impression and the literal truth. Either, as here and in *h. Apollo* 163, it marks simply an element of conscious exaggeration in a statement, or else appearance is more sharply perceived to be at odds with the reality of a situation (III.220, IV.429-30, XVII.366-67, iii.124-25, xviii.217-19). This disparity is widest at xxiii.135, where the phrase designates a clearly mistaken impression, arising from appearances that have been manipulated.

6. The remark of Forderer (1971, 98-99) on this device drew my attention to it. Miller (1977, 56-57) finds a different significance (he also discusses *kharis*, "grace," in *h. Apollo* 153).

7. On this theme see Solmsen (1954), 3-4, Heitsch (1964)—who lists some of the examples that follow here, but without discussion—and Pucci (1977), 2-3, 97-98. (Pp. 97-98 are concerned with the significance of Pandora and the meaning of her name; these things will be touched on briefly later in this chapter.)

8. Slightly in favor of the first interpretation is ἄμβροτα ("immortal"), but it is not decisive. For the sense "the gods' gifts to men" see Heitsch (1964), and for the contrary view, Càssola (1975), 498-99. The plural *tlēmosunas* is well explained by Heitsch (p. 263) as "the many and recurrent cases of endurance." Hence the translation given in the quotation of the whole passage.

9. Cf. iv.190–202. When weeping fills Menelaos's hall, Peisistratos protests that it is inappropriate after dinner (a way of expressing the idea of limit), but adds that he does not begrudge (i.e., feel *nemesis* in regard to) mourning the dead. That, he says, is the only honor that can be paid to "wretched [*oïsduroi*] mortals" (on this adjective see discussion later in this chapter).

10. Hesiod also uses ἀκηδής of Zeus at *Theog.* 489, where it is "equivalent to *securus*" (West, 1966, 301, who compares XXI.123) and thus is not pertinent here.

11. *Theog.* 102 (cf. 98), xv.344. These lines will be quoted and discussed later in this chapter.

12. E.g., XVIII.8, XXI.524 (but cf. 525), XXIV.617 (cf. 639), i.244, v.207, ix.15, xiv.197–98, *W.D.* 49, 95. The Hesiodic lines are especially noteworthy. They contain the same phrasing and refer to Zeus and Pandora respectively: "he / she devised baneful *kēdea* for men." Evidently the similarity shows how faithfully Pandora fulfills Zeus's design. Most important for our purpose, however, is the use of *kēdea* in these lines to denote miseries that are clearly inflicted by the gods and are a permanent part of the human condition.

13. E.g., I.417, XIII.2, XVII.446, iv.197–98 (cf. XIII.569, the only other occurrence of the formula "for woeful mortals," used of the place in the body where men are most vulnerable to fatal wounds), vii.211, xi.620–21 (although he was a son of Zeus, Herakles had "boundless woe"), xv.342 (cf. 343–45), xx.195–96, *Theog.* 214, *W.D.* 113, 177, 195. The examples from the *Works and Days* are particularly clear. In XIII.1–6, also, there is a dramatic contrast between man's inability to escape hardship and a god's freedom to take refuge in more pleasant spectacles. Having brought the fighting at Troy to a critical point, Zeus leaves the mortals "to have toil [*ponon*] and woe [*oïsdun*] unceasingly," and turns his eyes away toward Thrace and the semimythical peoples dwelling there.

14. E.g., XIII.2 (see n.13), *W.D.* 113. Cf. *W.D.* 91.

15. That this diction is conventional in such contexts is suggested by its use in Arkhilokhos fr. 13W, where the poet tries to assuage grief at death by a reminder that every man at some time must suffer, and that the gods have given endurance to offset woe. Note κήδεα (*kēdea*) in line 1, τλημοσύνην (*tlēmosunēn*) in line 6 (in a sentence that expresses the same idea as XXIV.49), and τλῆτε (*tlēte*) in line 10.

16. For a fuller discussion of this passage, see Solmsen (1954), 3–4. He would omit line 731, but though it is weakly attested, it is not out of place in this context. Its reference to dancing, lyre playing, and song would provide an antithesis to the warlike deeds mentioned in line 730 (see p. 174). Other passages concerning possession of one gift and lack of another are IX.37–39 and viii.166–77.

17. Or "gave her a gift." But the distinction is unimportant since, as West observes (1978, 167), "insofar as [the gods] 'all' contribute something to her, she can be considered as their joint gift to men." For the connection of Pandora of the *Works and Days* with the idea of the gods' gifts, see Heitsch (1964), 262, n. 2. But the corresponding passage in the *Theogony* expresses the associated motifs more fully. See also Pucci (1977), 97–98. The fullest study of these motifs, as they appear in both Hesiodic versions of the myth, however, is Vernant's (1981a, 1981b). Prominent in his treatment are sacrifice and eating; these will be discussed later in this chapter.

18. This line at first seems inappropriate to its context; but when it is considered in relation to the theme of the gods' gifts, it appears clearly in place

and should not be excised. For "mingle" here Hesiod uses a form of the same verb, μειγνύναι, as appears for the "mixture" of gifts in Achilles' speech on the jars (XXIV.529; for this parallel see Diller, 1966, 262).

19. The consequences of the difference between men and gods have recently been well expressed by Griffin (1980), 93, 162.

20. This is not the place to discuss why explicit mention of the Judgment of Paris is not made until so late in the poem. The most recent treatment of the question is by Davies (1981).

21. So, at any rate, the Akhaians believe: see III.351–54, 365–68, IV.155–68, 234–39, 270–71, XIII.620–39.

22. See Stanford (1967), I, 211 (on i.33–34).

23. The Moirai are born twice in the *Theogony,* as daughters first of Night (*Theog.* 217) and then of Zeus and Themis. This appears to be a way of saying that Zeus incorporates older powers into his reign. The Moirai and the gifts they bestow on men thus take on a different value as a result of their place in the new order. See Solmsen (1949), 37.

24. For the meaning of this word, see Svenbro (1976), 52–53. On the semantic range of *gastēr,* see his pp. 50–59, and for fuller discussion of "the belly's" significance and of Svenbro's argument, see pp. 143–46. Besides those mentioned here, other references by Odysseus to the compulsion of the belly are xvii.286–89 and xviii.52–54. A beggar can apparently achieve mock-heroic stature by his prodigious appetite: Iros "was outstanding among the Ithakans at eating and drinking endlessly with greedy belly," although he lacked true heroic strength and comeliness (xviii.2–4).

25. E.g., *tlēnai:* xiii.306–7, xix.347. xi.181–83 = xvi.37–39; *kēdea,* etc.: iv.107–108, v.5, 207, vii.215, ix.12, 15, xiii.307, xiv.197–98, xxiii.306–7; *oïsdus,* etc.: v.105, 289 (with vii.270), vii.211, xi.182 = xvi.38, xiii.337, xxiii.210–12, 307. The use of this diction reinforces the idea that Penelope, passive on Ithaka, undergoes trials of the same kind and intensity as Odysseus does in the wide range of his wanderings. Note especially the formula that is applied to her mental state at xi.181 and xvi.37: τετληότι θυμῷ, *tetlēoti thumōi,* which Odysseus also uses, in a general reflection, of the man afflicted with adversity (xviii.135, cited earlier). In Book 23, Telemakhos and Odysseus both apply this phrase to Penelope in turn, now to accuse her of insensitivity in holding back from the man who claims to be her husband (xxiii.100 = 168). The phrase thus undergoes a change—if not of meaning, at least of tone and nuance—but there is continuity with the other occurrences. Endurance and impassivity have been engrained in Penelope by long hardship. They have been her means of survival through the years of waiting; and to abandon them too soon, to commit herself too readily to belief that the stranger is really Odysseus, would be to leave herself open to disappointment. Suffering teaches prudence. In the same way, Odysseus did not rush to his home and family on landing in Ithaka before he found out whether or not his wife was loyal to him, as Athena admiringly remarks (xiii.333–38).

26. The connection between the experience of suffering and an understanding of the need to have compassion for others is also suggested by a speech of Menelaos (iv.30–36). To the suggestion that he turn away the two strangers (Telemakhos and Peisistratos) who have just arrived in his hall, he replies, "We ourselves, after eating many meals of hospitality in other men's houses, came back here—let us hope that Zeus prevents us in the future from woe [*oïsduos*]." The woe is the misery of wandering, apparently (see Stanford, 1967, I, 269), and the reference is to the obstacles Menelaos faced in his re-

turn from Troy, which he will describe to Telemakhos later in this book. In his wandering and the wisdom it has taught him, as in other respects, Menelaos is a minor version of Odysseus (the equally significant differences between them will be explored in Chapter 6).

27. The eating of raw flesh is typical of beasts: see Vernant (1981b), 72–77, and Detienne (1981). Desire to eat an enemy's raw flesh is thus an example of man's tendency towards animal behavior mentioned at the beginning of this chapter. Cf. Redfield (1975), 197–99, and Segal (1971), 38–41, 61–62. In a world where a goddess (Hera) threatens to move to the opposite extreme to her divinity, it becomes all the harder to maintain one's humanity.

28. On this speech see Redfield (1975), 99–101.

29. The similarity among these poems in this respect may not be coincidental. An epiphany would have been a natural part of a hymn and may well have been conventional in hymns with extended narrative sections. And since the nature of gods and of men was generally considered as we have described it, so that contacts between them were inevitably problematical, episodes that contained ephiphanies would be similar in character. For epiphanies as typical in the hymns, see Webster (1975), 88–89 (I would argue, however, that they serve a more complex function in these poems than simply "to express the power of these gods in relation to men"—though of course they do that), and —with fuller details—Richardson (1974), 208–9 (on h. Dem. 188–90).

30. It is interesting, and perhaps an indication of the thematic similarity between the two passages, that the papyrus reading for h. Dem. 256 gives diction much like that of h. Apollo 532.

31. There is a similar effect when the innocent Nausikaa offers the same consolation to Odysseus, who has had vast experience of the gods' gifts and the need for endurance (vi.186–90).

32. This somewhat resembles Apollo's less menacing but equally impressive epiphany in h. Apollo 440–47, which also inspires fear in mortals.

33. This and several of the other aspects of the hymn mentioned here are succinctly summarized by Richardson in the last paragraph of his note on lines 147–48 (1974, 194).

34. This mediating role is implied by the diction. Demeter says that she would have made Dēmophon "immortal and ageless" and given him "undying honor" (ἀφϑιτον . . . τιμήν, aphthiton timēn, ll. 259–61). As it is, she continues, he will not evade death, but he will receive "honor undying" (τιμή . . . ἀφϑιτος, timē aphthitos, l. 263)—that is, one of the privileges of divinity, but not full immortality.

35. This is not necessarily a sign of the imitation of one poem by another. If both poems present epiphanies as part of their concern with the relations between men and gods (see note 29, above), and if such scenes, being similar in feeling and tone, contain the same elements, they would naturally use similar language, which may well have been traditional. That the diction in this case has no parallels elsewhere in extant early epic may just be coincidence. But even if there is influence, it is more important to recognize that both hymns treat the same theme and are concerned with the same problems. On the whole question, see Richardson on h. Dem. 188–89 (1974, 209–10), who, though properly cautious, thinks that if the two poems are related, h. Dem. echoes h. Aphr.

36. The similarity is also noted by Reinhardt (1956), 13, and by Smith (1981b), 65, 125.

37. Boedecker (1974), 78–81. For other views, see Allen, Halliday, and

Sykes (1936), 363-64. In view of the participle ζῶντα ("living") in line 188, it is unlikely that Ankhises fears death, as those editors imply. The adjective ἀμενηνός (amenēnos) is used of the dead (e.g., xi.49), but means "without the vital force [menos]." Cf. V.887, where Ares, speaking of what almost happened to him as a result of the wound dealt him by Diomedes, says that he might have been "amenēnos though alive." Ankhises fears a "living death" like impotence or physical decay.

38. XXIV.537, Hesiod fr. 211. Partial exceptions are Ōriōn and Iasiōn, who paid for their good fortune by being killed by other gods out of jealousy (v.121-28); but for the reasons given in the foregoing note, that is probably not what Ankhises has in mind.

39. Segal (1974). Smith (1981b) takes essentially the same structuralist approach (but with differences of interpretation).

40. For a detailed study of this theme in early Greek poetry, but with different emphases from the present discussion, see Nagy (1979), Chapter 10 (pp. 174-210).

41. This disruption can be felt most directly in the blinded Polyphēmos's address to his pet ram (ix.447-60). Indifferent to human culture, the Kyklōps has a sympathetic bond with his animals. The portrayal of the Golden Age in this episode takes the specific form of pastoralism—a natural development, since pastoralism also, by definition, implies an opposition to the city and cultural institutions.

42. The story of Tantalos had many versions, which differed widely on the nature of his sin. This happens to be the only account known in hexameter poetry that specifies his crime (the description of his punishment in xi.582-92 is silent on this matter).

43. For this concept as it appears in hexameter poetry, and for Eastern parallels (including Genesis 6, which implies a story much like the one we shall find later in this chapter in fragments from the Catalogue of Women), see Matthiessen (1977), 181-86.

44. The meaning given here to ὁμόθεν in W.D. 108 is supported by h. Aphr. 135. For other examples, see West (1978), 178 (who concludes that "Hesiod means here that they started on the same terms"—but there seems no reason to weaken the adverb's literal force). We do not know who the common parents might have been: perhaps the Titans, as in h. Apollo 336 (similarly, the Golden Age, the time of the first race of men, is set in Kronos's reign—W.D. 111) or Earth, ancestress of the gods in the Theogony, and of men in Asios fr. 8 K.

45. Cf. West (1966), 317-18 (who quotes only a different part of the scholium).

46. The conjunction γάρ ("for") in line 6 indicates that mortal women's bearing of children to the gods is to be explained by this intimacy.

47. Cf. Hesiod frr. 2 and 4, and Schmitt (1975), 19-22.

48. See Leaf (1900-1902), II, 569, and the Lexikon des frühgriechischen Epos, s.v. ἀγαπάζω.

49. Cf., however, iii.420, where Nestor says that Athena has dined with him enargēs. But it might be claimed that the adjective is used loosely, in view of what actually has happened. Athena was in fact disguised throughout the meal, and only her departure in the form of a bird enabled Nestor to guess her identity (that she did finally give herself away perhaps justifies Nestor's manner of speaking). The adjective is also used elsewhere of gods appearing (or not appearing) in their own form, but a disguise is evidently not the only

way they can conceal themselves when they wish: Hesiod fr. 165.5 (gods have appeared to a mortal *enargees* and have spoken to him); XX.131 ("gods are fearsome when they appear *enargeis*"); xvi.161 ("gods do not appear *enargeis* to everyone"—here it is a matter of Athena being visible at all). For the general idea of the gods easily concealing themselves from mortals, see x.573–74 (they readily recognize each other, however: v.77–80). On the Phaiakians' meals with the gods, cf. Vidal-Naquet (1981), 91–92.

50. I.423–24, XXIII.205–7, i.22–26, discussed by Nagy (1979), 213. For a different and interesting account of the theme of feasting, which includes discussion of Hesiod frr.1 and 204, see his entire Chapter 11 (pp. 213–21).

51. Cf. Griffin (1980), 59, n.17; Clay (1981–82).

52. Cf. Segal (1962), 38. Although Odysseus stays with Kalypsō until his raft is built, we do not hear again of his eating a meal with her. The *effect* (though surely contrary to the literal truth) is that the meal described solemnizes their separation (as in the episode at Mēkonē).

53. Pausanias (8.2.4) preserves the story of men's original closeness to the gods, expressed in just these terms (I quote from the translation of W. H. S. Jones in Vol. 4 of the Loeb edition, Cambridge, Mass. 1935; repr. 1965, Harvard University Press): "For the men of those days, because of their righteousness and piety, were guests of the gods, eating at the same board; the good were openly [ἐναργῶς, *enargōs*] honored by the gods, and sinners were openly visited with their wrath." In the light of the foregoing examples, we can appreciate the age and pervasiveness of the tradition behind this statement. The adverb "openly" used by Pausanias may be a reflex of poetic diction.

54. Cf. Rudhardt (1978), 6–7; Vernant (1981a), 54–55, and (1981b), 59–61; Detienne (1981), 217–19. Both of the latter writers stress that sacrifice sets man apart from animals as well as from gods and thus defines his intermediate position.

55. See West (1978), 174–77, and in addition to the bibliography given there, Matthiessen (1977), 178, 180.

56. It is unclear whether or not the *hēmitheoi* were thought to comprise all of humanity during that age. Hesiod gives the impression that they did, but the Homeric poems do not, and neither do the fragments of the *Catalogue of Women*. This is a point on which conceptions of the Heroic Age would naturally vary.

57. There is a general similarity here between the *Catalogue* and the *Kypria*, since the latter poem also attributed the Trojan War to a plan of Zeus (fr. 1 Allen). But the two poems seem to have differed on details. According to the *Kypria*, Zeus caused the war to relieve the earth of overpopulation. To suggest, as Stiewe does (1963, 7–9), that the poet of the *Catalogue* drew on the *Kypria* as a source and tried to combine that version with the Hesiodic myth of the Five Ages may be misleading. It is, in any case, unnecessary, because a different interpretation of Hesiod fr. 204.98–103 is possible that is simpler and avoids risky assumptions about influence (see the discussion of the fragment below, and especially note 63).

58. The syntax and interpretation of lines 99–100 are uncertain. Homeric parallels (XIX.262, 302) show that πρόφασιν is an adverbial accusative (meaning approximately "with the declared reason [or intention] that . . . "). It is then most probable that ὥστε should be supplied before the infinitive ὀλέσθαι (Wilamowitz, 1907, 34). A conceivable, though rather awkward, alternative is Stiewe's suggestion (1963, 14–15) that the construction shifts from an

infinitive (ἀϊστῶσαι) to accusative plus infinitive (ψύχας, ὀλέσθαι), both dependent on σπεῦδε. On either view, Rzach's emendation ὀλέσαι for ὀλέσθαι in line 99 would ease both syntax and meaning somewhat, but is not really necessary.

59. The only serious competitor known to me is the text that would result from the supplements proposed by West for lines 100–101 (see the apparatus in his and Merkelbach's edition, 1967, 102). It involves awkward syntax: after the negative final clause introduced by μή in line 100, ἵνα would have to be supplied for the positive final clause in lines 103–4. The interpretation West proposes is: "Zeus is planning a world catastrophe; for he wishes the ἡμίθεοι [hēmitheoi], the children of the gods, whose birth and descendants form the subject of Hesiodic *Catalogues,* to be able to live as formerly, undefiled by contact with mortals like us" (West, 1961, 133). This explanation leaves vague the nature of the problem created by the gods' begetting of the *hēmitheoi;* and it is difficult to extract the notion of defilement from the verb West supplies in line 101, μινύθηι (literally, "waste away"). His view seems also to involve understanding "the blessed ones" in line 102 as the heroes themselves or at least as including them, although the word, used by itself as it is, would more naturally refer to the gods. The name μακάρων νῆσοι ("Islands of the Blessed Ones," *W.D.* 171) does not prove the contrary, since it can hardly apply in the first instance to the heroes. These become "blessed" by virtue of their translation to those islands after death. Of course, the *Catalogue* also might have envisioned that as the ultimate fate of the heroes, just as, according to the *Aithiopis,* Thetis rescued Achilles' body from the funeral pyre and took him to dwell on the "White Island" (Allen V, 106). But there is not the slightest trace of such a conclusion in any of the extant fragments of the *Catalogue,* and it is improbable for another reason. This poem seems to have stressed mortality as the *difference* between gods and men that caused them to *separate;* its outlook in this regard was the same as that of the Homeric epics. Any mitigation of death would have weakened one of the poem's main points.

60. Or simply "mingle" in the sense of "have contact with": the verb (if it is right here) can have either meaning. The ambiguity makes no difference to the interpretation. The problem confronting Zeus is the birth of mortal offspring to the gods, and this, as the poem's opening lines show, is a consequence of the close contact between mortals and immortals. The two orders must be separated entirely to avoid further mating. The meaning given in the translation is simply more specific than the alternative.

61. τέκνα would thus be used as παῖδες often is; see Schwartz (1960), 418. Cf. also Matthiessen (1977), 184, for Old Testament parallels for this phrase, and (for discussion of this interpretation and of the alternative, to understand the phrase as equivalent to *hēmitheoi*), Stiewe (1963), 15.

62. Wilamowitz (1907), 42. On the next page, however, he concedes that the lines which follow ought to give Zeus's true reason, although he says that he cannot restore them accordingly. I am conscious of the presumption of venturing where Wilamowitz felt he could not. I take comfort, however, in the reflection that the text of which I am offering an interpretation is all the more likely to be sound because it incorporates supplements he proposed on grounds other than the lines' potential meaning. That gives a measure of probability and objective control to my view of this fragment.

63. In itself, πρόφασις can imply either a pretended but false reason or a genuine one. It appears in each sense at XIX.302 and XIX.262 respectively—

the only other occurrences of πρόφασις in hexameter poetry. For illustrations of the meaning "true reason" elsewhere in Greek, see the examples in LSJ *s.v.* πρόφασις, II.1. On this word in later Greek prose, see Pearson (1952), especially 206 (I should add that his view of XIX.262—expressed on p. 207, n. 11 —is not the only possible one, and may be oversubtle). Pearson concentrates on usages in which the word indicates insincerity to one degree or another. As he says (p. 206), it frequently has this overtone "because we most commonly offer explanations for our behavior if it appears reprehensible or if we wish to conceal our true intentions or motives." Perhaps also the nature of many incidents recounted by Herodotus and Thucydides makes it inevitable that the word should appear so often in their writings with a negative color. All this compels no conclusions about its usage in hexameter poetry; and Pearson also indicates that the explanation to which πρόφασις refers can be a true one.

In the Hesiodic fragment, however, the particle μέν that follows the word (it does not occur in either of the Homeric parallels) would seem to indicate that the reason Zeus gave was false, the true motive being either implied or expressed in the very fragmentary lines that follow this passage, in a clause with an answering δέ. But those lines do not seem to have supplied such a reason, and if it had been only implied, the result would have been hopeless vagueness on a very important matter. If we had the complete text, of course, there would be no uncertainty; but μὲν may have had, and for the reason just given probably did have, a force other than the strongly adversative "his alleged motive was . . . but his real motive was. . . . " (1) It may not have been followed by a complementary δέ, but may have been simply emphatic (Denniston, 1966, 359–61). (2) It may have been preparatory, but the coordinated ideas may not have been antithetical, only complementary according to the habit of the paratactic style (Denniston, p. 370). Thus the sequence might have been, "his reason was the following . . . and [therefore] he did the following." Lines 104–6 look, in fact, as though they might have described Zeus's actions, especially if they are given supplements like those printed by Evelyn-White (1914, 200). In that case the other μέν, in line 102, would have been emphatic. But the complementary idea need not have been expressed at all (Denniston, pp. 380–81).

There remains Stiewe's suggestion (1963, 7–9) that πρόφασις does imply a false reason, but that Zeus's real motive—his desire to destroy all of mankind for a reason like that attributed to him in the *Kypria*—is expressed in the immediately preceding clause. This is a possible explanation (cf. Denniston, 1966, 377–78); and although it would weaken my interpretation, the fragment could still be said to refer to the gods' dismay at having to witness the deaths of their mortal offspring. After all, even if Zeus's alleged motive was false, it still must have been plausible, and therefore a problem must have existed in the close contacts between mortals and immortals. Since this motif has such serious implications, however, one would expect it to serve as more than mere dressing for a fundamental divine malevolence toward mankind; and the fragment would still not have told why Zeus wanted to destroy all men—an odd silence, even if there was an allusion to the *Kypria*.

On balance, then, I would prefer one of the two alternative explanations of μέν listed above (and of them, the second). Zeus's πρόφασις was either his true motive or—in the neutral sense—his declared intention, which, however, there is no reason to think was anything but sincere.

64. (*a*) with each other: West (1961), 141, Schmitt (1975), 24; (*b*) with the gods: Treu (1957), 178–80, Stiewe (1962), 297–99; (*c*) with men of the

present time: Merkelbach (1968b), 129. Somewhat in favor of (*a*) is ἠΐθεοι in line 12, but there is much to be said for Stiewe's ἠ⟨μ⟩ΐθεοι.

65. This agrees with Stiewe's interpretation of fr. 1.8-13 (1962, 298-99), according to which two not-quite-compatible ideas are expressed in these lines: that on the one hand man's lot was unhappy in earlier times too (as compared with that of the ageless and immortal gods), but on the other hand it was far better than it is now.

66. On many of these matters—the *hēmitheoi,* the Akhaian wall in the *Iliad,* and stories of the destruction of an earlier, and superior, race—and discussion of the relevant texts, see now Scodel (1982), especially pp. 36-39, 46-49.

67. For brief treatment of this subject against the background of other divine attitudes, see Griffin (1980), 195, 201. So far as I can discover, only Schwartz draws a connection between fragment 204 and an episode elsewhere in hexameter poetry (Zeus's grief for his son Sarpēdōn), and he does so only in passing (1960, 419).

68. Or at least one mortal—the bridegroom—was present. The *Iliad* has only one explicit reference to this fateful occasion, XXIV.62-63, in a context where, to judge by lines 27-30, the ultimate causes of the Trojan War are a prominent concern (note especially δαίνυο, line 63, which implies the sharing of a feast). The wedding is alluded to in XVIII.84-85 and probably also in XVI.141-44 (= XIX.388-91). It was described at length in the *Kypria* (fr. 3 Allen; cf. Proklos in Allen V, 102). The *Catalogue of Women* apparently referred to it (Hes. fr. 211.7-9). Of later poets, Pindar uses the story movingly, along with the parallel case of Kadmos's marriage to Harmonia, to describe the possibilities and limits that determine human life, its mixture of outstanding good fortune and disaster (*P.* 3.86-103, especially 93-95). Cf. also *N.* 4.66-68. In a fragment from an unknown play, Aeschylus represents Thetis as reflecting bitterly on Apollo's perfidy when she recalls her wedding feast and the god's prophecy of Achilles' extraordinary life (fr. 284M = 350N^2, quoted by Plato, *Republic* II, 383b; her words deepen the reproach aimed at Apollo by Hera in XXIV.62-63). In his treatment of the wedding of Peleus and Thetis, Catullus (poem 64) preserves several of the ideas we have been discussing. He represents this marriage as characteristic of the age of heroes, whom he addresses as "offspring of the gods," *deum genus* (ll. 22-30). At the end of the poem (ll. 384-408), he explains more fully that the gods used to visit mortals freely in the age of heroes, when mankind was virtuous, but that they became remote when men grew wicked. This notion is generally in accord with Hesiod's myth of the Five Ages. Lines 384-86 deserve particular notice:

praesentes namque ante domos invisere castas
heroum, et sese mortali ostendere coetu,
caelicolae nondum spreta pietate solebant.

For in former times the heaven-dwellers were accustomed to visit in their
    own forms [*praesentes*]
the pure houses of the heroes, and to show themselves in mortal gatherings,
    when virtue had not yet been scorned.

Here *praesentes* seems to translate the Greek ἐναργεῖς (*enargeis*) of vii.201 (discussed earlier): see Fordyce's notes on lines 384-407 and 384 (1961, 322-23).

69. This diction is used of the suffering of divinities in one other place in the Homeric poems: V.381-404, when Diōnē comforts Aphrodite for the

wound she has suffered at Diomedes' hands. Words for "endure" (*tlēnai*) and pain (*kēdos, algos*) are heavily concentrated in this speech, and with an effect as telling as when they are used of Thetis. They underline the incongruity and the outrage of gods being injured by mortals—something that can happen only when the gods themselves are at cross-purposes with each other and champion different men. As Diōnē says, "many of us who live on Olympos suffer [*tlēmen*] at the hands of men, when we inflict severe pains [*algea*] on each other" (V.383-84; cf. V.873-74, spoken by Ares when complaining to Zeus after Diomedes has wounded him as well). From this, it is a short step to the notion (expressed in passages cited earlier, such as XXI.462-67) that the gods should not trouble themselves on men's account if it means that they too will suffer. In a way, the cases of Thetis and of other divinities who have mortal sons dramatize the truth of this idea.

70. For the parallel between Thetis's situation and that of the immortal horses, see Wilson (1974), 388, and note 40 to Chapter 2, above.

71. For the rarity in Homer of the antithetical use of two adjectives from the same root (here ϑνητῷ and ἀϑανάτῳ, *thnētōi, athanatōi,* "mortal" and "immortal"), see Sellschopp (1934), 38. The only other Homeric instance she cites is IV.43. The balance here of the two adjectives—one at the beginning, the other at the end of the line—is therefore quite striking.

72. xviii.130-31, which has, instead of "more woeful," a more general word for inferiority.

73. The stories of Ōriōn and Iasiōn (v.121-29) may show a sinister form of the same theme. These men were killed by Artemis and Zeus respectively, because—so Kalypsō claims—the gods begrudged Ēōs and Demeter their mortal lovers. If this was really their motive, it may have been, not petty jealousy, but a feeling that such mixed unions were improper, possibly for the reasons that emerge from the passages discussed here. We then have a parallel, in two individual cases, with Zeus's plan in the *Catalogue* to destroy the entire race of *hēmitheoi* because of the consequences of these unions.

74. See now Smith (1981a), who argues impressively that there was no such family, and that there is no reference to it either in the Hymn or in *Iliad* 20. In his study of the hymn, Smith notes the theme of the gods' grief for mortals and the parallel with Thetis (1981b, 40, 111, 134), but does not give this matter particular prominence.

75. See Chapter 2, Section h. When and by whom the poems were joined is irrelevant here. Their union was in accordance with conventional notions, whoever made it. I need hardly point out that the example of the *Hymn to Aphrodite* supports my interpretation of Hesiod fr. 204. The parallel also shows what deep significance a genealogical catalogue could have for its audience.

76. Cf. Reinhardt (1956), 12-13. For a speculative discussion of how Aineias and Achilles—and poetic traditions about them—might be related, see Nagy (1979), 265-75.

77. These lines follow the stories of others in Ankhises' family who were loved by divinities, Ganymede and Tithōnos. For a fine treatment of the function of their stories in the hymn, see Smith (1981b), 71-82.

78. Virgil apparently exploits this idea in his depiction of Juturna who, given immortality by Jupiter, must see her brother Turnus doomed and wishes impotently to join him in death (*Aeneid* 12.878-86). Cf. Hercules' grief for Pallas and Jupiter's speech of consolation, *Aeneid* 10.464-73. Milton later put the theme to new and more complex use in *Paradise Lost*

(9.877–85) when Eve, tempting a yet unfallen Adam, claims that a taste of the forbidden fruit has enabled her to approach "Godhead,"

which for thee
Chiefly I sought, without thee can despise.
For bliss, as thou hast part, to me is bliss,
Tedious, unshar'd with thee, and odious soon.
Thou therefore also taste, that equal Lot
May join us, equal Joy, as equal Love;
Lest thou not tasting, different degree
Disjoin us, and I then too late renounce
Deity for thee, when Fate will not permit.

4. THE POETS ON THEIR ART, I:
THE PERFORMANCE OF HEXAMETER POETRY

1. Cf. Greene (1951), 28: "Memory is indeed the mother of the Muse, who reminds the poet of the right formula; but it is she also who is the memory of the race, preserving myths and traditions and proverbs, heroic legends and characters, religious rites and folkways." Havelock (1963), Chapters 7 and 8, argues the same point at greater length and from his own point of view; cf. also p. 100: "Oral verse was the instrument of a cultural indoctrination, the ultimate purpose of which was the preservation of group identity. It was selected for this role because, in the absence of the written record, its rhythms and formulas provided the sole mechanism of recall and re-use." On the social function of oral poetry, see also Notopoulos (1964), 41–45.

2. Concerning meter, cf. Porter (1951), 8: "The hexameter may be defined as the sum total of all metrical usages of all the poets who composed in the form. However, in this mass of disparate metrical phenomena we can, by statistical analysis, perceive a norm, or rather a system of norms. This system of norms is no mere scholar's abstraction but is rather *a pattern of expectancy present in the mind of the listener or reader*" (emphasis added). On formulae, see Parry (1971), 260: "And if we, reading a strange tongue, come thus to read by a fixed scheme, how much deeper must this scheme have been pressed upon the mind of Homer's hearers, knowing as they did the epic style with its traditional diction; for they heard it since their first years, in the tales of many Singers, and in verses far outnumbering those of our sole *Iliad* and *Odyssey*."

3. The *Works and Days*, which shows the poet at odds with his society, is the apparent exception that proves the rule. Hesiod reasserts traditional social norms in the face of their disintegration at the hands of dishonest citizens and unscrupulous rulers. In a well-governed and harmonious city there would be no conflict. But even under the conditions Hesiod depicts, we can observe the poet performing a crucial service to society by rebuking those who act wrongfully and admonishing them of the consequences of their actions. In default of just rulers, it is the poet's duty, as the guardian of tradition, to say these things. If he did not do so, who would?

4. Finnegan (1977), 205–6. Cf. pp. 44–46. Properly wary as she is of cross-cultural generalizations, Finnegan is also careful to point out that every culture must be examined individually in regard to such matters. What will be said below about Greek hexameter poetry would surely fall within the bounds of the possible functions of oral poetry that she describes.

5. Cf. M. I. Finley (1978).

6. For the transmission of values and ideas through time and over space by means of poetry, see Finnegan (1977), 244–45.

7. The leaders of the lament for Hektor in XXIV.719–76 are often imagined by modern readers as professional mourners (see Leaf, 1900–1902, II, 588). But they are referred to as *aoidoi,* the regular word for singers, and are surely no different from the performers of other types of song.

8. No manuscript includes references to a singer or his performance in XVIII.603–6. Wolf's suggestion (based on Athenaeus V, 180e–82a) that the sentence mentioning a singer should be restored here from the corresponding scene in iv.17–19 has been plausibly defended by Pagliaro (1953, 20–23; for the contrary view see Leaf, 1900–1902, II, 315). Athenaeus's testimony is very problematical. But the absence of a singer, and of any mention of instrumental accompaniment, in such a context would be very odd.

The *kōmos* in *Aspis* 281–84 also raises difficulties. Solmsen (1970) eliminates it by rejecting line 281 as well as the clearly interpolated line 283, but there is no compelling reason for doing so. See Russo (1965), 148.

9. On the nature of the performances discussed in what follows, see Diehl (1940), 98–113, and Wegner (1968), 29–40 (on song), 40–68 (on the dance).

10. For salutary caution about an imitative dance in this passage, see Stanford (1967), I, 338. For a reply (not wholly satisfactory), see Austin (1975), 160.

11. For *molpē* as a combination of song and rhythmical body movements, see Wegner (1968), 43, and the detailed discussion by Pagliaro (1953), 19–27. The latter argues that the word originally signified dance and song in celebration of a god, as it does several times in the *Iliad,* and that its use in the *Odyssey* to designate purely secular singing and dancing represents a development in meaning. There seems no good evidence, however, that the word at first was associated only with religious performances rather than all performances that combined singing and dancing, of which some might have taken place in honor of a god and others might have been secular in nature. As Pagliaro himself recognizes, the word occurs in connection with both types of occasion even in the *Iliad.* The use of *molpē* in vi.101 to describe the game played with the ball by Nausikaa and her maidservants may be irregular, for the musical element seems to be lacking. Note, however, Stanford's suggestion that even here it "refers to rhythmical ball-play controlled by a tune" (1967, I, 312).

12. For illustrations of tumblers in vase paintings, see Wegner (1968), Plate VI, a and d.

13. Pan plays the syrinx in *h.* 19.15, but he cannot do so if he joins in singing the hymn described in lines 27 ff.

14. Cf. Pagliaro (1953), 27–34. In discussing this scene, he distinguishes between the *thrēnos* sung by the *aoidoi* and the *goos,* or lamentation, delivered by each of the three women. If this is correct, and it may well be, the latter do not necessarily sing.

15. See Koller (1956), 161–62. Cf. West's suggestion that Stēsikhoros's poetry was similarly performed by a solo singer with musical instrument, whom nonsinging dancers may have accompanied (1971, 309, 313–14).

16. Music and the dance can, however, be used as a grimly incongruous metaphor for combat. "I know how, in the standing fight, to tread fierce Ares' measure [μέλπεσθαι, *melpesthai*]," Hektor tells Aias (VII.241). Cf. XVI.617, cited by Leaf (1900–1902), 316.

17. West (1966), 44–45, after a suggestion by Wade-Gery. His arguments are highly speculative, however.

18. Latte (1968), 74—again on speculative grounds; Walcot (1960), 38–39.

19. Murray (1934), 187–92. His argument is elaborated by Whitman (1958), 81–83, and Webster (1964), 267–72. For a dissenting view, see Notopoulos (1964), 12–18. This matter is bound up with the vexed questions of whether written texts would have been a precondition for such continuous performances, and if so how early and how widely these texts were available.

20. It would have included that class of Ionians described in the *Hymn to Apollo* as participants in the Delian festival, whom Webster (1975, 86) imagines as affluent but not necessarily aristocratic.

21. *H. Aphr.* 293, *h.* 9.9, 31.18, 32.18. Cf. *h.* 1.17–18.

22. Cf. Richardson (1974), 3–4. The theory of Bethe (1931), 28–37, would set the longer hymns in a different category from the shorter, introductory invocations as independent compositions in their own right. But the distinction upon which it rests, between *humnos* and *prooimion*, is inconsistent with the use of the former term in hexameter poetry.

23. So Càssola (1975), xv–xvi, xix.

24. For various theories, see Allen, Halliday, and Sykes (1936), xciii–xcv; Wünsch in *R.-E.* 9, 148–51 (*s.v.* "Hymnos"); Koller (1956); Càssola (1975), xvii–xxi.

25. Schadewaldt (1944), 59–62; Càssola (1975), xxii–xxv. The tendency of Pagliaro's argument would also be against the position I have adopted (1953, especially pp. 17–19). But although he makes good sense of the various terms used in descriptions of performances, the developments he finds in terminology and musical practice, particularly those that the *Odyssey* is supposed to represent by comparison with the *Iliad*, do not seem justified by the evidence (see, for example, note 11, above).

26. Paus. 9.30.3, 10.7.3. Some modern scholars have accepted his testimony, but it is worthless.

27. Koller (1956), 165–66. He thinks that the hexameter could be sung, but that our poems had no musical accompaniment (see his p. 204). If δρέψασθαι were certainly to be read at *Theog.* 31, it would rule out thoughts of the rhapsode's staff. Kambylis (1965), 65–66, defends this reading (the laurel staff would therefore be indisputably a sign of inspiration); but there are reasons for hesitating to adopt it (see West, 1966, 165). It must be admitted that the word Hesiod uses for the branch, σκῆπτρον (*skēptron*), is the term used in the Homeric poems for the staff carried by kings, speakers in the assembly, priests, and prophets, and it is tempting to connect it with the staff later carried by rhapsodes. That is usually referred to by a different word (ῥάβδος, *rhabdos*), however; on the whole matter, see West (1966), 163–64. This is very slender evidence on which to conclude that Hesiod could not play the phorminx.

28. ἐνέπειν, i.1, καταλέγειν, viii.496. In xi.368, the latter term is used by Alkinoos of Odysseus's story, but that merely indicates that the same word, if it refers to content, can be used indifferently of spoken or poetic narrative. See Pagliaro (1953), 16.

29. *Theog.* 95 (equivalent to *h.* 25.3) does not necessarily imply a distinction between poets and musicians. Cf. Hesiod fr. 305.2 and West (1966), 187.

30. This essentially agrees with the conclusion of West (1981), 115: "that Homeric 'singing' was truly singing, in that it was based on definite notes and intervals, but that it was at the same time a stylized form of speech, the rise and fall of the voice being governed by the melodic accent of the words." On the whole question of delivery, see his pp. 113–15.

31. Schadewaldt (1944), 60. West (1981), 122-23, also suggests that the singer may have paused at the end of each line "and filled the hiatus with instrumental flourishes."

32. *Theog.* 1 and 36 and the formulaic line at (e.g.) *h. Aphr.* 293 indicate that in viii.499 ϑεοῦ should be taken with ἄρχετο. If it is understood instead with ὁρμηϑείς, the resulting phrase signifies inspiration, and reference to an invocation is excluded. This view is favored by many modern editors (e.g., Stanford, 1967, I, 344–45). The scholia and Eustathios recognize both meanings as possible. For discussion, and formidable objections to taking ὁρμηϑείς ϑεοῦ together, see Calhoun (1938).

33. Cf. Schadewaldt (1944), 72-73, who gives a convenient list of the conventions of performance.

34. Pagliaro (1953), 41–52. He rightly rejects the identification of *anabolē* as an instrumental prelude, but does not consider the possibility that the word refers to a sung *prooimion* in which the singer would begin with and invoke a god. Consequently, he views Dēmodokos's procedure at viii.499 (which he explains much as I have done) as a special instance, different from what *aneballeto . . . aeidein* implies. But surely an opening invocation must have been the rule.

35. Schadewaldt (1944), 72–73; Wegner (1968), 17; Stanford (1967) I, 222; West (1981), 122.

36. Koller (1956) understands *anabolē* as "kitharodic prelude" (see especially pp. 161–62), and this seems the most likely view, whatever one feels about the conclusions reached in his article. The evidence provided by the usage of *anabolē* and related words in hexameter and lyric poetry is ambiguous; but it does not contradict, and in one or two cases tends to support, the interpretation "sung prelude" (*h. Hermes* 426, Pind. *Nem.* 10.33; doubtful instances are XXII.476, Pind. *Pyth.* 1.1–4, *Nem.* 7.77).

37. A. B. Lord (1960), 16. Concerning the cooperation of singer and audience of Greek hexameter poetry, see also Bassett (1938), Chapter 5, especially pp. 128–40; van Groningen (1958), 55; Havelock (1963), 124–25; Notopoulos (1949), 18–20; Notopoulos (1964), 51–54; and (with comparative material from the oral poetry of other cultures) Finnegan (1977), 54–56, 122, 231–33.

38. For the implications of the concept of poetic "paths," see Schadewaldt (1944), 74–75, and Nilsson (1952), 751–52, who connects this notion with the "theme" or outline of the plot of an oral poem, which the singer could reproduce in performance with the aid of traditional formulae and typical scenes. Pagliaro (1953), 36–38, followed by Lanata (1963), 11–12, derives οἴμη and οἶμος from a root meaning "join" or "connect." The former word thus means "legame, traccia," he says, and took on a technical significance with regard to epic poetry as "l'argomento, la traccia narrativa che il poeta segue" (p. 39). In its final result, the difference between this explanation and the traditional one is small.

39. Cf. A. B. Lord (1960), 95–97, and see the analyses of the plots of the *Odyssey* and the *Iliad* respectively in his Chapters 8 and 9.

40. The genitive οἴμης in this line is usually explained as partitive (e.g., Pagliaro, 1953, 39; Stanford, 1967, I, 333), but it could also be local (Chantraine, 1963, 58), with the meaning "on the path." This significance would accord with the metaphor suggested by the verbs of motion that describe poetic activity. The local genitive is related to the use of the same case to indicate the space over which a movement takes place (although the genitive in

this sense usually occurs with verbs of motion); and both are actually forms of the partitive genitive (Chantraine, 58–59). It is also possible that οἴμης has been "attracted" into the case of the following relative pronoun (Chantraine 237–38), but I cannot understand Chantraine's own explanation of the word as "peut être un génitif dépendant de κλέα" (p. 238).

41. After I had completed this chapter, Penelope Murray's article (1981) appeared, which covers many of the topics treated in the following pages. I have not felt it necessary to curtail my own discussion, because I disagree with her on fundamental points, one or two of which are specified below.

42. Schadewaldt (1944), 78–79; Lanata (1963), 13–14. Cf. Kranz (1924), 72.

43. Pagliaro (1953), 12; Lanata (1963), 14. This idea assumes that Dēmodokos is Homer's individual self-portrait and mouthpiece, rather than a typical representative of the singer—hardly a compelling view. And originality of this kind is a modern obsession irrelevant to the concept of poetry that we are examining. Attempts to leach clues to Homer's personality out of his poetry can only blind us to what he really is saying.

44. Cf. also line 979, which corresponds metrically with 991 (with Fraenkel's notes on both lines: 1950, II, 444, 446). Pagliaro (1953, 12), also cites this passage, but rather confusingly as support for the sense he wants to give autodidaktos in viii.347.

45. "Spontaneous" is the explanation of Denniston and Page (1957), 156. Cf. Fraenkel (1950) II, 451: "The θυμός, which learned it [the song of fear] from no one, sings it from within" (emphasis added).

46. Murray (1981), 96–97, also considers these clauses complementary, and rejects their identification with form and content respectively. But she understands autodidaktos as the equivalent of the English self-taught and accepts other scholars' interpretation of Phēmios's words as a claim that he creates original poetry (as opposed to repeating the poems of others).

47. Dēmodokos's words thus strikingly resemble a Kirghiz minstrel's account of his art as recorded by Radlov: "I can sing any song whatever; for God has implanted this gift of song in my heart. He gives me the word on my tongue, without my having to seek it. I have learnt none of my songs. All springs from my inner self" (H. M. and N. K. Chadwick, The Growth of Literature III [Cambridge, Cambridge University Press, 1940], 182, quoted in Finnegan, 1977, 193).

48. Cf. Dodds (1951), 80–82; Tigerstedt (1970); Murray (1981), 87–89. Tigerstedt presents convincing objections to the view represented by Kranz (1924), Sperduti (1950), and Schadewaldt (1944), 77–78; but he seems in reaction to go rather too far towards the other extreme, and to make our poets' conception of their art more rational than it really is.

49. On this subject, see Murray (1981), 98–99 (her discussion has different emphases from my own). The claim to divine inspiration even by poets who have acquired their art through professional training is evidently typical of oral poets in various places. See Finnegan (1977), 193.

50. For the thought in this passage, see Görgemanns (1976), 124–26 (but I doubt that conclusions can be drawn from it about the date of the hymn, as he attempts to do). The participial phrase in line 486 is difficult: "'avoiding (denying itself to) painful working,' painful that is to the instrument" (Allen, Halliday, and Sykes, 1936, 338); "die Lyra 'flieht schmerzhafte Bearbeitung,' sie wünscht, dass mit ihr gespielt wird, nicht dass harte Arbeit mit ihr geleistet wird, die nicht schönend ist (μαλακῇσιν), sondern ihr Schmerzen bereitet"

(Görgemanns, p. 125). But why must pain be referred to the instrument, and does the issue lie between hard work and amusement—that is, is "working" an adequate translation of ἐργασίην? Allen, Halliday, and Sykes (1936) go on to observe (p. 339) that the word means "practice," and this provides a clue to a different interpretation. The whole passage contrasts the man who has art and long experience in playing the phorminx (ll. 483, 485) with one who approaches it for the first time and therefore ignorantly, whose touch is violent (l. 487). It is the latter whom the phorminx avoids, because he will need practice that is painful to the instrument, or to himself, or both. But in view of line 489 (= 474), there seems also to be a suggestion that laborious practice will take the player only so far, that he needs an innate talent to handle the phorminx with gentle deftness and so to produce harmonious notes. This interpretation has the advantage of fitting the phrase into its context; otherwise, we must assume a change of thought in what follows ("ein wenig anders wird seine Spielweise im zweiten Abschnitt geschildert"—Görgemanns, pp. 125-26). My view has something in common with that of Radermacher (1931), 159, although there are substantial differences.

51. This phrase can also mean "you are present to help the poet" (see Leaf, 1900-1902, I, 85), but this is less probable in view of the clauses that precede and follow it.

52. For this phrase, and its equivalent in viii.496, see Lanata (1963), 12-13; Adkins (1972), 16-17.

53. On the relation between poetry and prophecy, see Vernant (1965), 53-54; Kambylis (1965), 18-23; Koller (1965, 1972). It seems doubtful, however, that poetry actually developed from prophecy (so Sperduti, 1950, 213-18). On the other hand, Tigerstedt denies any relation between the two activities, asserting that *Theog.* 32 was borrowed from 1.70 and "was evidently an old formula, expressing divine omniscience, which Hesiod inadvertently applied to himself" (1970, 173). The adverb in the last clause is suspicious. The formula may be traditional, but if it can be applied to both prophecy and poetry, that surely indicates that they have something in common. For parallels in other cultures to a poet claiming the gift of prophecy and a sensible discussion of that claim (with a demonstration in particular that it does not imply frenzy or ecstasy), see Finnegan (1977), 207-10.

54. E.g., i.346-47, viii.44-45, *h. Apollo* 170. Cf. Phēmios's patronymic, Terpiadēs ("son of Pleasure-Giver"), xxii.330.

55. Perhaps not too much should be made of the literal meaning of the adverbs in the phrases ἐρατὸν / ἱμερόεν κιθαρίζειν (*h. Hermes* 423, 455, XVIII. 570; cf. *h. Apollo* 185). Cf. ἱμερόεις χορός / ἀοιδή, XVIII.603, xviii.194, i.421), ἔπε' ἱμερόεντα (xvii.519).

56. The lacunae after lines 409 and 415 make the precise nature of the situation uncertain, but Apollo's words in lines 407-8 do seem to contain a threat.

57. For this sense of the line (which is not entirely certain), see Allen, Halliday, and Sykes (1936), 335, and Görgemanns (1976), 122. In support of this meaning, cf. the case of Achilles, whose singing and harping at IX.186-89 have at least in part the function of calming him, filling his idleness, and temporarily diverting him from his anger against Agamemnon. For another view, see Càssola (1975), 537. His interpretation ("song which inspires irresistible passions") strains the meaning of μελεδών (*W.D.* 65-66 is hardly an unambiguous parallel for the sense he assigns it).

58. E.g., Schadewaldt (1944), 83-85, who says of the Greeks of the archaic

age, "sie genossen die Dinge des Wissens, so wie sie umgekehrt in Bildern dachten" (p. 85).

59. On the relation between the utilitarian value of poetry in an oral society and the pleasure it gives, see also Finnegan (1977), 227–30.

60. Cf. scholium on viii.44: οἰκεῖον τὸ ὄνομα διὰ τὴν παρὰ τῷ δήμῳ ὑποδοχήν.

61. For the appearance, in this list, of beggars, whom Eumaios considers mere parasites, see the discussion of beggars and singers in the next chapter.

Of the four types of oral poets described by Finnegan (1977), 188–201, there is no sign in Greek hexameter poetry of the first (the official court or religious poet who has had special training, often in a formal school, and who earns his livelihood completely by the practice of his art under a single patron). The *aoidos* does correspond rather strikingly, however, with her second category: the "free-lance or unattached practitioner" who is often itinerant and attaches himself to a series of patrons. He too can profit materially, and even support himself completely, by his singing. His training is relatively informal; it often consists merely of listening to other poets and absorbing techniques and stylistic conventions. But there are signs too of less professional singers: those who support themselves by other activities and have no formal training but are sufficiently skilled to sing "on ceremonial occasions when convention demands poetry and song. . . . These occasions are often crucial points in the social life cycle." Of this third category, the boy who sings in the vineyard on the Shield of Achilles might be an example (XVIII.569–72). And finally there are complete amateurs (Finnegan's fourth category), of whom Achilles, who sings during his withdrawal from battle, is one (IX.186–89). That these three separate, though perhaps overlapping, types are represented is consistent with the pervasiveness of song and the variety of occasions on which performances might take place. It is also not unusual; for as Finnegan writes (p. 200), "In some societies—especially those with a marked division of labour and enough economic resources to support specialists in what is not an economically productive role—all or several of these categories often co-exist."

62. Cf. Theognis 22–23. In lines 237–54, Theognis also uses the traditional diction of hexameter poetry to describe the nature and purpose of his art (κλέος, ἄφθιτον . . . ὄνομα, καὶ ἐσσομένοισιν ἀοιδή).

63. E.g., VI.208, XI.784.

64. Cf. viii.74: the *kleos* of an *oimē* that reaches the broad heaven.

65. Cf. Stanford (1967), I, 332.

5. THE POETS ON THEIR ART, II:
THE INTRODUCTION TO HESIOD'S *THEOGONY*
AND THE SELF-REFLECTIVENESS OF HEXAMETER POETRY

1. Friedländer (1966b). See especially pp. 291–93 of this reprint of his 1914 article.

2. This view has been maintained most recently by Verdenius (1972), 225–26. See also Minton (1970), 368–69, and Kambylis (1965), 35–38 (the latter believes that a Helikonian cult of the Muses was formed under Hesiod's influence). The idea has a long history, however. For cricitisms of it, see von Fritz (1966), 299.

3. Latte (1968), 63–67.

4. This point was noticed already by Friedländer (see 1966b, 291, n. 21),

who cautioned against making too sharp a distinction between the goddesses of these two mountains. It has been taken into account sporadically since then (e.g., by Kambylis, as cited in note 2 above, who apparently believes that there is no difficulty).

5. Minton (1970), 358. His suggestions as to the meaning of the structure that results (pp. 369, 375) are very attractive. Janko (1981), 20-22, limits his discussion of the proem to the way in which formal elements appear in it, without exploring the possibilities this matter may hold for interpretation and without taking Minton's article into consideration.

6. Walcot (1957), 46; Bradley (1966), 37-39. See also Minton (1970), 369. There is clearly ring composition within various sections, but the case for such a pattern in the proem as a whole seems weak. The categories by which Walcot classifies the various sections are very general and slightly misleading, and Bradley's attempt to make them more specific does not make the alleged correspondences between passages entirely convincing. The symmetry of Walcot's scheme, moreover, depends on the running together of the Muses' performances in lines 65-67 and 68-74, but surely these are distinct (the former represents the Muses' typical activities on Olympos, the latter their actions at the specific time of their birth). I agree with these writers, however, about the importance of the various lists of the contents of the Muses' songs and of their interrelation.

7. Schwabl (1963), 409-10; (1966), 176-78. His view of the structure of the proem in the former article (and of other passages of the *Theogony* in the latter), based as it is on counting lines in the various subsections, is too bookish to be plausible (the analogies he draws with music are too vague to inspire confidence that the audience of a performance would have been aware of these numbers). That is why in my discussions of structure throughout I may seem to have slighted what others have considered a promising approach.

8. On this alternation of typical description with narrative, see West (1966), 151: "Hesiod keeps returning to these descriptions because it is only from passages of this type that he can readily pass to the narrative and other passages that he wants to bring in." We should not imagine, however, that Hesiod was uninterested in the descriptive passages for their own sake; they are not just transitional but basic to the meaning of the whole proem.

9. Explanations of the different verb tenses in *Theog.* 1-10 have been suggested (e.g., by Kambylis, 1965, 49-52) that rival in their complexity those given for the similar mixture in *h. Apollo* 1-13. This elaborateness by itself makes them suspect. Any such explanation, to be convincing, would have to account for similar inconsistencies in other passages cited by West (1966), 155, on *Theog.* 6 (i.e., *h.* 19.10-15, 27-29; *h. Aphr.* 260-61). His solution to the problem, that the verbs in all these passages are timeless, is more economical and more plausible than its convoluted rivals. Verdenius takes issue with West on this point; but his own explanation (1972, 227, on *Theog.* 5)—that the narrative of a particular event begins at line 5 and continues through line 35—ignores ποτε (l. 22) and drives him to an untenable view (p. 249) of τότε in line 68.

10. I have in mind here the theory of Mircea Eliade about the significance of myths of origin. Here, for example, is his description of "the 'strong time' of myth" (1968, 19): "it is prodigious, 'sacred' time when something *new, strong,* and *significant* was manifested. To reexperience that time, to re-enact it as often as possible, to witness again the spectacle of the divine works, to meet with the Supernaturals and relearn their creative lesson is the desire that

runs like a pattern through all the ritual reiterations of myths. In short, myths reveal that the World, man, and life have a supernatural origin and history, and that this history is significant, precious, and exemplary." Compare also p. 34: "The time that has passed between the *origin* and the present moment is neither 'strong' nor 'significant' . . . and for this reason it is neglected or an attempt is made to abolish it." Eliade regards literature as representing a more developed stage of thinking than the purely mythic; but in many ways these statements describe the very reason for the existence of the *Theogony* as a whole as well as of the narrative of the Muses' birth in particular.

11. For specifics, see Walcot (1957), 44–45; West (1966), 180–81.

12. The adverbial phrase δεύτερον αὖτε (*deuteron aute,* "in second place again") in line 47 cannot be purely temporal, because Zeus must be included with the Olympians mentioned in line 46. It, and πρῶτον (*prōton,* "first," 44), which it answers, must have a logical force here (*h. Apollo* 158–59 is exactly the same and should be similarly interpreted). Praise of Zeus and of his rule is thus superposed upon a chronological account of cosmic development, as happens in the body of the *Theogony* itself (see Chapter 2, Section a). In line 50, αὖτις (*autis,* "again") has a similar implication. The birth of men and Giants would be included in the genealogies of lines 45–46 (for the Giants see *Theog.* 185, and for the origin of men under Kronos's rule see *W.D.* 109–11). On the relation between the songs in lines 11–21 and 43–50, cf. Siegmann (1966), 318–19.

13. With θεῶν γένος αἰδοῖον ("the revered race of the gods," l. 44), cf. ἀθανάτων ἱερὸν γένος αἰὲν ἐόντων ("the holy race of the immortal ones who live forever," l. 21). The descriptions of the Muses' voice in lines 65 and 67 resemble those in lines 10 and 43 (on the text of l. 67, see von Fritz, 1966, 304–7, and West, 1966, 178–79). With lines 69–71, cf. 42–43. Κάρτει ("with strength") appears in praise of Zeus in lines 49 and 73.

14. For the summary statement of the subject in line 105, cf. ll. 21, 44. Κλείετε ("celebrate," l. 105): cf. ll. 44, 67 (and 32). Ἐξ ἀρχῆς ("from the beginning," l. 115): cf. l. 45. Line 106 resembles 45 in substance, and line 111 is identical with 46 (I follow Solmsen's text (1970) as opposed to West's (1966), with the excision of lines 108–10 and the retention of line 111). The division of privileges among the Olympians (l. 112) has appeared in the Muses' song on their way to Olympos (ll. 73–74), as has the overthrow of the Titans (probably indicated by the occupation of Olympos, l. 113—see West, 1966, 191). The *Theogony,* with its time scheme, combines the order of the first two lists (ll. 11–21, 43–50): it begins in Zeus's reign but also proceeds in chronological order "from the beginning." See Chapter 2, Section a.

15. If *Theog.* 48 could be satisfactorily emended so as to scan, it would strengthen the depiction of the Muses as intermediaries between the gods and men. The Muses would begin and end their song with Zeus, just as Hesiod sings the Muses first and last (l. 34; cf. ll. 1 and 36; elsewhere in hexameter poetry, "to sing first and last" evidently is not intended literally but means "to honor particularly," although it happens that the *Theogony* opens and concludes with Zeus's reign and the Muses' birth). The device of the "song-within-the-song" is the mortal poet's way of "beginning and ending" with Zeus. But no reliance can be placed on line 48. The essential point is clear enough without it anyway.

16. Singers "are from" (have their calling from) the Muses and Apollo, says Hesiod, and rulers "are from" Zeus. But the Muses' influence, since it is felt in both the poetic performance and the agora, produces a crossover in

these relationships. The Muses bring the poet into relation with Zeus, as we have seen, and on the other hand they aid the "Zeus-cherished kings." That is why Hesiod can then go from a summary statement of the Muses' benefits to *all* men (ll. 96–97) to the example of poets (rulers having already been treated). For views that differ in varying degrees from this, see von Fritz (1966), 313, and Verdenius (1972), 257. I see no inconsequence in lines 94–97, as West does (1966, 186).

17. Kalliopē, through whom the transition is made from the Muses' names to mortal rulers (ll. 79–80), implies beauty of voice, which confers the power of persuasion on the ruler and earns him the citizens' respect. For lines 80–93 as a progressively more profound explication of this name and a justification of the ruler's epithet *aidoios,* see Neitzel (1977), 38–39. Cf. also Solmsen (1954), 7. Whatever may be the truth about the much-discussed question of how (if at all) these lines are related to viii.169–73, I regard this whole passage as genuine Hesiod.

18. Solmsen (1954), 3–5, followed by Lanata (1963), 31. For the Muses' association with rhetoric, however, see Paus. 2.31.3—a passage that associates them also with sleep (cf. *h. Hermes* 449). It may also be significant that Odysseus spares Medōn with Phēmios when he kills the suitors (xxii.357–60, where the sight of the poet seems to remind Odysseus of the herald). We should not be unduly concerned with the question of whether Hesiod invented the connection between rhetoric and song, or feel that his "originality" has been disappointingly lessened if it turns out that he did not. The important point is what he made of the idea as part of his overall statement about poetry (Homer, as we shall see immediately below, used the same idea in quite different contexts and for different ends). That is a more important kind of literary artistry, or so it seems to me; and in any case, worry about who originated a particular concept is inappropriate when we are dealing with a poetry that drew so heavily on traditional stock.

19. This assumption is made by Solmsen (1954, 8)—among others.

20. This is a general form of an argument that has been made in regard to the particular instance of nouns that can receive the same epithet, and that are therefore (so it is maintained) semantically related to each other. See Ritoók (1968).

21. West (1966), 171. Among the passages he cites, see especially XVIII. 570–71. The Trojan elders exemplify the way in the Homeric poems that warfare and eloquence (which is exercised by the giving of wise advice in the assembly) usually alternate and are not found simultaneously in the same person. As we shall find in Chapter 6, this matter is involved in the issue of song's relation to action. For now we should note that the elders resemble Nestor, who still goes to battle but fights ineffectually. Like him, in the absence of youthful strength, they excel in speech and have poetlike qualities.

22. See the authors cited in note 6, above. To recognize a relation between these two sections is not, of course, to accept a detailed scheme of ring composition for the proem as a whole.

23. West (1966), 160, 161–62. Cf. *h. Dem.* 256–58, *h. Apollo* 532–33, and Webster (1975), 88–89.

24. Svenbro (1976), 50–59. He also argues (pp. 60–73) that the Muses' speech distinguishes between self-sufficiency, which the poet needs if he is to utter truth, and dependence on others, which hinders truthful discourse.

25. This passage is discussed by Svenbro (1976), 54, but without consideration of the context or the details of the diction.

26. Odysseus is exceptional, however, because telling his tale reawakens his own grief (ix.12–13). An explanation will be suggested in Chapter 6.

27. Some understand the lines in this way, but also—unnecessarily—as polemic against Homer: e.g., Lanata (1963), 24–25, von Fritz (1966), 302–4, and Kambylis (1965), 62–63. Kambylis in particular bases his view on a distinction between form and content that is alien to the hexameter poets' conception of their art.

28. For a review and criticisms of previous views of the Muses' words, see Stroh (1976), 90–97. Stroh himself argues that the lines refer to Hesiod's own poem, the *Theogony*, in which he gave poetic embroidery to the events he recounted, and that Hesiod considers the ability to give falsehood the artful appearance of truth not an evil but a matter for pride. It will be obvious from the discussion below where I differ from this position. For a reply to Stroh, and an argument (on—to my mind—unconvincing grounds) that *both* "lies like the truth" *and* "true things" refer to non-Hesiodic poetry, see Neitzel (1980).

29. Vernant (1965), 53–60. The quotations in the last sentence are from his summary on p. 299.

30. For its part, prophecy is not limited to prediction. Epimenidēs, who combined the functions of poet and seer, was said to have practiced the latter art in regard, not to the future, but to things that were in the past but obscure (fr. 4 K). For prophecy concerning the present, cf. Hdt. 1.46.3–49. And for the statement that "the Muse" knows all things and not just the present, see *PMG* 947.

31. Detienne (1960); cf. Detienne (1963), Chapter 4, where he applies this concept of "truth" to the *Works and Days*. His arguments are supported by Heitsch (1962), who collects passages that reflect the connection between *lēthē* and *alētheia*. The demonstration by Adkins (1972, 5–11) that there are many other passages in which *alētheia* is opposed to falsehood (as it is in *Theog.* 27–28) is not incompatible with Detienne's conclusions. In the latter's view, such an opposition would simply reflect a later, nonmythic type of thought.

32. Detienne (1967), 22. Cf. Sappho 55 L-P, which opposes death to Mnēmosynē (here associated explicitly with poetry).

33. Pucci (1977), especially Chapter 1 (pp. 8–44). Cf. Detienne (1967), 67–69.

34. See Chapter 3, above. The connection between poetry and the theme of divine gifts is also made by Solmsen (1954), 1–4 (but without stress on the ambiguous value of such gifts) and by Pucci (1977), 2–3, 29–33.

35. From "Chocorua to Its Neighbor," in *The Collected Poems of Wallace Stevens* (1978: New York, Alfred A. Knopf).

36. In performance elsewhere than Delos, the address to the Delian maidens and the adverb ἐνθάδε ("here") in line 168 would mean that the poet was imagining himself on Delos and inviting his audience to do the same. The passage on the festival thus would have had essentially the same effect then as in its first performance.

37. See Friedländer (1966b), 282.

38. Ibid.; Minton (1970), 359–62; Janko (1981), 19–20.

39. On the effect of these songs-within-the-song, see also Koller (1956), 161.

40. Many of the characteristics that set this poem apart from the other Homeric Hymns and have led scholars to assign it a late date may be explained

as elements of parody and cannot be dated. The hymn's relation to its tradition, not its chronological place, is what finally matters anyway. It may well
be—in fact, it probably is—a later composition than the other major hymns;
but I am skeptical of arguments for dating it as recently as the third quarter
of the sixth century B.C. (Brown, 1947, 102-32) or even the fifth century B.C.
(Görgemanns, 1976, especially pp. 127-28).

41. Cf. Eitrem (1906), 280; Radermacher (1931), 158.

42. Maehler (1963), 49, n. 2; Nagy (1979), 303-5. The connection with
the *Hymn to Hermes* was proposed by the original publisher of the inscription, M. Kontoleon, but has been disputed. For discussion, see Kambylis
(1965), 143. The differences that Kambylis emphasizes seem trivial; and I do
not see the distinction here between "eine äussere Ähnlichkeit in der Grund-
form des Motivs" and "eine echte Paralletität."

43. Diog. Laert. 1.109 (H. Diels, *Die Fragmente der Vorsokratiker*, 7th ed.,
revised by W. Kranz [Berlin, 1954; Weidmann], I, 27-28).

6. POETRY IN THE *ODYSSEY*

1. On this subject see Redfield (1973), 151-52, and Marg (1957), 13-15.

2. It was perhaps out of failure to appreciate this point, as well as through
ignorance of how formulaic diction works, that ancient scholars (Aristarkhos
among them) athetized these lines on the grounds that they are more appropriate where they occur in nearly identical form at VI.490-93 and xxi.350-
53. See the scholia on i.356.

3. Cf. vi.62-65 and (for the contrast with heroic standards) XXIV.260-61
and III.54-55, 390-94.

4. Lanata (1963), 17; Nagy (1979), 98-101.

5. Here I owe a debt to Marg (1957), whose remarks on pp. 13-15 and 18-
19 stimulated my thinking, especially the following: "Leiden ist im Weltlauf
beschlossen. Hört man vom Leide im Lied, auch von eigenem, so ordnet man
es ein ins Ganze, das fremde Leid hebt über eigenes heraus" (p. 14). I do not
agree, however, that Phēmios's song in Book 1 of the *Odyssey* could have this
effect on Penelope.

6. This passage sheds light on xii.212, where Odysseus encourages his men
by saying, "I think that perhaps we shall remember these things also." Pleasure
is of course implied, but the act of memory in itself is what matters most. In
his imitation of the line (*Aeneid* 1.203), Virgil obscures this fact by stressing
pleasure: "forsan et haec olim meminisse iuvabit" ("perhaps someday it will
be pleasant to remember even these things").

7. And yet this tale is supposed to be true! Thus this poem constantly con-
fuses our sense of the distinction between truth and falsehood. A detail is
symptomatic. Eumaios's experiences are supposed to have taken place in the
known world, and yet the land of his birth has the quality of what I have
called (in Chapter 3) a paradisal place. Neither want nor disease is ever known
there, but when people grow old, the bolts of Apollo and Artemis kill them
gently (xv.407-11). Cf. *W.D.* 90-92, 116.

8. Modern readers, impatient of poetic catalogues, are apt to find Odysseus's recapitulation of his story in this scene tedious, or at best an example
of the oral style's necessary disadvantages. Although summaries of the main
events of the plot occur in several other places in both Homeric poems, this
passage is unique. It repeats in indirect statement episodes earlier narrated as

past within the main framework of the poem. Its striking character accords with the essential function it performs.

Since doubts have been cast on the authenticity of this scene and of all that follows it until the end of Book 24, I should add that I consider the whole concluding section well integrated in the design of the poem and even indispensable. For a masterful summary of the question and relevant scholarship, see Stanford (1967) II, 404-6. Page (1955), 101-36, argues vigorously against authenticity. Wender (1978) has given the most recent and the most detailed defense of the disputed scenes. I agree with her arguments, and I hope in addition that I have shown from a different perspective that the storytelling by Odysseus and Penelope is anything but otiose. The second Underworld scene will be discussed later in this chapter; and on Odysseus's reunion with Laertes, see note 28. But justification for including these scenes in the present discussion need not rest on so extreme a position. As Moulton (1974) has observed, the burden of proof rests on those who reject the ending, and their arguments do not so far add up to proof. It is thus only reasonable to give the disputed section its place in an interpretation of the *Odyssey* as a whole. All too often, in fact, this approach, which ought to be primary, has been subordinated to the defense of authenticity, although many perceptive observations have been made in the course of the debate.

A few words must be said here about one of the main objects of contention. The scholia on xxiii.296 say that Aristophanes and Aristarkhos considered Odysseus and Penelope going to bed the τέλος or πέρας of the *Odyssey*. On the possible meanings of these terms see Stanford (1965), 5 and 18, n. 2. If the language attributed to those scholars means that they considered xxiii. 296 the end of the poem—and Moulton (1974), 154-57, considers it prudent to assume that it does—that is not sufficient reason for rejecting everything in our text that follows the line. The basis of this opinion may just as well have been subjective judgment and taste as factual evidence no longer available to us. On the other hand, the Alexandrian scholars may have meant only that the *Odyssey* reaches its goal at this point, as Eustathios thought. Scott (1916- 17), 398-400, has maintained that xxiii.296 cannot be the climax (or the ending; his other arguments apply only to concluding the poem here) on the grounds that Odysseus's longing all along has been, not for his wife, but for regaining home, property, and kingdom. This seems to me an artificial distinction. Penelope *is* important to Odysseus personally, even though she may be only part of what home means to him (so Stanford, 1965, 11-12). The reunion of husband and wife matters greatly; why else did the poet devote the bulk of Books 19 and 23 to it? The poem does reach its culmination here from the point of view of the plot and—though this goes far beyond what Aristophanes and Aristarkhos would have meant—in another respect as well. For if we consider not only the fact of Odysseus and Penelope going to bed but also the conversation they hold there, we can appreciate how this scene resolves the issue of poetry in the *Odyssey* (a subject that is, after all, intimately related to the reunion). It does not follow, of course, that the section xxiii.344- xxiv.548 is either boring or superfluous. Other concerns of the poem receive their necessary conclusion there.

I had already completed a draft of this chapter when I saw Wender's monograph. I am pleased to find that we share a similar understanding of the *Odyssey* as a whole and of particular episodes within it (see especially her remarks on pp. 4 and 74-75).

9. In general, the cyclic *Nostoi* agreed with the *Odyssey*'s version of these

events. See the summary of Proklos, Allen V, 108-9. Perhaps one poem influenced the other; but both may have drawn on the same store of tradition.

10. Cf. D'Arms and Hulley (1946), 211-12, and (for details of the contrast between the homecomings of Agamemnon and Odysseus) Bassett (1917-18), 522.

11. These are the terms of Polyphēmos's curse: ix.532-35.

12. This parallel is noted also by Nagy (1979), 101. On the simile, see Moulton (1977), 130-31, who rather indirectly notes the comment on the Trojan War but also associates the grieving woman with Penelope. This seems a tenuous, or at best a secondary, connection.

13. There is, however, the same contrast here as in the case of Nestor. Odysseus must struggle to reinstate himself at home and thereby wins glory. Menelaos faces no obstacles at home—Orestes' revenge has paved the way for him—but therefore has no opportunity to gain *kleos* by the manner of his return.

14. Cf. Austin (1975), 127-28, who implies, but does not draw explicitly, the parallel between Helen and the poet.

15. The sadness of Menelaos's life may be indicated in the name of his son, Megapenthēs ("he who has great grief," iv.11). As is well known, in the Homeric epics sons are often named for characteristics of their fathers. With this name contrast the transient effect of Helen's anodyne, described as *nēpenthes* ("without grief") in iv.221.

16. For details of these anticipations of the plot of the *Odyssey* in the anecdotes at Sparta, see Andersen (1977), 8-13.

17. This has also been remarked by Nagy (1979), 39.

18. See Thornton (1970), 5-6.

19. Cf. Bassett (1923), 50-51, who may go too far, however, in saying that Agamemnon never makes proper amends to Achilles in the *Iliad*. But his contention that this scene is an epilogue to both the *Iliad* and the *Odyssey* implies an important perception about how these poems are related.

20. On Agamemnon's speech, see Nagy (1979), 36-38. It seems more natural to understand the *kleos* and *aretē* as belonging to Penelope, not (as he does) to Odysseus: "it is his *aretē* 'merit' to have won a Penelope (rather than a Clytemnestra)." Agamemnon immediately goes on to contrast the songs Penelope and Klytaimēstra will receive, and the shift from Penelope to Odysseus and back to Penelope would be very abrupt and not at all clearly marked. Still (as I say below), the import of the speech as a whole is that having Penelope as a wife does credit to Odysseus, whereas marriage to Klytaimēstra has led to Agamemnon's ignominious death and shame.

21. For the function of the second Underworld scene as contrasting Odysseus with Agamemnon and Achilles, see Segal (1962), 44, and Wender (1978), 40-43. Compare also the interesting remarks on the arrangement of the scene by Bassett (1923), 47-48. There are, he observes, two pairs of speeches in chiastic order. Each consists of a long narrative joined with a shorter speech: lines 24-34 (Achilles) with 36-97 (Agamemnon) and lines 121-90 (Amphimedōn) with 192-202 (Agamemnon). These pairs concern the *kleos* of Achilles and Odysseus respectively, and each of the shorter speeches contrasts Agamemnon's fate with the other man's fortune. The symmetry, it might be added, also suggests that Odysseus's victory balances and even surpasses Achilles' achievements. Cf. also Bassett's earlier article (1917-18, 523).

22. Dēmodokos's two songs in Book 8—the first recounting an episode from the start of the Argive expedition, the second the strategem by which Troy was taken—bracket the entire ten years of the war.

23. Arkhilokhos (fr. 1W) gives us our earliest example of a man who claims literally to be both a poet and a soldier. On this, and on Odysseus as poet, see Seidensticker (1978), 13–15.

24. Cf. G. DeF. Lord (1963), 44.

25. Cf. Nagy (1979), 235: the word "designates praise poetry within the traditional diction of epinician praise poetry."

26. Redfield (1973), 148–49. On these tales, and on the appropriateness of each to the particular circumstances and audience, see Trahman (1952).

27. The relation between the two lines has been much discussed, but conclusions about the dependence of one text upon another when traditional diction is likely to be in question seem unwarranted—and unnecessary. In the Odyssean version of the line, ἴσκε presents a problem. For discussion, see Maehler (1963), 40, n. 2, who understands it as "make similar" ("gleich machen"), but argues that the participle λέγων is not in that case superfluous. The important parallel for this sense of ἴσκε is iv.279, where it is used of Helen imitating the voices of the Akhaians' wives. The parallel is especially significant in view of the poetlike qualities that she displays.

28. Odysseus spins another tall tale about his past to Laertes in xxiv.302–14. But it is perfunctory; it is shorter than his other false stories and lacks the circumstantial detail that gives them the ring of truth. On the other hand, I find it natural that Odysseus, who has lied to others before revealing his identity, should—practically as a reflex—treat his father the same way. When he sees the effect of his words on Laertes, the profundity of which he failed to anticipate, Odysseus drops even this thin disguise and the tone of the scene modulates into seriousness. But in Odysseus's speech itself we might justly detect an affectionate humor, almost satire, on the part of the poet towards his hero. The poet can afford to take this tone here because he has already depicted all the important elements of Odysseus's character. We would do wrong to solemnize the scene and speak of Odysseus's heartlessness, as Page does (1955, 112). For a rather similar view of the scene to mine, see Moulton (1974), 163–64.

29. M. Parry (1971), 154, 156–57. This is, of course, not the same as saying, as I have, that the word is "the quintessential description of Odysseus," but in this case it amounts to the same thing, because the word is used in the first line of the Odyssey to characterize the hero.

30. It may be significant that this epithet is first used of Hermes at the moment of his birth, and stands first in a series of descriptive words and phrases that reflects the poet's concern to characterize the god as fully as possible (h. Hermes 13–16; cf. Radermacher, 1931, 61). The word thus has the same function as in the first line of the Odyssey and is given a somewhat similar prominence. For the association of Hermes with Odysseus on the basis of polutropos, see now van Nortwick (1980), 5 (that the similarity between god and hero consists of their sharing characteristics typical of women, as he maintains, seems to me doubtful, however).

31. H. 28.2—of Athena, to whom Odysseus is similar in character (xiii. 291–99). It is interesting to note that in h. Hermes 319 Apollo is called πολυμήχανος ("resourceful")—an adjective elsewhere in hexameter poetry given only to Odysseus. The play of the two epithets in the same line emphasizes that Hermes has met his match.

32. Cf. Dimock (1963), especially 55–58. For Hermes' role as Odysseus's patron in the Odyssey itself, see Wender (1978), 31–32. Perhaps the division of functions in the poem that she makes (following Anne Amory) between

Hermes and Athena is too sharp. Athena cannot be *only* "the divine representative of Odysseus' civilized wisdom" in view of xiii.296-99.

33. See especially Moulton (1977), 145-53, and Seidensticker (as cited in note 23, above).

34. III.54-55 (Hektor rebuking Paris for his cowardice). For the antithesis between action and song (or the related art of dancing), cf. viii.246-49, XXIV.260-62. For the somewhat problematical XIII.730-34, see Chapter 3, note 16.

35. This agrees with the suggestion of Pucci (1979) that the diction of the Sirens' song suggests that they are tempting Odysseus to desert the *Odyssey* and become a character in the *Iliad* once again.

36. On this passage, see Segal (1962), 5, and the brief but judicious remarks by Moulton (1977), 151-52. Lines 410-11 faintly resemble the descriptions of playing the phorminx in *h. Hermes* 53-54, 419-20, 501-2. For the comparison of the sound to the swallow's voice, cf. *h.* 19.16-18 (Pan's piping compared to the nightingale's song). Moulton (1977, 138-39) connects this comparison with Athena's assumption of the swallow's shape as she watches the battle with the suitors (xxii.239-40): "The short swallow similes unobtrusively underline her partnership with Odysseus and the certainty that she will champion his cause" (p. 139). This is perhaps oversubtle, since Athena's metamorphosis can hardly be anticipated when Odysseus strings his bow. What is mainly important is that these lines stress the similarity of the bow to a musical instrument.

37. Schadewaldt (1944), 65. I would agree instead with Marg (1957), 16. Another character who occupies his idleness with music is Ankhises, whose companions have left him behind while they tend the livestock (*h. Aphr.* 80).

38. My colleague Sheila Murnaghan (who kindly read this chapter in manuscript) suggests to me that the contrast between these heroes might be formulated in this way: Achilles is a poet when he is most outside society; Odysseus becomes a poet as a sign of his return to society.

39. For discussion, see Solmsen (1954), 9-13, who decides (against Wilamowitz) that Hesiod imitated the passage in the *Odyssey*. But because the phrasing in neither passage is entirely satisfactory, this is probably an instance of two poets adapting traditional diction to particular contexts without complete success (note how the same ideas, with some similarity in diction, are applied to Arētē, vii.69-74). In his recent examination of the question, Neitzel (1977) is properly skeptical about the use of style as a criterion, but gives his own reasons for considering the Odyssean passage earlier than the Hesiodic (pp. 42-44). Even if chronological priority and influence can be satisfactorily demonstrated, however, these are not the most interesting—or even the essential—questions to raise.

40. For the connection between these passages, see Austin (1975), 199-200, who considers viii.170 directly related to xi.367. I follow Neitzel's convincing interpretation of viii.170, however (1977, 27-28), although I adhere to the more traditional view of viii.175 (pace Neitzel, pp. 28-30, who also denies any connection with xi.367).

41. A line with the same structure is *h.* 22.5, which gives complementary functions of Poseidon.

42. Cf. Solmsen (1954), 1-3, for more detailed treatment of the passages referred to here. Solmsen observes that the two qualities "are not normally found in one and the same Homeric character" (p. 1), but does not consider Odysseus in the *Odyssey*. Actually, the figure in the *Iliad* who comes nearest

to fulfilling the ideal is also Odysseus, but no special point is made in that poem of the range of his abilities because he must take second place to Achilles. His qualities are prominent enough, however, for him to serve as a foil to the central hero.

43. Before enumerating Agamemnon's gifts, Odysseus mentions the plight of the Akhaians, Achilles' quickness to anger (here he invokes the authority of Pēleus), and the irrevocability of a rash act (IX.225–29). At the end of the speech (ll. 300–306), he says that if Agamemnon and his gifts are hateful (a possibility he has foreseen), Achilles should pity his comrades; and besides— here Odysseus appeals to Achilles' heroic instincts—the chance is at hand to kill Hektor. In addition, the opening lines of the speech (225–27), in which Odysseus says that Achilles does not lack an "equal" or "fair" portion of the banquet in Agamemnon's hut, serve a twofold purpose. They assure Achilles that Agamemnon is now anxious to do him honor; but also, because a share in the feast is a reward for fighting among the foremost men, they subtly re-mind Achilles of his duty (cf. IV.257–64, 338–48, VII.319–22, XII.310–21).

44. For fuller discussion of the contrast between Achilles and Odysseus— in regard to their ways of speaking, and particularly in regard to their assump-tions about how word and deed are related—see Cramer (1976). Cf. also Friedrich and Redfield (1978), especially 270–271, 275–77.

45. Nagy (1979), especially 23–25, 64–65. Cf. also Austin (1975), 109.

46. Cf. ii.272, xvi.241–42. Occasionally other figures are described as ex-celling in both counsel and warfare. Cf. Hesiod fr. 25.37: ὅς ῥ' ἀγαθὸς μὲν ἔην ἀγορῇ, ἀγαθὸς δὲ μάχεσθαι ("who was good at speaking [agorēi] and a good fighter [makhesthai]"). This describes another unusual figure, Amphi-araos, who was both a seer and a warrior. Pindar praises him in similar terms (Ol. 6.17: ἀμφότερον μάντιν τ' ἀγαθὸν καὶ δουρὶ μάρνασθαι) but substitutes his gift as a seer for his speaking in council. At Nem. 8.7–8, in bestowing on Aiakos what he must intend as the highest possible praise, Pindar also uses the terms of the heroic ideal: χειρὶ καὶ βουλαῖς ἄριστος ("best in might and coun-sels"). This, of course, does not affect the Odyssey's portrayal of Odysseus as unique; Pindar has his own reasons for idealizing Aiakos. In the Iliad (III.179), Helen describes Agamemnon as "both a good king and a mighty warrior." But that is not quite the same as calling him a wise and persuasive counsellor, and in fact his quarrel with Achilles in the first book has shown him as lacking this quality (and also as less than kingly).

🔲 Bibliography of Works Cited 🔲

Abbreviations of journal titles are those of *L 'Année Philologique.*

Adkins, A. W. H. 1972. "Truth, ΚΟΣΜΟΣ, and ΑΡΕΤΗ in the Homeric Poems." *CQ* 66:5–18.
Allen, T. W., ed. 1946. *Homeri Opera.* Vol. V. Corrected reprint of 1912 edition. Oxford, Clarendon Press.
Allen, T. W., Halliday, W. R., and Sykes, E. E., eds. 1936. *The Homeric Hymns.* 2nd ed. Oxford, Clarendon Press. Rpt. ed. Amsterdam: Adolf M. Hakkert, 1963.
Andersen, Ø. 1977. "Odysseus and the Wooden Horse." *SO* 52:5–18.
Angier, C. 1964. "Verbal Patterns in Hesiod's *Theogony.*" *HSCP* 68:329–44.
Austin, N. 1975. *Archery at the Dark of the Moon: Poetic Problems in Homer's* Odyssey. Berkeley and Los Angeles, University of California Press.

Baltes, M. 1981. "Die Kataloge im homerischen Apollonhymnus." *Philologus* 125:25–43.
Bassett, S. E. 1917–18. "The Second Necyia." *CJ* 13:521–26.
———. 1920. ""ΥΣΤΕΡΟΝ ΠΡΟΤΕΡΟΝ 'ΟΜΗΡΙΚΩΣ (Cicero, Att. 1, 16, 1)." *HSCP* 31:39–62.
———. 1923. "The Second Necyia Again." *AJPh* 44:44–52.
———. 1938. *The Poetry of Homer.* Berkeley and Los Angeles, University of California Press.
Baumeister, A., ed. 1860. *Hymni Homerici.* Leipzig, B. G. Teubner.
Bertman, S. 1966. "The *Telemachy* and Structural Symmetry." *TAPA* 97: 15–27.
Bethe, E. 1922. *Homer, Dichtung und Sage.* Vol 2. Leipzig and Berlin, B. G. Teubner.
———. 1931. *Der homerische Apollonhymnos und das Prooimion* (Leipzig). Berichte über die Verhandlungen der sächsischen Akademie der Wissenschaften 83.
Beye, C. R. 1972. "The Rhythm of Hesiod's *Works and Days.*" *HSCP* 76:23–43.
Blusch, J. 1970. *Formen und Inhalt Hesiods individuellem Denken.* Bonn, H. Bouvier.
Boedeker, D. 1974. *Aphrodite's Entry into Greek Epic. Mnemosyne* suppl. 32. Leiden, E. J. Brill.

Bowra, C. M. 1930. *Tradition and Design in the* Iliad. Oxford, Clarendon Press.
———. 1952. *Heroic Poetry.* London, Macmillan.
Bradley, E. M. 1966. "The Relevance of the Prooemium to the Design and Meaning of Hesiod's *Theogony.*" *SO* 41:29–47.
Brown, N. O. 1947. *Hermes the Thief.* Madison, University of Wisconsin Press.
———. 1952. "The Birth of Athena." *TAPA* 83:130–43.
Bruneau, P. 1970. *Recherches sur les cultes de Délos à l'époque hellénistique et à l'époque impériale.* Bibliothèque des écoles françaises d'Athènes et de Rome 217. Paris, E. de Boccard.
Burkert, W. 1979. "Kynaithos, Polycrates, and the *Homeric Hymn to Apollo.*" In *Arktouros: Hellenic Studies Presented to Bernard M. W. Knox.* Ed. Glen W. Bowersock, Walter Burkert, and Michael C. J. Putnam. Berlin and New York, Walter de Gruyter. Pp. 53–62.

Calhoun, G. M. 1938. "ΟΡΜΗΘΕΙΣ ΘΕΟΥ ΑΡΧΕΤΟ, *Odyssey* VIII.499." *CP* 33:205–6.
Càssola, F. 1975. *Inni Omerici.* Milan, Fondazione Lorenzo Valla.
Chantraine, P. 1963. *Grammaire homérique.* Vol. 2. Paris, Librarie C. Klincksieck.
Clark, M. E., and Coulson, W. D. E. 1978. "Memnon and Sarpedon." *MH* 35: 65–73.
Claus, D. B. 1977. "Defining Moral Terms in the *Works and Days.*" *TAPA* 107:73–84.
Clay, D. 1969. "Aeschylus' Trigeron Mythos." *Hermes* 97:1–9.
Clay, J. D. 1980. "Goat Island: *Od.* 9.116–141." *CQ* 74:261–64.
———. 1981–82. "Immortal and Ageless Forever." *CJ* 77:112–17.
Cook, R. M. 1937. "The Date of the Hesiodic *Shield.*" *CQ* 31:204–14.
Cramer, O. C. 1976. "Speech and Silence in the *Iliad.*" *CJ* 71:300–304.

D'Arms, E. F., and Hulley, K. K. 1946. "The Oresteia-Story in the *Odyssey.*" *TAPA* 77:207–13.
Davies, M. 1981. "The Judgement of Paris and *Iliad* Book XXIV." *JHS* 101: 56–62.
Denniston, J. D. 1966. *The Greek Particles.* Corrected reprint of 2nd ed. Oxford, Clarendon Press.
Denniston, J. D., and Page, D. 1957. *Aeschylus* Agamemnon. Oxford, Clarendon Press.
Detienne, M. 1960. "La notion mythique d' ΑΛΗΘΕΙΑ." *REG* 73:27–35.
———. 1963. *Crise agraire et attitude religieuse chez Hésiode.* Collection Latomus 68. Brussels, Latomus.
———. 1967. *Les maîtres de vérité dans la Grèce archaïque.* Paris, François Maspero.
———. 1981. "Between Beasts and Gods." In *Myth, Religion, and Society.* Ed. R. L. Gordon. Cambridge: Cambridge University Press. Pp. 215–28. First published in *Nouvelle revue de psychanalyse* 6(1972):231–46. Reprinted in M. Detienne, *Dionysos mis à mort.* Paris: Gallimard, 1977. (English translation, Baltimore: Johns Hopkins University Press, 1979.)

Detienne, M., and Vernant, J.-P. 1979. *Cunning Intelligence in Greek Culture and Society.* Sussex, England, Harvester Press, and Atlantic Highlands, N.J., Humanities Press. First published as *Les ruses d'intelligence: la mētis des Grecs.* Paris: Flammarion, 1975.

Deubner, L. 1938. "Der homerische Apollonhymnus." *SPAW,* 248–77.

Dickie, M. W. 1978. "'Dikē' as a Moral Term in Homer and Hesiod." *CP* 73: 91–101.

Diehl, E. 1940. "Fuerunt ante Homerum Poetae." *RhM* 89:81–114.

Diller, H. 1966. "Die dichterische Form von Hesiods Erga." In *Hesiod.* Ed. E. Heitsch. Darmstadt, Wissenschaftliche Buchgesellschaft. First published in Abhandlungen der Akad. der Wissenschaften und der Literatur, Mainz, nr. 2 (1962):41–69.

Dimock, G. E., Jr. 1963. "The Name of Odysseus." In *Essays on the* Odyssey. Ed. C. H. Taylor, Jr. Bloomington: Indiana University Press. Pp. 54–72. First published in *Hudson Review,* spring, 1956, 9:52–70.

Dodds, E. R. 1951. *The Greeks and the Irrational.* Berkeley and Los Angeles, University of California Press.

Drerup, E. 1937. "Der homerische Apollonhymnos: eine methodologische Studie." *Mnemosyne,* 3rd ser., 5:81–134.

Edwards, G. P. 1971. *The Language of Hesiod in Its Traditional Context.* Oxford, Basil Blackwell.

Edwards, M. W. 1980. "The Structure of Homeric Catalogues." *TAPA* 110: 81–105.

Eitrem, S. 1906. "Der homerische Hymnus an Hermes." *Philologus* 65:248–82.

Eliade, M. 1968. *Myth and Reality.* New York, Harper and Row. 1st ed. 1963.

Evelyn-White, H. G., ed. and trans. 1914. *Hesiod, the* Homeric Hymns, *and* Homerica. Cambridge, Mass., Harvard University Press, Loeb Classical Library.

Fenik, B. 1968. *Typical Battle Scenes in the* Iliad: *Studies in the Narrative Techniques of Homeric Battle Descriptions.* Hermes Einzelschriften 21. Wiesbaden, F. Steiner Verlag.

———. 1974. *Studies in the* Odyssey. Hermes Einzelschriften 30. Wiesbaden, F. Steiner Verlag.

Finley, J. H., Jr. 1978. *Homer's* Odyssey. Cambridge, Mass., Harvard University Press.

Finley, M. I. 1978. *The World of Odysseus.* 2nd rev. ed. New York, Viking Press.

Finnegan, R. 1977. *Oral Poetry.* Cambridge, Cambridge University Press.

Fontenrose, J. 1959. *Python: A Study of Delphic Myth and Its Origins.* Berkeley and Los Angeles, University of California Press.

Forderer, M. 1971. *Anfang und Ende der abendlandischen Lyrik.* Amsterdam, B. R. Grüner.

Fordyce, C. J., ed. 1961. *Catullus.* Oxford, Clarendon Press.

Fraenkel, E. 1950. *Aeschylus,* Agamemnon. 3 vols. Oxford, Clarendon Press.

Fraenkel, H. 1921. *Die homerischen Gleichnisse.* 2nd ed. Göttingen: Vandenhoeck & Ruprecht.

Fraenkel, H. 1960. "Eine Stileigenheit der frühgriechischen Literatur" and "Drei Interpretationen aus Hesiod." In his *Wege und Formen frühgriechischen Denkens*. 2nd ed., Munich, C. H. Beck. Pp. 40–96, 316–34.

———. 1973. *Early Greek Poetry and Philosophy*. Oxford: Basil Blackwell. Translation of *Dichtung und Philosophie des frühen Griechentums*, 2nd ed., Munich: C. H. Beck, 1962.

Friedländer, P. 1966a. "Hesiods ΥΠΟΘΗΚΑΙ." In *Hesiod*. Ed. E. Heitsch. Darmstadt, Wissenschaftliche Buchgesellschaft. Pp. 223–38. First published in *Hermes* 48 (1913):558–72.

———. 1966b."Das Proömium von Hesiods Theogonie." In *Hesiod*. Ed. E. Heitsch. Darmstadt, Wissenschaftliche Buchgesellschaft. Pp. 277–94. First published in *Hermes* 49 (1914):1–16.

Friedrich, P., and Redfield, J. 1978. "Speech as a Personality Symbol: The Case of Achilles." *Language* 54:263–88.

Frolíková, A. 1963. "Some Remarks on the Problem of the Division of the *Homeric Hymn to Apollo*." In Γέρας: *Studies Presented to G. Thomson on the Occasion of his Sixtieth Birthday*. Ed. L. Varcl and R. F. Willetts. Acta Univ. Carolinae 1963 Philosophica et Historica 1 Graecolatina Pragensia II. Prague, Charles University. Pp. 99–109.

Gagarin, M. 1973. "Dikē in the *Works and Days*." *CP* 68:81–94.

———.1974. "Hesiod's Dispute with Perses." *TAPA* 104:103–11.

Gemoll, A. 1886. *Die Homerischen Hymnen.* Leipzig, B. G. Teubner.

Gordon, R. L., ed. 1981. *Myth, Religion, and Society: Structuralist Essays by M. Detienne, L. Gernet, J.-P. Vernant, and P. Vidal-Naquet.* Cambridge, Cambridge University Press.

Görgemanns, H. 1976. "Rhetorik und Poetik im homerischen Hermes-hymnus." In *Studien zum antiken Epos*. Ed. H. Görgemanns and E. A. Schmidt. Meisenheim, A. Hain. Pp. 113–28.

Greene, W. C. 1951. "The Spoken and the Written Word." *HSCP* 60:23–59.

Griffin, J. 1977. "The Epic Cycle and the Uniqueness of Homer." *JHS* 97: 39–53.

———. 1980. *Homer on Life and Death*. Oxford, Clarendon Press.

Havelock, E. A. 1963. *Preface to Plato*. Cambridge, Mass., Harvard University Press.

Heitsch, E. 1962. "Die nicht-philosophische ΑΛΗΘΕΙΑ." *Hermes* 90:24–33.

———. 1964. "ΤΛΗΜΟΣΥΝΗ." *Hermes* 92:257–64.

———. ed. 1966. *Hesiod*. Wege der Forschung 44. Darmstadt: Wissenschaftliche Buchgesellschaft.

Heubeck, A. 1966. "Thukydides III 104." *WS* 79:148–57.

———. 1972. "Gedanken zum homerischen Apollonhymnus." In *Festschrift für Konstantinos J. Merentitis*. Athens. Pp. 131–46.

Hoekstra, A. 1969. *The Sub-Epic Stage of the Formulaic Tradition: Studies in the* Homeric Hymns to Apollo, to Aphrodite, and to Demeter. Amsterdam, North Holland Publishing Co.

Jacoby, F. 1933. "Der homerische Apollonhymnus." *SPAW*, 682–751.

Janko, R. 1981. "The Structure of the Homeric Hymns: A Study in Genre." *Hermes* 109:9–24.

———. 1982. *Homer, Hesiod, and the Hymns: Diachronic Development in Epic Diction.* Cambridge Classical Studies. Cambridge, Cambridge University Press.

Kakridis, T. J. 1937–38. "Zum homerischen Apollonhymnus." *Philologus* 92: 104–8.

Kambylis, A. 1965. *Die Dichterweihe und ihre Symbolik: Untersuchungen zu Hesiodos, Kallimachos, Properz, und Ennius.* Heidelberg, C. Winter.

Kamerbeek, J. C. 1967. "Remarques sur l'Hymne à Aphrodite." *Mnemosyne* 20:385–95.

Kinkel, G. 1877. *Epicorum Graecorum Fragmenta.* Leipzig, B. G. Teubner.

Kirk, G. S. 1962. *The Songs of Homer.* Cambridge, Cambridge University Press.

———. 1970. *Myth: Its Meaning and Functions in Ancient and Other Cultures.* Berkeley and Los Angeles, University of California Press. Paperback edition: 1973.

Koller, H. 1956. "Das kitharodische Prooimion." *Philologus* 100:159–206.

———. 1965. "ΘΕΣΠΙΣ ΑΟΙΔΟΣ." *Glotta* 43:277–85.

———. 1972. "Ἔπος." *Glotta* 50:16–24.

Kranz, W. 1924. "Das Verhältnis des Schöpfers zu seinem Werk in der althellenischen Literatur." *NJA* 53:65–86.

Kumaniecki, K. 1963. "The Structure of Hesiod's *Works and Days.*" *BICS* 10:79–96.

Lanata, G. 1963. *Poetica Pre-Platonica: Testimonianze e Frammenti.* Florence, La Nuova Italia.

Latte, K. 1968. "Hesiods Dicterweihe." In his *Kleine Schriften.* Munich, C. H. Beck. Pp. 60–75. First published in *Antike und Abendland* 2 (1946):152–63.

Leaf, W., ed. 1900–1902. *The Iliad.* 2nd ed. 2 vols. London. Reprint ed., Amsterdam: Adolf M. Hakkert, 1971.

Leinieks, V. 1973. "A Structural Pattern in the *Iliad.*" *CJ* 69:102–7.

Lloyd, G. E. R. 1966. *Polarity and Analogy: Two Types of Argumentation in Early Greek Thought.* Cambridge, Cambridge University Press.

Lobel, E., and Page, D. L., eds. 1955. *Poetarum Lesbiorum Fragmenta.* Oxford, Clarendon Press.

Lord, A. B. 1951. "Composition by Theme in Homer and Southslavic Epos." *TAPA* 82:71–80.

———. 1960. *The Singer of Tales.* Cambridge, Mass., Harvard University Press.

Lord, G. DeF. 1963. "The *Odyssey* and the Western World." In *Essays on the Odyssey.* Ed. C. H. Taylor, Jr. Bloomington, Indiana University Press. Pp. 36–53. First published in the *Sewanee Review* (summer 1954) 62:406–27.

Lord, M. L. 1967. "Withdrawal and Return: An Epic Story Pattern in the *Homeric Hymn to Demeter* and in the Homeric Poems." *CJ* 62:241–48.

Lynn-George, J. M. 1978. "The Relationship of Σ 535–540 and Scutum 156–160 Re-examined." *Hermes* 106:396–405.

Maehler, H. 1963. *Die Auffassung des Dichterberufs im frühen Griechentum bis zur Zeit Pindars.* Hypomnemata 3. Göttingen, Vandenhoeck & Ruprecht.

Marg, W. 1957. *Homer über die Dichtung.* Münster, Aschendorff.

Matthiessen, K. 1977. "Das Zeitalter der Heroen bei Hesiod." *Philologus* 121: 176–88.

Mazon, P., ed. and trans. 1928. *Hésiode: Théogonie, les Travaux et les Jours, le Bouclier.* Paris: Société d'édition "Les belles lettres."

Merkelbach, R. 1968a. "Les papyrus d'Hésiode et la géographie mythologique de la Grèce." *CE* 43:132–55.

———. 1968b. "Das Prooemium des hesiodischen Katalogs." *ZPE* 3:26–33.

Merkelbach, R., and West, M. L., eds. 1967. *Fragmenta Hesiodea.* Oxford, Clarendon Press.

Miller, A. M. 1977. *Form and Generic Intention in the* Homeric Hymn to Apollo. Ann Arbor, Mich., University Microfilms.

———. 1979. "The 'Address to the Delian Maidens' in the *Homeric Hymn to Apollo:* Epilogue or Transition?" *TAPA* 109:173–86.

Minton, W. W. 1960. "Homer's Invocations of the Muses: Traditional Patterns." *TAPA* 91:292–309.

———. 1970. "The Proem-Hymn of Hesiod's *Theogony.*" *TAPA* 101:357–77.

Monro, D. B. 1901. *Homer's* Odyssey: *Books XIII–XXIV.* Oxford, Clarendon Press.

Moulton, C. 1974. "The End of the *Odyssey.*" *GRBS* 15:153–69.

———. 1977. *Similes in the Homeric Poems.* Hypomnemata 49. Göttingen, Vandenhoeck & Ruprecht.

Murray, G. 1934. *The Rise of the Greek Epic.* 4th ed. Oxford, Oxford University Press.

Murray, P. 1981. "Poetic Inspiration in Early Greece." *JHS* 101:87–100.

Myres, J. L. 1930. *Who Were the Greeks?* Berkeley and Los Angeles, University of California Press.

———. 1941. "Hesiod's *Shield of Herakles:* Its Structure and Workmanship." *JHS* 61:17–38.

Nagler, M. N. 1967. "Towards a Generative View of the Homeric Formula." *TAPA* 98:269–311.

———. 1974. *Spontaneity and Tradition: A Study in the Oral Art of Homer.* Berkeley and Los Angeles, University of California Press.

Nagy, G. 1974. *Comparative Studies in Greek and Indic Meter.* Cambridge, Mass., Harvard University Press.

———. 1979. *The Best of the Achaeans: Concepts of the Hero in Archaic Greek Poetry.* Baltimore, Johns Hopkins University Press.

Neitzel, H. 1976. "Pandora und das Fass: zur Interpretation von Hesiod, Erga 42–105." *Hermes* 104:387–419.

———. 1977. "Zum zeitlichen Verhältnis von Theogonie (80–93) und Odyssee (8, 166–177)." *Philologus* 121:24–44.

———. 1980. "Hesiod und die lügende Musen: zur Interpretation von Theogonie 27 f." *Hermes* 108:387–401.

Nicolai, W. 1964. *Hesiods Erga: Beobachtungen zum Aufbau.* Heidelberg, C. Winter.

BIBLIOGRAPHY OF WORKS CITED /243/

Niles, J. D. 1979. "On the Design of the *Hymn to Delian Apollo*." *CJ* 75:36–39.

Nilsson, M. P. 1952. "Der homerische Dichter in der homerischen Welt." In his *Opuscula Selecta*. Lund, C. W. K. Gleerup. 2:745–61. First published in *Die Antike* 14 (1938):22–35.

Northrup, M. D. 1979. "Tartarus Revisited: A Reconsideration of *Theogony* 711–819." *WS* n.f. 13:22–36.

Notopoulos, J. A. 1949. "Parataxis in Homer." *TAPA* 80:1–23.

———. 1951. "Continuity and Interconnexion in Homeric Oral Composition." *TAPA* 82:81–101.

———. 1964. "Studies in Early Greek Oral Poetry." *HSCP* 68:1–77.

Page, D. L. 1955. *The Homeric* Odyssey. Oxford, Clarendon Press.

———. 1959. *History and the Homeric* Iliad. Berkeley and Los Angeles, University of California Press.

———, ed. 1962. *Poetae Melici Graeci*. Oxford, Clarendon Press.

Pagliaro, A. 1953. "Aedi e Rapsodi." In his *Saggi di Critica Semantica*, Messina and Florence, G. d'Anna. Pp. 3–62.

Parry, M. 1971. *The Making of Homeric Verse: The Collected Papers of Milman Parry*. Ed. A. Parry. Oxford, Clarendon Press.

Pearson, L. 1952. "*Prophasis* and *Aitia*." *TAPA* 83:205–23.

Perry, B. E. 1937. "The Early Greek Capacity for Viewing Things Separately." *TAPA* 68:403–27.

Philippson, P. 1966. "Genealogie als mythische Form: Studien zur Theogonie des Hesiod." In *Hesiod*. Ed. E. Heitsch. Darmstadt, Wissenschaftliche Buchgesellschaft. Pp. 651–87. First published in *SO* suppl. 7 (Oslo), 1936.

Porter, H. N. 1949. "Repetition in the *Homeric Hymn to Aphrodite*." *AJPh* 70:249–72.

———. 1951. "The Early Greek Hexameter." *YClS* 12:1–63.

Pucci, P. 1977. *Hesiod and the Language of Poetry*. Baltimore, Johns Hopkins University Press.

———. 1979. "The Song of the Sirens." *Arethusa* 12:121–32.

Radermacher, L. 1931. "Der homerische Hermeshymnus." *SAWW* 213, pt. 1.

Redfield, J. M. 1973. "The Making of the *Odyssey*." In *Parnassus Revisited*. Ed. A. C. Yu. Chicago, American Library Association. Pp. 141–54. First published in *Essays in Western Civilization in Honor of Christian W. Mackauer*. Ed. L. Botstein and E. Karnofsky. Chicago: The College of the University of Chicago, 1967. Pp. 1–17.

———. 1975. *Nature and Culture in the* Iliad: *The Tragedy of Hector*. Chicago, University of Chicago Press.

Reinhardt, K. 1956. "Zum homerischen Aphroditehymnus." In *Festschr. Bruno Snell*. Munich, C. H. Beck. Pp. 1–14.

Richardson, N. J., ed. 1974. *The Homeric Hymn to Demeter*. Oxford, Clarendon Press.

Ritoók, Zs. 1968. "The Epithets for Minstrels in the *Odyssey*." *AAntHung* 16:89–92.

Robert, C. 1966. "Zu Hesiods Theogonie." In *Hesiod*. Ed. E. Heitsch. Darmstadt, Wissenschaftliche Buchgesellschaft. Pp. 153–74. First published in *Mélanges Nicole* (Geneva, 1905): 461–87.

Robertson, N. 1978. "The Myth of the First Sacred War." *CQ* 72:38–73.

Rudhardt, J. 1978. "A propos de l'hymne homérique à Déméter." *MH* 35:1–17.

Russo, C. F. 1965. *Hesiodi Scutum.* 2nd ed. Florence, La Nuova Italia.

Schadewaldt, W. 1944. "Die Gestalt des homerischen Sängers." In his *Von Homers Welt und Werk.* 1st ed. Leipzig, Koehler & Amelang. Pp. 54–86.

———. 1951. "Einblick in die Erfindung der Ilias: Ilias und Memnonis." In his *Von Homers Welt und Werk.* 2nd ed. Stuttgart, K. F. Koehler. Pp. 155–202.

Schmitt, A. 1975. "Zum Prooimion des hesiodischen Frauenkatalogs." *Würzburger Jahrbücher für die Altertumswissenschaft* n.f. 1:19–31.

Schubart, W., and Wilamowitz-Moellendorff, U. von, eds. 1907. *Griechische Dichterfragmente.* Berliner Klassikertexte 5. Berlin, Weidmann.

Schwabl, H. 1963. "Aufbau und Struktur des Prooimions der hesiodischen Theogonie." *Hermes* 91:385–415.

———. 1966. "Beispiele zur poetischen Technik des Hesiod." In *Hesiod.* Ed. E. Heitsch. Darmstadt, Wissenschaftliche Buchgesellschaft. Pp. 175–219.

———. 1969. "Der homerische Hymnus auf Pan." *WS* n.f. 3:5–14.

Schwartz, J. 1960. *Pseudo-Hesiodeia: Recherches sur la composition, la diffusion et la disparition ancienne d'oeuvres attribuées à Hésiode.* Leiden, E. J. Brill.

Schwenn, F. 1934. *Die Theogonie des Hesiodos.* Heidelberg, C. Winter.

Scodel, R. 1982. "The Achaean Wall and the Myth of Destruction." *HSCP* 86:33–50.

Scott, J. A. 1916–17. "The Close of the *Odyssey.*" *CJ* 12:397–405.

Scott, W. C. 1974. *The Oral Nature of the Homeric Simile. Mnemosyne* suppl. 28. Leiden, E. J. Brill.

Segal, C. P. 1962. "The Phaeacians and the Symbolism of Odysseus' Return." *Arion* 1 (no. 4):17–64.

———. 1971. *The Theme of the Mutilation of the Corpse in the Iliad. Mnemosyne* suppl. 17. Leiden, E. J. Brill.

———. 1974. "The *Homeric Hymn to Aphrodite:* A Structuralist Approach." *CW* 67:205–12.

Seidensticker, B. 1978. "Archilochus and Odysseus." *GRBS* 19:5–22.

Sellschopp, I. 1934. *Stilistische Untersuchungen zu Hesiod.* Diss. Hamburg, O. Schneider.

Sheppard, J. T. 1922. *The Pattern of the Iliad.* London, Methuen.

Siegmann, E. 1966. "Zu Hesiods Theogonieproömium." In *Hesiod,* ed. E. Heitsch. Darmstadt, Wissenschaftliche Buchgesellschaft. Pp. 316–23. First published in *Festschr. Ernst Kapp.* Hamburg: M. von Schröder, 1958. Pp. 9–14.

Sinclair, T. A., ed. 1932. *Hesiod,* Works and Days. London, Macmillan.

Singleton, C. S., trans. 1975. *The Divine Comedy of Dante Alighieri,* vol. III, *Paradiso.* Bollingen Series 80. Princeton, N.J., Princeton University Press.

Skafte Jensen, M. 1966. "Tradition and Individuality in Hesiod's *Works and Days.*" *C&M* 27:1-27.

Slater, W. J. 1969. *Lexicon to Pindar.* Berlin, Walter de Gruyter.

Smith, P. M. 1981a. "The Aeneiadai as Patrons of *Iliad* XX and the Homeric *Hymn to Aphrodite.*" *HSCP* 85:17-58.

———. 1981b. *Nursling of Mortality: A Study of the* Homeric Hymn to Aphrodite. Studien zur klassischen Philologie 3. Frankfurt and Bern, P. Lang.

Solmsen, F. 1949. *Hesiod and Aeschylus.* Ithaca, N.Y., Cornell University Press.

———. 1954. "The 'Gift' of Speech in Homer and Hesiod." *TAPA* 85:1-15.

———. 1960. "Zur Theologie im grossen Aphrodite-Hymnus." *Hermes* 88:1-13.

———. 1965. "Ilias Σ 535-540." *Hermes* 93:1-6.

———. 1982. "The Earliest Stages in the History of Hesiod's Text." *HSCP* 86:1-31.

———, ed. 1970. *Hesiodi Theogonia Opera et Dies Scutum.* Oxford Classical Text. Oxford, Clarendon Press.

Sperduti, A. 1950. "The Divine Nature of Poetry in Antiquity." *TAPA* 81:209-40.

Stanford, W. B. 1965. "The Ending of the *Odyssey:* An Ethical Approach." *Hermathena* 100:5-20.

———, ed. 1967. *The* Odyssey *of Homer.* 2 vols. 2nd ed., reprinted with alterations and additions. New York and London, St. Martin's Press.

Stiewe, K. 1962, 1963. "Die Entstehungszeit der hesiodischen Frauenkataloge." *Philologus* 106:291-99 (pt. 1), 107:1-29 (pt. 2).

Stroh, W. 1976. "Hesiods lügende Musen." In *Studien zum antiken Epos.* Ed. H. Görgemanns and E. A. Schmidt. Meisenheim: A. Hain. Pp. 85-112.

Svenbro, J. 1976. *La Parole et le marbre: aux origines de la poëtique grecque.* Lund, Studentlitteratur.

Thornton, A. 1970. *People and Themes in the* Odyssey. London and Dunedin, University of Otago Press.

Tigerstedt, E. N. 1970. "Poetic Inspiration in Greek Literature." *JHI* 3:163-78.

Trahman, C. R. 1952. "Odysseus' Lies (*Odyssey,* Books 13-19)." *Phoenix* 6:31-43.

Treu, M. 1957. "Das Proömium der hesiodischen Frauenkataloge." *RhM* 100:169-86.

Van der Valk, M. 1953. "A Defence of Some Suspected Passages in the *Scutum Hesiodi.*" *Mnemosyne,* 4th ser., 6:265-82.

———. 1966. "Le *Bouclier* du Pseudo-Hésiode." *REG* 79:450-81.

Van Groningen, B. A. 1957. *Hésiode et Persès* (Amsterdam), Mededelingen der Koninklijke Nederlandse Akademie van Wetenschappen, Afd. Letterkunde, n.r. 20, no. 6.

———. 1958. *La composition littéraire archaïque grecque.* Amsterdam, North Holland Publishing Co.

Van Nortwick, T. 1980. "Apollōnos Apatē: Associative Imagery in the Homeric *Hymn to Hermes* 227-292." *CW* 74:1-5.

Van Otterlo, W. A. A. 1944. *Untersuchungen über Begriff, Anwendung, und Entstehung der griechischen Ringkomposition* (Amsterdam), Mededelingen der Koninklijke Nederlandse Akademie van Wetenschappen, Afd. Letterkunde, n.r. 7, no. 3.

———. 1944-45. "Eine merkwürdige Kompositionsform der älteren griechischen Literatur." *Mnemosyne* 12:192-207.

———. 1948. *De Ringcompositie als Opbouwprincipe in de Epische Gedichten van Homerus* (Amsterdam), Verhandelingen der Koninklijke Nederlandsche Akademie van Wetenschappen, Afd. Letterkunde, n.r. 51, no. 1.

Verdenius, W. J. 1960. "L'association des idées comme principe de composition dans Homère, Hésiode, Théognis." *REG* 73:345-61.

———. 1962. "Aufbau und Absicht der Erga." In Fritz, K. von et al. *Hésiode et son influence*. Fondation Hardt, Entretiens sur l'antiquité classique 7. Geneva, Vandoeuvres-Genève. Pp. 111-59.

———. 1972. "Notes on the Proem of Hesiod's *Theogony*." *Mnemosyne* 25:225-60.

Vernant, J.-P. 1965. *Mythe et pensée chez les Grecs: études de psychologie historique*. Paris, Maspero.

———. 1981a. "The Myth of Prometheus in Hesiod." In *Myth, Religion, and Society*. Ed. R. L. Gordon. Cambridge, Cambridge University Press. Pp. 43-56. First published in his *Mythe et société en Grèce ancienne*. Paris: Maspero, 1974.

———. 1981b. "Sacrificial and Alimentary Codes in Hesiod's Myth of Prometheus." In *Myth, Religion and Society*. Ed. R. L. Gordon. Cambridge, Cambridge University Press. Pp. 57-79. First published in *Annali della Scuola Normale di Pisa* 7(1977):905-40.

Vidal-Naquet, P. 1981. "Land and Sacrifice in the *Odyssey*: A Study of Religious and Mythical Meanings." In *Myth, Religion, and Society*. Ed. R. L. Gordon. Cambridge, Cambridge University Press. Pp. 80-94. With alterations and corrections. First published in *Annales ESC* 25 (1970):1278-97.

Vivante, P. 1982. *The Epithets in Homer: A Study in Poetic Values*. New Haven, Yale University Press.

Von Fritz, K. 1966. "Das Proömium der hesiodischen Theogonie." In *Hesiod*. Ed. E. Heitsch. Darmstadt, Wissenschaftliche Buchgesellschaft. Pp. 295-315. First published in *Festschr. Bruno Snell*. Munich: C. H. Beck, 1956. Pp. 29-45.

Walcot, P. 1956. "The Text of Hesiod's *Theogony* and the Hittite *Epic of Kumarbi*." *CQ* 50:198-206.

———. 1957. "The Problem of the Prooemium of Hesiod's *Theogony*." *SO* 33:37-47.

———. 1958. "Hesiod's Hymns to the Muses, Aphrodite, Styx, and Hecate." *SO* 34:5-14.

———. 1960. "Allusion in Hesiod." *REG* 73:36-39.

———. 1961. "The Composition of the *Works and Days*." *REG* 74:1-19.

———. 1966. *Hesiod and the Near East*. Cardiff, University of Wales Press.

Webster, T. B. L. 1964. *From Mycenae to Homer.* 2nd ed. New York, W. W. Norton & Co.

———. 1975. "Homeric Hymns and Society." In *Le monde grec: hommages à Claire Préaux.* Brussels, University of Brussels. Pp. 86–93.

Wegner, M. 1968. *Musik und Tanz.* Archaeologia Homerica 3. Göttingen, Vandenhoeck & Ruprecht.

Wender, D. 1978. *The Last Scenes of the* Odyssey. *Mnemosyne* suppl. 52. Leiden, E. J. Brill.

West, M. L. 1961. "Hesiodea." *CQ* 55:130–45.

———. 1963. Review of E. Lobel, *The Oxyrhynchus Papyri,* Part 28. *Gnomon* 35:752–59.

———. 1971. "Stesichorus." *CQ* 65:302–14.

———. 1975. "Cynaethus' *Hymn to Apollo.*" *CQ* 69:161–70.

———. 1981. "The Singing of Homer and the Modes of Early Greek Music." *JHS* 101:113–29.

———, ed. 1971. *Iambi et Elegi Graeci.* Vol. I. Oxford, Clarendon Press.

———, ed. 1978. *Hesiod,* Works and Days. Oxford, Clarendon Press.

Whitman, C. H. 1958. *Homer and the Heroic Tradition.* Cambridge, Mass., Harvard University Press. Paperback edition, New York: W. W. Norton & Co., 1965.

Wilamowitz-Moellendorff, U. von. 1905. "Lesefrüchte." *Hermes* 40:116–24. (Discussion of *Aspis.*)

———. 1907. See above: Schubart, W., and Wilamowitz-Moellendorff, U. von. 1907.

———. 1920. *Die Ilias und Homer.* Berlin, Weidmann.

———, ed. 1928. *Hesiodos Erga.* Berlin, Weidmann.

Wilson, J. R. 1974. "The Wedding Gifts of Peleus." *Phoenix* 28: 385–89.

▣ Index of Subjects ▣

▣ Index of Passages ▣

Aeschylus: *Ag. 168-75:* 200n.35;
  979: 224n.44; *990-94:* 127;
  Cho. 274: 200n.35; *Cho. 556-
  59:* 200n.35; *1065-76:* 200
  n.35; *fr. 284M (=350N²):* 218
  n.68
Aristotle: Poet. *1450ᵇ21-1451ᵃ6:* 5;
  Rh. 3.9 (1409ᵃ27-37): 4
Arkhilokhos: *fr. 1W:* 234n.23; *fr.
  13W:* 211n.15
Asios: *fr. 8K:* 214n.44
Aspis. See [Hesiod]
Athenaeus: *V, 180e-182a:* 221n.8

Bacchylides: *5.9-10:* 196n.80; *19.8:*
  196n.80

Catullus: *64:* 218n.68

Diogenes Laertius: *1.109:* 231n.43

Epic Cycle: *Kypria, fr. 1:* 75, 215
  n.57; *fr. 3:* 218n.68; *Nostoi,
  fr. 10:* 98
Epimenides: *fr. 4K:* 230n.30

Herodotus: *1.46.3-49:* 230n.30
Hesiod: *Theogony: 1-115:* 40, 134-
  50, 151-152; *1-21:* 136, 138; *1-
  10:* 227n.9; *1:* 223n.32, 228
  n.15; *3-8:* 118; *4:* 143; *9-21:*
  118, 143; *10:* 228n.13; *11-21:*
  138-39, 228n.14; *21:* 139, 228
  n.13, 228n.14; *22-52:* 135-36;
  22-35: 136; *22:* 128, 136; *23:*
  143; *25:* 134-35, 136, 143; *26-
  28:* 143-44, 146-49; *27:* 172;
  28: 149; *30-31:* 121; *31-32:*
  126, 129; *31:* 222n.27; *32-34:*
  138; *32:* 42, 129, 131, 136,

225n.53, 228n.14; *33:* 139; *34:*
  228n.15; *35:* 134; *36-52:* 136,
  138; *36:* 223n.32, 228n.15; *38:*
  42, 129, 136; *39-40:* 140; *40-
  42:* 142; *42-43:* 228n.13; *43-52:*
  138-39; *43-50:* 228n.12, 228
  n.14; *43:* 228n.13; *44:* 131, 139,
  228n.13, 228n.14; *45:* 228n.14;
  46: 228n.14; *48:* 228n.15; *49:*
  228n.13; *50:* 150; *52:* 136; *53-
  103:* 136; *53-67:* 40; *53-62:*
  136; *54-55:* 138, 145, 148; *55:*
  83, 130, 166; *61:* 83; *63-67:*
  118, 136; *64:* 130; *65-67:* 227
  n.6; *65:* 228n.13; *66-67:* 138-
  39; *67:* 131, 228n.13, 228n.14;
  68-79: 136; *68-75:* 118; *68-74:*
  227n.6; *68:* 138; *69-71:* 228
  n.13; *71-75:* 138-39; *71-73:* 41;
  73-74: 41, 228n.14; *73:* 228
  n.13; *77-79:* 138; *79-93:* 179;
  79-80: 229n.17; *80-103:* 136,
  138, 139-40; *80-93:* 229n.17;
  83-84: 140; *86:* 148; *88-90:*
  141; *90:* 148; *93:* 87, 149; *94-
  97:* 228-29n.16; *95:* 222n.29;
  97: 140; *98-103:* 87, 130, 138,
  166; *98:* 145, 211n.11
    102-3: 144-45, 148; *102:* 211
  n.11; *103:* 148, 149; *104-15:*
  126, 136, 139, 228n.14; *105:*
  131; *115-22:* 41; *116-210:* 40;
  124-25: 187n.2; *132-38:* 14;
  137-58: 13-14; *138:* 191n.38,
  192n.39; *139-53:* 41, 191n.38,
  191-92n.39, 196n.79; *141:* 40;
  146: 192n.40; *153:* 192n.40;
  154-56: 191n.38; *154:* 191
  n.39; *155-56:* 191-92n.39; *155:*
  191n.38; *156-59:* 192n.39; *157:*

William G. Thalmann is associate professor of classics at Hobart and William Smith Colleges and the author of *Dramatic Art in Aeschylus's "Seven Against Thebes."*